Ken-ichi Sakura

When I'm at work I often think about doing this or that for my health, but as soon as work is over the feeling drifts away and I wind up doing nothing. If only I could be more active...sigh...

(It's hopeless.)

Ken-ichi Sakura's manga debut was *Fabre Tanteiki*, which was published in a special edition of *Monthly Shonen Jump* in 2000. Serialization of *Dragon Drive* began in the March 2001 issue of *Monthly Shonen Jump* and the hugely successful series has inspired video games and an animated TV show. Sakura's latest title, *Kotokuri*, began running in the March 2006 issue of *Monthly Shonen Jump*. *Dragon Drive* and *Kotokuri* have both become tremendously popular in Japan because of Sakura's unique sense of humor and dynamic portrayal of feisty teen characters.

DRAGON DRIVE

DRAGON DRIVE
VOLUME 10

The SHONEN JUMP Manga Edition

STORY AND ART BY
KEN-ICHI SAKURA

Translation/Martin Hunt, HC Language Solutions, Inc.
English Adaptation/Ian Reid, HC Language Solutions, Inc.
Touch-up Art & Lettering/Jim Keefe
Design/Sam Elzway
Interior Design/Julie Behn
Editor/Shaenon K. Garrity

Editor in Chief, Books/Alvin Lu
Editor in Chief, Magazines/Marc Weidenbaum
VP of Publishing Licensing/Rika Inouye
VP of Sales/Gonzalo Ferreyra
Sr. VP of Marketing/Liza Coppola
Publisher/Hyoe Narita

Printed in the U.S.A.

Published by VIZ Media, LLC
P.O. Box 77010
San Francisco, CA 94107

SHONEN JUMP Manga Edition
10 9 8 7 6 5 4 3 2 1
First printing, October 2008

www.viz.com

PARENTAL ADVISORY
DRAGON DRIVE is rated
A and is suitable for
readers of all ages.
ratings.viz.com

THE WORLD'S
MOST POPULAR MANGA

www.shonenjump.com

DRAGON DRIVE

SHONEN JUMP MANGA EDITION

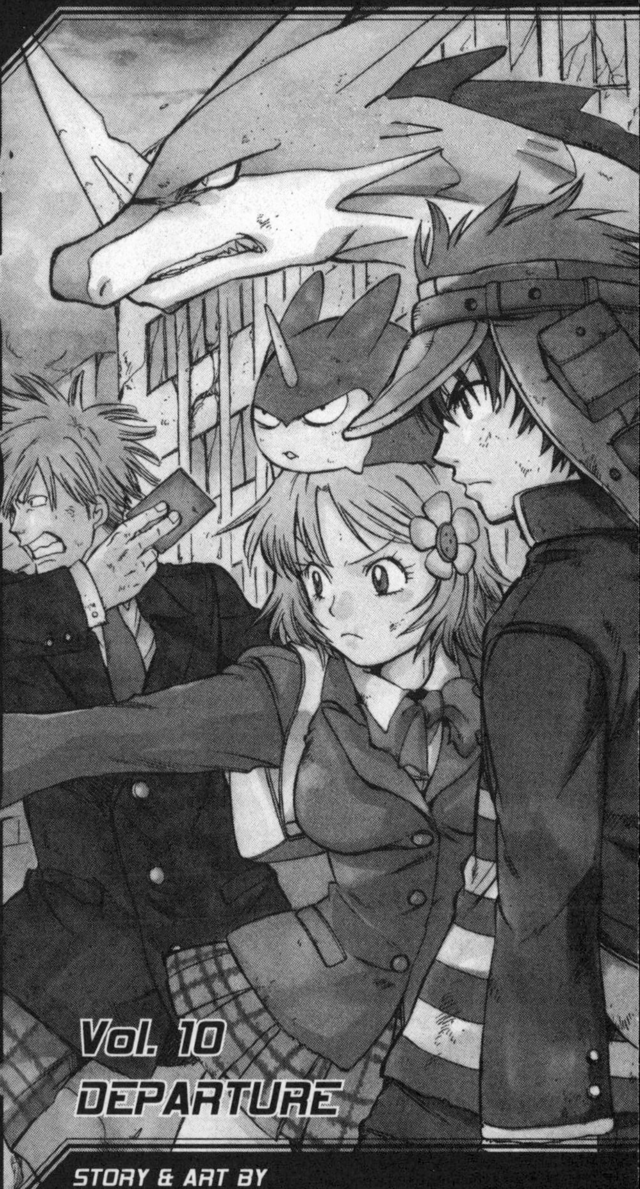

Vol. 10

DEPARTURE

STORY & ART BY

KEN-ICHI SAKURA

IN COLLABORATION WITH BANDAI • CHAN'S • ORG

CHARACTERS

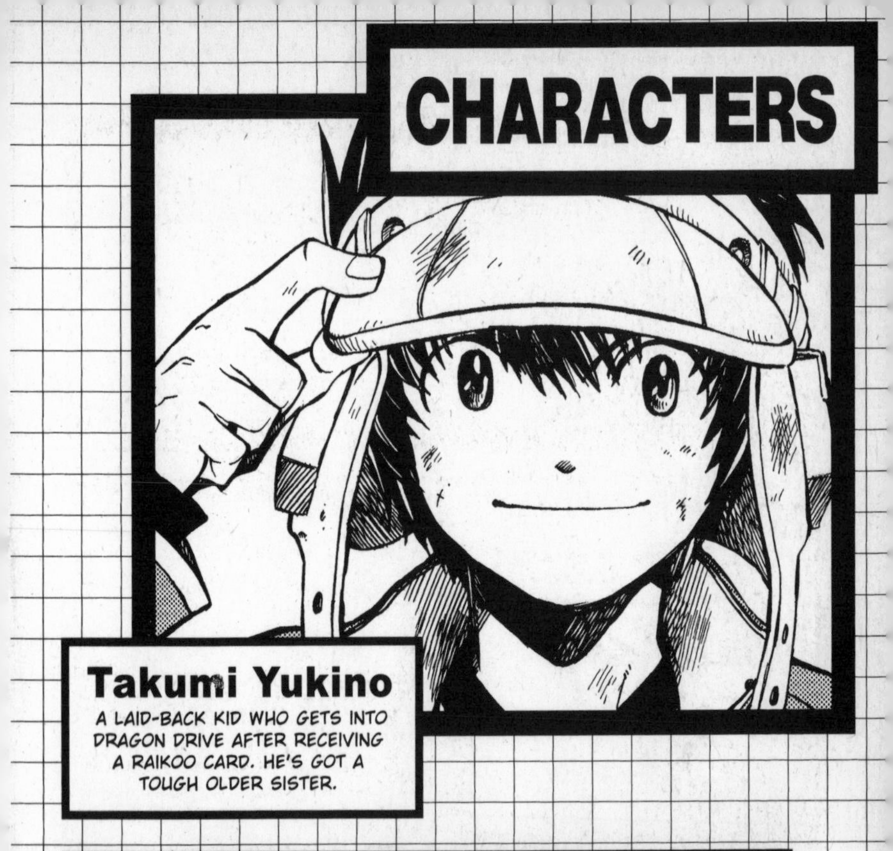

Takumi Yukino

A LAID-BACK KID WHO GETS INTO DRAGON DRIVE AFTER RECEIVING A RAIKOO CARD. HE'S GOT A TOUGH OLDER SISTER.

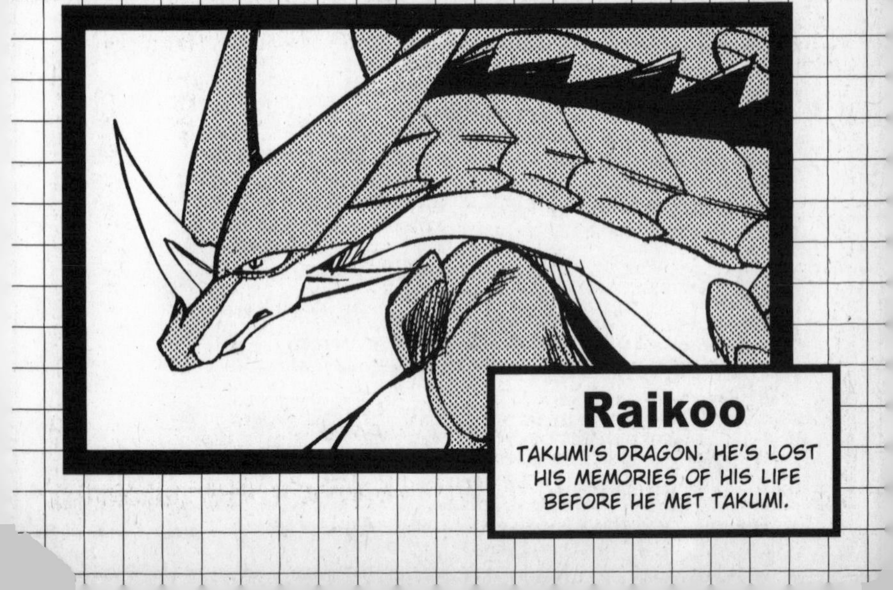

Raikoo

TAKUMI'S DRAGON. HE'S LOST HIS MEMORIES OF HIS LIFE BEFORE HE MET TAKUMI.

Kenji Koto

AN EXPERIENCED DRAGON DRIVE PLAYER WHO SHOWS TAKUMI THE ROPES.

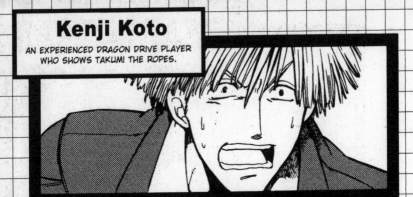

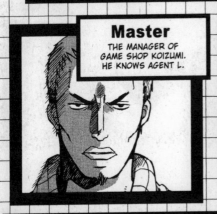

Neko Chihoda

A GIRL WHO WAS LEFT BEHIND ON EARTH.

Master

THE MANAGER OF GAME SHOP KOIZUMI. HE KNOWS AGENT L.

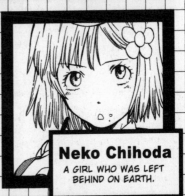

STORY

A GAME CALLED DRAGON DRIVE BECOMES WILDLY POPULAR WITH KIDS ALL OVER THE WORLD. ONE DAY, TAKUMI YUKINO RECEIVES A DECK OF D.D. CARDS FROM A MYSTERIOUS OLD MAN. EVEN THOUGH HIS SISTER HAS FORBIDDEN HIM TO PLAY, TAKUMI ENTERS A LOCAL D.D. TOURNAMENT, UNABLE TO IGNORE HIS NEW THIRST FOR EXCITEMENT.

FOR HIS FIRST MATCH, TAKUMI ACCIDENTALLY ENTERS THE TOURNAMENT FINALS, FACING AN EXPERIENCED PLAYER. EVEN THOUGH HE'S NEVER PLAYED BEFORE, THE STRENGTH OF RAIKOO HELPS HIM WIN.

AFTERWARDS, TAKUMI HAS A STRANGE DREAM. HE'S TOLD THAT TO AWAKEN THE TRUE RAIKOO FROM AMONG THE 99 RAIKOO CARDS, ALL THE RAIKOOS MUST FIGHT EACH OTHER. THE DREAM WORRIES TAKUMI, BUT HE HEADS FOR THE NATIONAL TOURNAMENT ANYWAY, HOPING TO RESTORE RAIKOO'S LOST MEMORIES. HOWEVER, AFTER REALIZING HOW MUCH HE STILL HAS TO LEARN, TAKUMU DROPS OUT OF THE TOURNAMENT TO CONCENTRATE ON HIS TRAINING.

A WEEK AFTER THE TOURNAMENT, A STRANGE DISASTER STRIKES. AN ORGANIZATION CALLED RI-IN HACKS INTO THE D.D. COMPUTER SYSTEM. THE D-ZONE DRAGONS TRADE PLACES WITH THE PEOPLE OF EARTH. TAKUMI IS AMONG THE FEW, SCATTERED HUMANS LEFT BEHIND...

Vol. 10 DEPARTURE
CONTENTS

DRAGON DRIVE

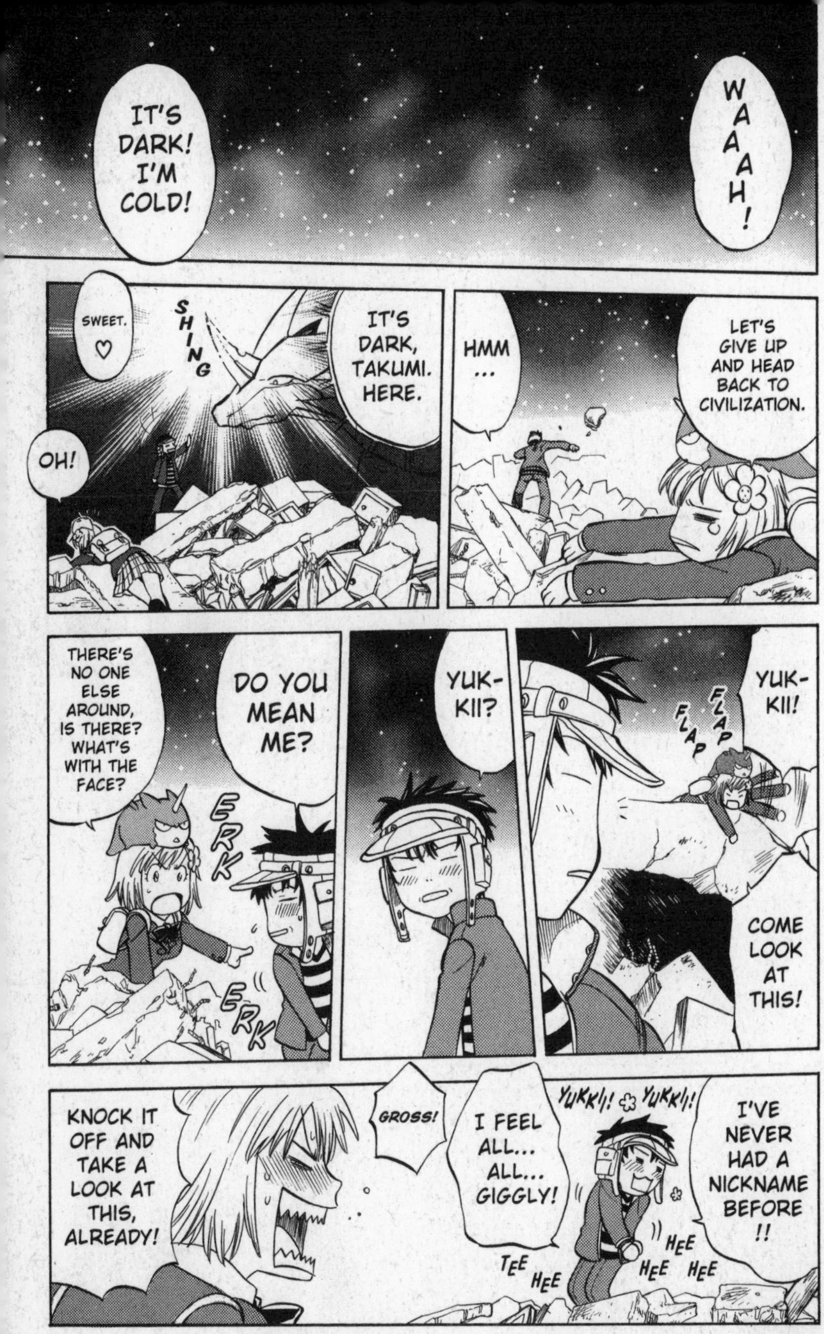
WAAAH!
IT'S DARK! I'M COLD!
LET'S GIVE UP AND HEAD BACK TO CIVILIZATION.
HMM...
IT'S DARK, TAKUMI. HERE.
SHING
SWEET. ♡
OH!
YUK-KII!
FLAP FLAP
COME LOOK AT THIS!
YUK-KII?
DO YOU MEAN ME?
THERE'S NO ONE ELSE AROUND, IS THERE? WHAT'S WITH THE FACE?
ERK
ERK
I'VE NEVER HAD A NICKNAME BEFORE!!
YUKKII! ✿ YUKKII!
I FEEL ALL... ALL... GIGGLY!
HEE HEE HEE
TEE HEE
GROSS!
KNOCK IT OFF AND TAKE A LOOK AT THIS, ALREADY!

8th turn Departure

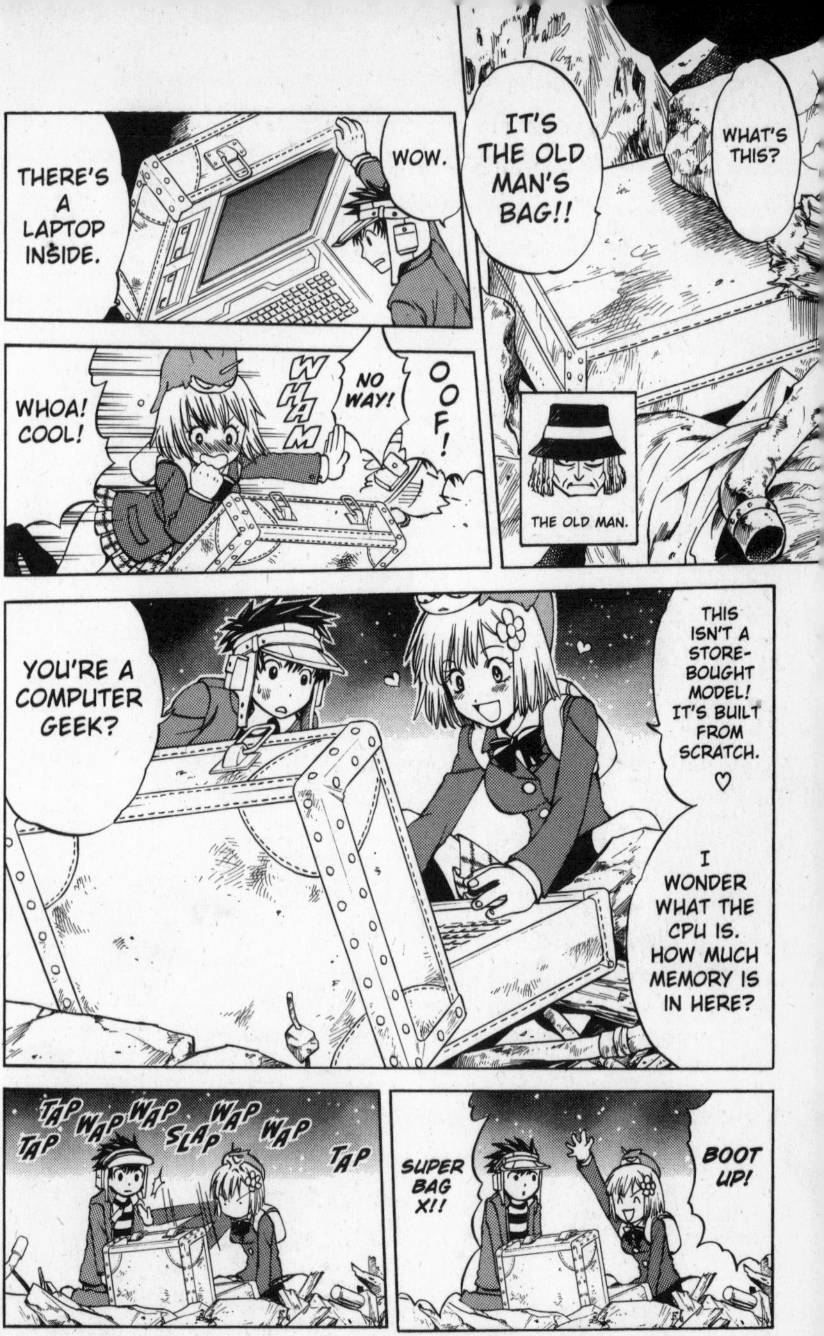
WHAT'S THIS?
IT'S THE OLD MAN'S BAG!!
THE OLD MAN.
WOW.
THERE'S A LAPTOP INSIDE.
OOF!
NO WAY!
WHAM
WHOA! COOL!
THIS ISN'T A STORE-BOUGHT MODEL! IT'S BUILT FROM SCRATCH. ♡
I WONDER WHAT THE CPU IS. HOW MUCH MEMORY IS IN HERE?
YOU'RE A COMPUTER GEEK?
BOOT UP!
SUPER BAG X!!
TAP
WAP
WAP
SLAP
WAP
WAP
TAP TAP

READ THIS WAY

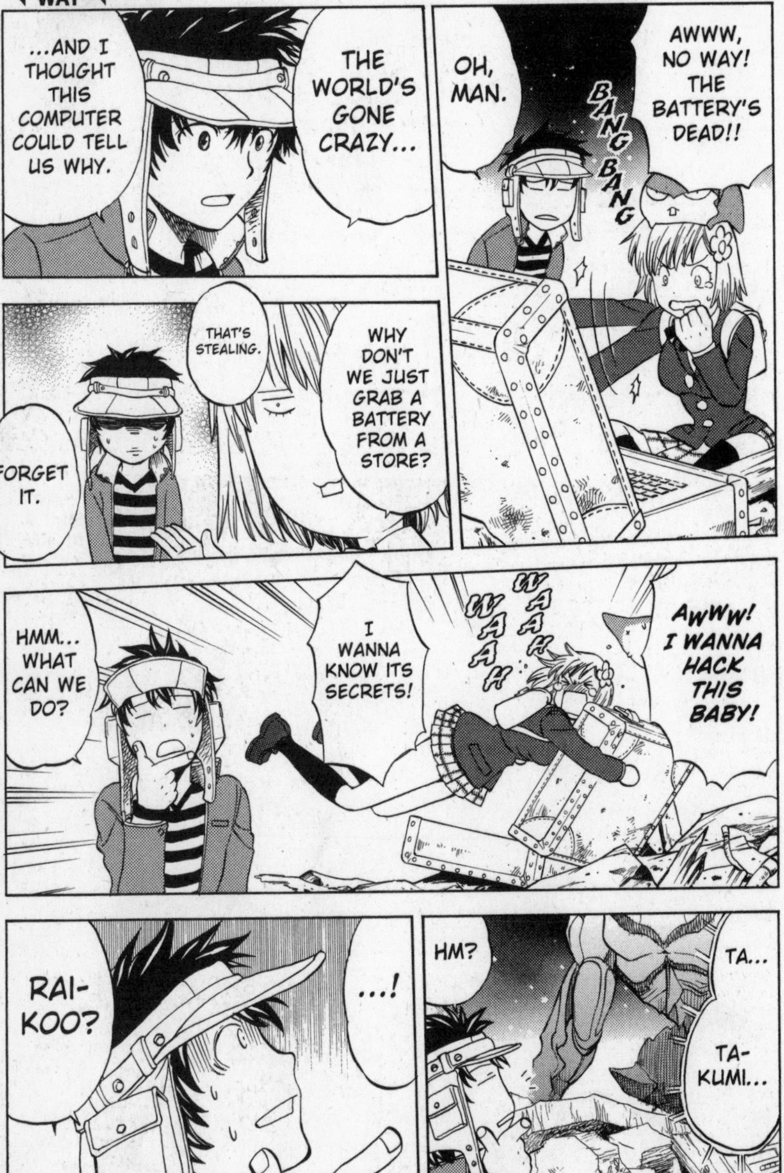
AWWW, NO WAY! THE BATTERY'S DEAD!!
BANG BANG
OH, MAN.
THE WORLD'S GONE CRAZY...
...AND I THOUGHT THIS COMPUTER COULD TELL US WHY.
WHY DON'T WE JUST GRAB A BATTERY FROM A STORE?
THAT'S STEALING.
FORGET IT.
AWWW! I WANNA HACK THIS BABY!
WAAH WAAH
I WANNA KNOW ITS SECRETS!
HMM... WHAT CAN WE DO?
TA...
TA-KUMI...
HM?
...!
RAI-KOO?

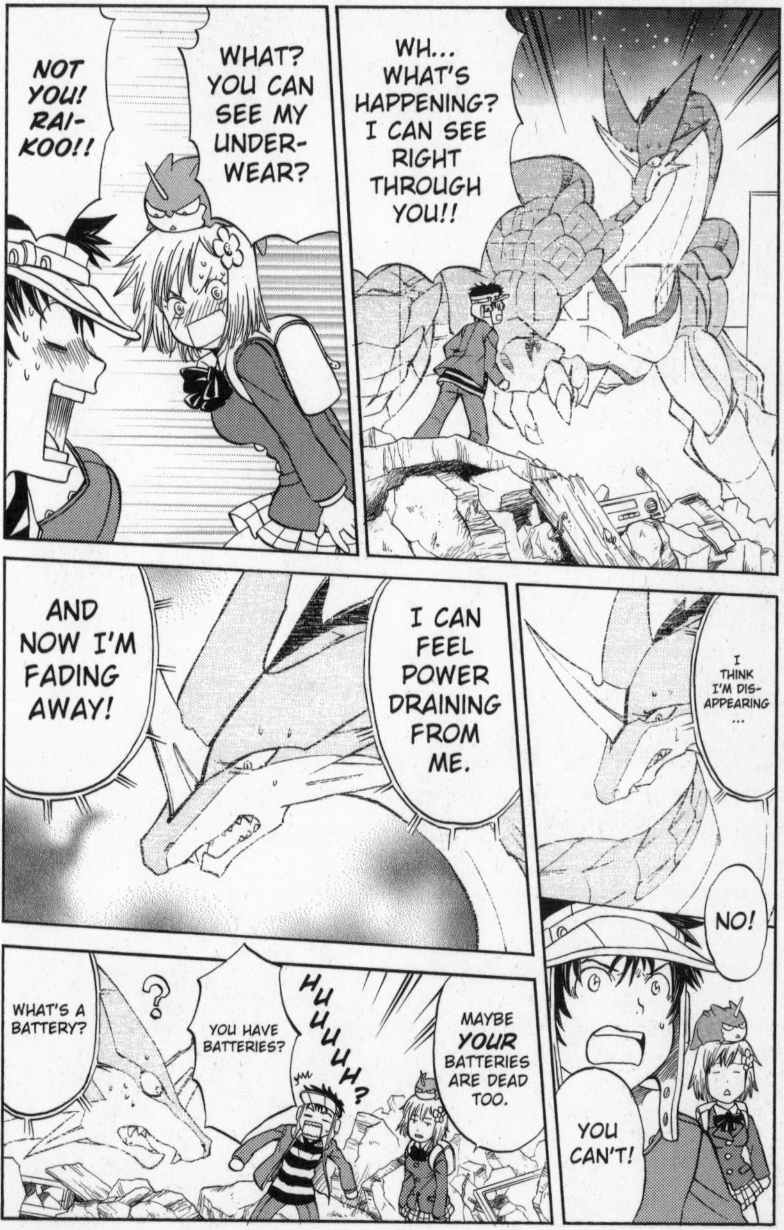
WH... WHAT'S HAPPENING? I CAN SEE RIGHT THROUGH YOU!!
WHAT? YOU CAN SEE MY UNDER-WEAR?
NOT YOU! RAI-KOO!!
I THINK I'M DIS-APPEARING ...
NO!
YOU CAN'T!
I CAN FEEL POWER DRAINING FROM ME.
AND NOW I'M FADING AWAY!
MAYBE YOUR BATTERIES ARE DEAD TOO.
HUUUUH?
YOU HAVE BATTERIES?
WHAT'S A BATTERY?
?

READ THIS WAY

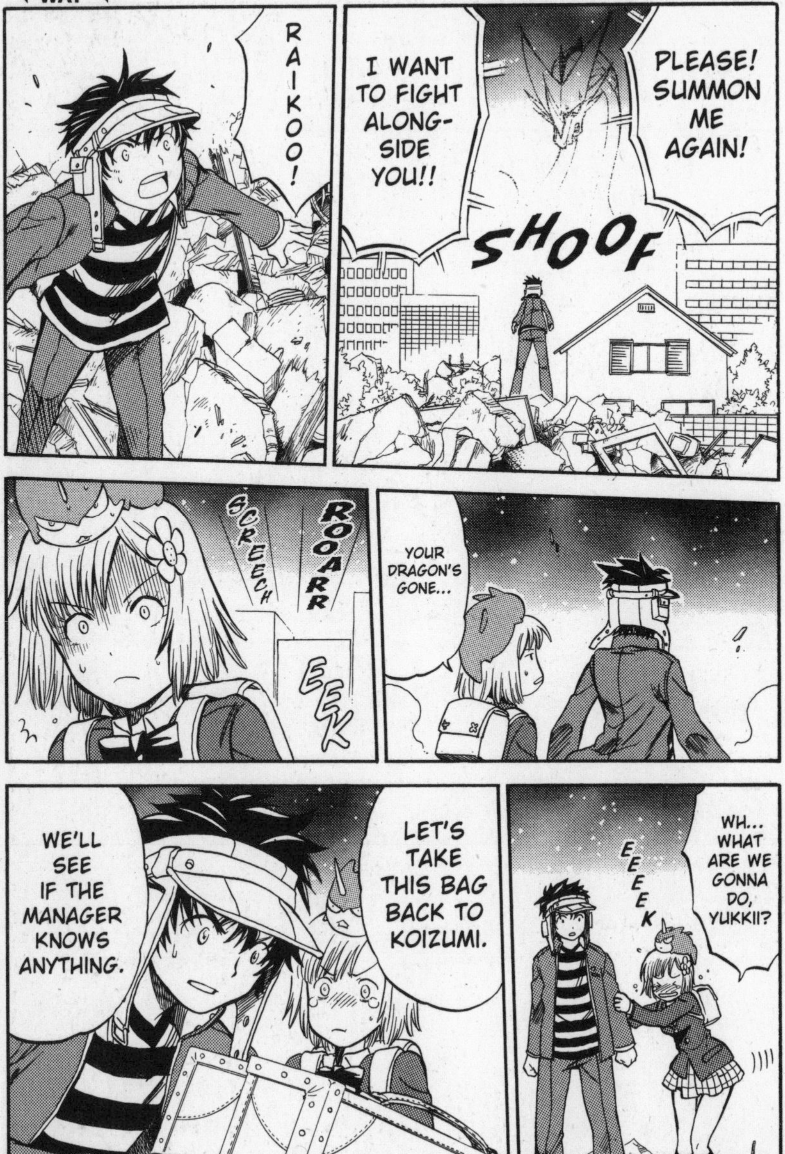

PLEASE! SUMMON ME AGAIN!
I WANT TO FIGHT ALONG-SIDE YOU!!
SHOOF
RAIKOO!
YOUR DRAGON'S GONE...
ROOARR
SCREEECH
EEK
WH... WHAT ARE WE GONNA DO, YUKKII?
EEEEK
LET'S TAKE THIS BAG BACK TO KOIZUMI.
WE'LL SEE IF THE MANAGER KNOWS ANYTHING.

CARD GAMES ·
GOODS · etc
TEL-0000-00-000
KOIZUMI
GAME SHOP
YOU IDIOT!
WHERE'D YOU RUN OFF TO?
YOU HAVE ANY IDEA HOW WORRIED WE WERE?
HEY, KENJI. LONG TIME NO SEE...
HOW MANY HOURS HAS IT BEEN?
YOU DON'T GET IT!
YOU DON'T GET IT AT ALL!
HYUP
THIS BEANPOLE IS KENJI KOTO.
HUH?
I'M NEKO CHI-HODA.

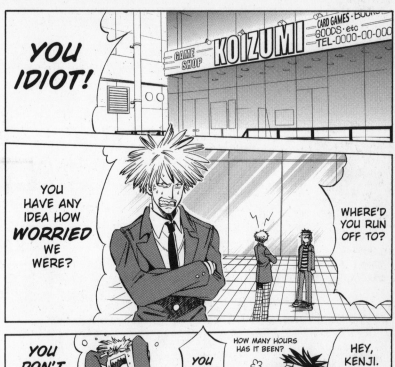

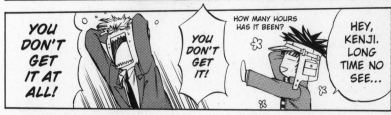

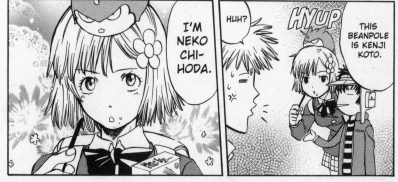

READ THIS WAY

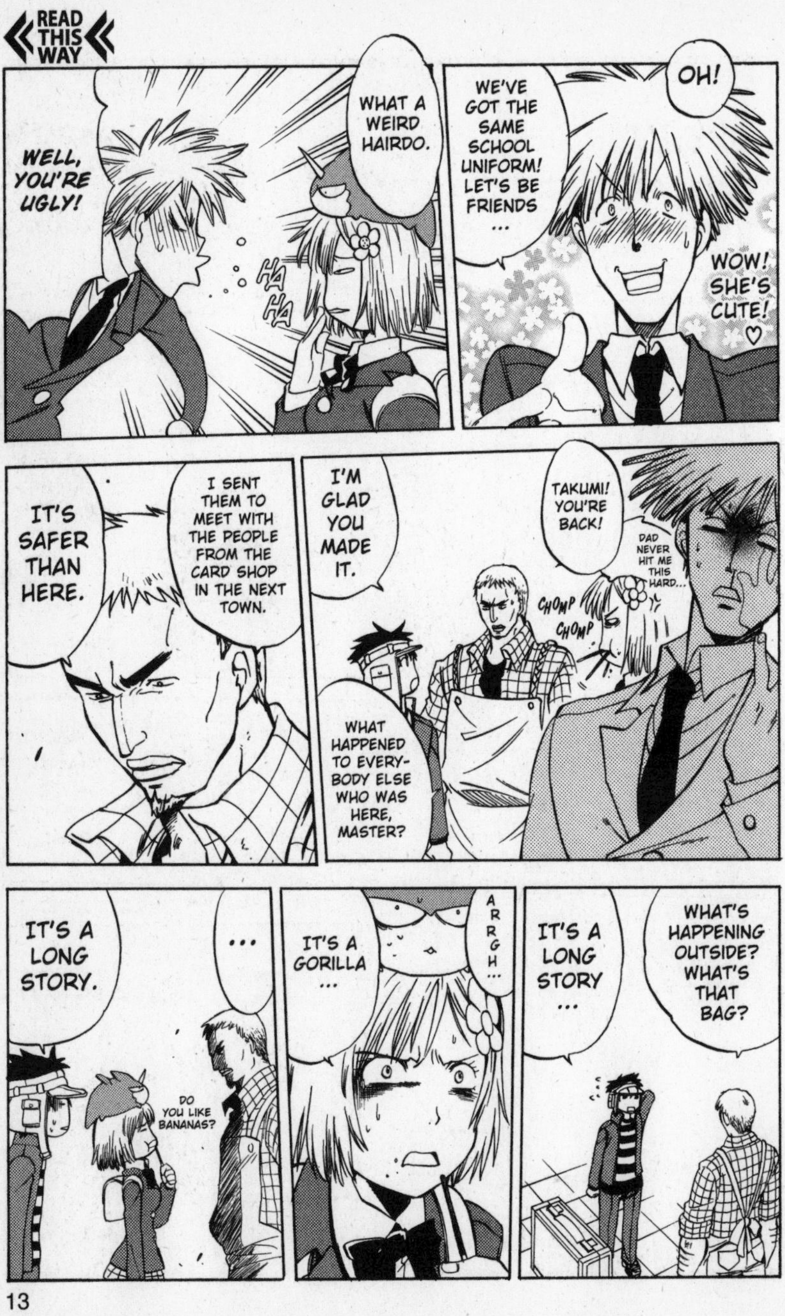
OH!
WE'VE GOT THE SAME SCHOOL UNIFORM! LET'S BE FRIENDS ...
WOW! SHE'S CUTE! ♡
WHAT A WEIRD HAIRDO.
HA HA
WELL, YOU'RE UGLY!
TAKUMI! YOU'RE BACK!
DAD NEVER HIT ME THIS HARD...
CHOMP CHOMP
I'M GLAD YOU MADE IT.
WHAT HAPPENED TO EVERY-BODY ELSE WHO WAS HERE, MASTER?
I SENT THEM TO MEET WITH THE PEOPLE FROM THE CARD SHOP IN THE NEXT TOWN.
IT'S SAFER THAN HERE.
WHAT'S HAPPENING OUTSIDE? WHAT'S THAT BAG?
IT'S A LONG STORY ...
ARRGH...
IT'S A GORILLA ...
...
IT'S A LONG STORY.
DO YOU LIKE BANANAS?

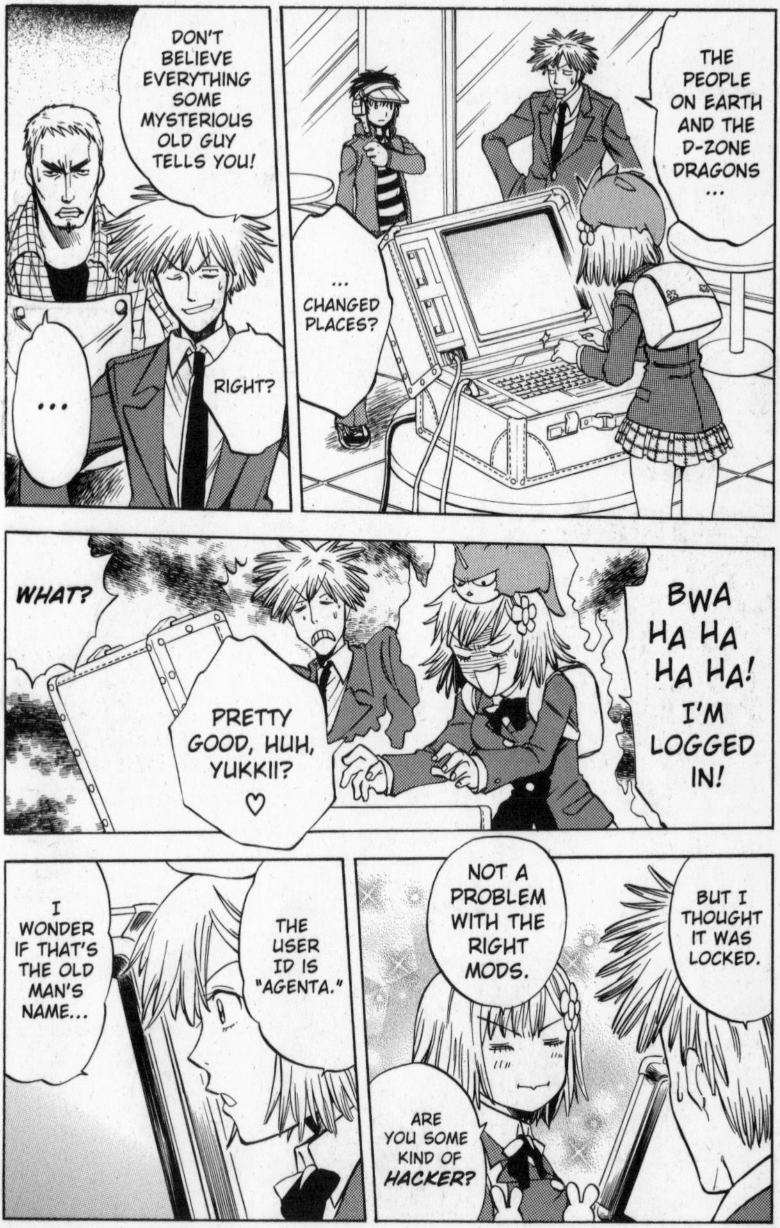
THE PEOPLE ON EARTH AND THE D-ZONE DRAGONS ...
... CHANGED PLACES?
DON'T BELIEVE EVERYTHING SOME MYSTERIOUS OLD GUY TELLS YOU!
RIGHT?
...
BWA HA HA HA HA! I'M LOGGED IN!
PRETTY GOOD, HUH, YUKKII? ♡
WHAT?
BUT I THOUGHT IT WAS LOCKED.
NOT A PROBLEM WITH THE RIGHT MODS.
ARE YOU SOME KIND OF HACKER?
THE USER ID IS "AGENTA."
I WONDER IF THAT'S THE OLD MAN'S NAME...

READ THIS WAY

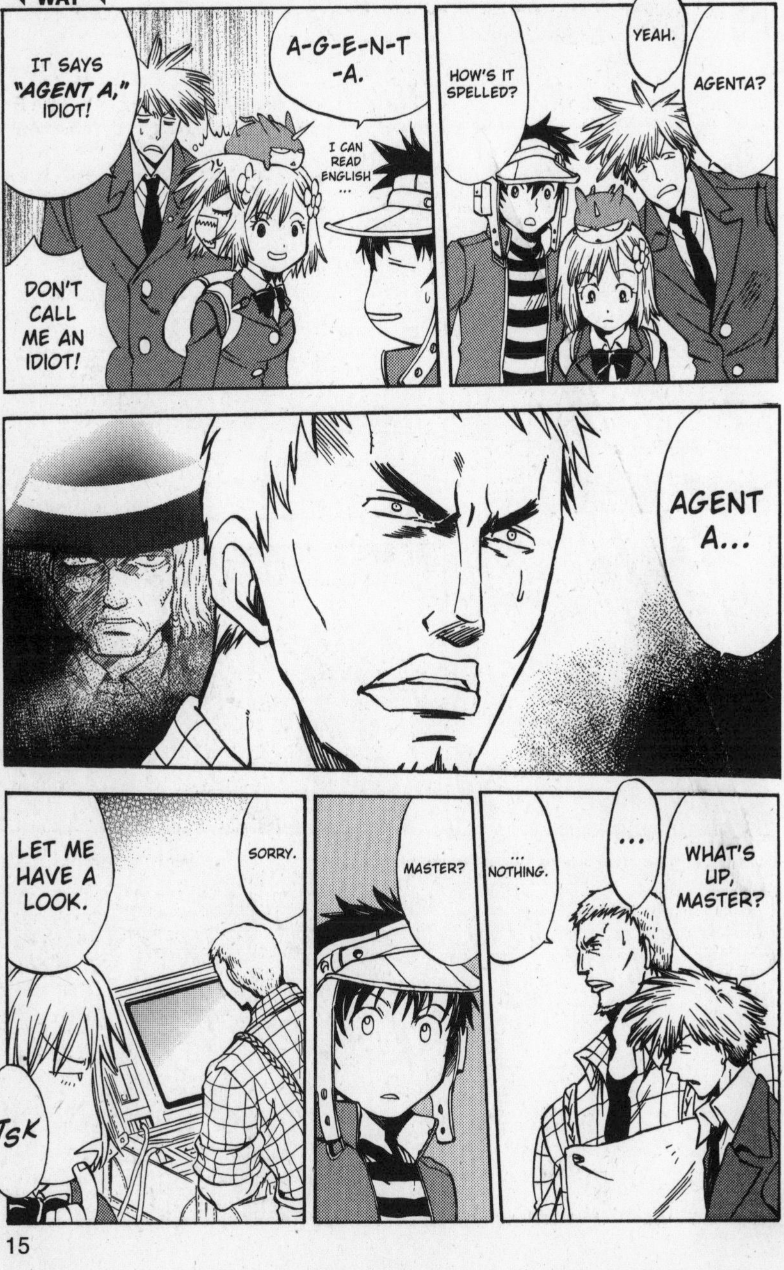
AGENTA?
YEAH.
HOW'S IT SPELLED?
A-G-E-N-T -A.
I CAN READ ENGLISH ...
IT SAYS "AGENT A," IDIOT!
DON'T CALL ME AN IDIOT!
AGENT A...
WHAT'S UP, MASTER?
...
... NOTHING.
MASTER?
SORRY.
LET ME HAVE A LOOK.
TSK

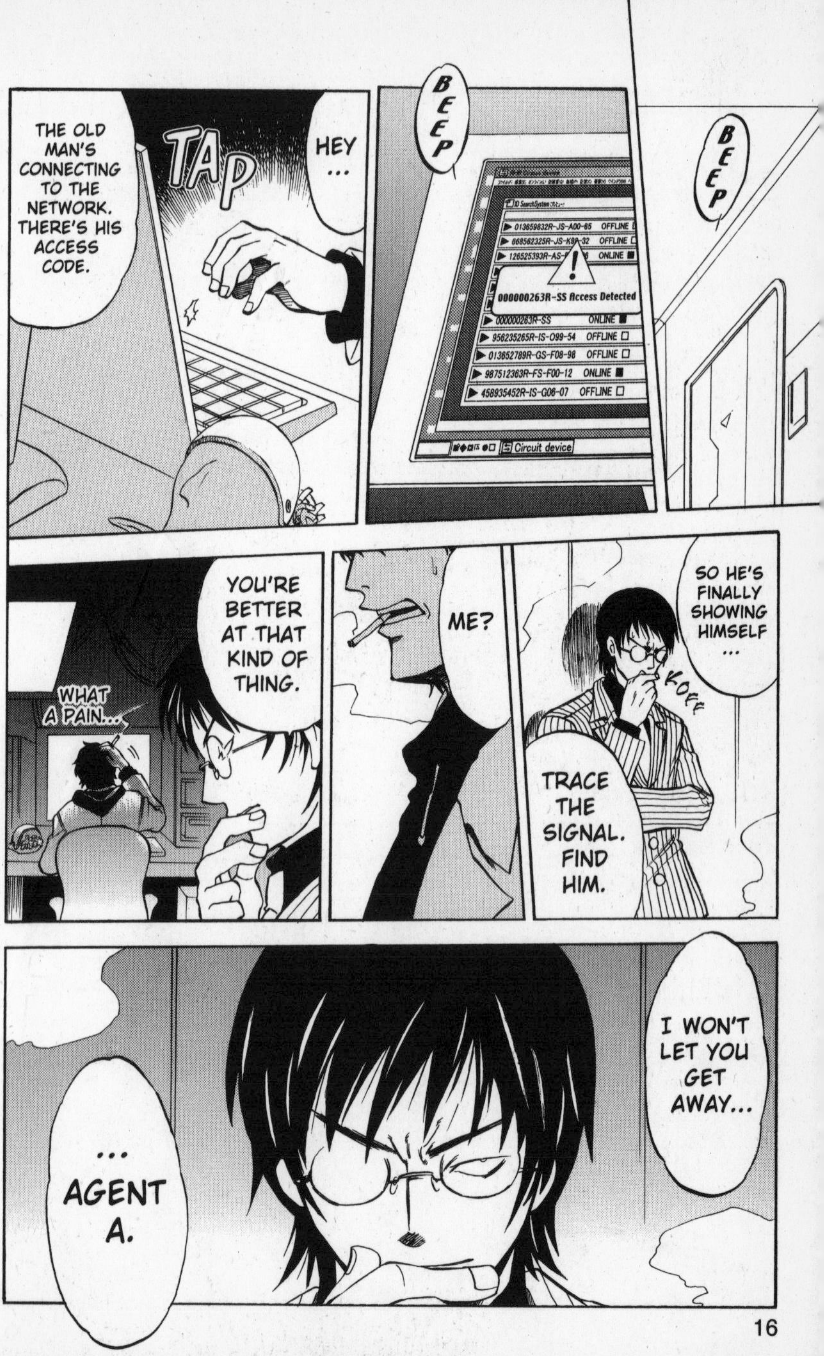
BEEP
BEEP
ID SearchSystem
013659832R-JS-A00-65 OFFLINE
668562325R-JS-K8 -32 OFFLINE
000000263R-SS Access Detected
000000263R-SS ONLINE
956235265R-IS-O99-54 OFFLINE
013652789R-GS-F08-98 OFFLINE
987512363R-FS-F00-12 ONLINE
458935452R-IS-G06-07 OFFLINE
Circuit device
HEY ...
TAP
THE OLD MAN'S CONNECTING TO THE NETWORK. THERE'S HIS ACCESS CODE.
SO HE'S FINALLY SHOWING HIMSELF ...
KOFF
TRACE THE SIGNAL. FIND HIM.
ME?
YOU'RE BETTER AT THAT KIND OF THING.
WHAT A PAIN...
I WON'T LET YOU GET AWAY...
... AGENT A.

READ THIS WAY

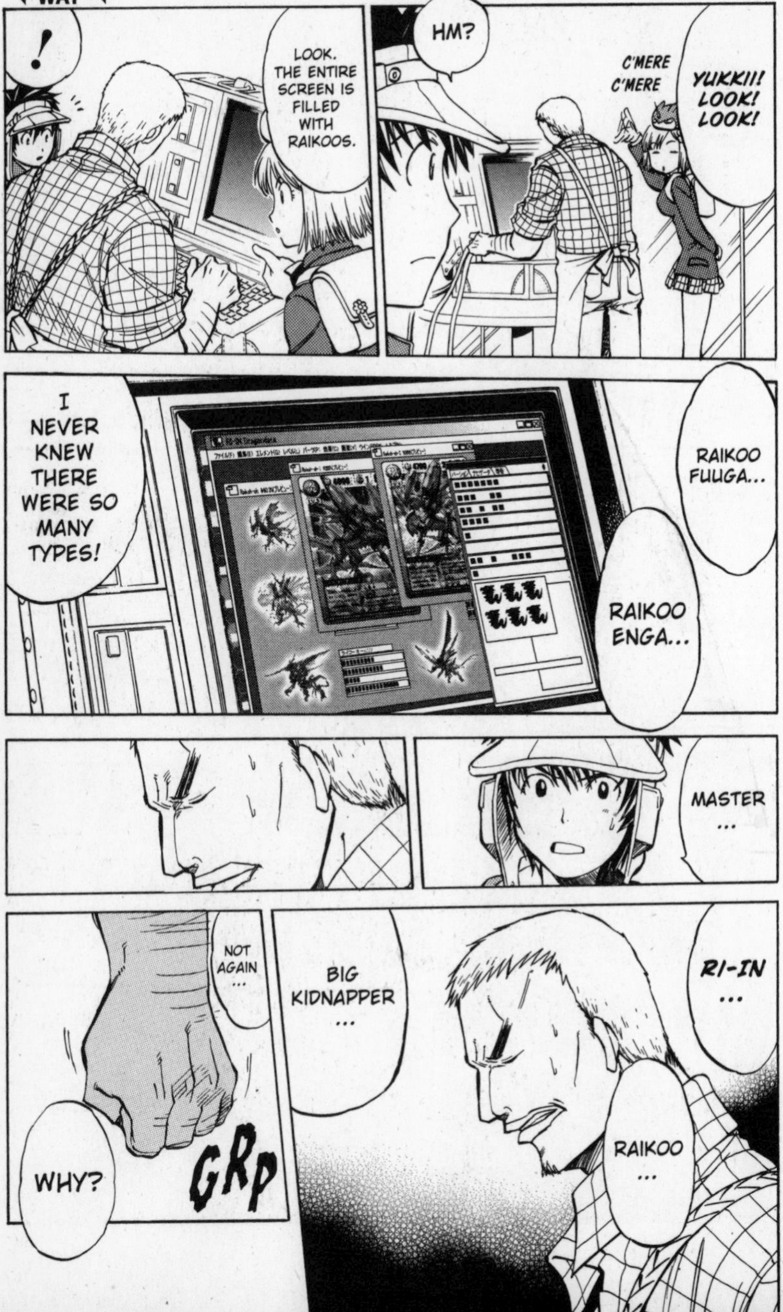
YUKKI!! LOOK! LOOK!
C'MERE C'MERE
HM?
LOOK. THE ENTIRE SCREEN IS FILLED WITH RAIKOOS.
!
RAIKOO FUUGA...
RAIKOO ENGA...
I NEVER KNEW THERE WERE SO MANY TYPES!
MASTER ...
RI-IN ...
RAIKOO ...
BIG KIDNAPPER ...
NOT AGAIN ...
GRP
WHY?

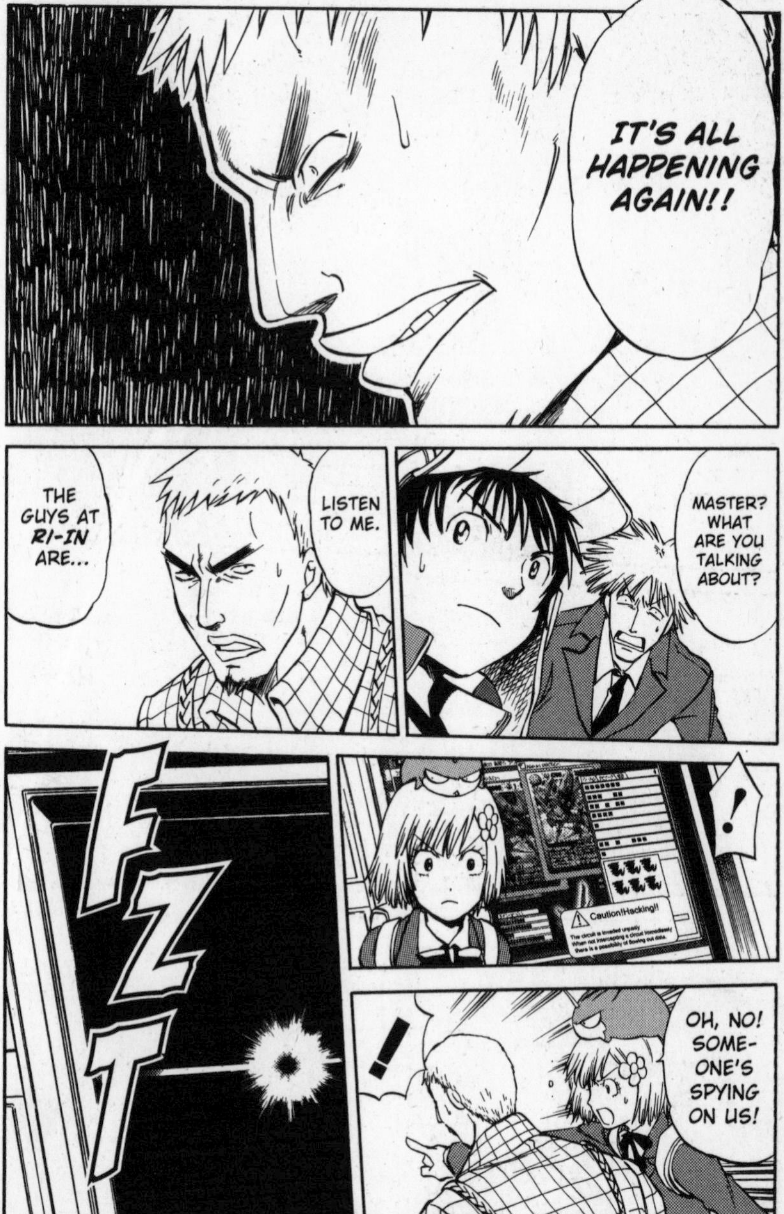
IT'S ALL HAPPENING AGAIN!!
MASTER? WHAT ARE YOU TALKING ABOUT?
LISTEN TO ME.
THE GUYS AT *RI-IN* ARE...
!
Caution!Hacking!!
OH, NO! SOME-ONE'S SPYING ON US!
!
FZT

READ THIS WAY

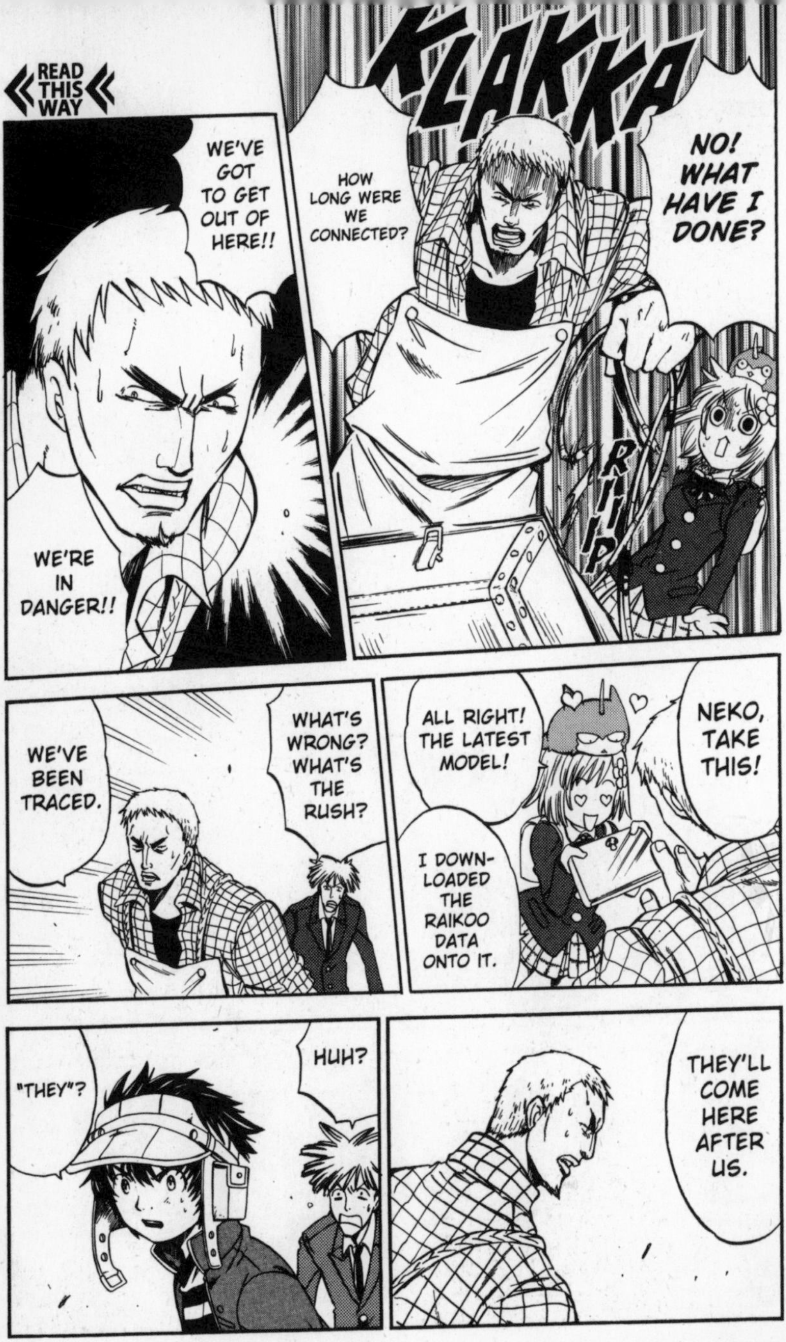
KLAKKA
NO! WHAT HAVE I DONE?
HOW LONG WERE WE CONNECTED?
RIIIP
WE'VE GOT TO GET OUT OF HERE!!
WE'RE IN DANGER!!
NEKO, TAKE THIS!
ALL RIGHT! THE LATEST MODEL!
I DOWN-LOADED THE RAIKOO DATA ONTO IT.
WHAT'S WRONG? WHAT'S THE RUSH?
WE'VE BEEN TRACED.
THEY'LL COME HERE AFTER US.
HUH?
"THEY"?

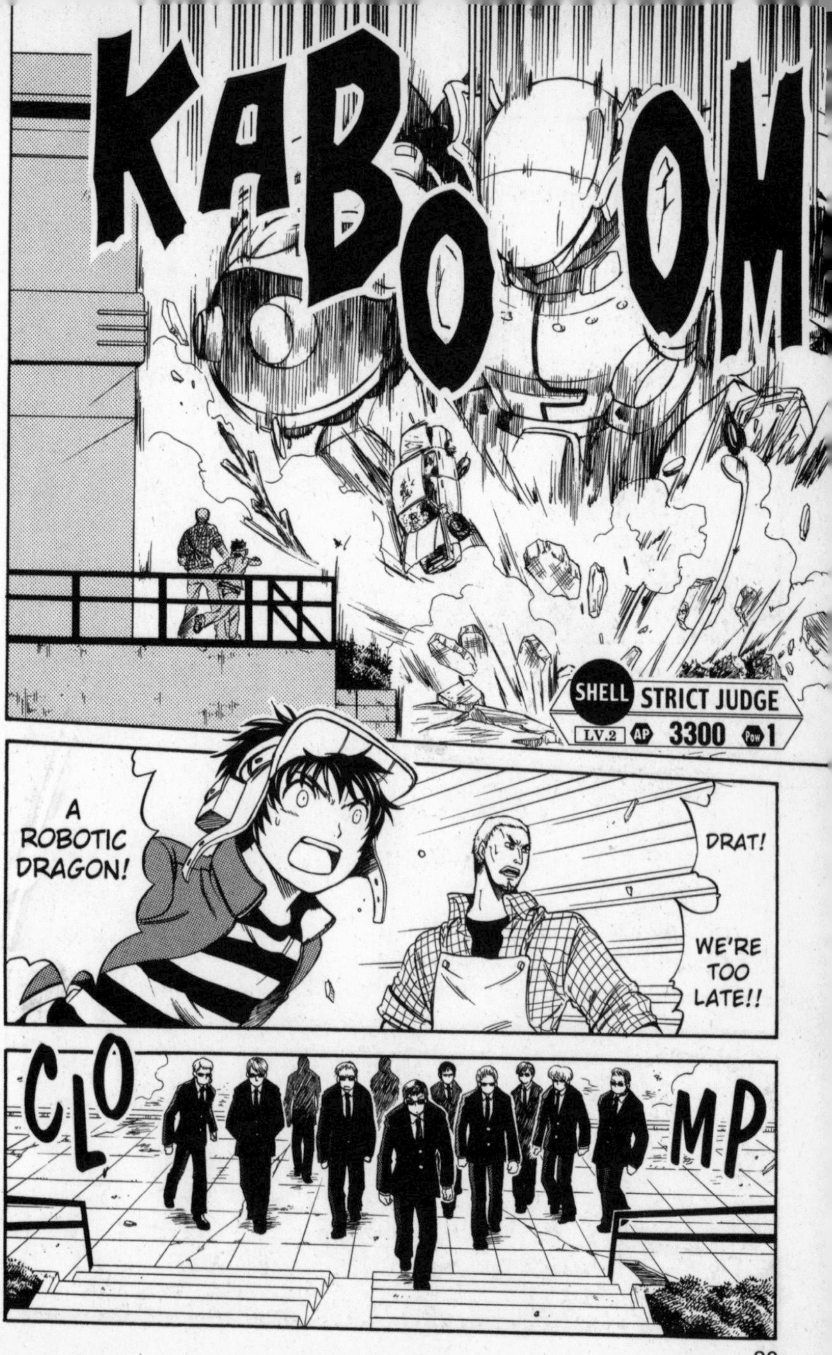
KABOOOM
SHELL
STRICT JUDGE
LV.2
AP
3300
Pow
1
A ROBOTIC DRAGON!
DRAT!
WE'RE TOO LATE!!
CLOMP

READ THIS WAY

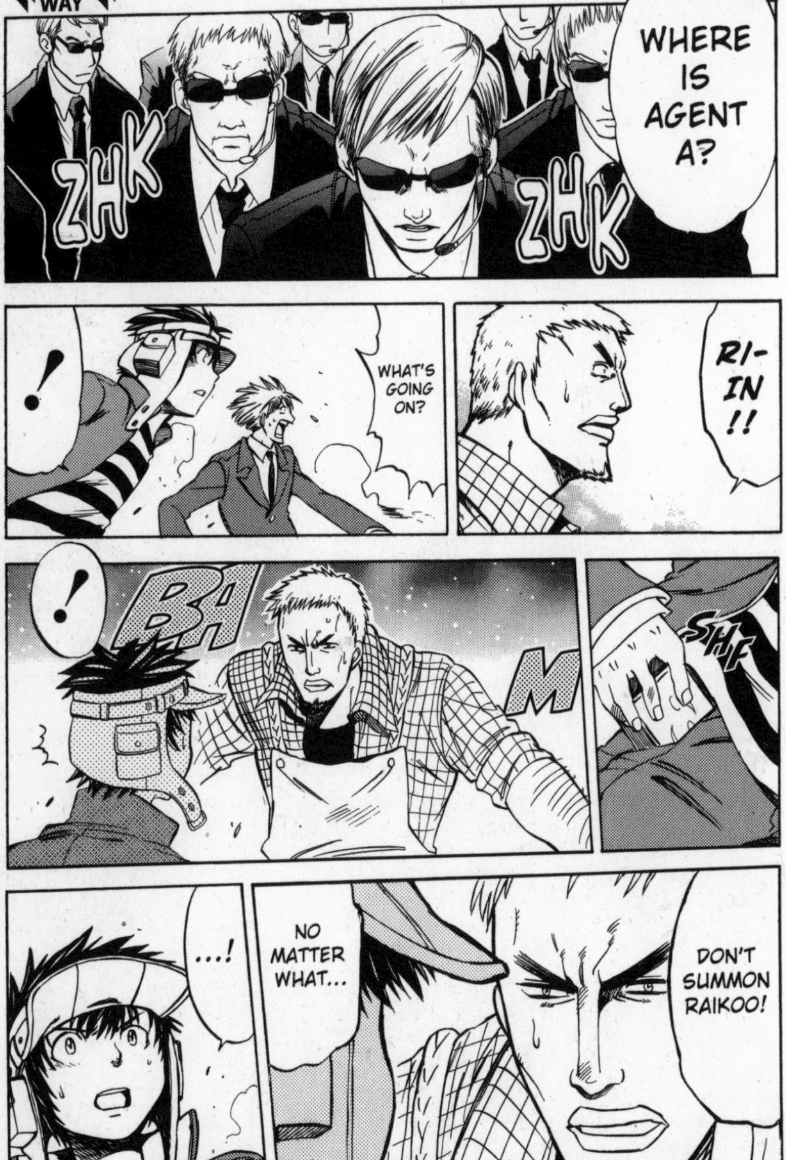
WHERE IS AGENT A?
ZHK
ZHK
RI-IN!!
WHAT'S GOING ON?
!
SHF
BAM
!
DON'T SUMMON RAIKOO!
NO MATTER WHAT...
...!

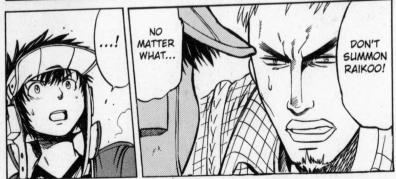

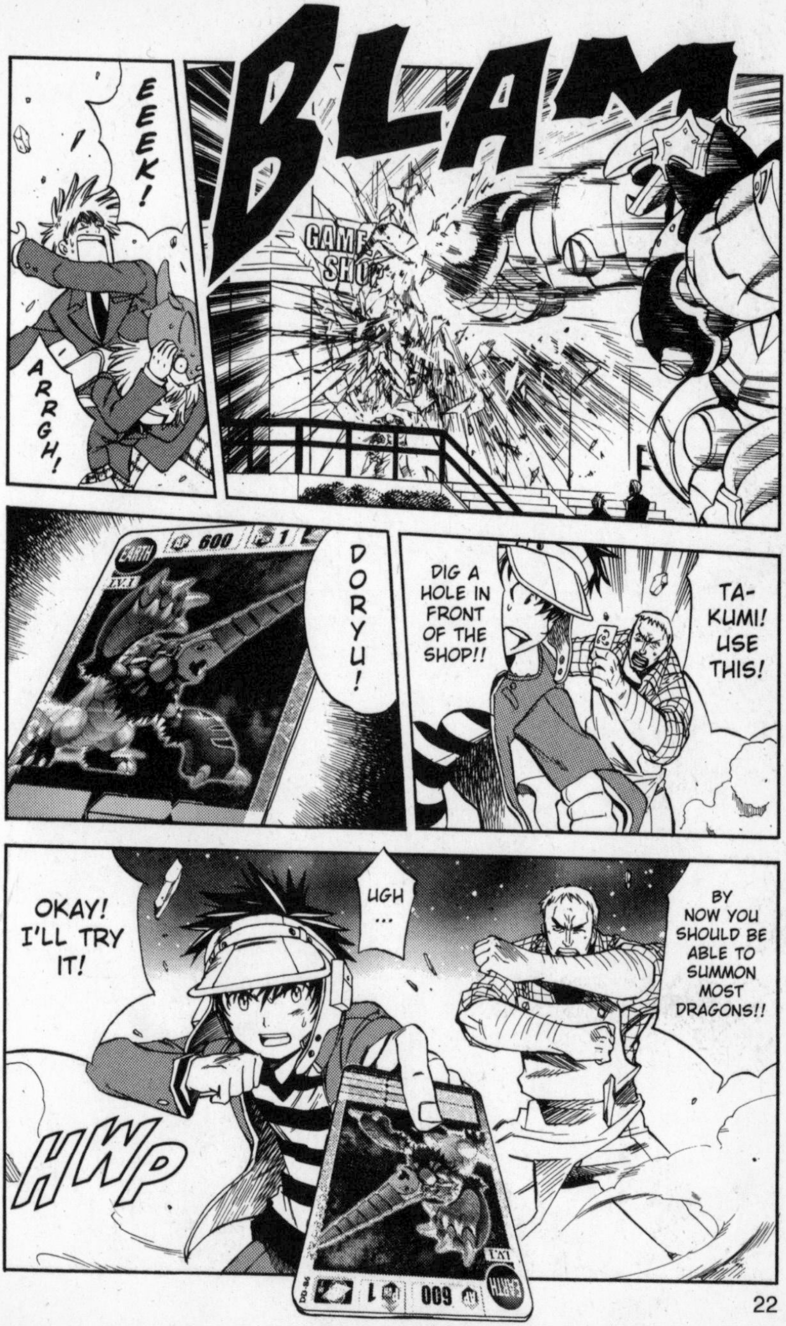
BLAM
GAME SHOP
EEEK!
ARRGH!
TA-KUMI! USE THIS!
DIG A HOLE IN FRONT OF THE SHOP!!
DORYU!
EARTH
600
1
LV.1
BY NOW YOU SHOULD BE ABLE TO SUMMON MOST DRAGONS!!
UGH...
OKAY! I'LL TRY IT!
HWP

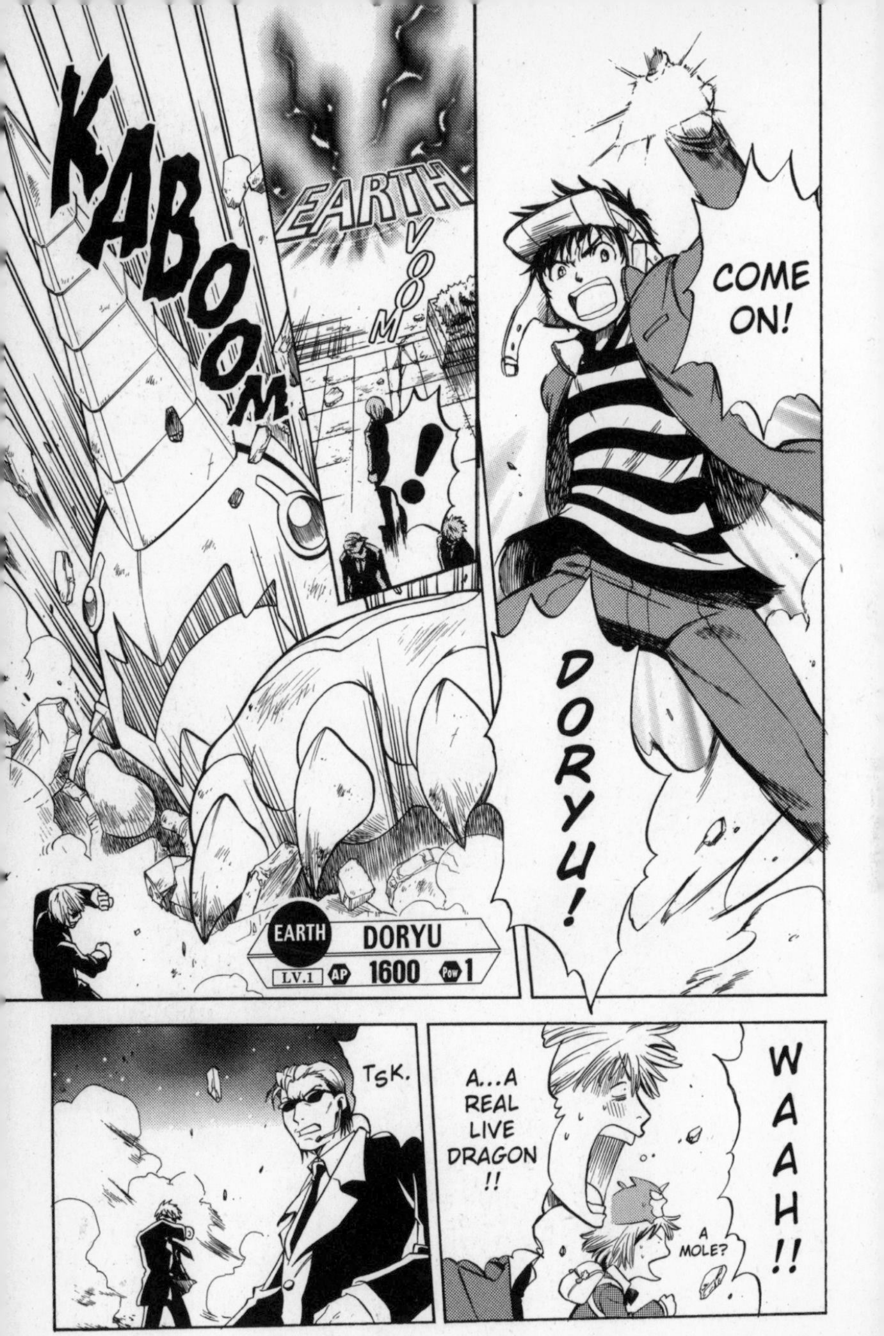
COME ON!
DORYU!
EARTH
VOOM
!!
KABOOM
EARTH
DORYU
LV.1 AP 1600 Pow 1
WAAH!!
A...A REAL LIVE DRAGON!!
A MOLE?
TSK.

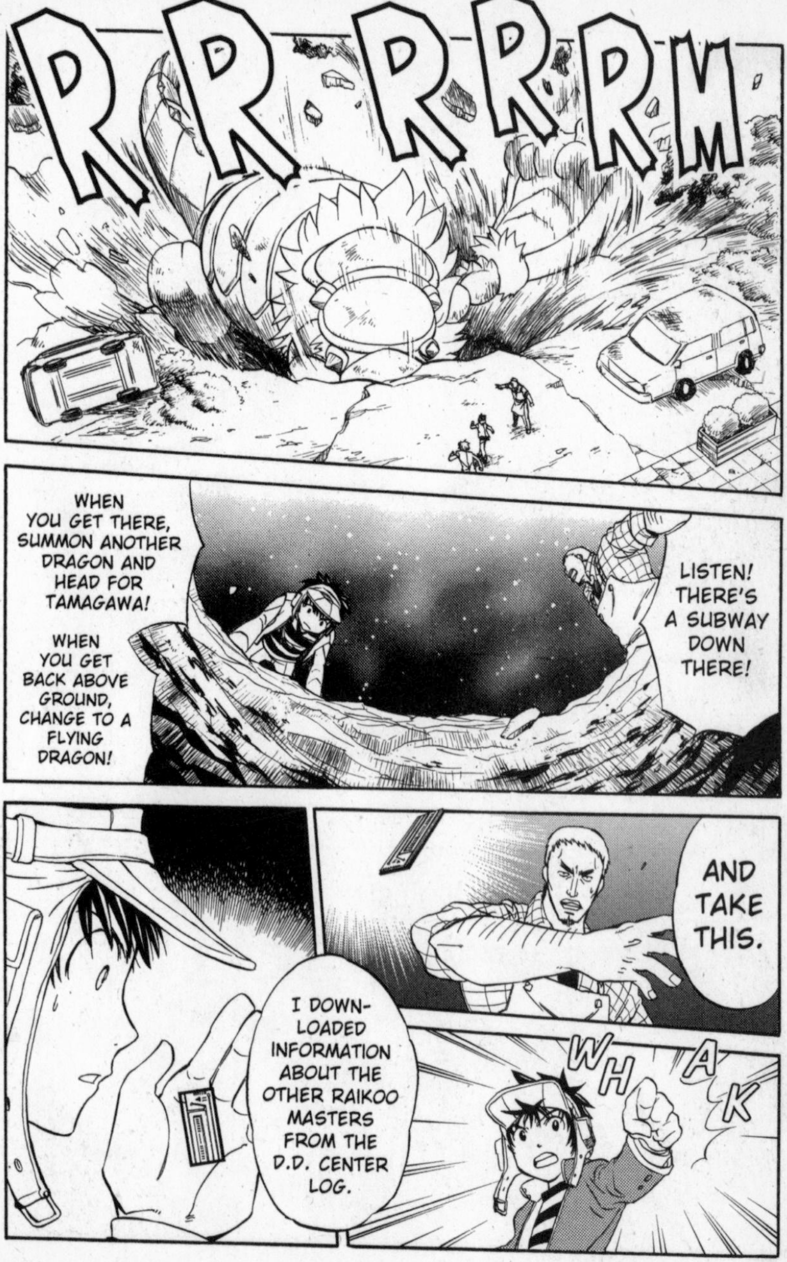
R-R-R-R-R-M
LISTEN! THERE'S A SUBWAY DOWN THERE!
WHEN YOU GET THERE, SUMMON ANOTHER DRAGON AND HEAD FOR TAMAGAWA!
WHEN YOU GET BACK ABOVE GROUND, CHANGE TO A FLYING DRAGON!
AND TAKE THIS.
WHAK
I DOWN-LOADED INFORMATION ABOUT THE OTHER RAIKOO MASTERS FROM THE D.D. CENTER LOG.

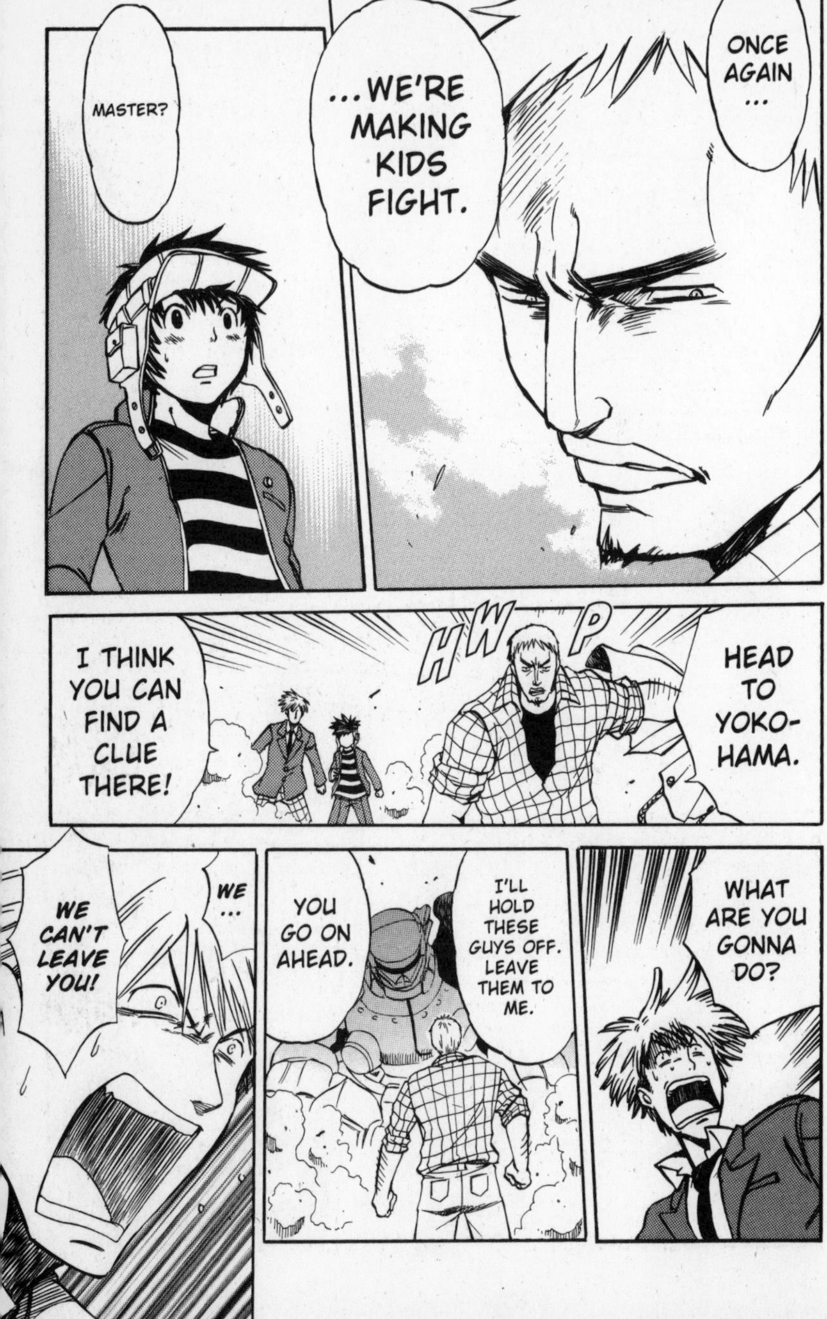
ONCE AGAIN ...
...WE'RE MAKING KIDS FIGHT.
MASTER?
HEAD TO YOKO-HAMA.
HWP
I THINK YOU CAN FIND A CLUE THERE!
WHAT ARE YOU GONNA DO?
I'LL HOLD THESE GUYS OFF. LEAVE THEM TO ME.
YOU GO ON AHEAD.
WE ...
WE CAN'T LEAVE YOU!

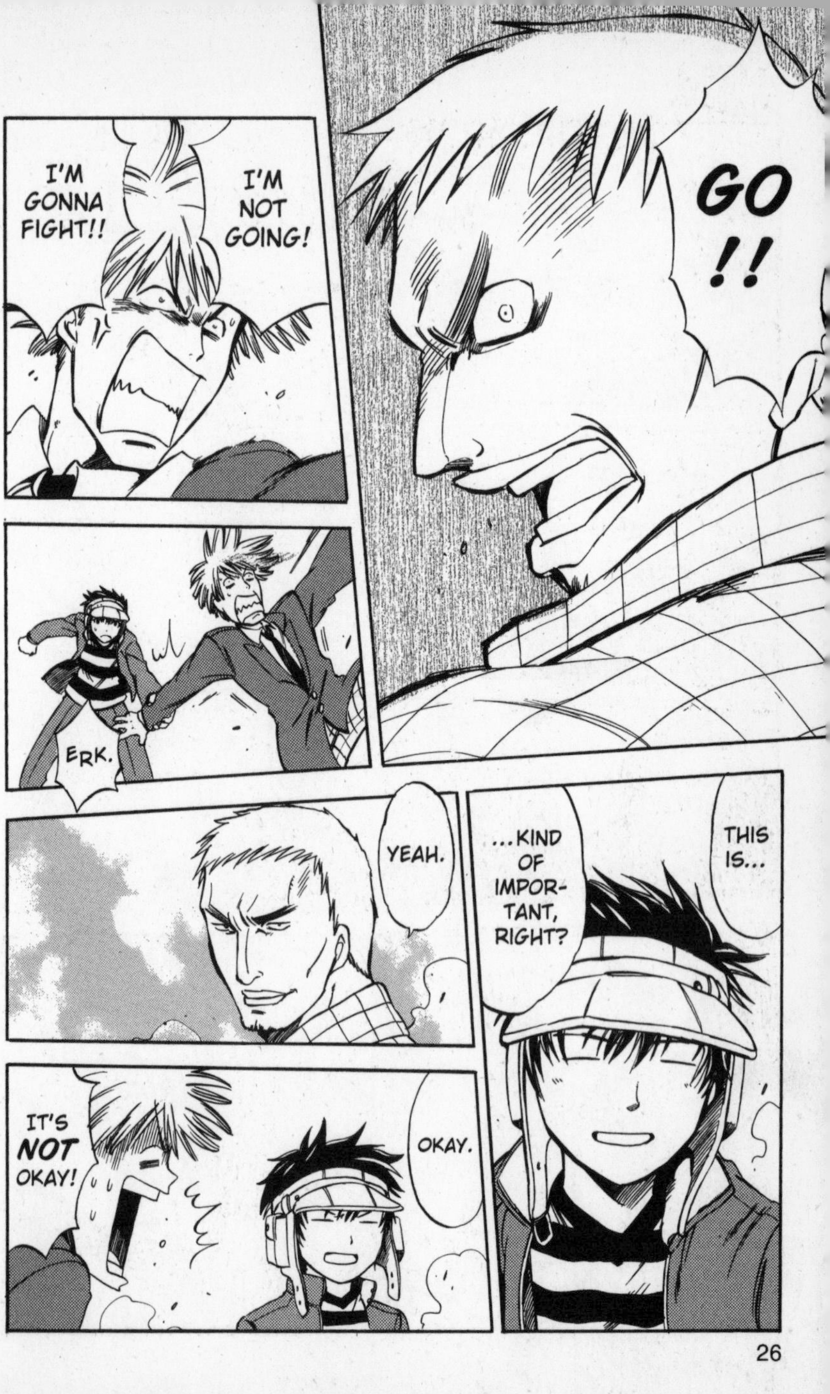
GO !!
I'M NOT GOING!
I'M GONNA FIGHT!!
ERK.
THIS IS...
...KIND OF IMPOR-TANT, RIGHT?
YEAH.
OKAY.
IT'S NOT OKAY!

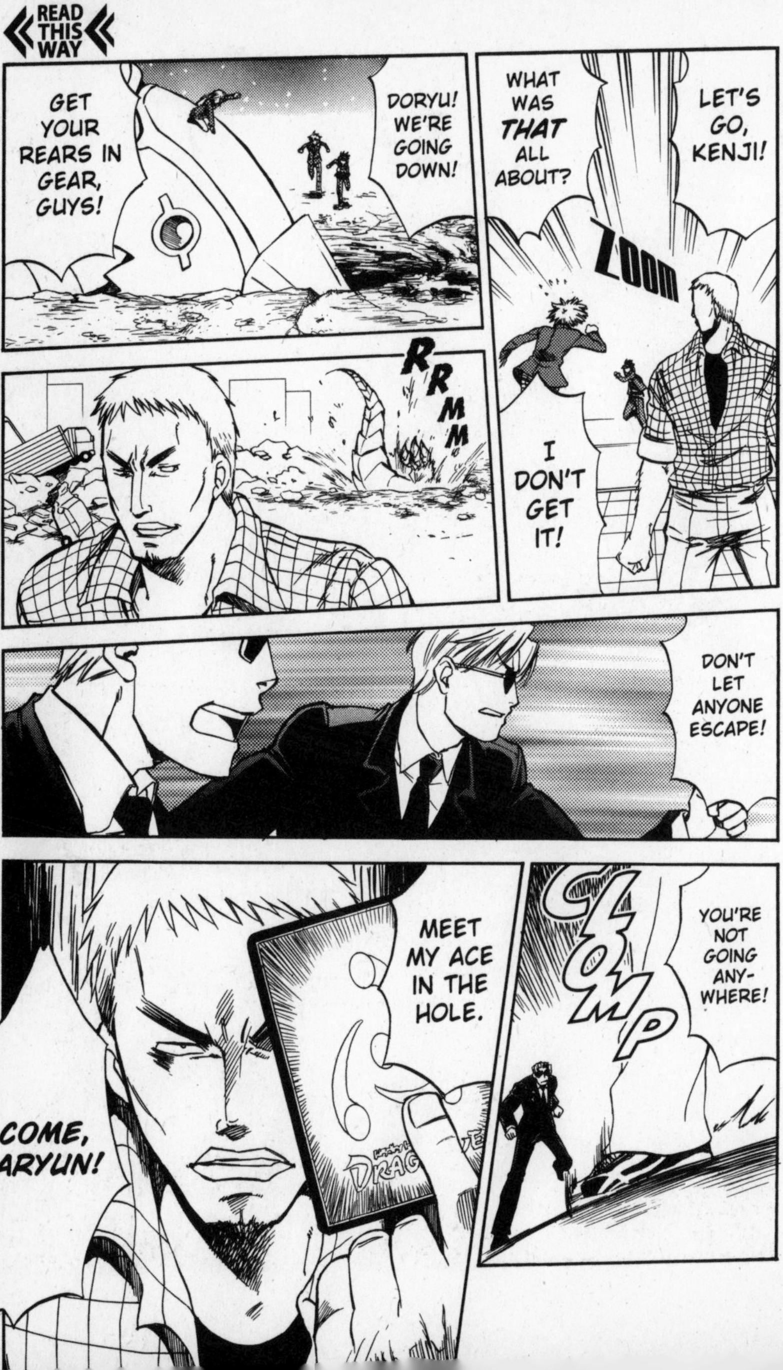
READ THIS WAY
LET'S GO, KENJI!
WHAT WAS THAT ALL ABOUT?
ZOOM
I DON'T GET IT!
DORYU! WE'RE GOING DOWN!
GET YOUR REARS IN GEAR, GUYS!
RRMM
DON'T LET ANYONE ESCAPE!
CLOMP
YOU'RE NOT GOING ANY-WHERE!
MEET MY ACE IN THE HOLE.
COME, ARYUN!

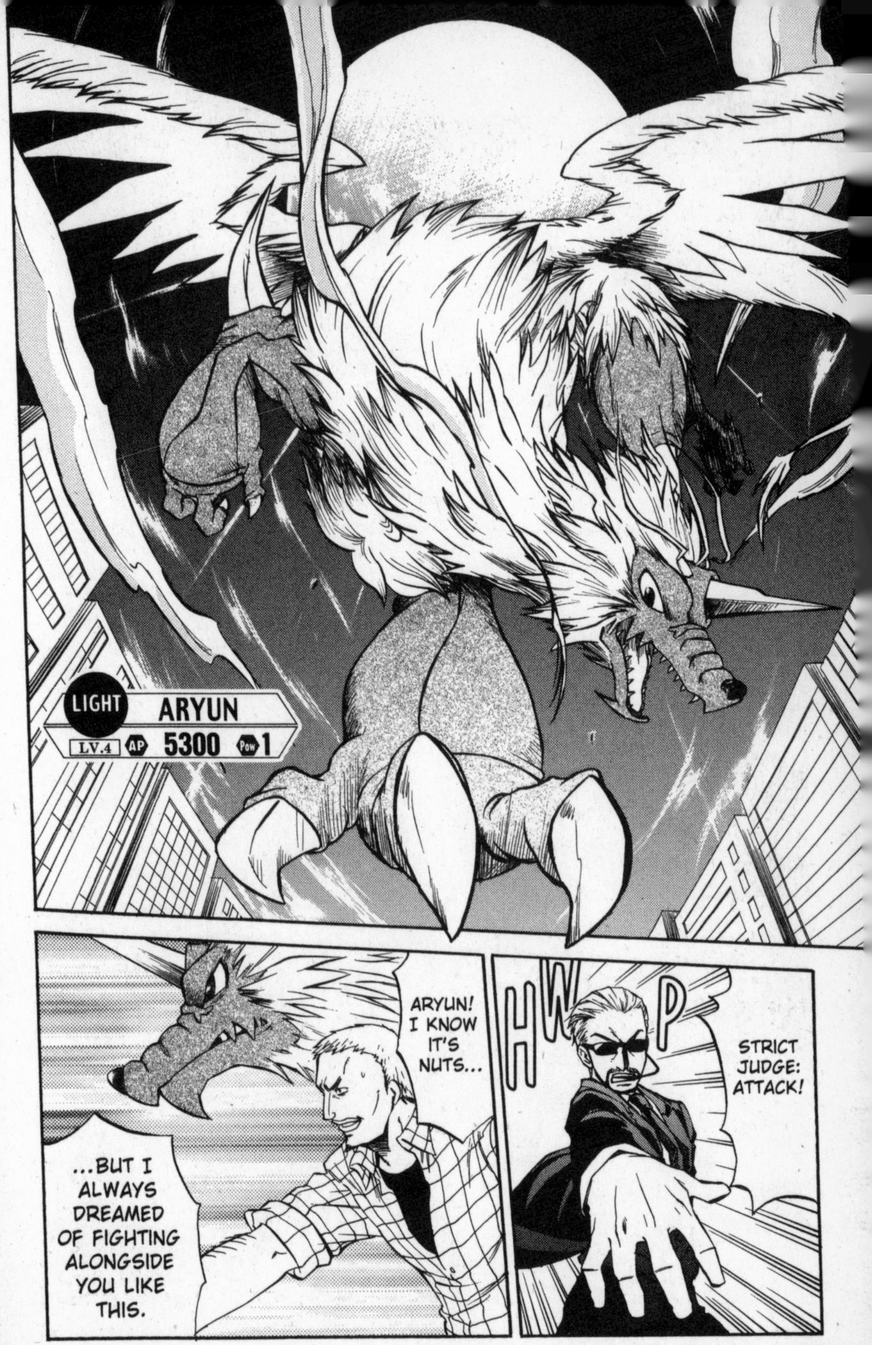
LIGHT
ARYUN
LV.4 AP 5300 Pow 1
HWP
STRICT JUDGE: ATTACK!
ARYUN! I KNOW IT'S NUTS...
...BUT I ALWAYS DREAMED OF FIGHTING ALONGSIDE YOU LIKE THIS.

READ THIS WAY

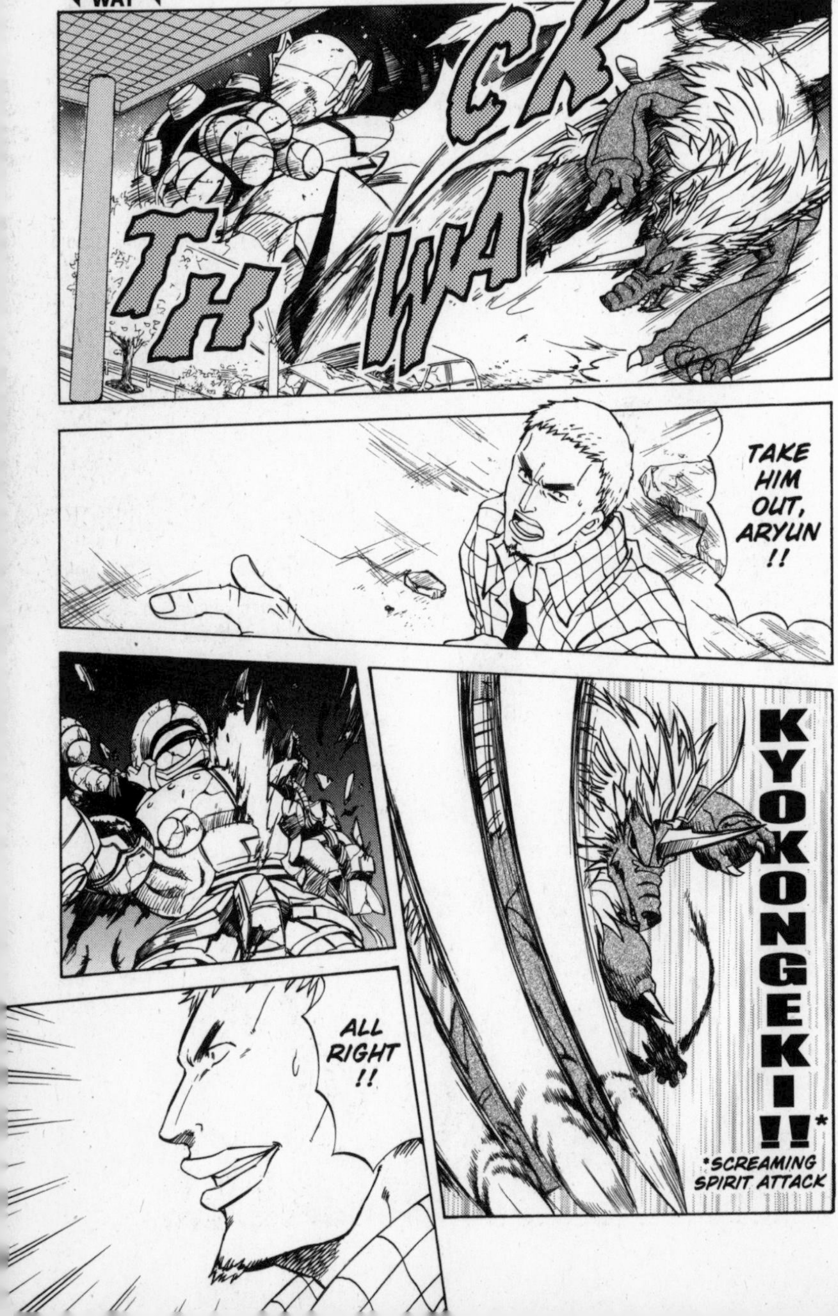
THWACK
TAKE HIM OUT, ARYUN!!
KYOKONGEKI!!*
*SCREAMING SPIRIT ATTACK
ALL RIGHT!!

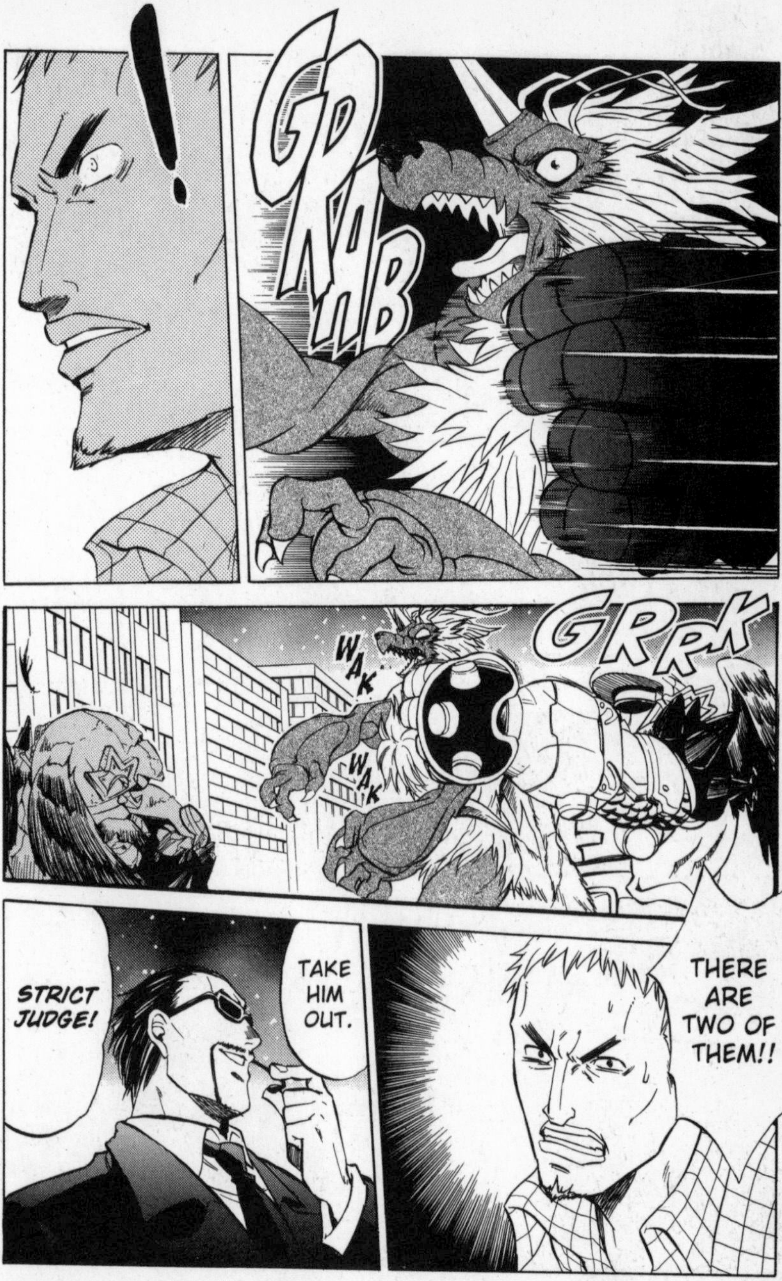
GRAB
!
GRRK
WAK
WAK
THERE ARE TWO OF THEM!!
TAKE HIM OUT.
STRICT JUDGE!

READ THIS WAY

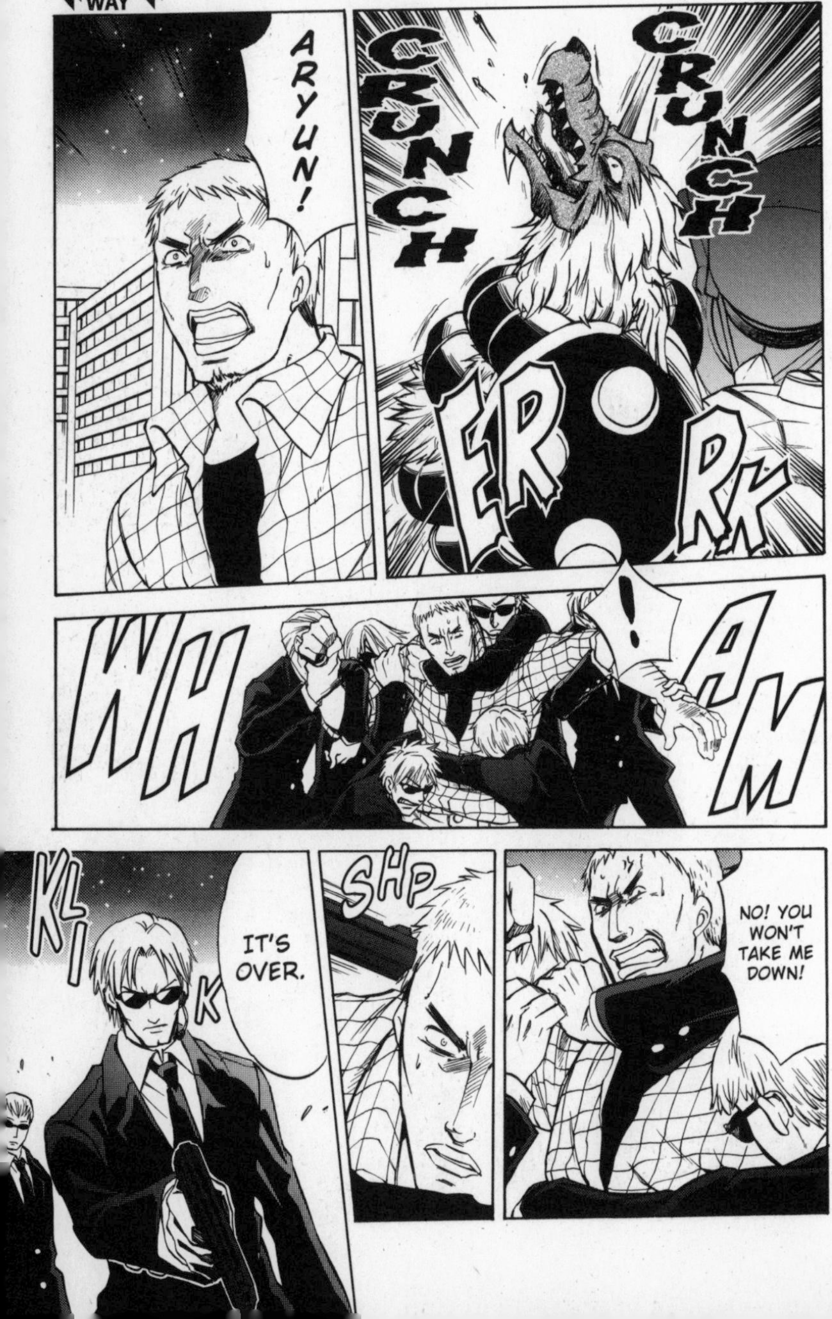
CRUNCH
CRUNCH
ERRK
ARYUN!
!
WHAM
NO! YOU WON'T TAKE ME DOWN!
SHP
IT'S OVER.
KLIK

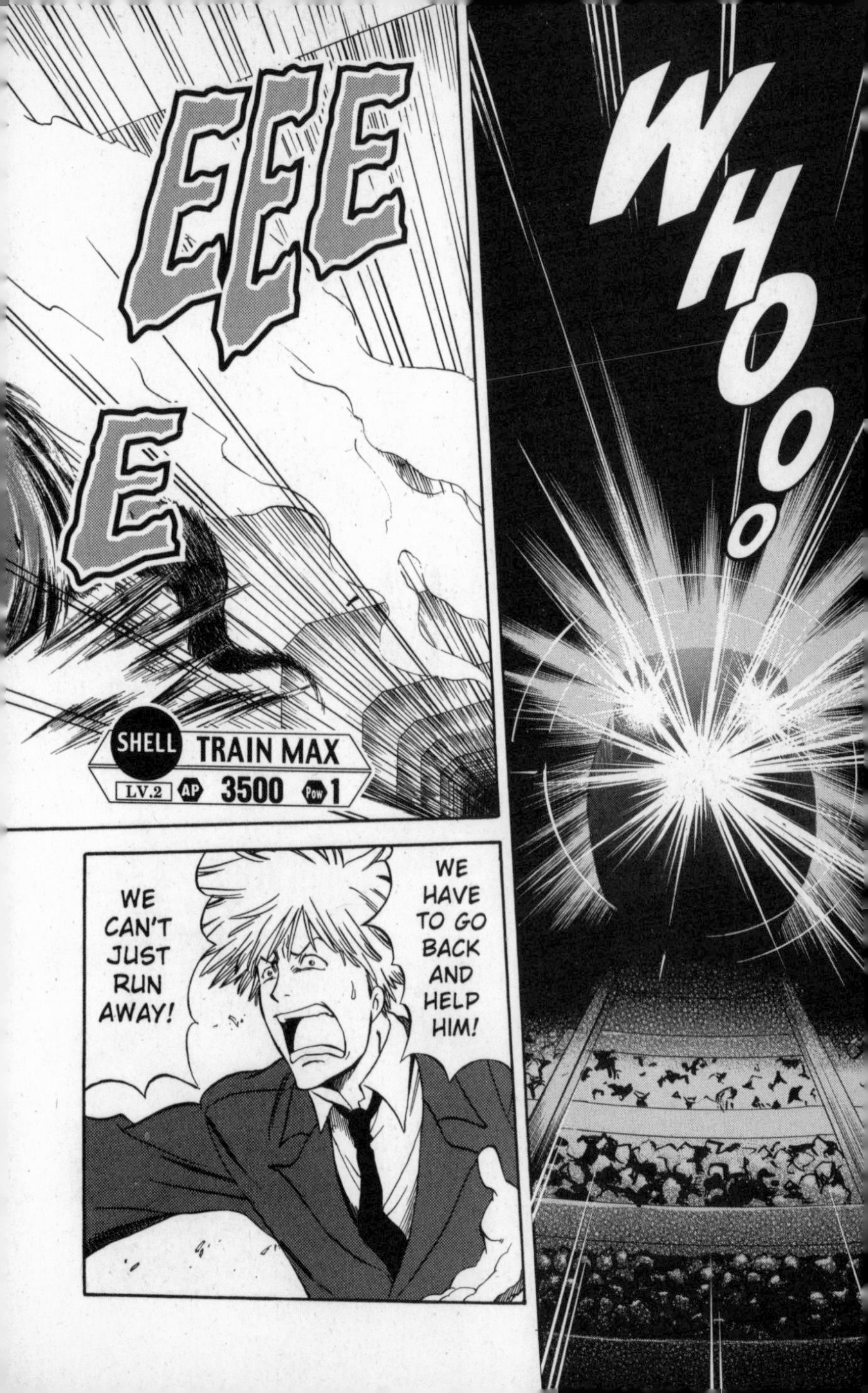
WHOOOO
EEEE
E
SHELL TRAIN MAX
LV.2 AP 3500 Pow 1
WE HAVE TO GO BACK AND HELP HIM!
WE CAN'T JUST RUN AWAY!

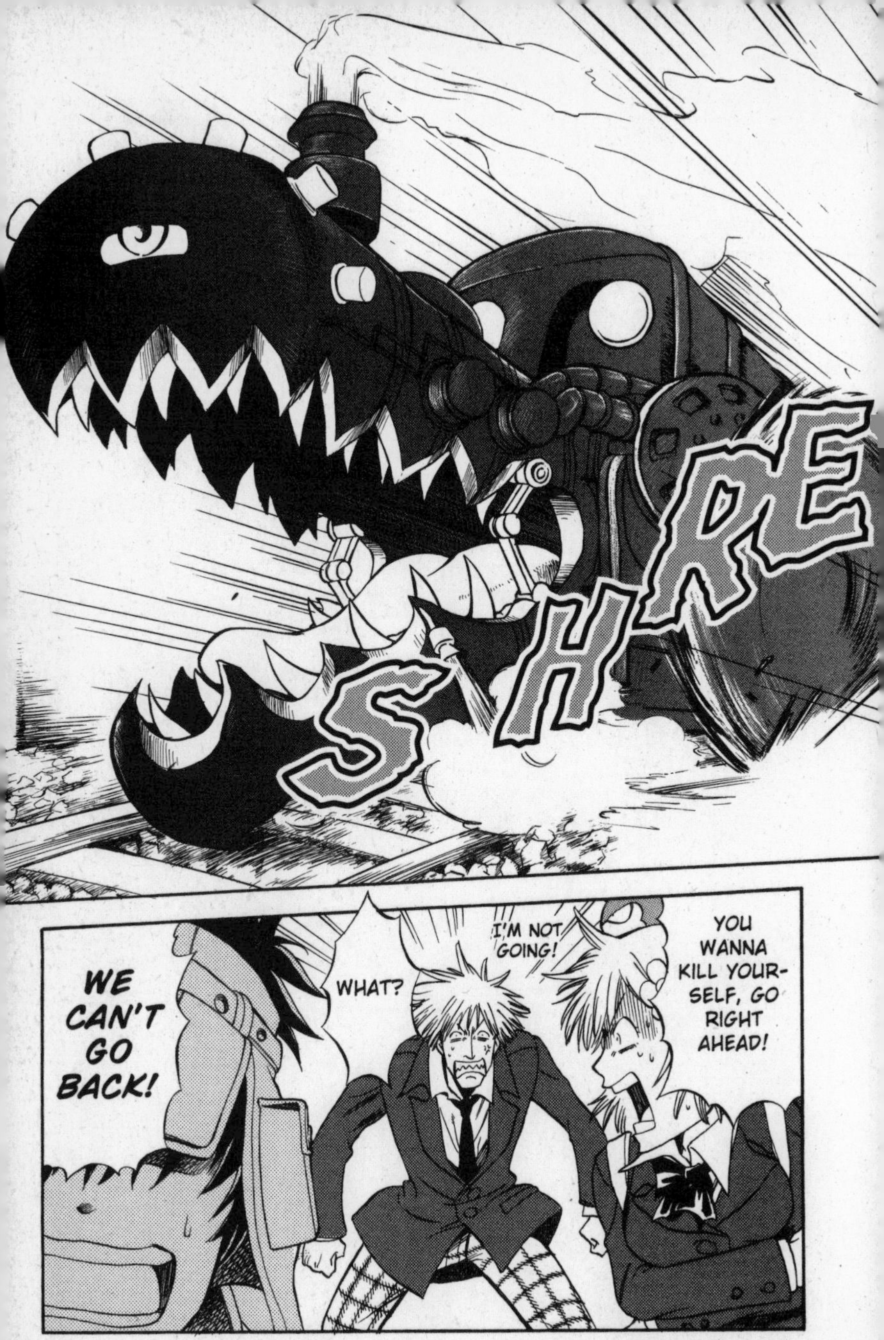
SHRE
YOU WANNA KILL YOUR-SELF, GO RIGHT AHEAD!
I'M NOT GOING!
WHAT?
WE CAN'T GO BACK!

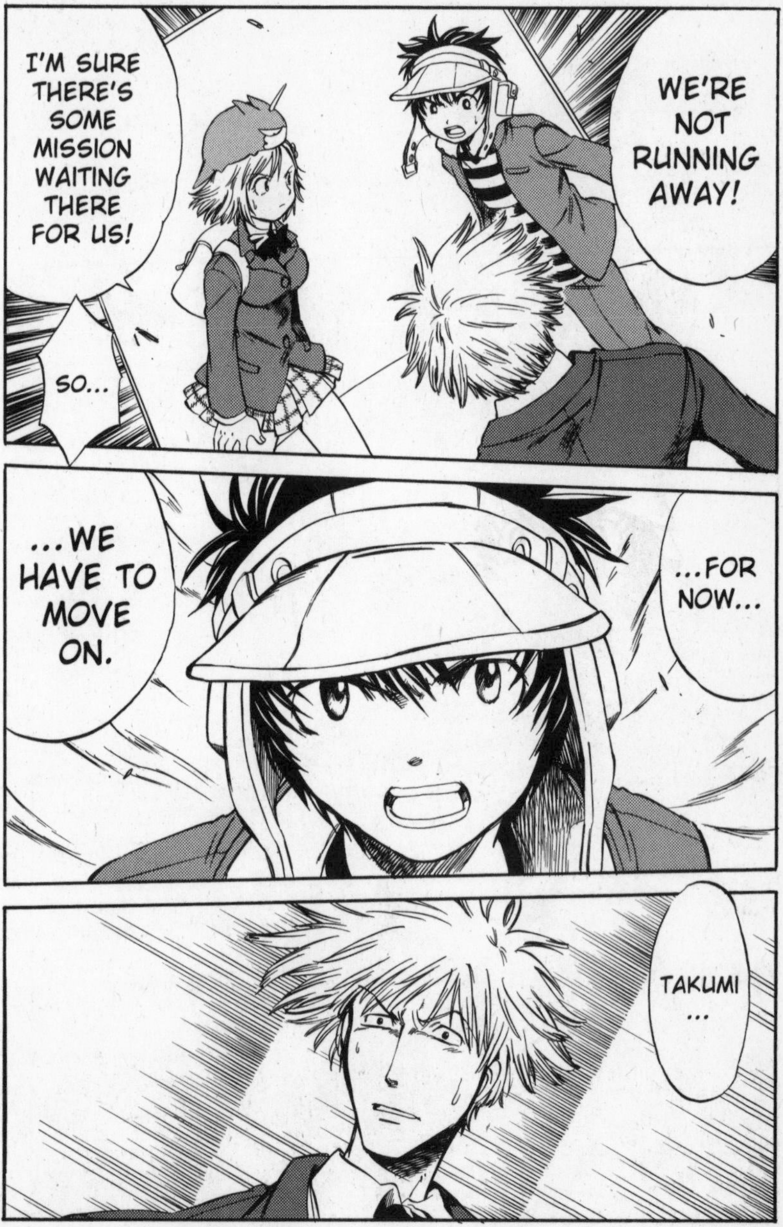
WE'RE NOT RUNNING AWAY!
I'M SURE THERE'S SOME MISSION WAITING THERE FOR US!
SO...
...FOR NOW...
...WE HAVE TO MOVE ON.
TAKUMI ...

READ THIS WAY

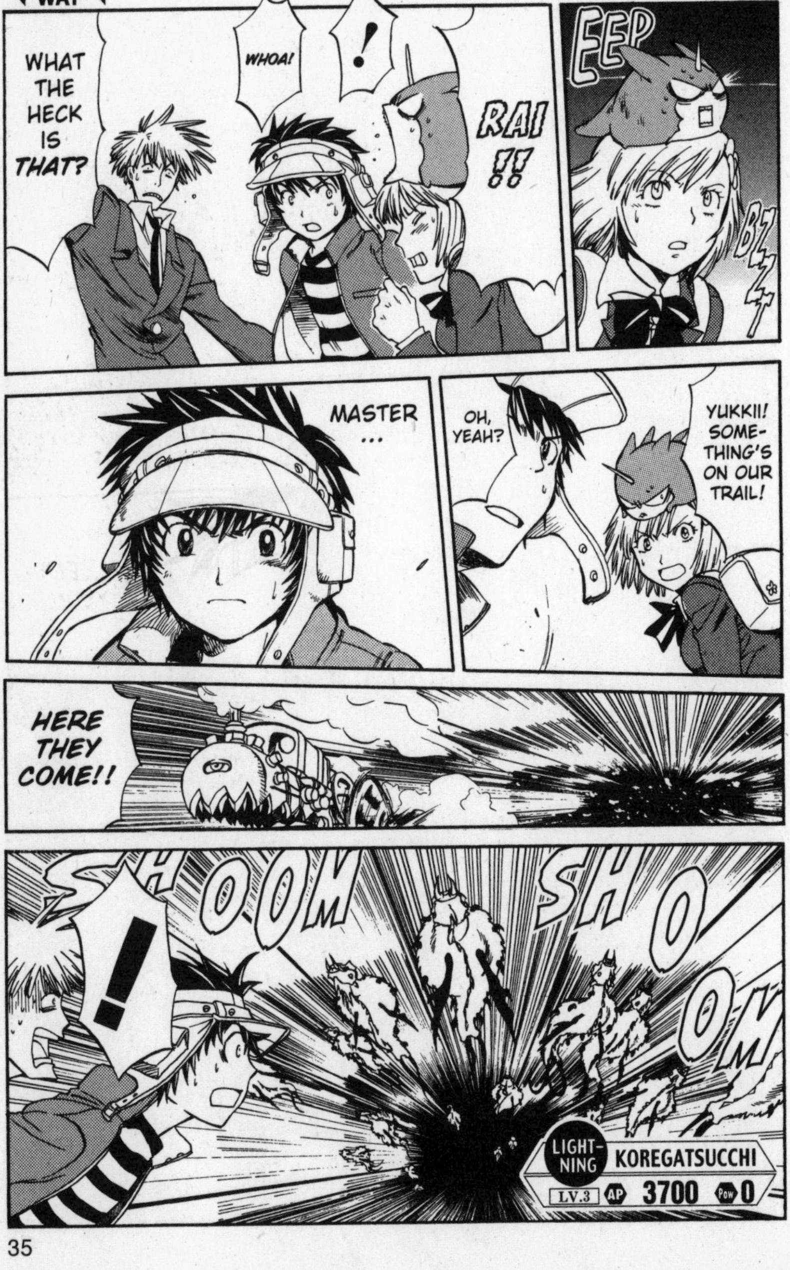
EEP
BZZT
RAI!!
!
WHOA!
WHAT THE HECK IS *THAT?*
YUKKII! SOMETHING'S ON OUR TRAIL!
OH, YEAH?
MASTER...
HERE THEY COME!!
SHOOM
SHOOM
!
LIGHTNING
KOREGATSUCCHI
LV.3
AP 3700
Pow 0

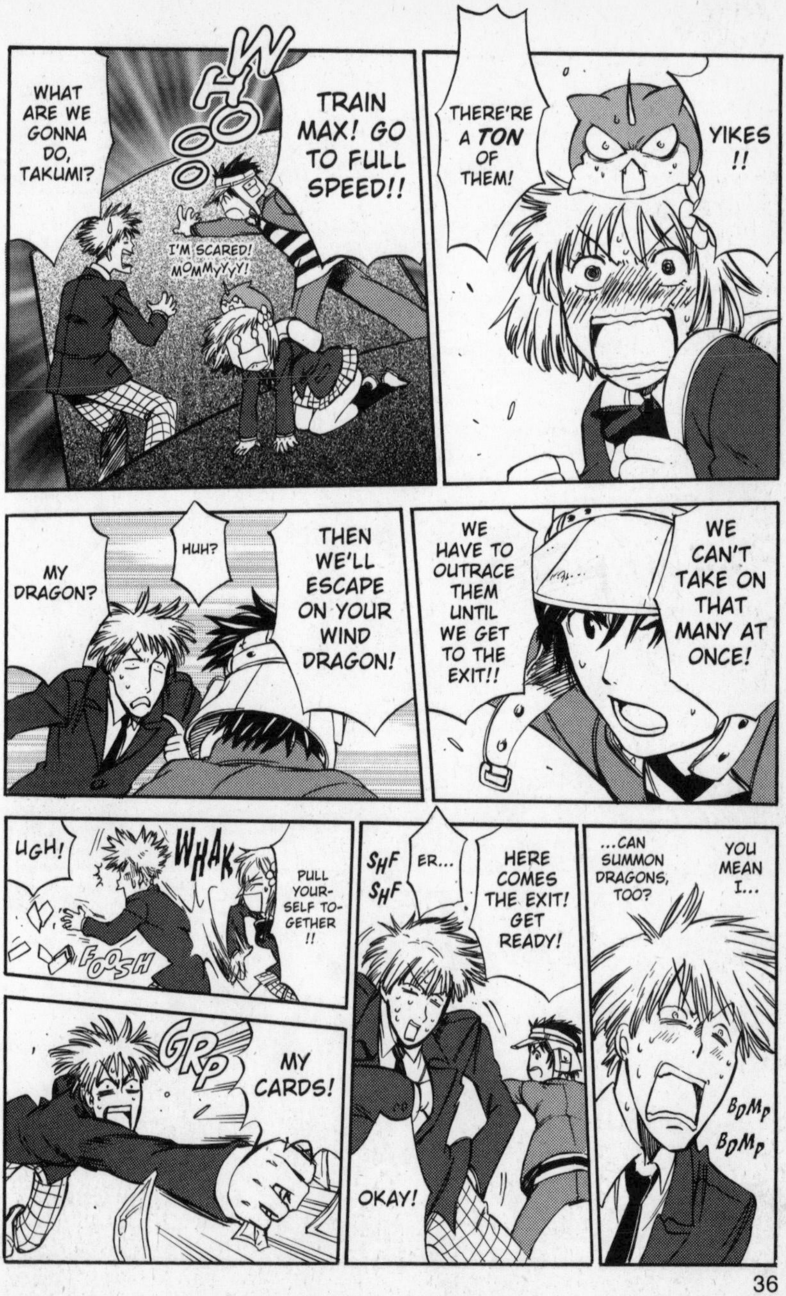

YIKES!!
THERE'RE A TON OF THEM!
TRAIN MAX! GO TO FULL SPEED!!
WHOOOO
WHAT ARE WE GONNA DO, TAKUMI?
I'M SCARED! MOMMYYY!
WE CAN'T TAKE ON THAT MANY AT ONCE!
WE HAVE TO OUTRACE THEM UNTIL WE GET TO THE EXIT!!
THEN WE'LL ESCAPE ON YOUR WIND DRAGON!
HUH?
MY DRAGON?
YOU MEAN I...
...CAN SUMMON DRAGONS, TOO?
BDMP
BDMP
HERE COMES THE EXIT! GET READY!
ER...
SHF
SHF
OKAY!
PULL YOURSELF TOGETHER!!
WHAK
UGH!
FOOSH
MY CARDS!
GRP

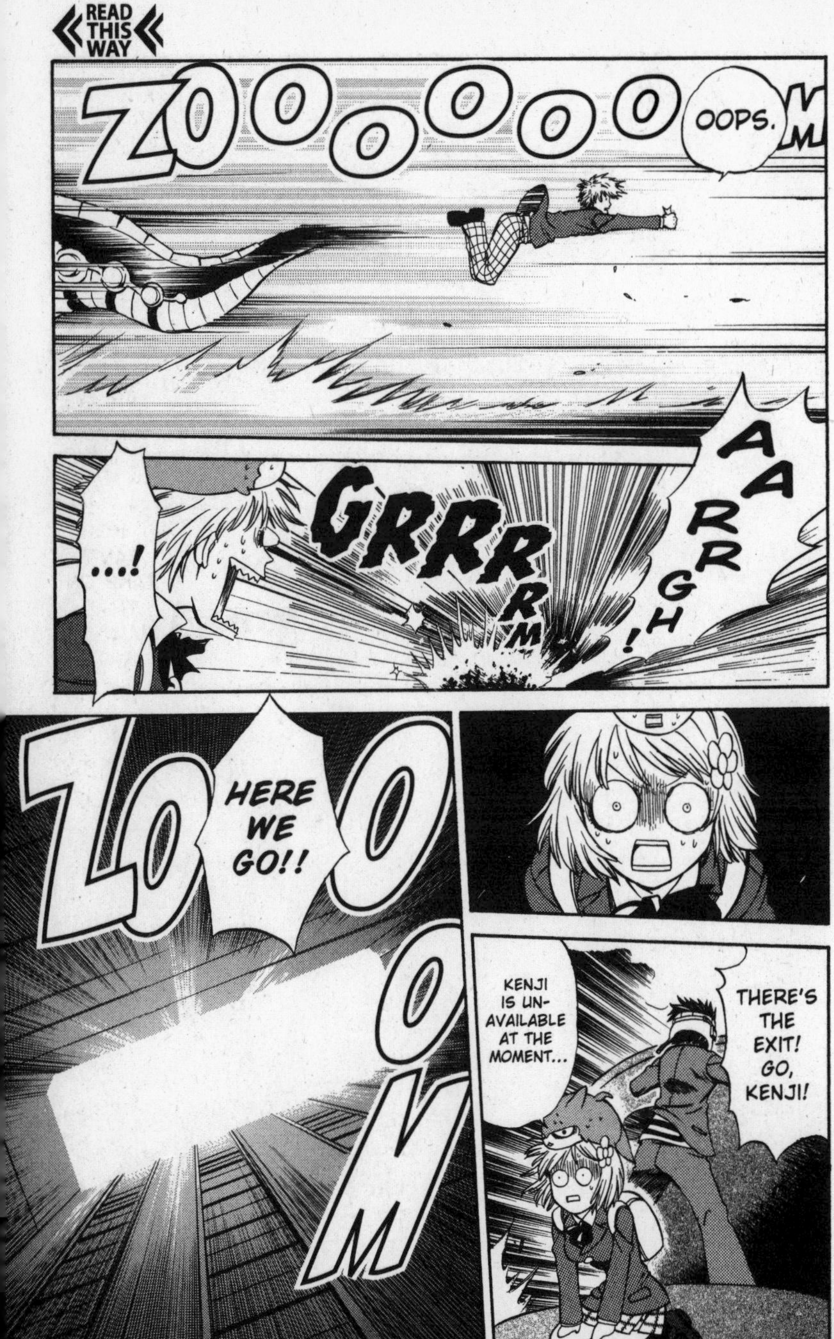
READ THIS WAY
ZOOOOOOOOMM
OOPS.
AARRGH!
GRRRRM
...!
THERE'S THE EXIT! GO, KENJI!
KENJI IS UN-AVAILABLE AT THE MOMENT...
ZOOOM
HERE WE GO!!

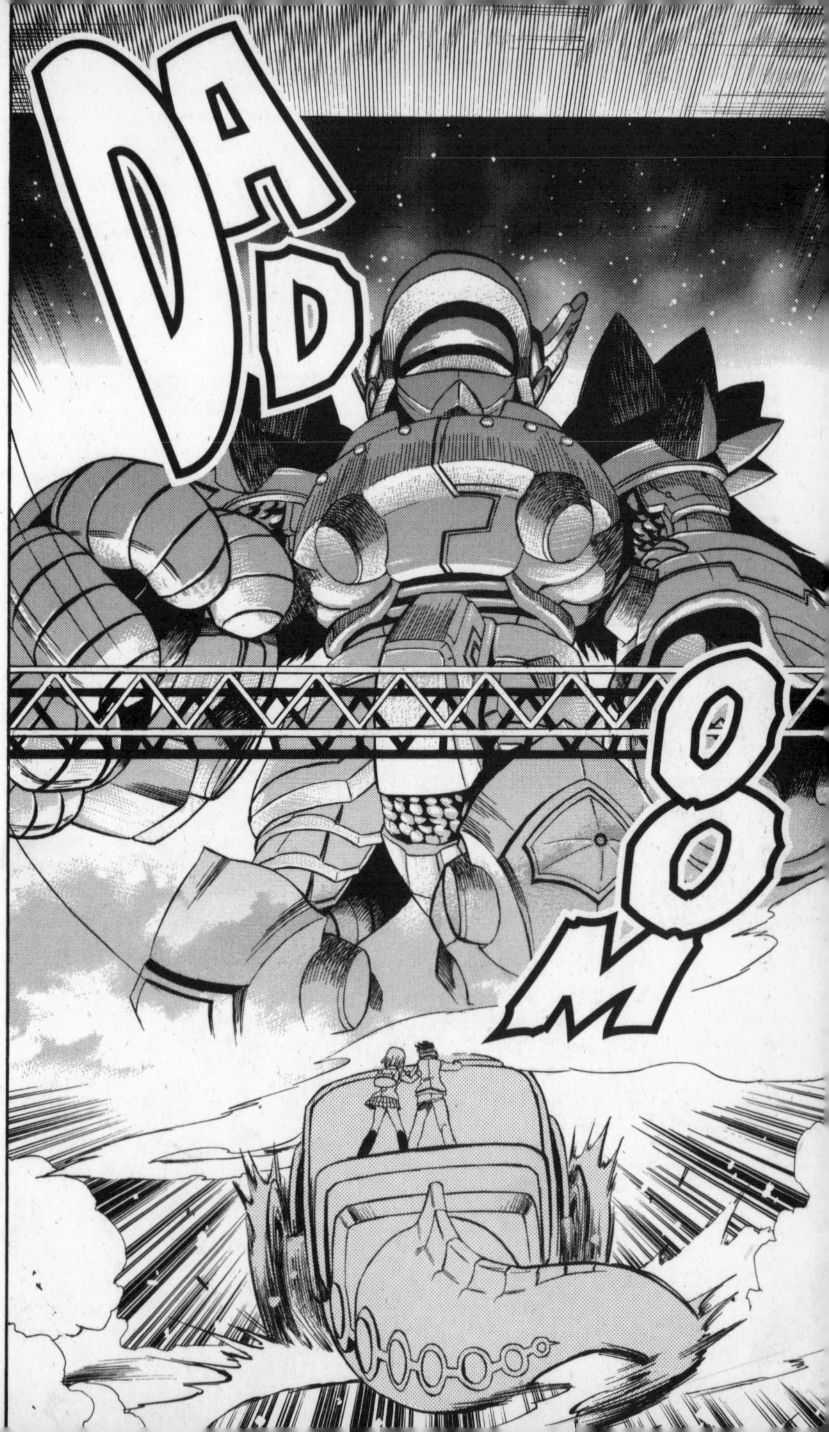
DADOOM

READ THIS WAY

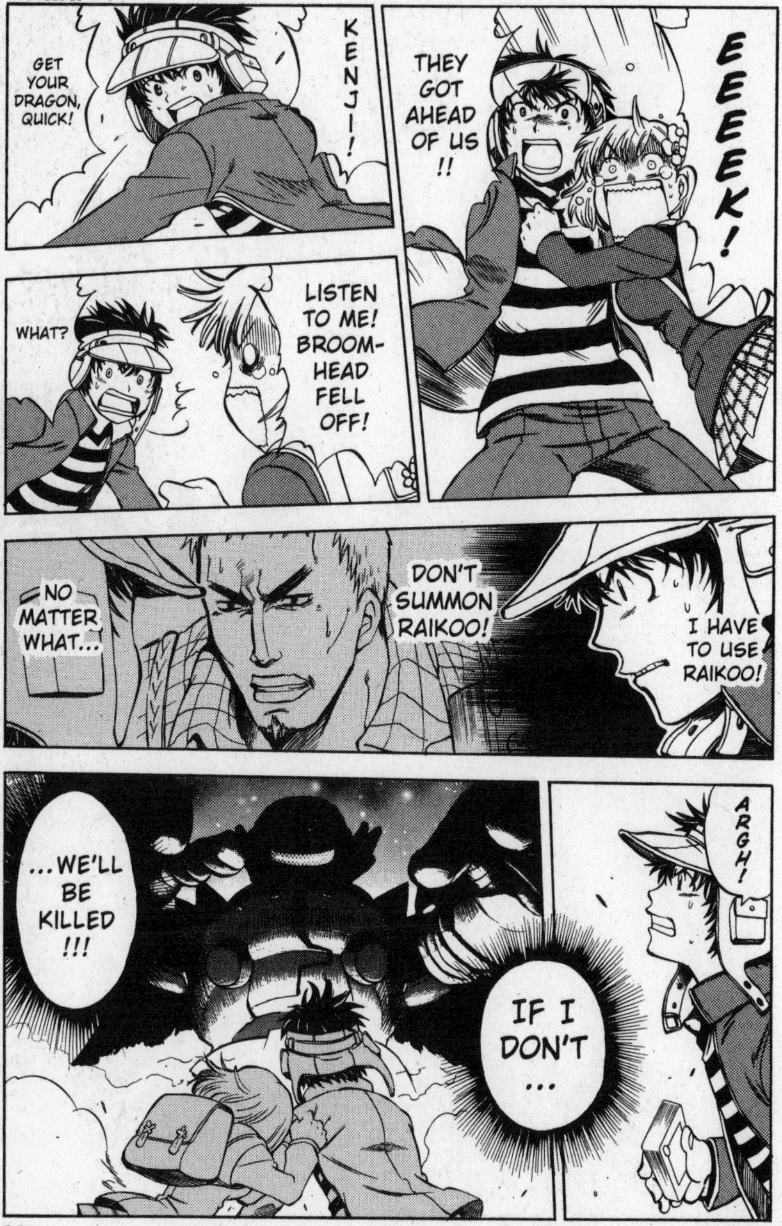
THEY GOT AHEAD OF US!!
EEEEEK!
KENJI!
GET YOUR DRAGON, QUICK!
LISTEN TO ME! BROOMHEAD FELL OFF!
WHAT?
I HAVE TO USE RAIKOO!
DON'T SUMMON RAIKOO!
NO MATTER WHAT...
ARGH!
IF I DON'T...
...WE'LL BE KILLED!!!

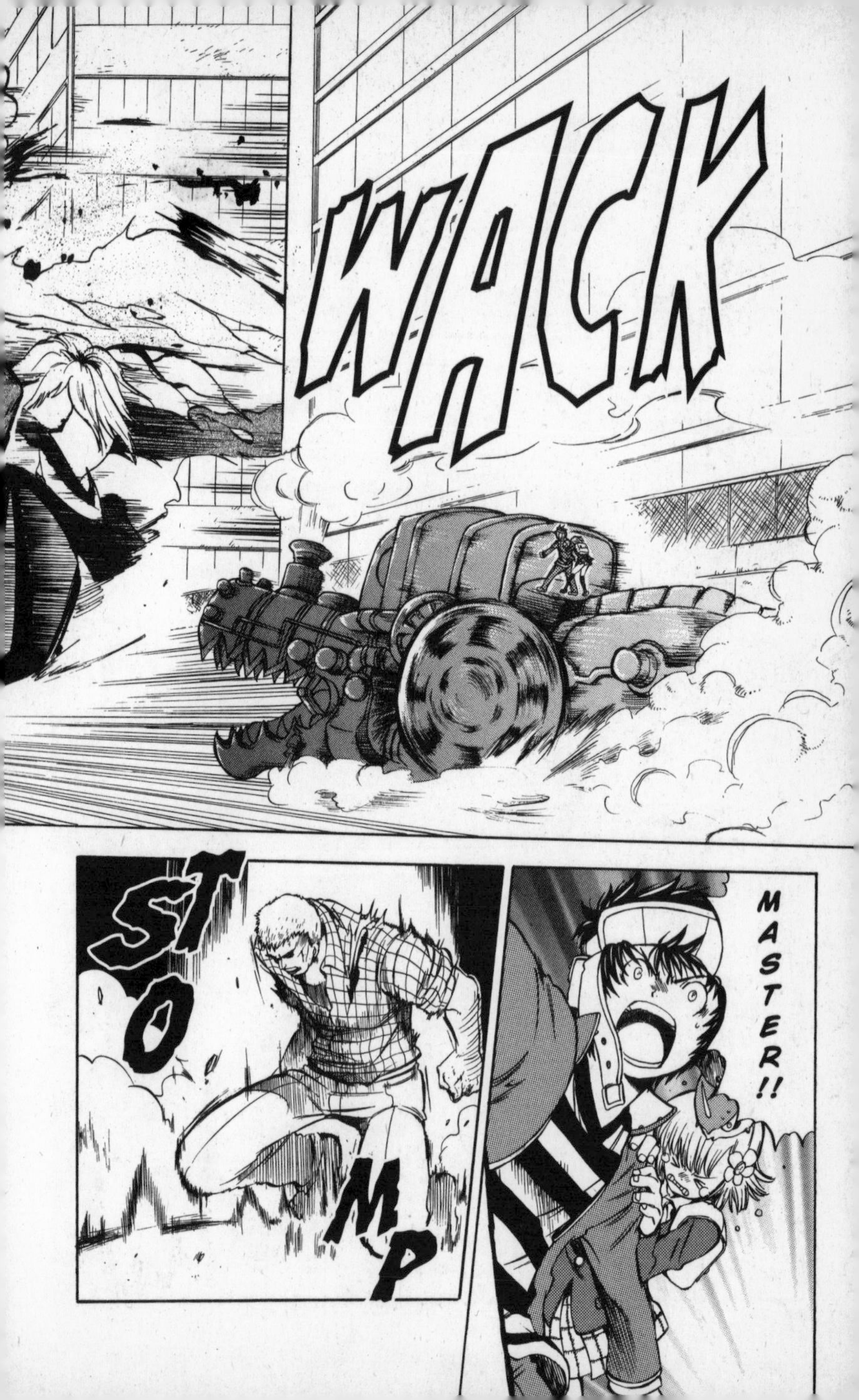
WACK
MASTER!!
STOMP

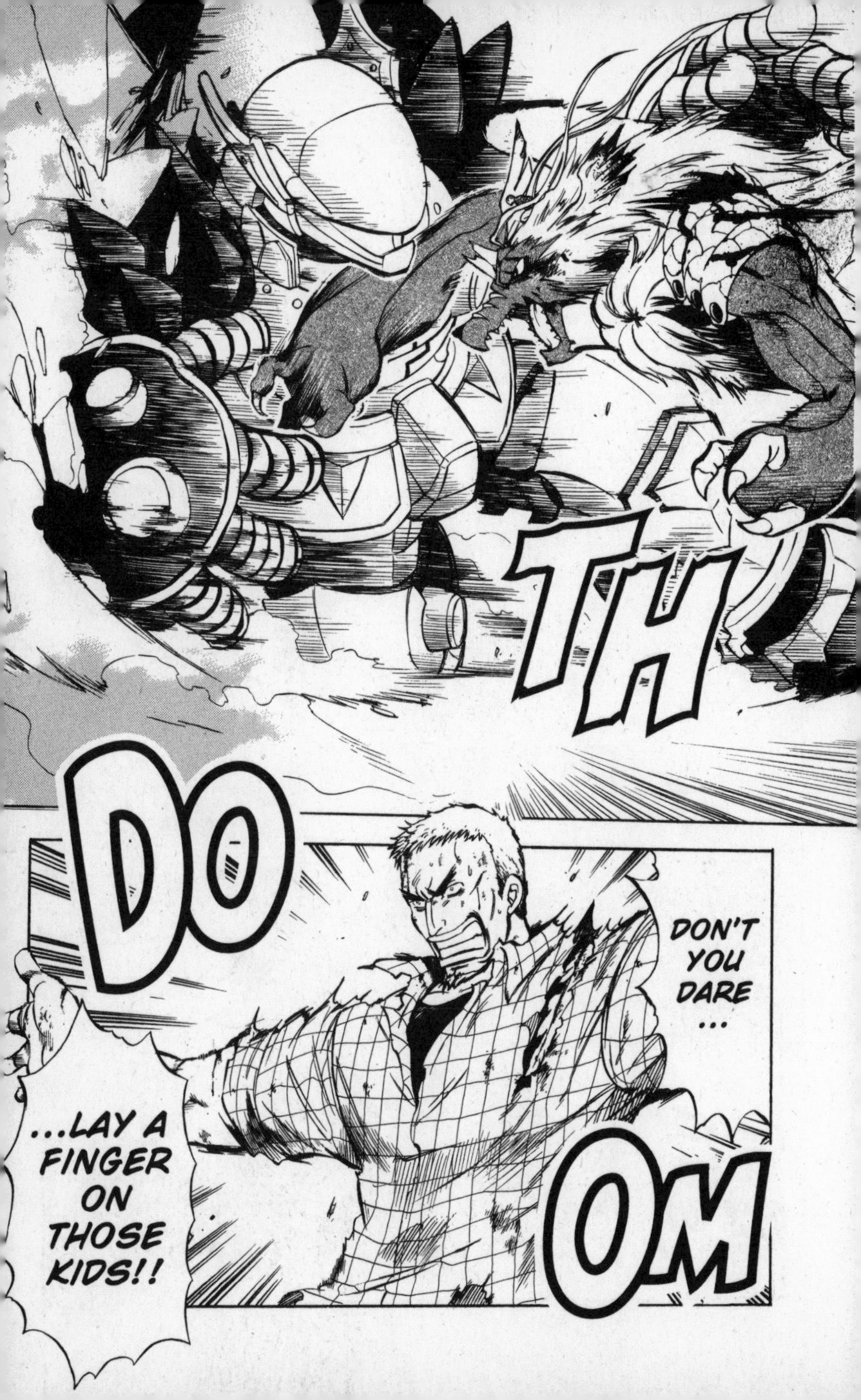
TH
DO
DON'T YOU DARE...
...LAY A FINGER ON THOSE KIDS!!
OM

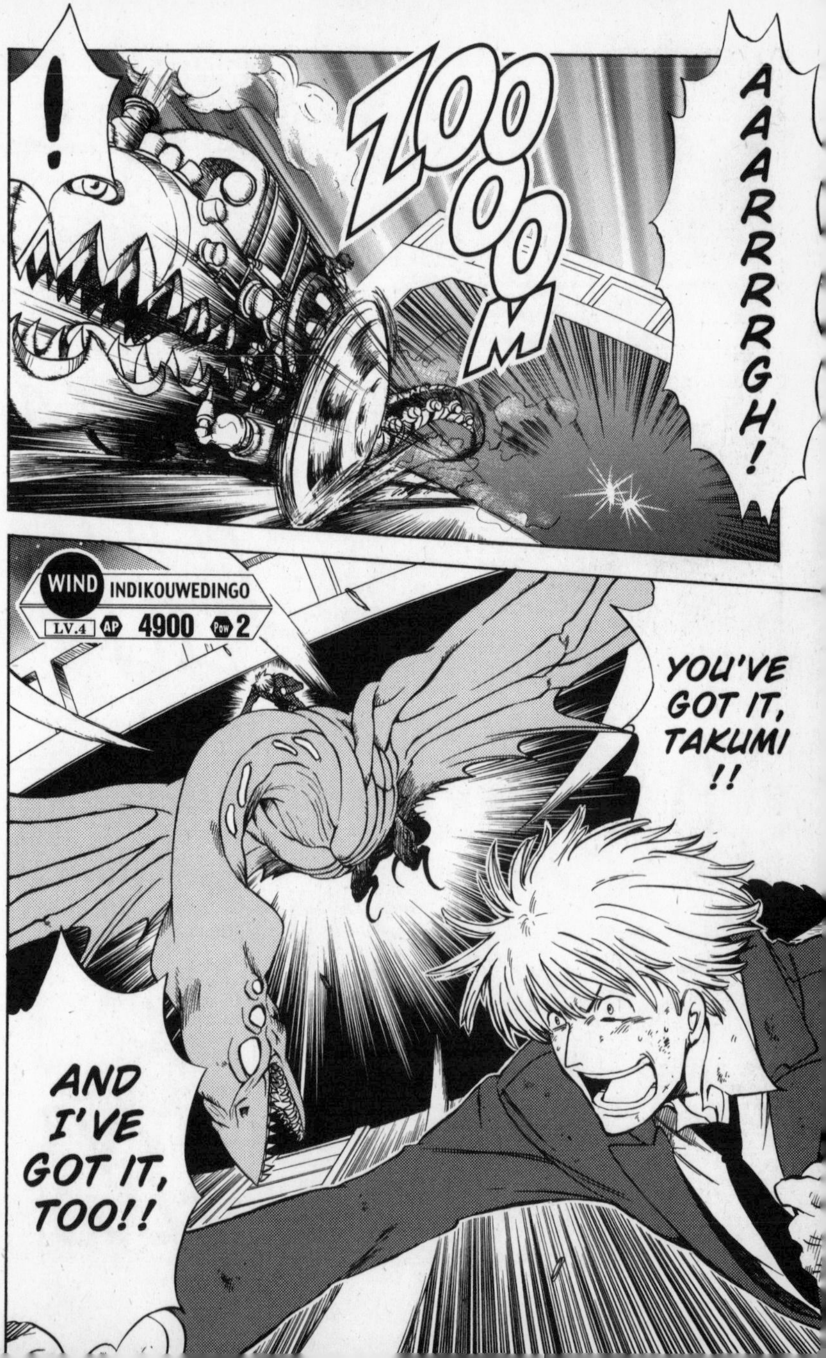
AAARRRGH!
ZOOOOM
!
WIND INDIKOUWEDINGO
LV.4 AP 4900 Pow 2
YOU'VE GOT IT, TAKUMI!!
AND I'VE GOT IT, TOO!!

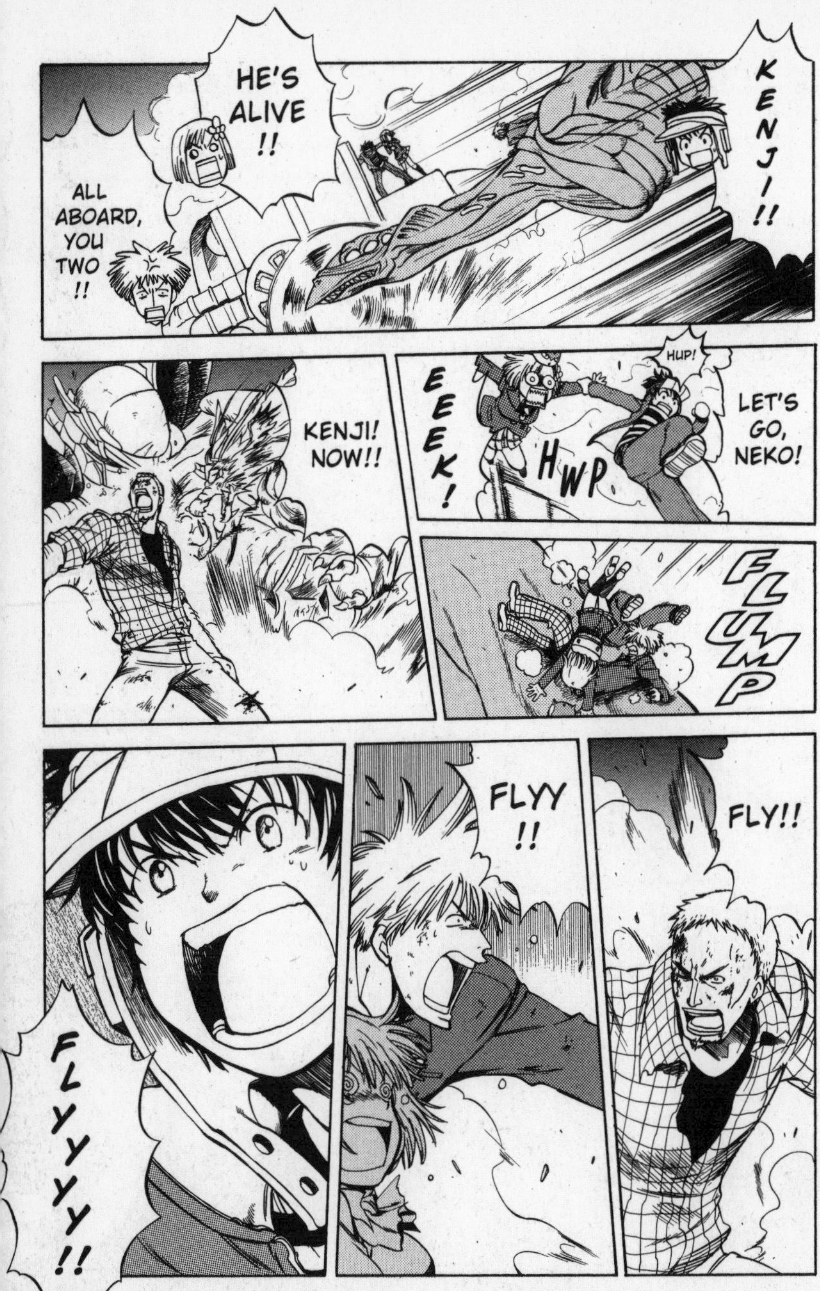
KENJI!!
HE'S ALIVE!!
ALL ABOARD, YOU TWO!!
HUP!
LET'S GO, NEKO!
HWP
EEEK!
FLUMP
KENJI! NOW!!
FLY!!
FLYY!!
FLYYYY!!

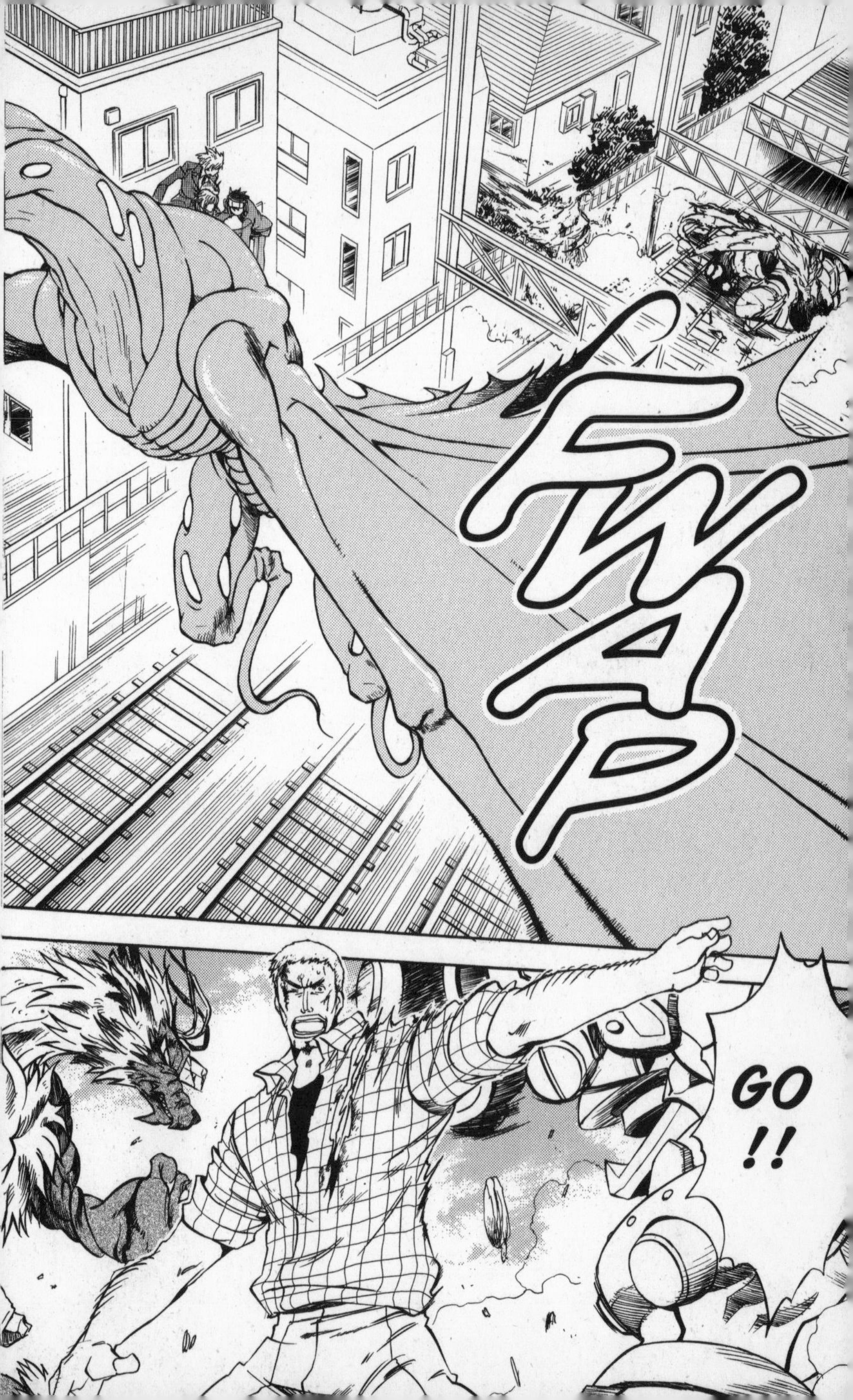
SNAP
GO !!

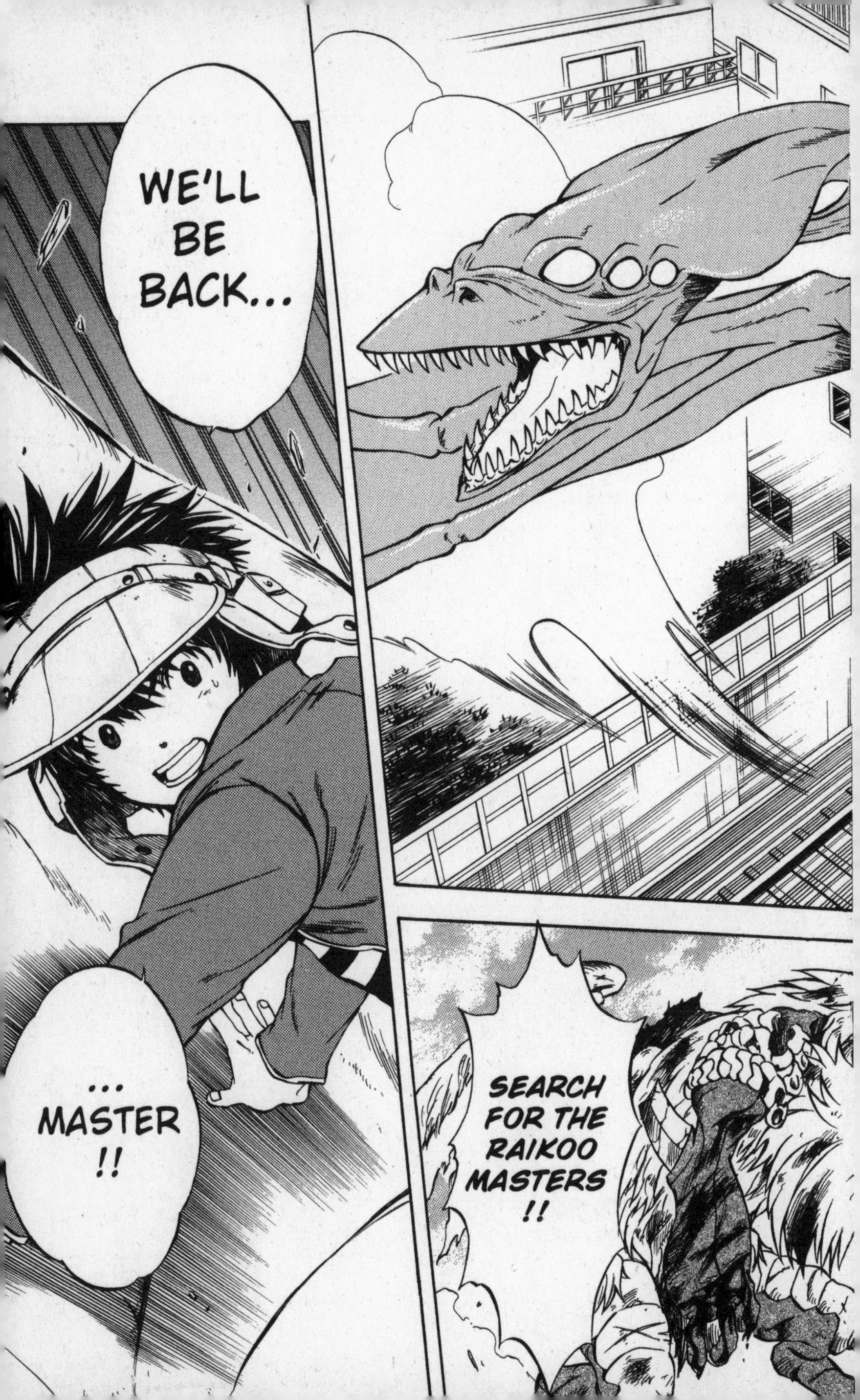
SEARCH FOR THE RAIKOO MASTERS !!
WE'LL BE BACK...
... MASTER !!

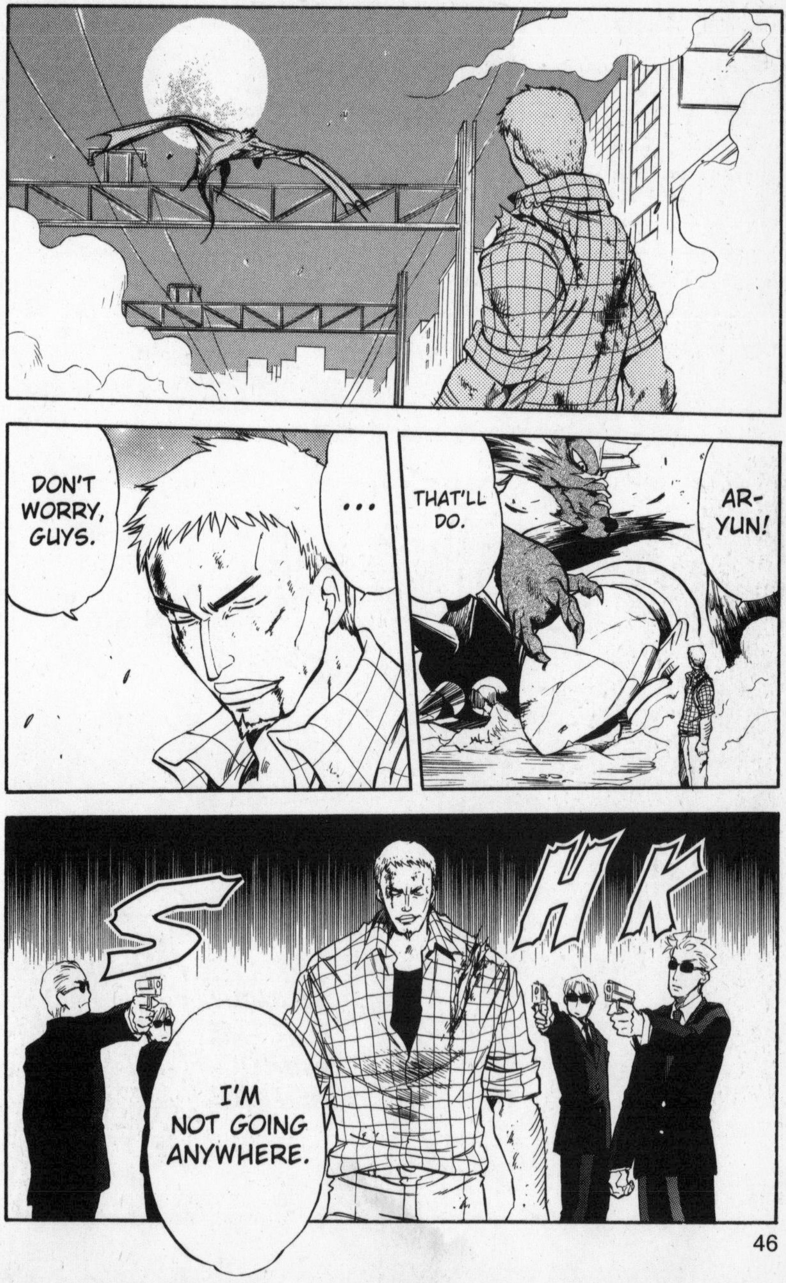
AR-YUN!
THAT'LL DO.
...
DON'T WORRY, GUYS.
SHK
I'M NOT GOING ANYWHERE.

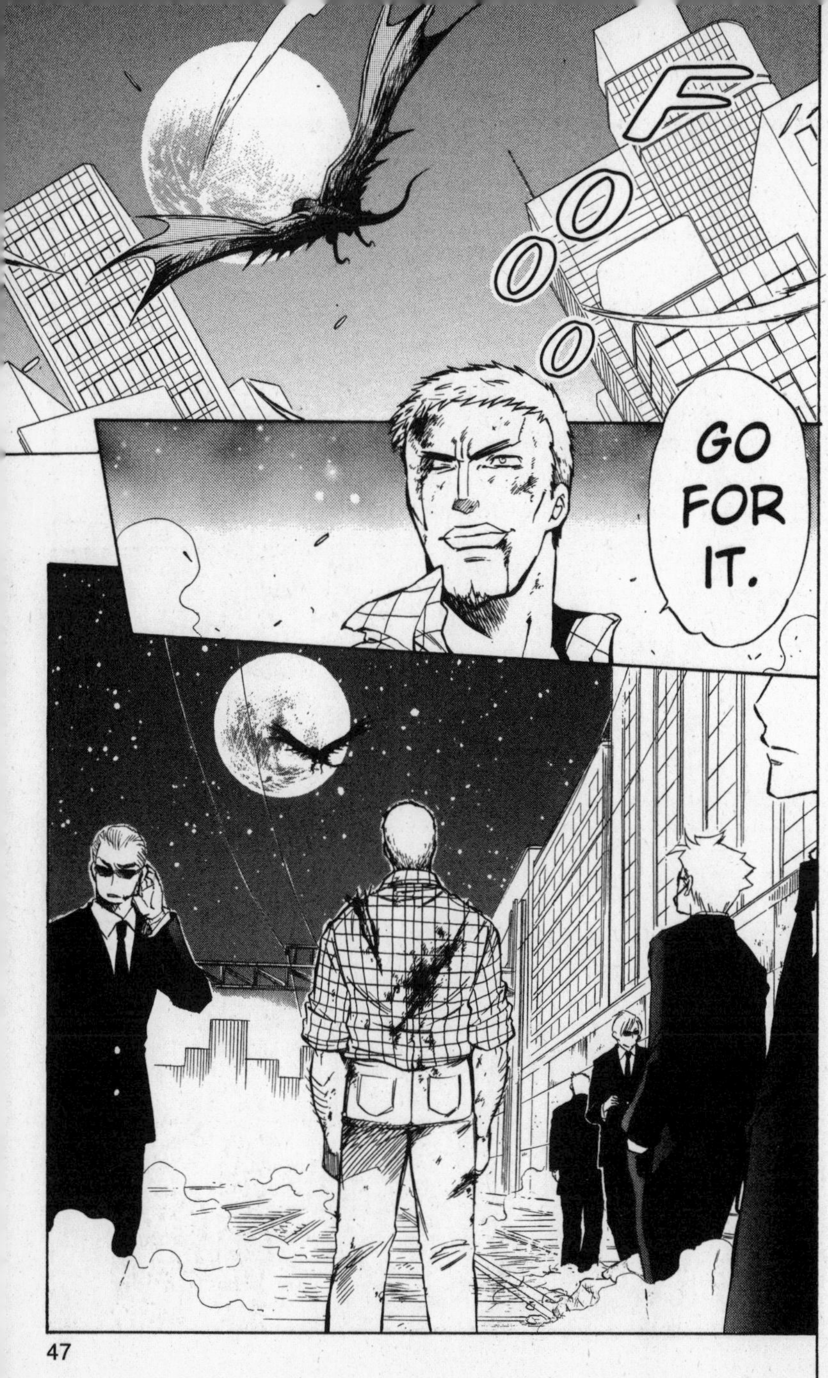
FOOOO
GO FOR IT.

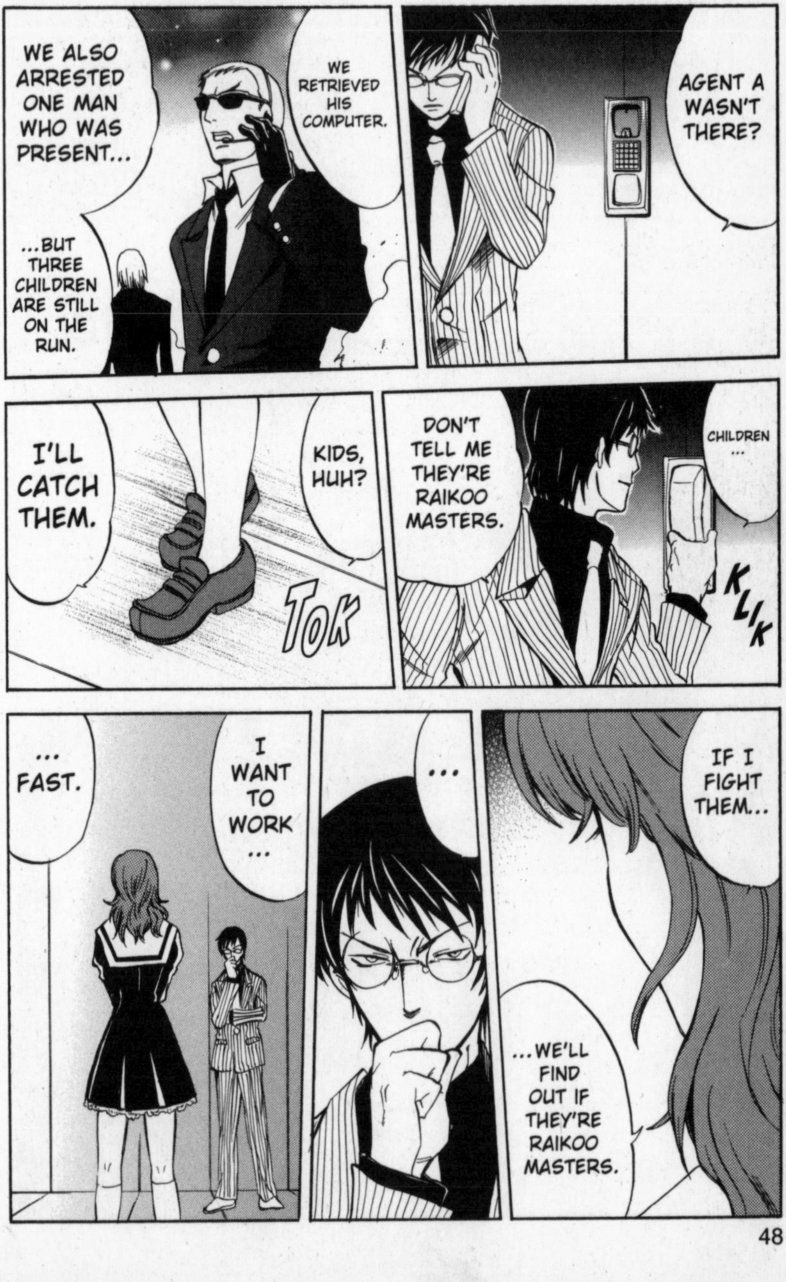
AGENT A WASN'T THERE?
WE RETRIEVED HIS COMPUTER.
WE ALSO ARRESTED ONE MAN WHO WAS PRESENT...
...BUT THREE CHILDREN ARE STILL ON THE RUN.
CHILDREN...
KLIK
DON'T TELL ME THEY'RE RAIKOO MASTERS.
KIDS, HUH?
I'LL CATCH THEM.
TOK
IF I FIGHT THEM...
...WE'LL FIND OUT IF THEY'RE RAIKOO MASTERS.
...
I WANT TO WORK...
...FAST.

READ THIS WAY

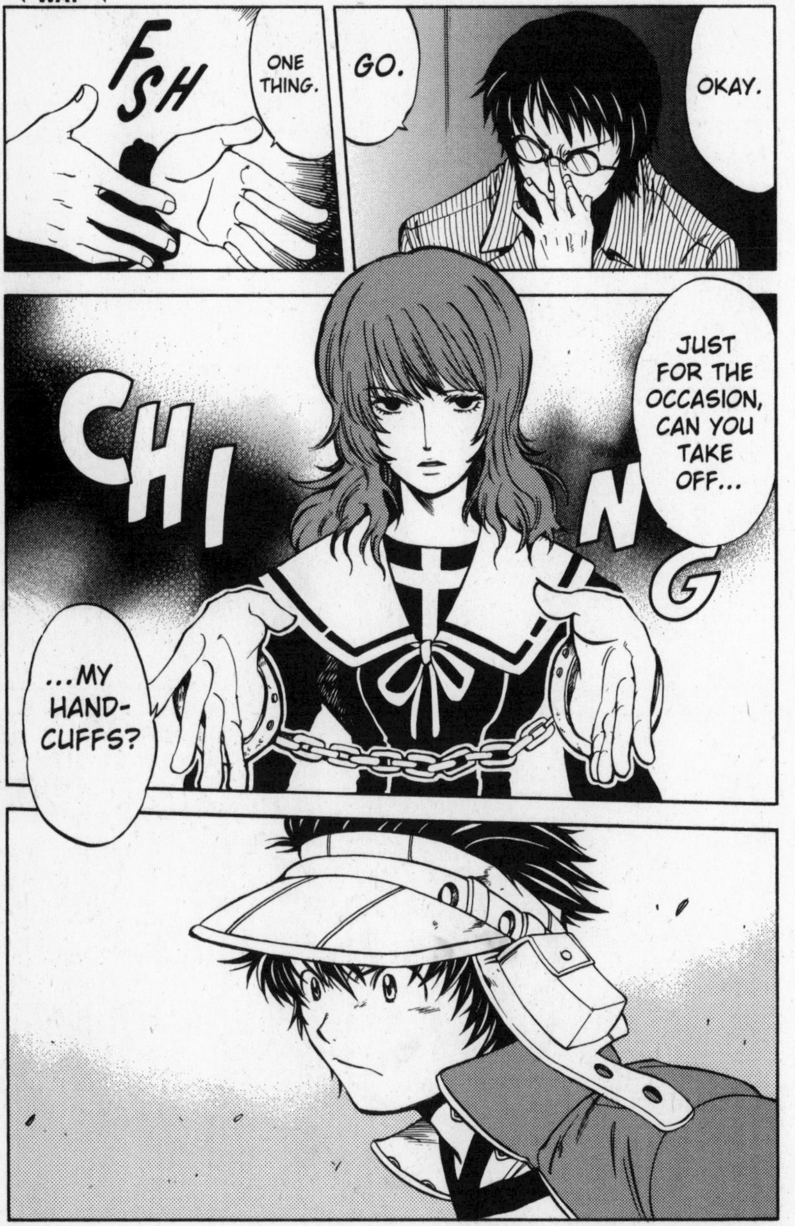
OKAY.
GO.
ONE THING.
FSH
JUST FOR THE OCCASION, CAN YOU TAKE OFF...
CHING
...MY HAND-CUFFS?

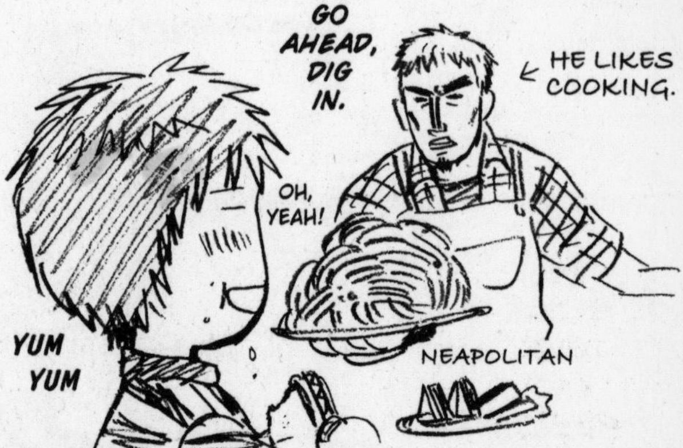
HE LIKES COOKING.
GO AHEAD, DIG IN.
OH, YEAH!
NEAPOLITAN
YUM YUM
TAKUMI GAINED A LITTLE WEIGHT AT KOIZUMI...

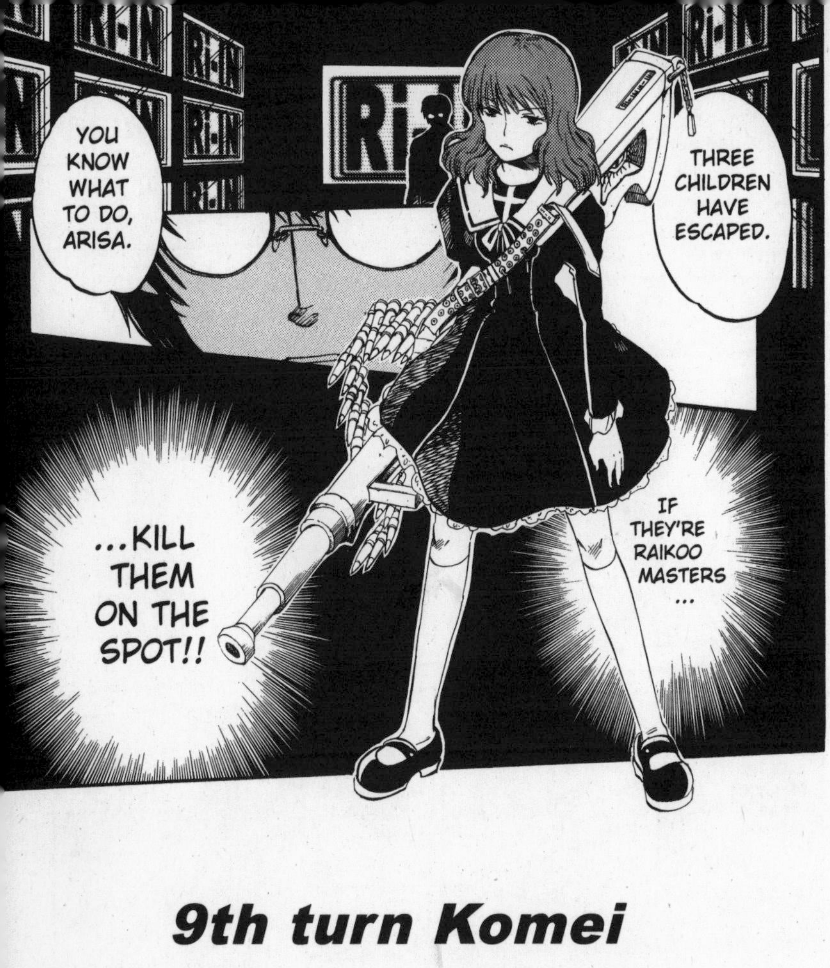
THREE CHILDREN HAVE ESCAPED.
YOU KNOW WHAT TO DO, ARISA.
IF THEY'RE RAIKOO MASTERS...
...KILL THEM ON THE SPOT!!

9th turn Komei

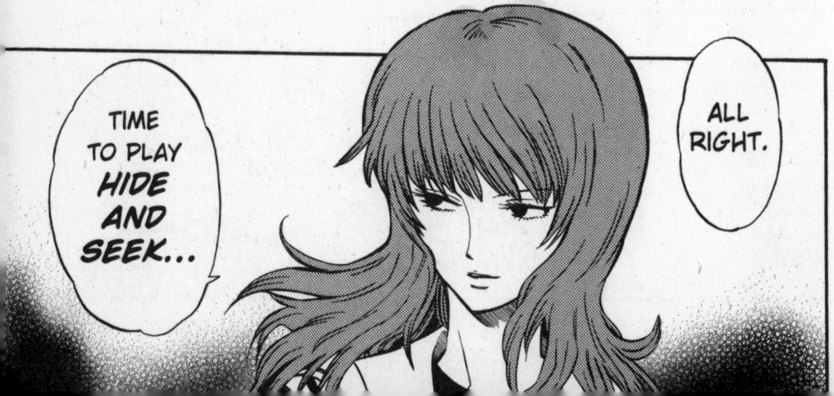
ALL RIGHT.
TIME TO PLAY *HIDE AND SEEK*...

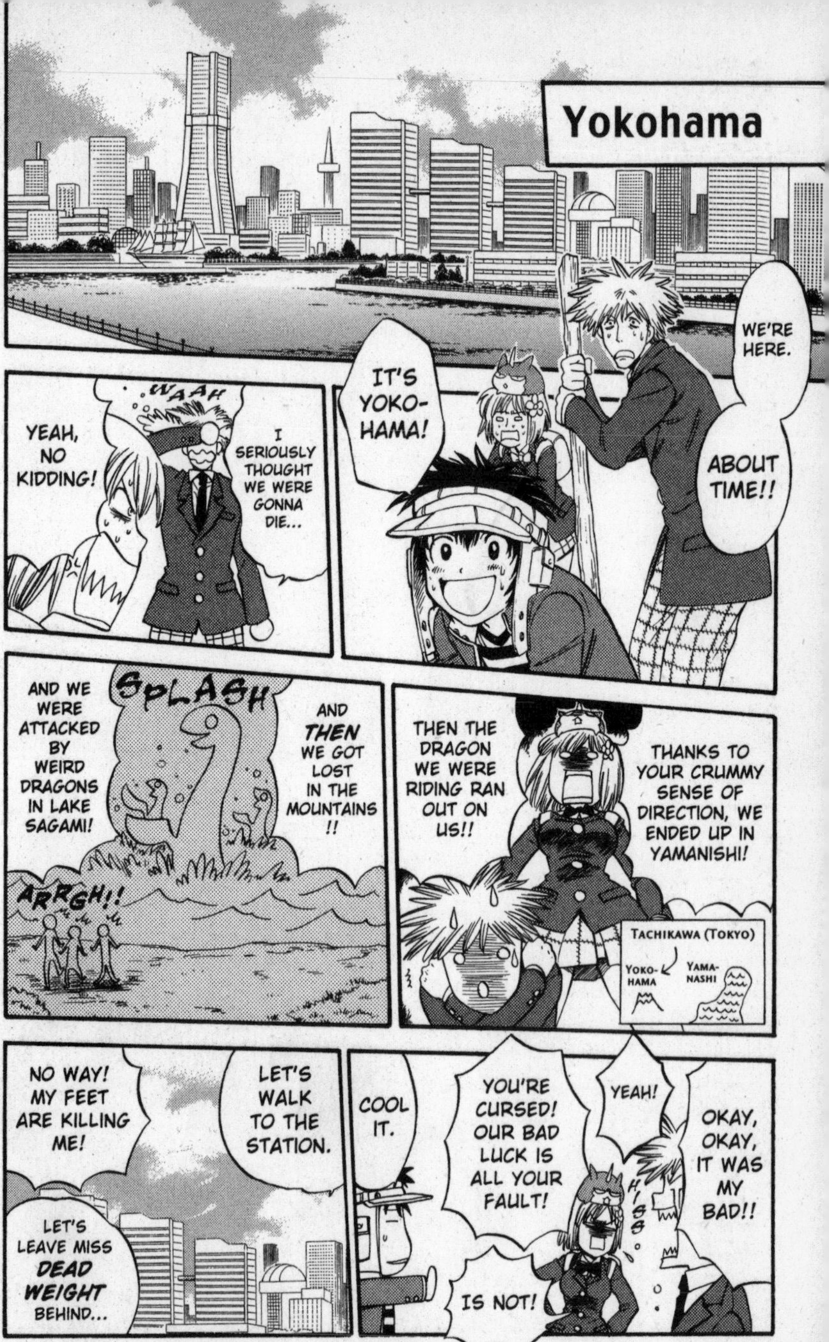
Yokohama
WE'RE HERE.
ABOUT TIME!!
IT'S YOKOHAMA!
I SERIOUSLY THOUGHT WE WERE GONNA DIE...
WAAH
YEAH, NO KIDDING!
THANKS TO YOUR CRUMMY SENSE OF DIRECTION, WE ENDED UP IN YAMANISHI!
THEN THE DRAGON WE WERE RIDING RAN OUT ON US!!
TACHIKAWA (TOKYO)
YOKOHAMA
YAMANASHI
AND THEN WE GOT LOST IN THE MOUNTAINS!!
SPLASH
AND WE WERE ATTACKED BY WEIRD DRAGONS IN LAKE SAGAMI!
ARRGH!!
OKAY, OKAY, IT WAS MY BAD!!
YEAH!
YOU'RE CURSED! OUR BAD LUCK IS ALL YOUR FAULT!
HISS
IS NOT!
COOL IT.
LET'S WALK TO THE STATION.
NO WAY! MY FEET ARE KILLING ME!
LET'S LEAVE MISS DEAD WEIGHT BEHIND...

READ THIS WAY

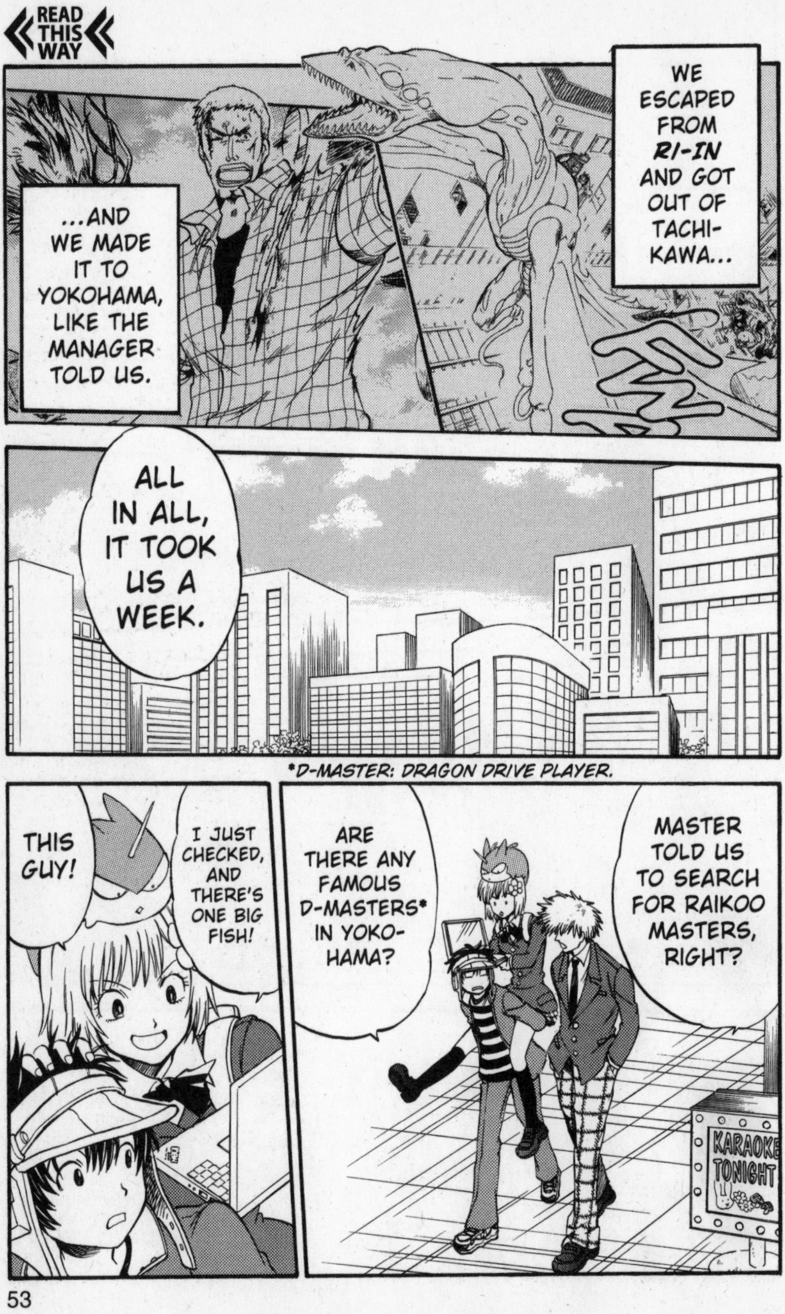
WE ESCAPED FROM *RI-IN* AND GOT OUT OF TACHI-KAWA...
...AND WE MADE IT TO YOKOHAMA, LIKE THE MANAGER TOLD US.
ALL IN ALL, IT TOOK US A WEEK.
MASTER TOLD US TO SEARCH FOR RAIKOO MASTERS, RIGHT?
ARE THERE ANY FAMOUS D-MASTERS* IN YOKO-HAMA?
KARAOKE TONIGHT
I JUST CHECKED, AND THERE'S ONE BIG FISH!
THIS GUY!

*D-MASTER: DRAGON DRIVE PLAYER.

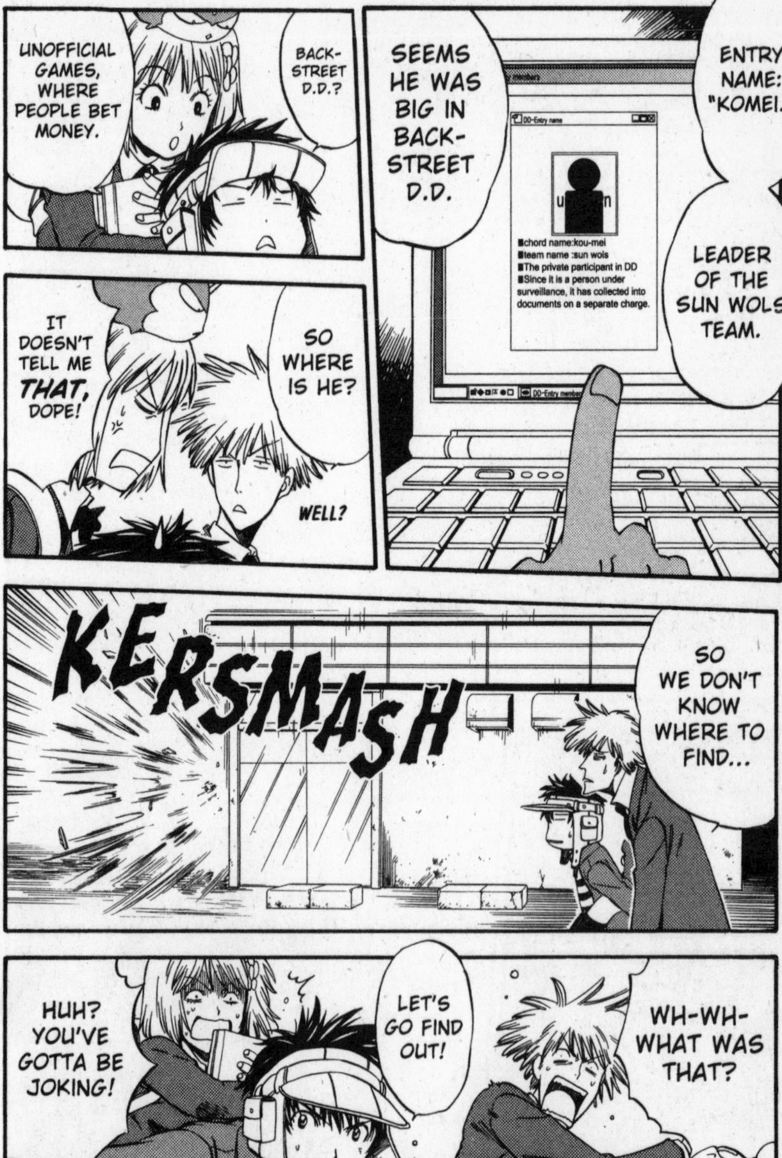
ENTRY NAME: "KOMEI."
LEADER OF THE SUN WOLS TEAM.
SEEMS HE WAS BIG IN BACK-STREET D.D.
DD-Entry name
■chord name:kou-mei
■team name :sun wols
■The private participant in DD
■Since it is a person under surveillance, it has collected into documents on a separate charge.
DD-Entry member
BACK-STREET D.D.?
UNOFFICIAL GAMES, WHERE PEOPLE BET MONEY.
SO WHERE IS HE?
WELL?
IT DOESN'T TELL ME *THAT*, DOPE!
SO WE DON'T KNOW WHERE TO FIND...
KERSMASH
WH-WH-WHAT WAS THAT?
LET'S GO FIND OUT!
HUH? YOU'VE GOTTA BE JOKING!

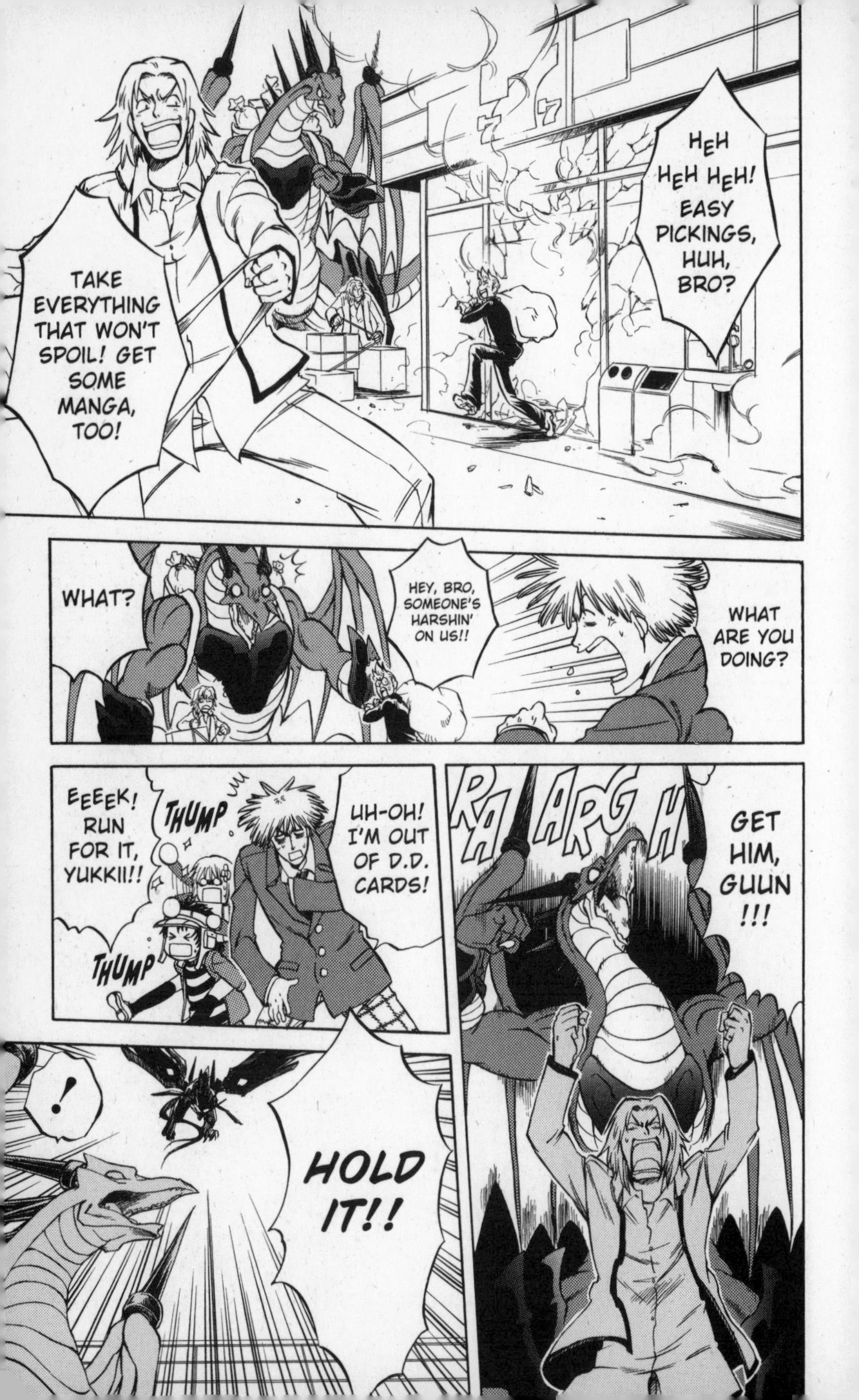
HEH HEH HEH! EASY PICKINGS, HUH, BRO?
TAKE EVERYTHING THAT WON'T SPOIL! GET SOME MANGA, TOO!
WHAT ARE YOU DOING?
HEY, BRO, SOMEONE'S HARSHIN' ON US!!
WHAT?
RAARGH
GET HIM, GUUN!!!
UH-OH! I'M OUT OF D.D. CARDS!
THUMP
EEEEK! RUN FOR IT, YUKKII!!
THUMP
HOLD IT!!
!

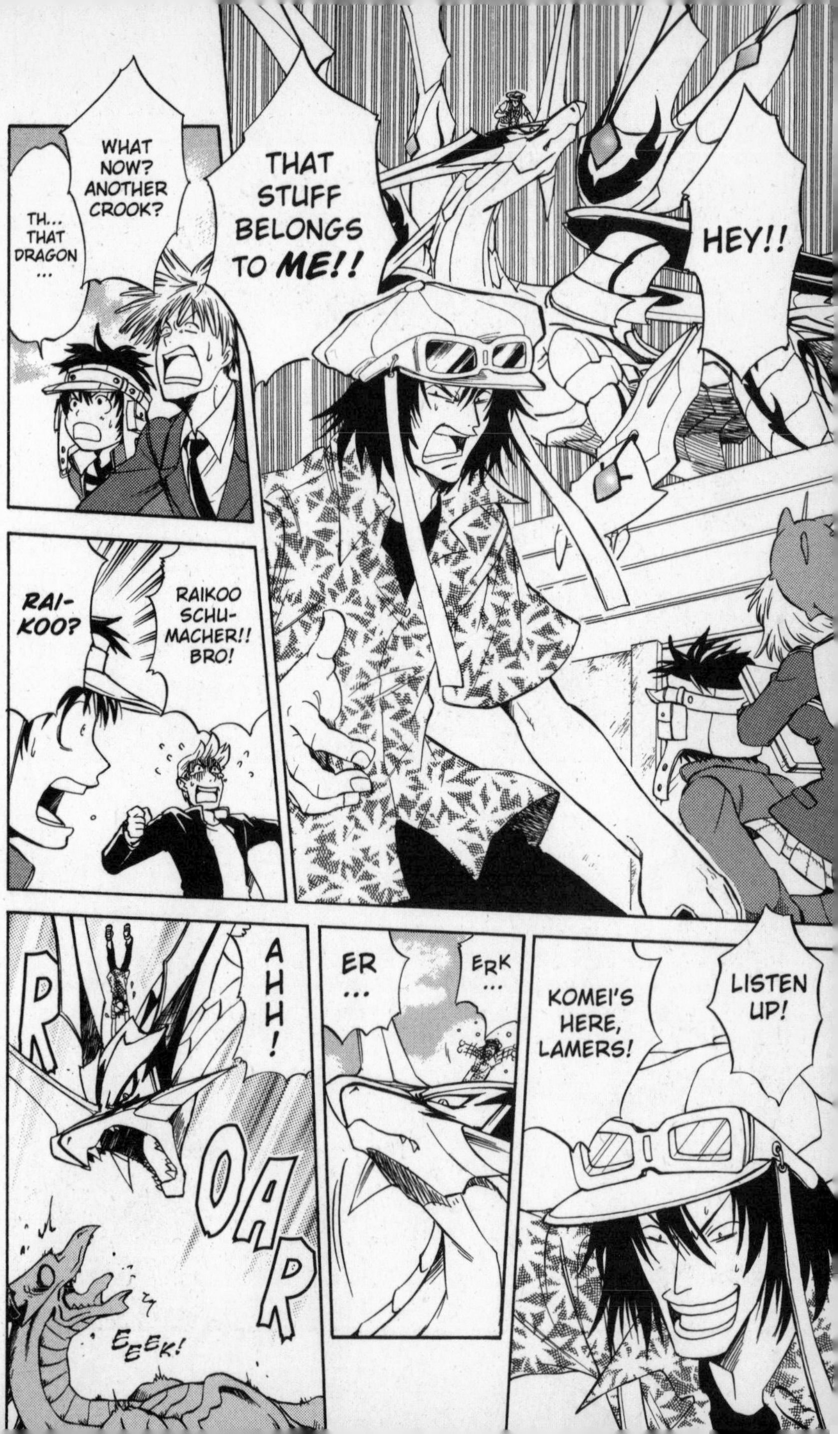
HEY!!
THAT STUFF BELONGS TO *ME!!*
WHAT NOW? ANOTHER CROOK?
TH... THAT DRAGON ...
RAIKOO SCHUMACHER!! BRO!
RAI-KOO?
LISTEN UP!
KOMEI'S HERE, LAMERS!
ERK ...
ER ...
AHH!
ROAR
EEEK!

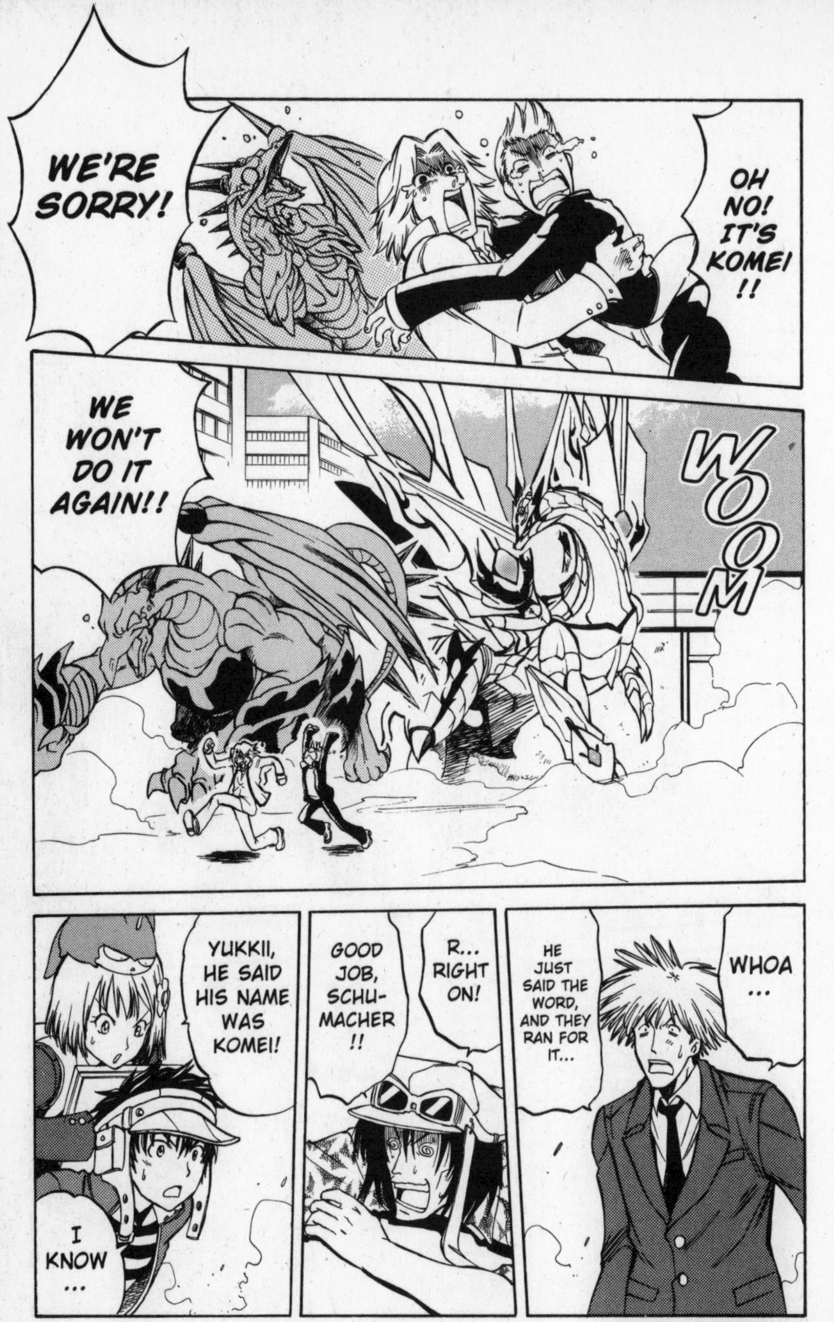
OH NO! IT'S KOMEI!!
WE'RE SORRY!
WE WON'T DO IT AGAIN!!
WOOM
WHOA...
HE JUST SAID THE WORD, AND THEY RAN FOR IT...
R... RIGHT ON!
GOOD JOB, SCHUMACHER!!
YUKKII, HE SAID HIS NAME WAS KOMEI!
I KNOW...

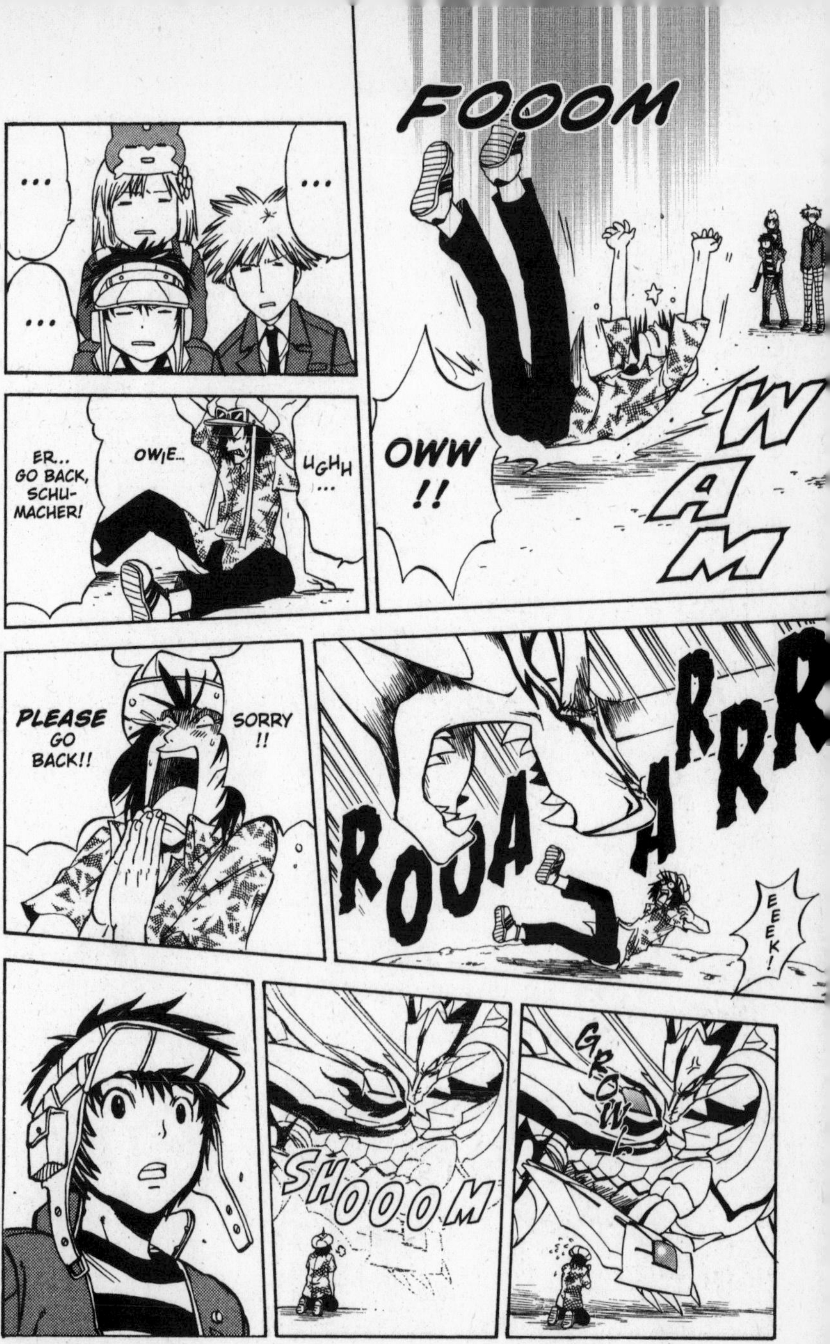

FOOOM
OWW!!
WAM
...
...
...
UGHH...
OWIE...
ER... GO BACK, SCHUMACHER!
ROOAARRR
EEEK!
SORRY!!
PLEASE GO BACK!!
GROWL
SHOOOM

READ THIS WAY

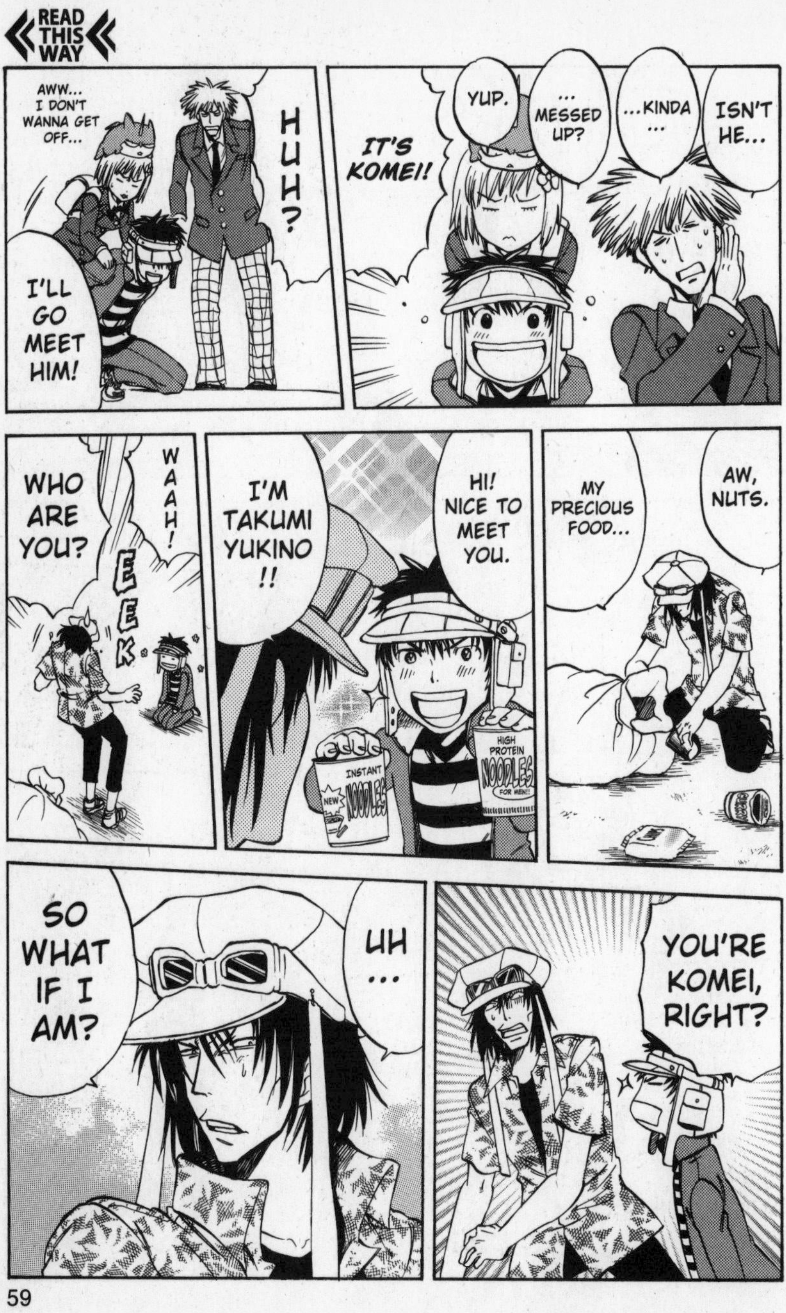
ISN'T HE...
...KINDA...
...MESSED UP?
YUP.
IT'S KOMEI!!
HUH?
AWW... I DON'T WANNA GET OFF...
I'LL GO MEET HIM!
AW, NUTS.
MY PRECIOUS FOOD...
HI! NICE TO MEET YOU.
HIGH PROTEIN NOODLES FOR MEN!!
I'M TAKUMI YUKINO!!
INSTANT
NEW
NOODLES
WAAAH!
EEK
WHO ARE YOU?
YOU'RE KOMEI, RIGHT?
UH...
SO WHAT IF I AM?

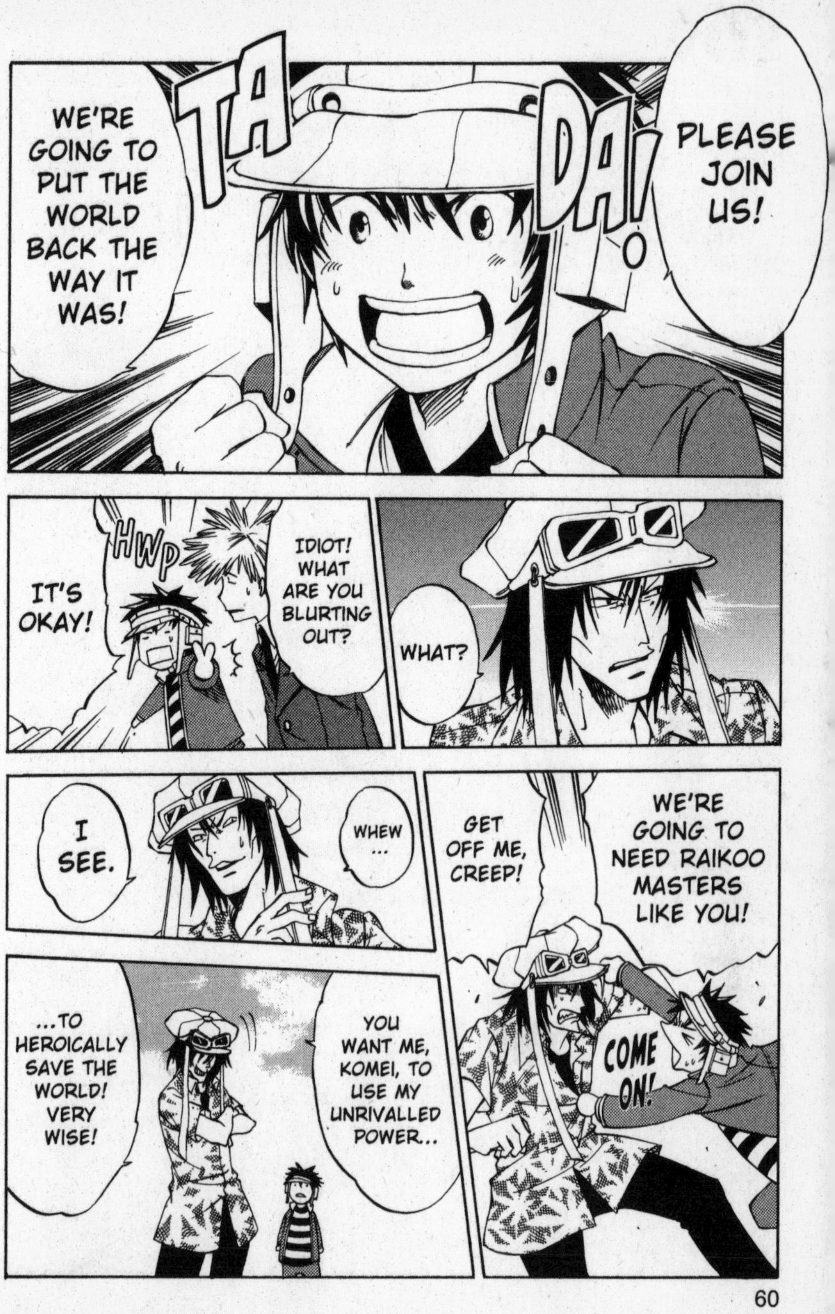
PLEASE JOIN US!
TA DA!
WE'RE GOING TO PUT THE WORLD BACK THE WAY IT WAS!
WHAT?
IDIOT! WHAT ARE YOU BLURTING OUT?
HWP
IT'S OKAY!
WE'RE GOING TO NEED RAIKOO MASTERS LIKE YOU!
GET OFF ME, CREEP!
COME ON!
WHEW ...
I SEE.
YOU WANT ME, KOMEI, TO USE MY UNRIVALLED POWER...
...TO HEROICALLY SAVE THE WORLD! VERY WISE!

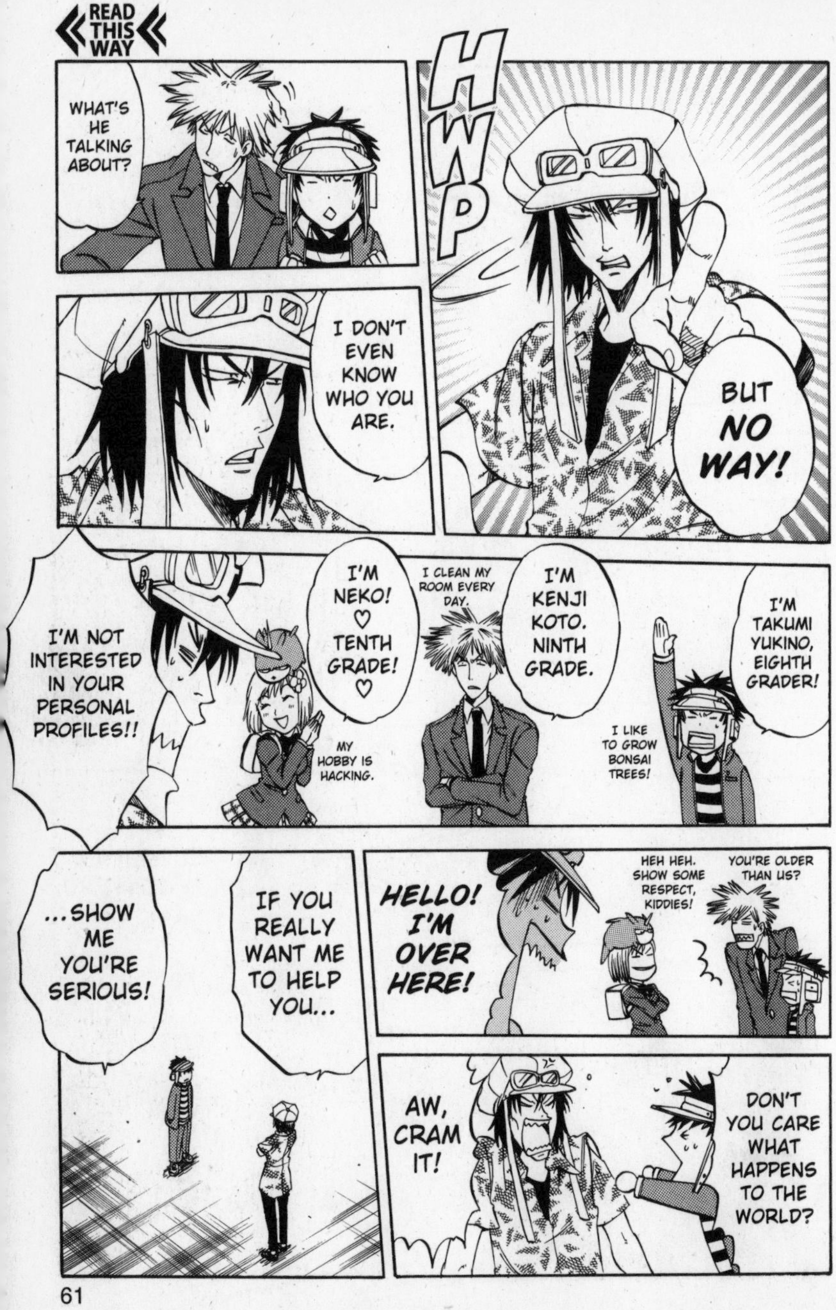
READ THIS WAY
HWP
BUT NO WAY!
WHAT'S HE TALKING ABOUT?
I DON'T EVEN KNOW WHO YOU ARE.
I'M TAKUMI YUKINO, EIGHTH GRADER!
I LIKE TO GROW BONSAI TREES!
I'M KENJI KOTO. NINTH GRADE.
I CLEAN MY ROOM EVERY DAY.
I'M NEKO! ♡ TENTH GRADE! ♡
MY HOBBY IS HACKING.
I'M NOT INTERESTED IN YOUR PERSONAL PROFILES!!
YOU'RE OLDER THAN US?
HEH HEH. SHOW SOME RESPECT, KIDDIES!
HELLO! I'M OVER HERE!
DON'T YOU CARE WHAT HAPPENS TO THE WORLD?
AW, CRAM IT!
IF YOU REALLY WANT ME TO HELP YOU...
...SHOW ME YOU'RE SERIOUS!

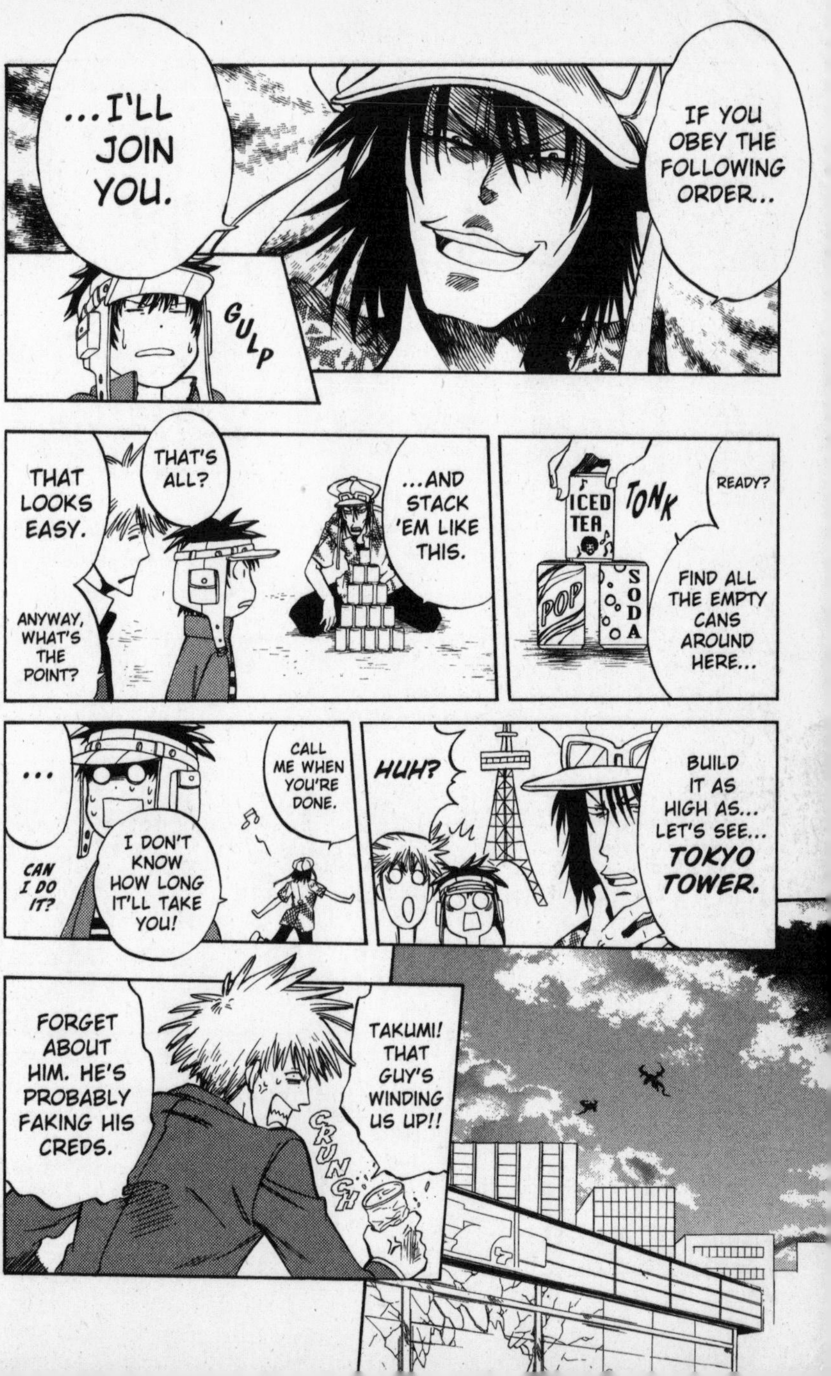
IF YOU OBEY THE FOLLOWING ORDER...
GULP
...I'LL JOIN YOU.
READY?
TONK
ICED TEA
POP
SODA
FIND ALL THE EMPTY CANS AROUND HERE...
...AND STACK 'EM LIKE THIS.
THAT'S ALL?
THAT LOOKS EASY.
ANYWAY, WHAT'S THE POINT?
BUILD IT AS HIGH AS... LET'S SEE... TOKYO TOWER.
HUH?
CALL ME WHEN YOU'RE DONE.
I DON'T KNOW HOW LONG IT'LL TAKE YOU!
...
CAN I DO IT?
TAKUMI! THAT GUY'S WINDING US UP!!
FORGET ABOUT HIM. HE'S PROBABLY FAKING HIS CREDS.
CRUNCH

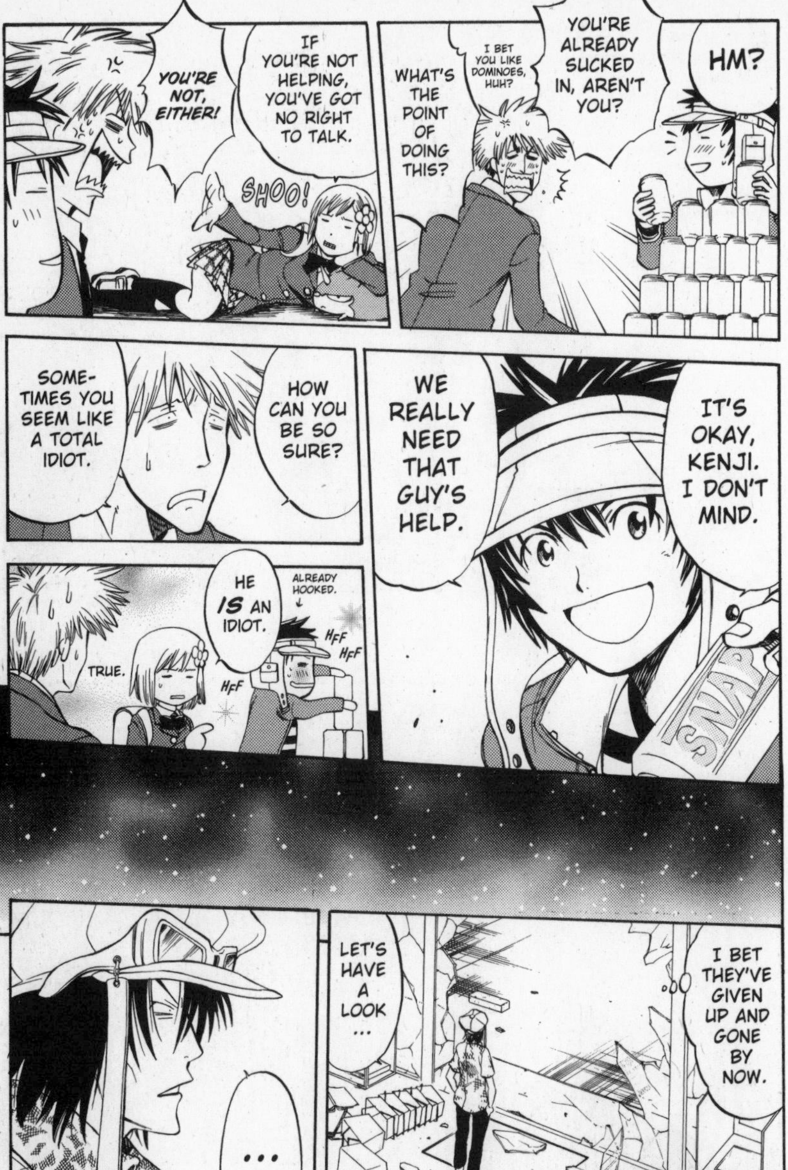
HM?
YOU'RE ALREADY SUCKED IN, AREN'T YOU?
I BET YOU LIKE DOMINOES, HUH?
WHAT'S THE POINT OF DOING THIS?
IF YOU'RE NOT HELPING, YOU'VE GOT NO RIGHT TO TALK.
SHOO!
YOU'RE NOT, EITHER!
IT'S OKAY, KENJI. I DON'T MIND.
WE REALLY NEED THAT GUY'S HELP.
SNAP
HOW CAN YOU BE SO SURE?
SOME-TIMES YOU SEEM LIKE A TOTAL IDIOT.
ALREADY HOOKED.
HFF HFF HFF
HE IS AN IDIOT.
TRUE.
I BET THEY'VE GIVEN UP AND GONE BY NOW.
LET'S HAVE A LOOK ...
...

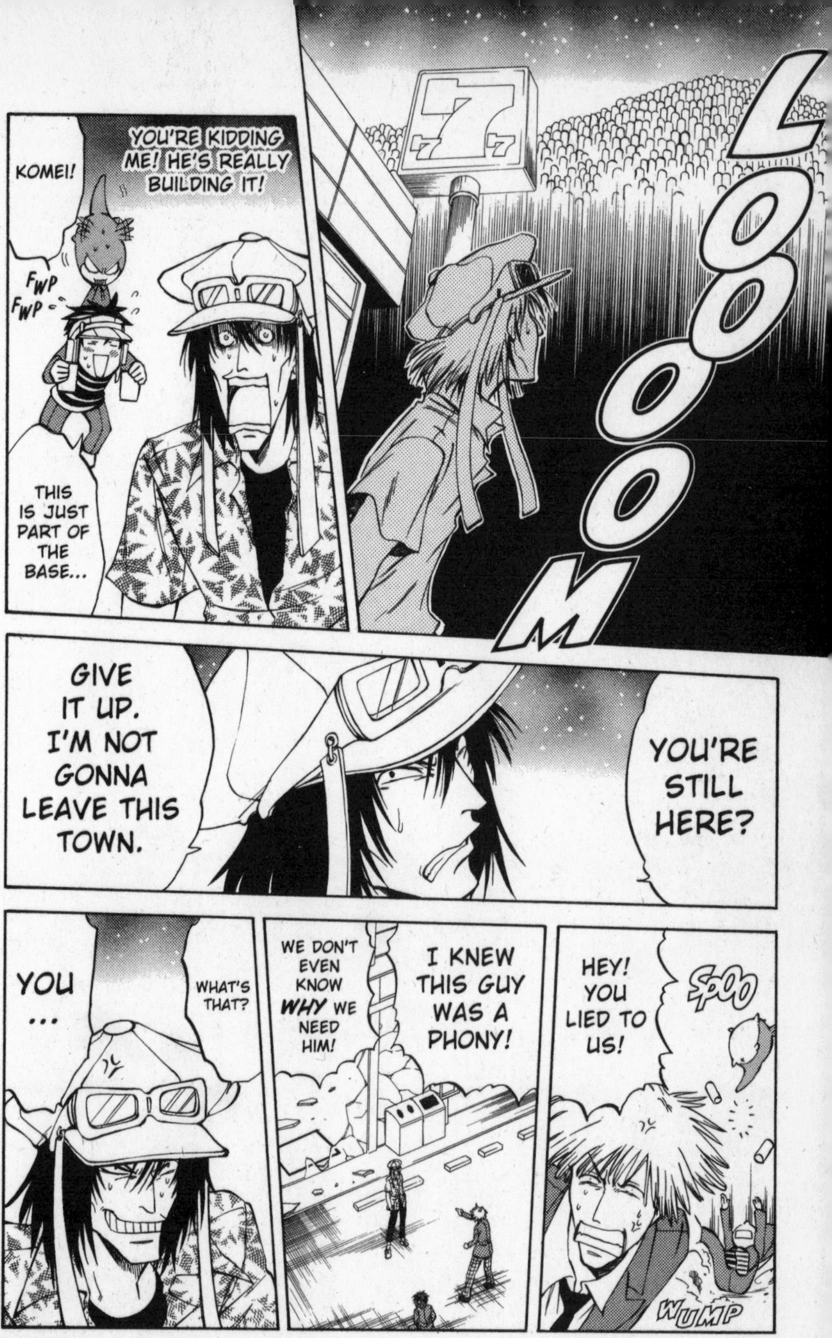
LOOOOOM
YOU'RE KIDDING ME! HE'S REALLY BUILDING IT!
KOMEI!
FWP FWP
THIS IS JUST PART OF THE BASE...
YOU'RE STILL HERE?
GIVE IT UP. I'M NOT GONNA LEAVE THIS TOWN.
SPOO
HEY! YOU LIED TO US!
WUMP
I KNEW THIS GUY WAS A PHONY!
WE DON'T EVEN KNOW WHY WE NEED HIM!
WHAT'S THAT?
YOU ...

READ THIS WAY

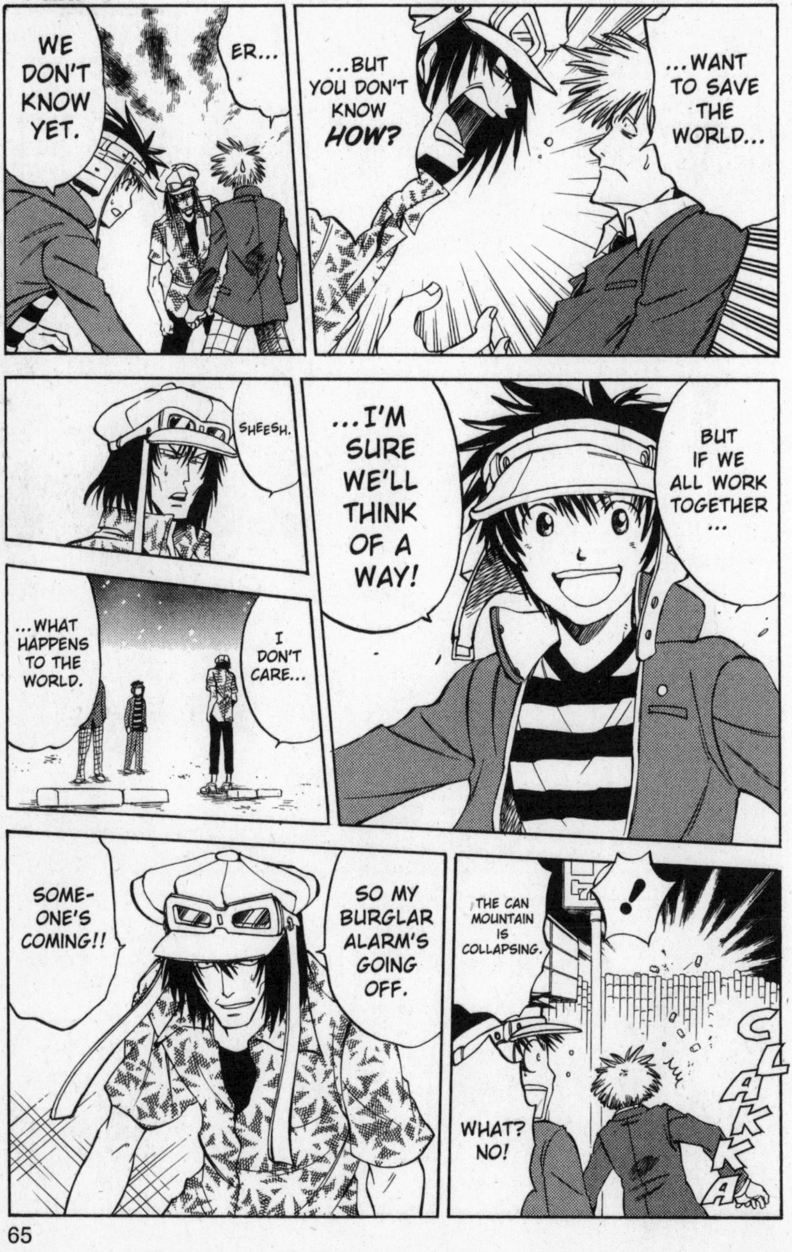
...WANT TO SAVE THE WORLD...
...BUT YOU DON'T KNOW *HOW?*
ER...
WE DON'T KNOW YET.
BUT IF WE ALL WORK TOGETHER ...
...I'M SURE WE'LL THINK OF A WAY!
SHEESH.
I DON'T CARE...
...WHAT HAPPENS TO THE WORLD.
!
THE CAN MOUNTAIN IS COLLAPSING.
CLAKKA
WHAT? NO!
SO MY BURGLAR ALARM'S GOING OFF.
SOME-ONE'S COMING!!

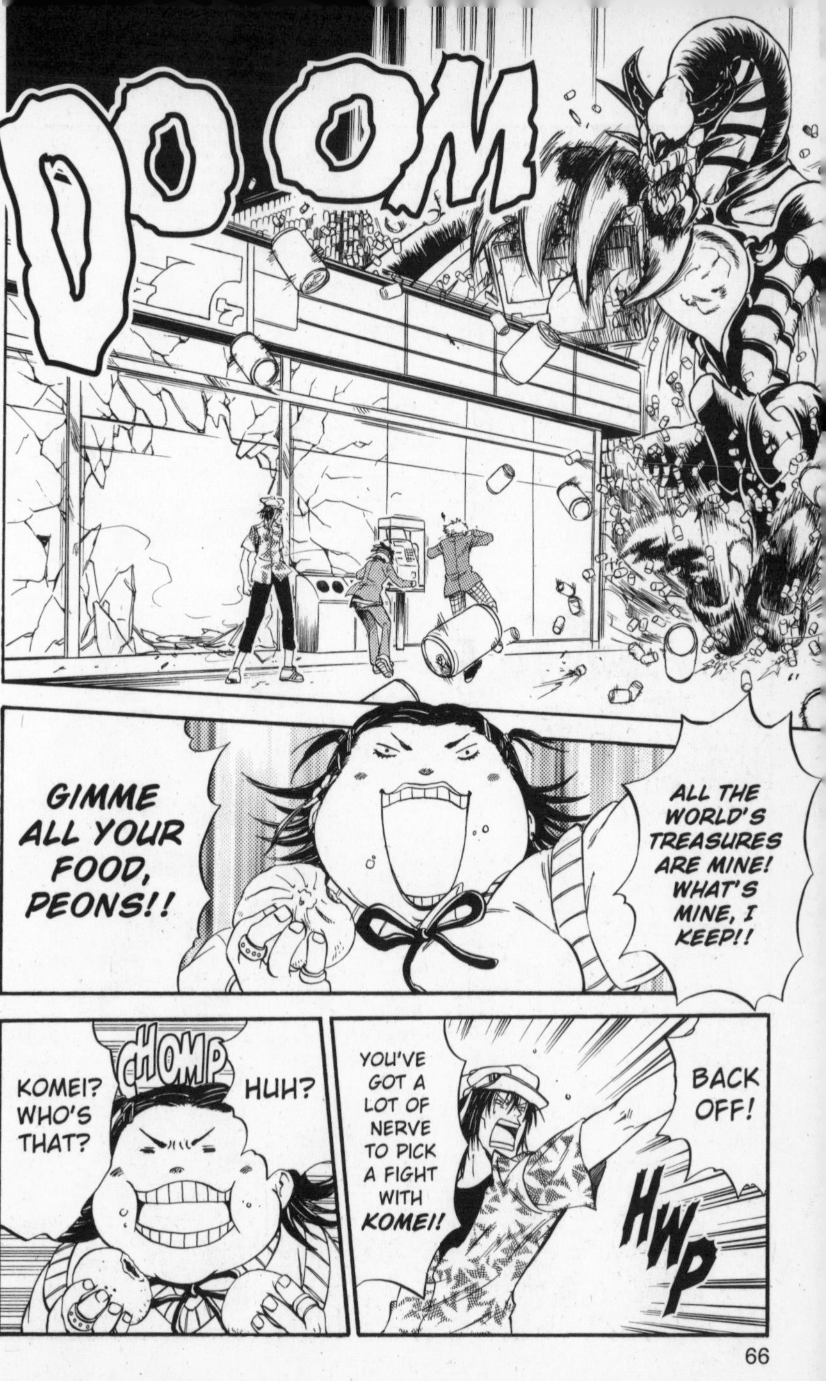
DOOM
ALL THE WORLD'S TREASURES ARE MINE! WHAT'S MINE, I KEEP!!
GIMME ALL YOUR FOOD, PEONS!!
BACK OFF!
YOU'VE GOT A LOT OF NERVE TO PICK A FIGHT WITH KOMEI!!
HWP
HUH?
CHOMP
KOMEI? WHO'S THAT?

READ THIS WAY

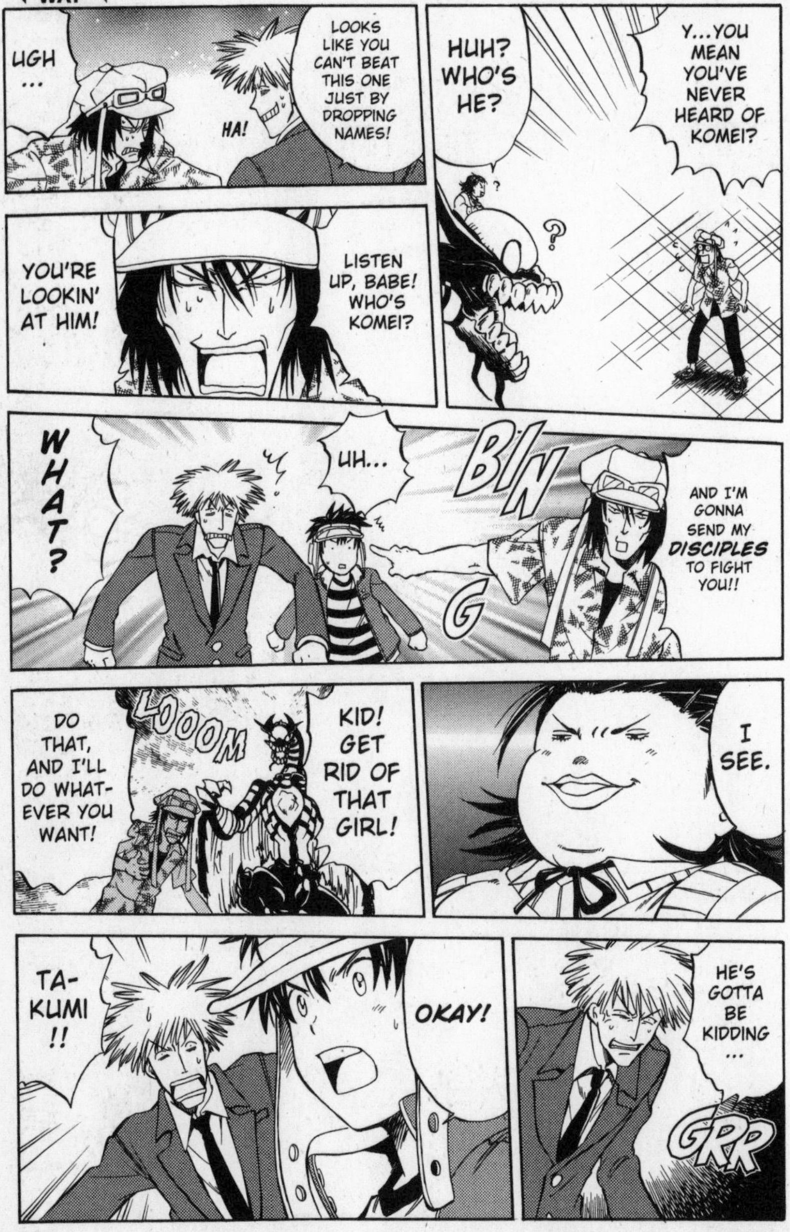

Y...YOU MEAN YOU'VE NEVER HEARD OF KOMEI?
HUH? WHO'S HE?
LOOKS LIKE YOU CAN'T BEAT THIS ONE JUST BY DROPPING NAMES!
HA!
UGH ...
LISTEN UP, BABE! WHO'S KOMEI?
YOU'RE LOOKIN' AT HIM!
AND I'M GONNA SEND MY **DISCIPLES** TO FIGHT YOU!!
BING
UH...
WHAT?
I SEE.
KID! GET RID OF THAT GIRL!
DO THAT, AND I'LL DO WHAT-EVER YOU WANT!
LOOOM
HE'S GOTTA BE KIDDING ...
GRR
OKAY!
TA-KUMI!!

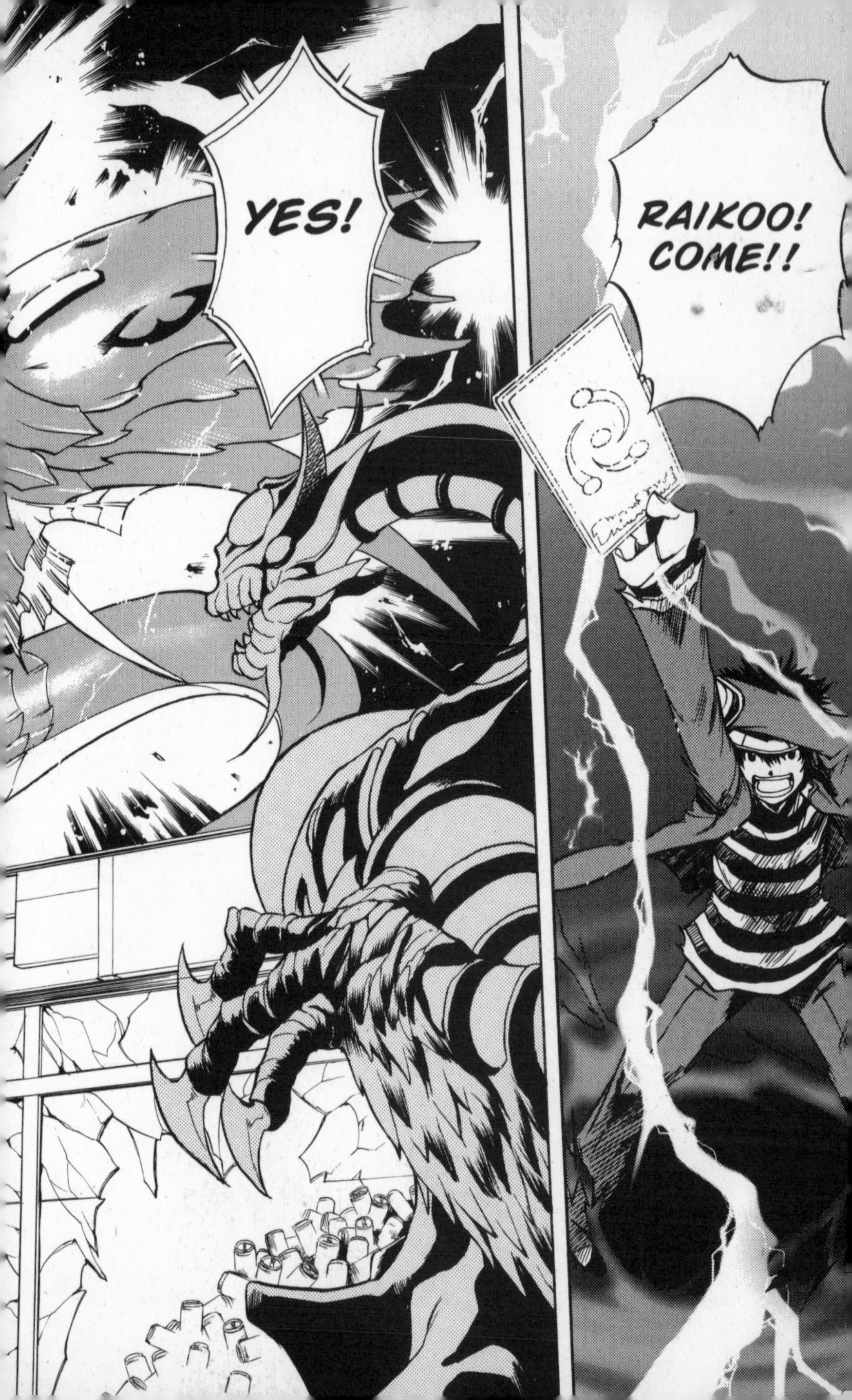
RAIKOO! COME!!
YES!

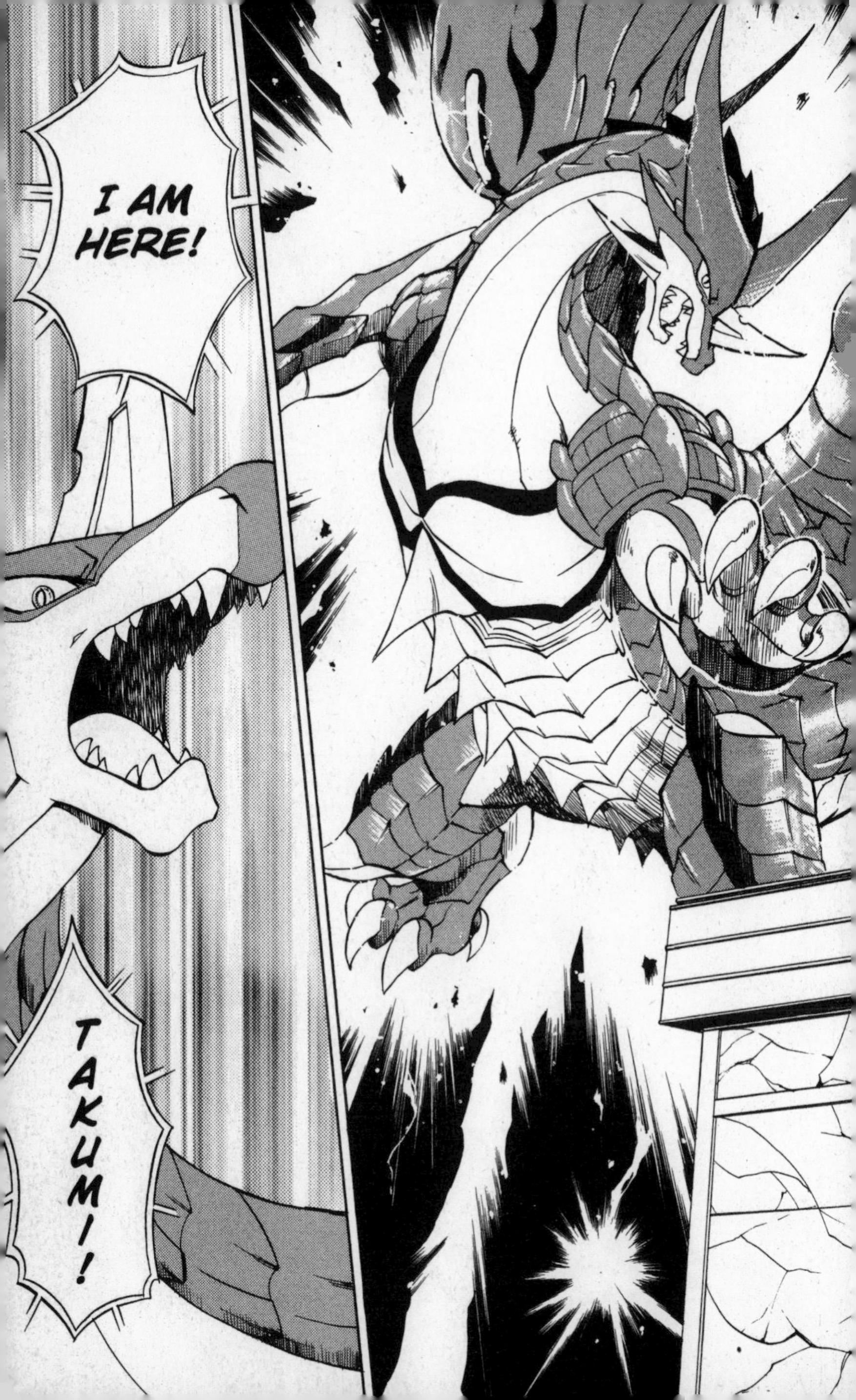
I AM HERE!
TAKUMI!

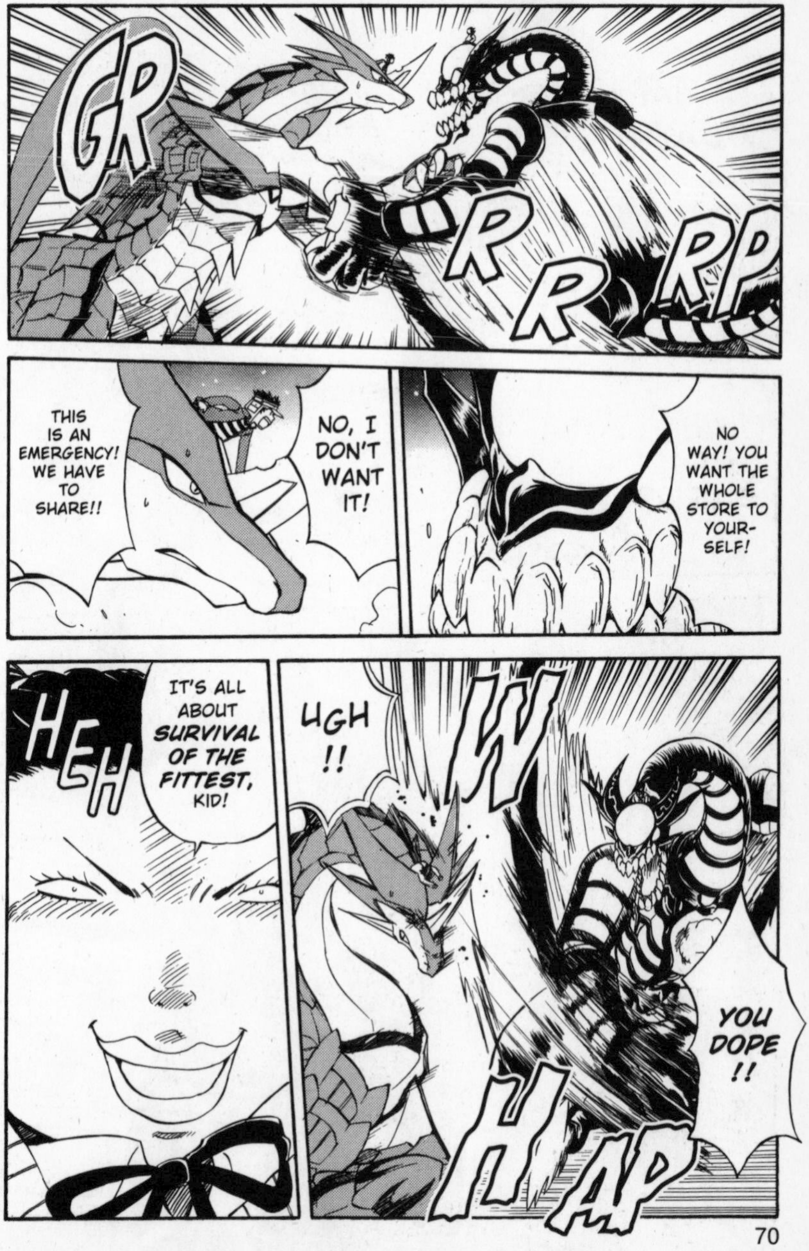
GR
R
R
RP
THIS IS AN EMERGENCY! WE HAVE TO SHARE!!
NO, I DON'T WANT IT!
NO WAY! YOU WANT THE WHOLE STORE TO YOUR-SELF!
HEH
IT'S ALL ABOUT SURVIVAL OF THE FITTEST, KID!
UGH!!
W
YOU DOPE!!
HAP

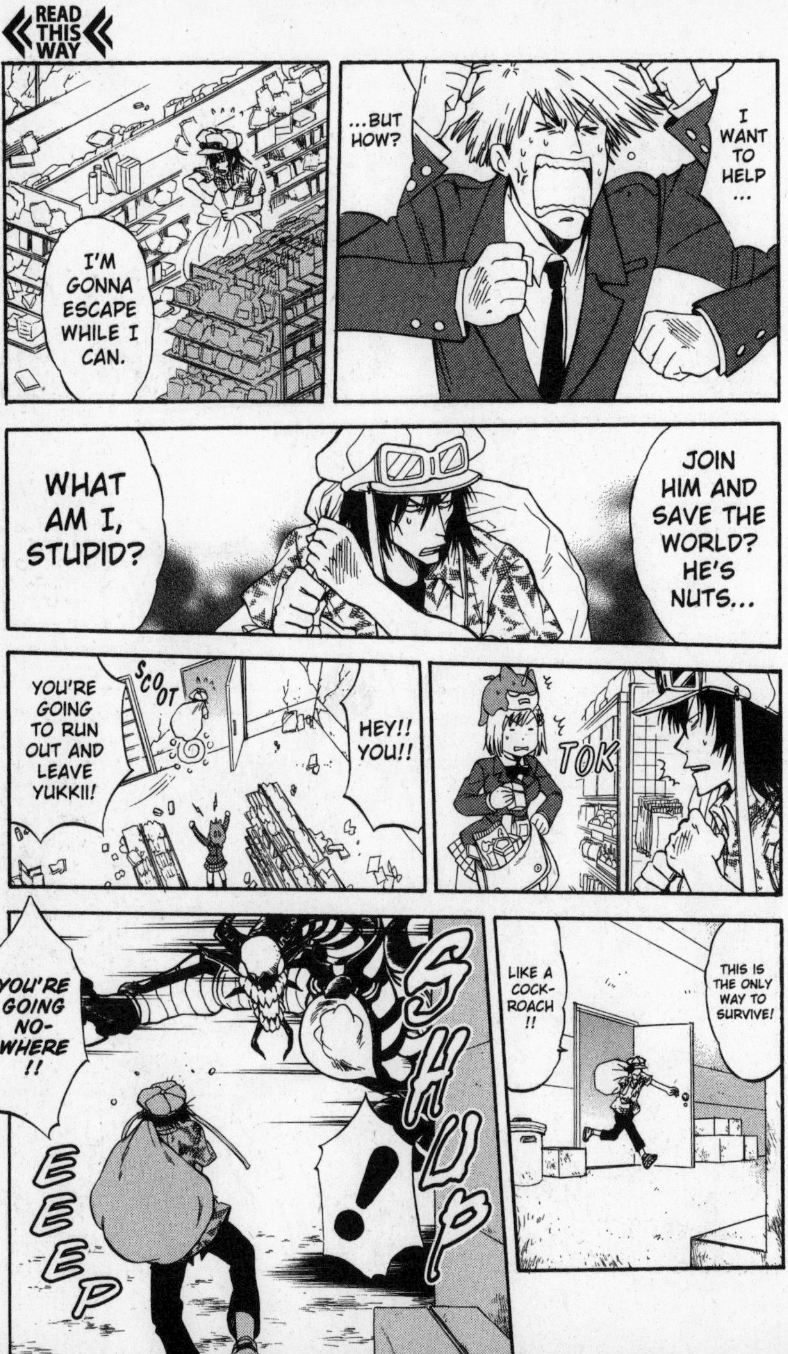
READ THIS WAY
I WANT TO HELP ...
...BUT HOW?
I'M GONNA ESCAPE WHILE I CAN.
JOIN HIM AND SAVE THE WORLD? HE'S NUTS...
WHAT AM I, STUPID?
TOK
HEY!! YOU!!
SCOOT
YOU'RE GOING TO RUN OUT AND LEAVE YUKKII!
THIS IS THE ONLY WAY TO SURVIVE!
LIKE A COCK-ROACH !!
SHUP
!
YOU'RE GOING NO-WHERE !!
EEEEP

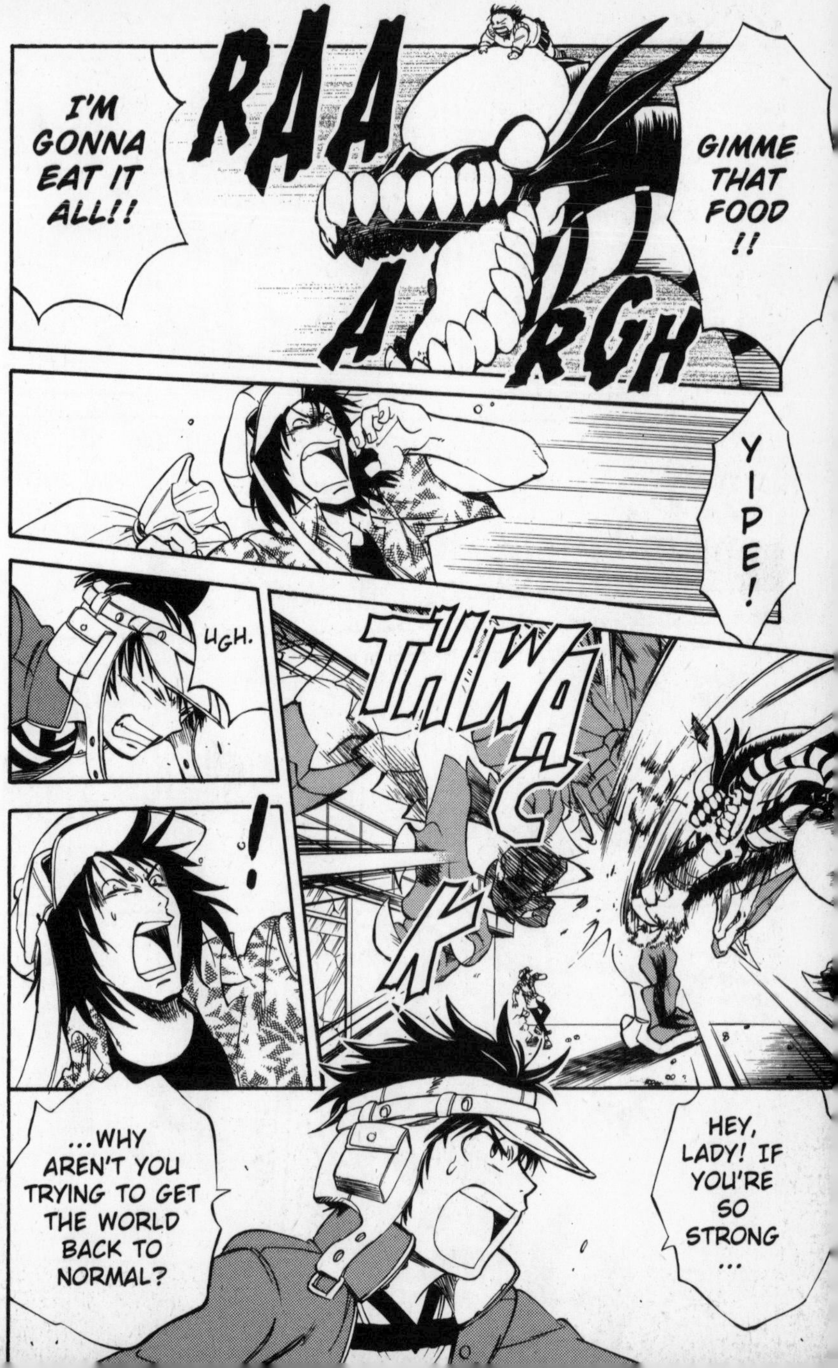
GIMME THAT FOOD!!
RAAAARGH
I'M GONNA EAT IT ALL!!
YIPE!
THWACK
UGH.
!
HEY, LADY! IF YOU'RE SO STRONG...
...WHY AREN'T YOU TRYING TO GET THE WORLD BACK TO NORMAL?

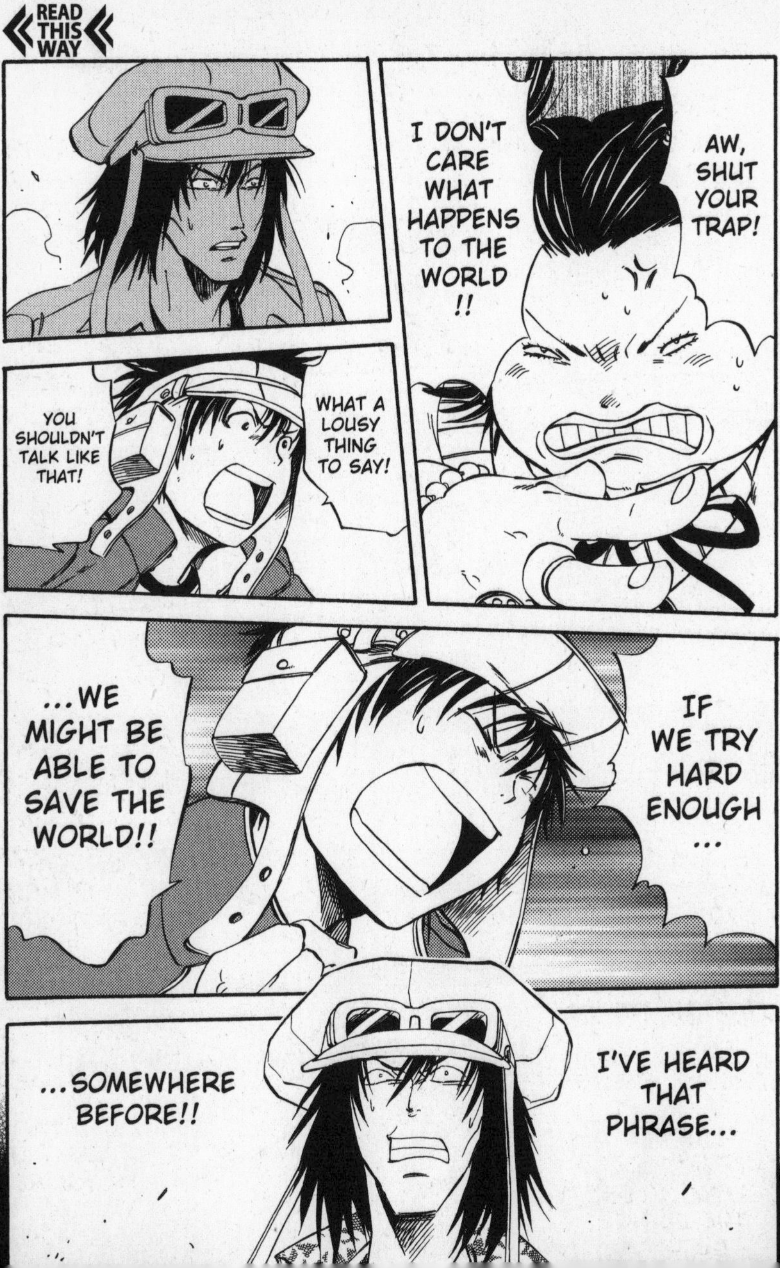
READ THIS WAY
AW, SHUT YOUR TRAP!
I DON'T CARE WHAT HAPPENS TO THE WORLD !!
WHAT A LOUSY THING TO SAY!
YOU SHOULDN'T TALK LIKE THAT!
IF WE TRY HARD ENOUGH ...
...WE MIGHT BE ABLE TO SAVE THE WORLD!!
I'VE HEARD THAT PHRASE...
...SOMEWHERE BEFORE!!

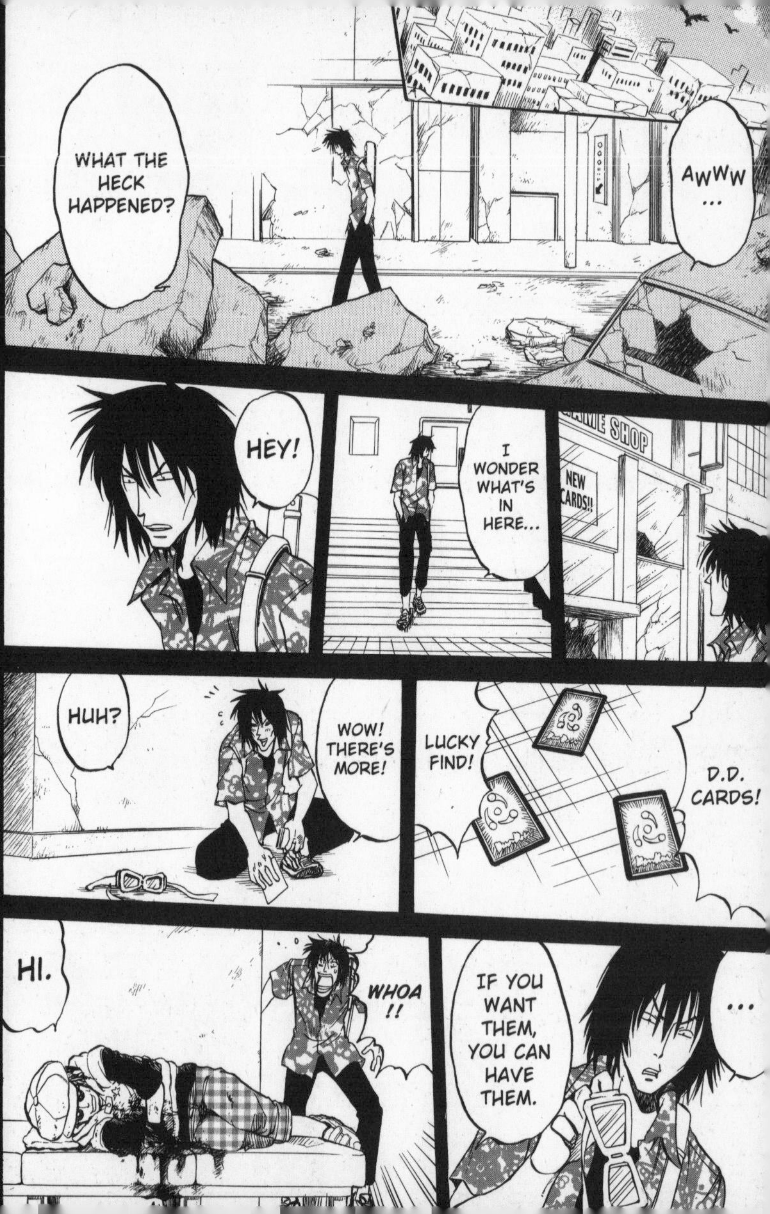
AWWW ...
WHAT THE HECK HAPPENED?
NEW CARDS!!
I WONDER WHAT'S IN HERE...
HEY!
D.D. CARDS!
LUCKY FIND!
WOW! THERE'S MORE!
HUH?
...
IF YOU WANT THEM, YOU CAN HAVE THEM.
WHOA !!
HI.

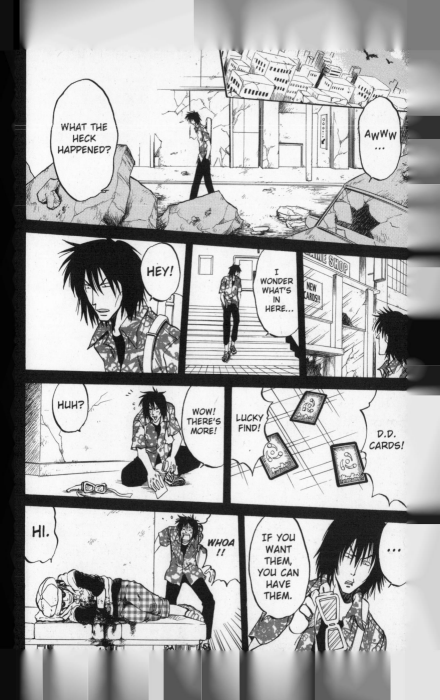

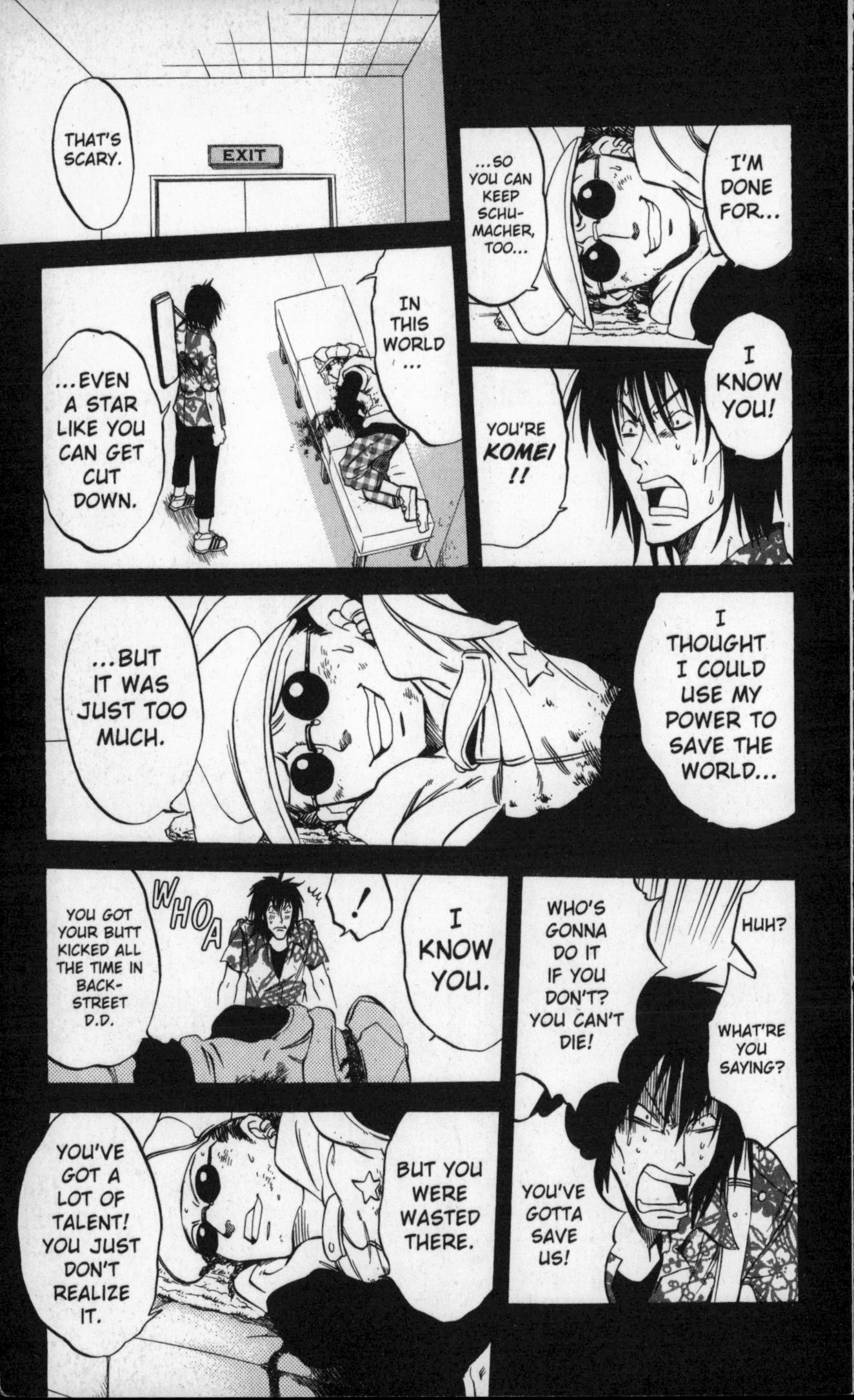
I'M DONE FOR...
...SO YOU CAN KEEP SCHUMACHER, TOO...
THAT'S SCARY.
IN THIS WORLD...
...EVEN A STAR LIKE YOU CAN GET CUT DOWN.
I KNOW YOU!
YOU'RE KOMEI!!
I THOUGHT I COULD USE MY POWER TO SAVE THE WORLD...
...BUT IT WAS JUST TOO MUCH.
HUH?
WHAT'RE YOU SAYING?
WHO'S GONNA DO IT IF YOU DON'T? YOU CAN'T DIE!
YOU'VE GOTTA SAVE US!
I KNOW YOU.
!
WHOA
YOU GOT YOUR BUTT KICKED ALL THE TIME IN BACK-STREET D.D.
BUT YOU WERE WASTED THERE.
YOU'VE GOT A LOT OF TALENT! YOU JUST DON'T REALIZE IT.

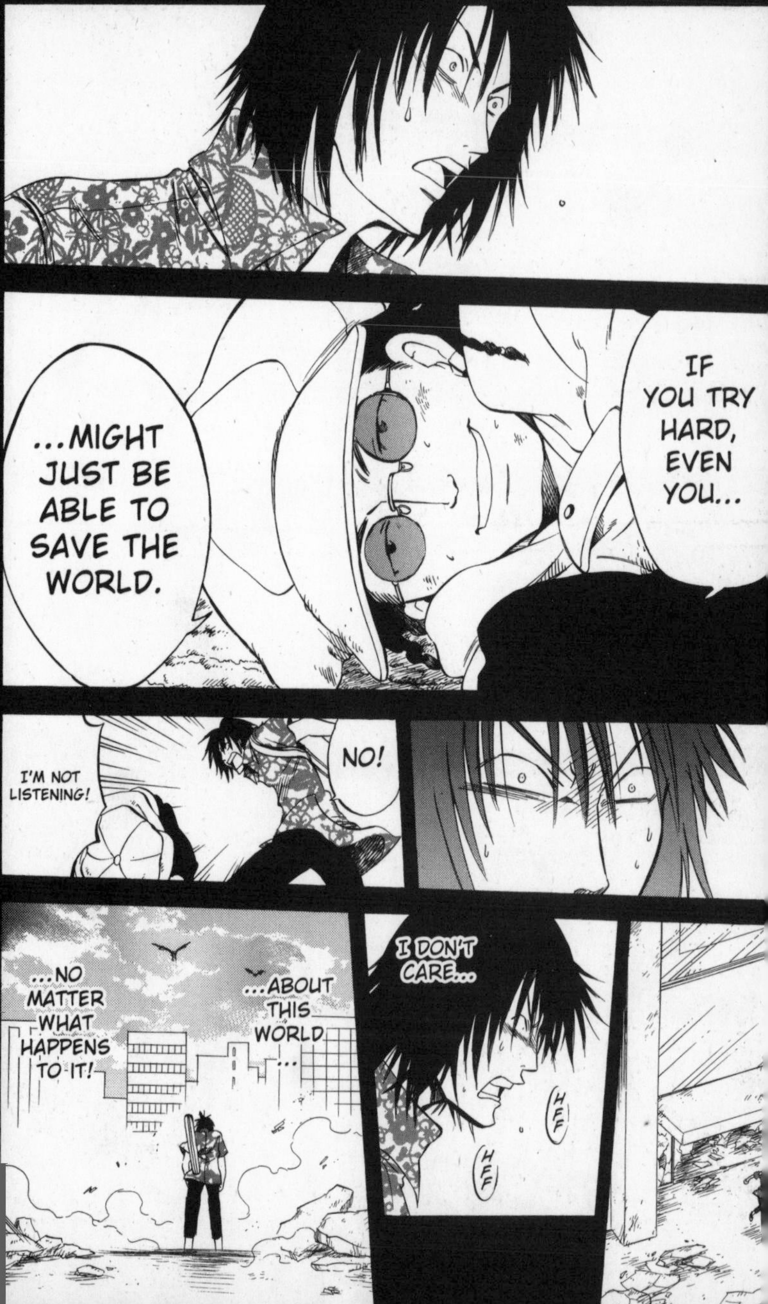
IF YOU TRY HARD, EVEN YOU...
...MIGHT JUST BE ABLE TO SAVE THE WORLD.
NO!
I'M NOT LISTENING!
I DON'T CARE...
HFF
HFF
...ABOUT THIS WORLD...
...NO MATTER WHAT HAPPENS TO IT!

READ THIS WAY

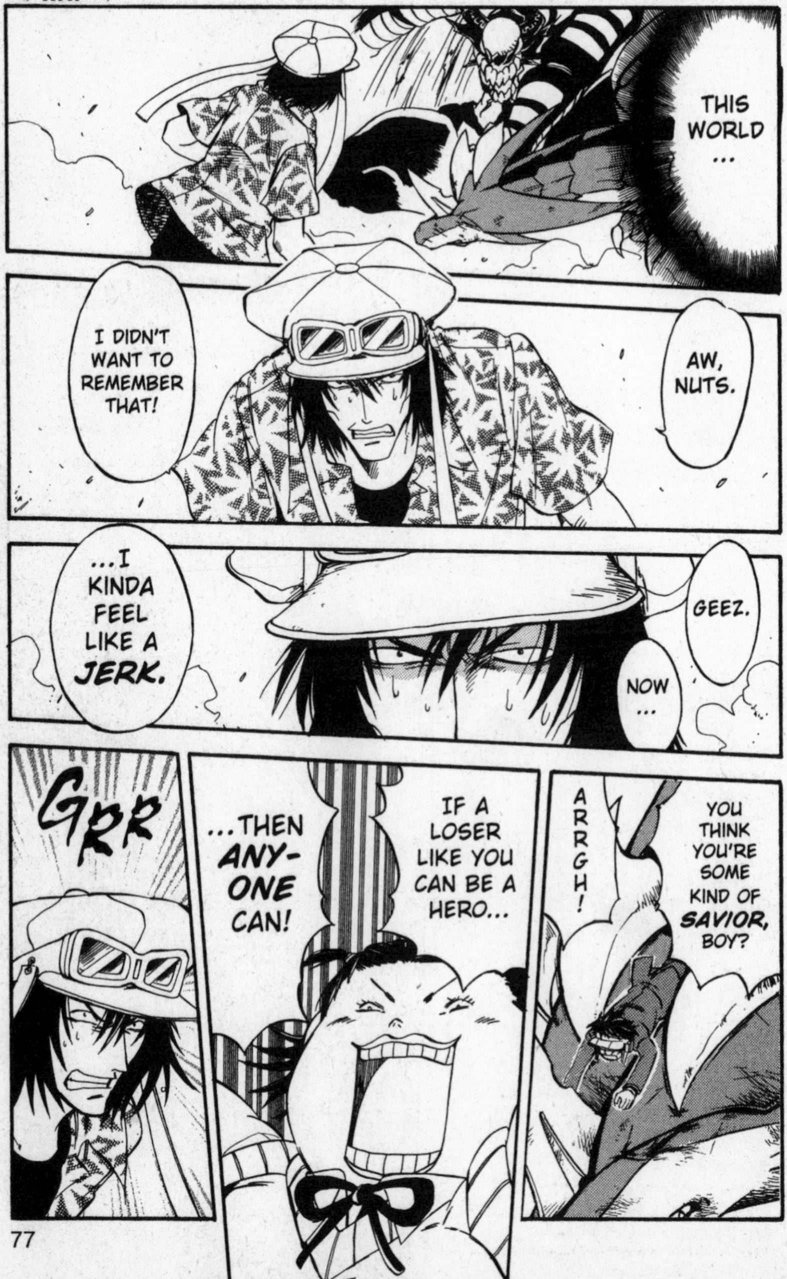
THIS WORLD ...
AW, NUTS.
I DIDN'T WANT TO REMEMBER THAT!
GEEZ.
NOW ...
...I KINDA FEEL LIKE A JERK.
YOU THINK YOU'RE SOME KIND OF SAVIOR, BOY?
ARRGH!
IF A LOSER LIKE YOU CAN BE A HERO...
...THEN ANY-ONE CAN!
GRR

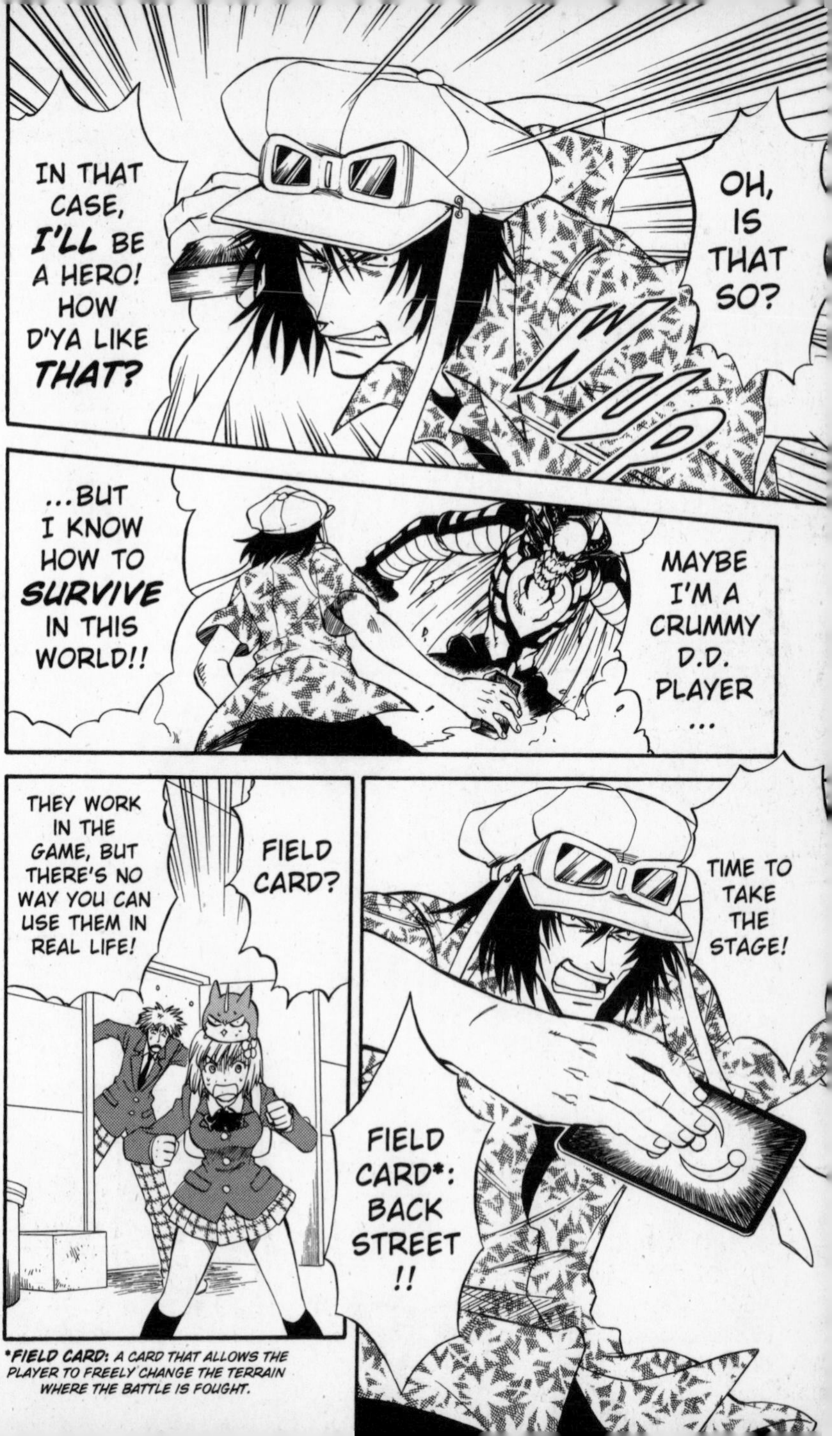
OH, IS THAT SO?
IN THAT CASE, I'LL BE A HERO! HOW D'YA LIKE THAT?
WHUP
MAYBE I'M A CRUMMY D.D. PLAYER...
...BUT I KNOW HOW TO SURVIVE IN THIS WORLD!!
TIME TO TAKE THE STAGE!
FIELD CARD*: BACK STREET!!
FIELD CARD?
THEY WORK IN THE GAME, BUT THERE'S NO WAY YOU CAN USE THEM IN REAL LIFE!

*FIELD CARD: A CARD THAT ALLOWS THE PLAYER TO FREELY CHANGE THE TERRAIN WHERE THE BATTLE IS FOUGHT.

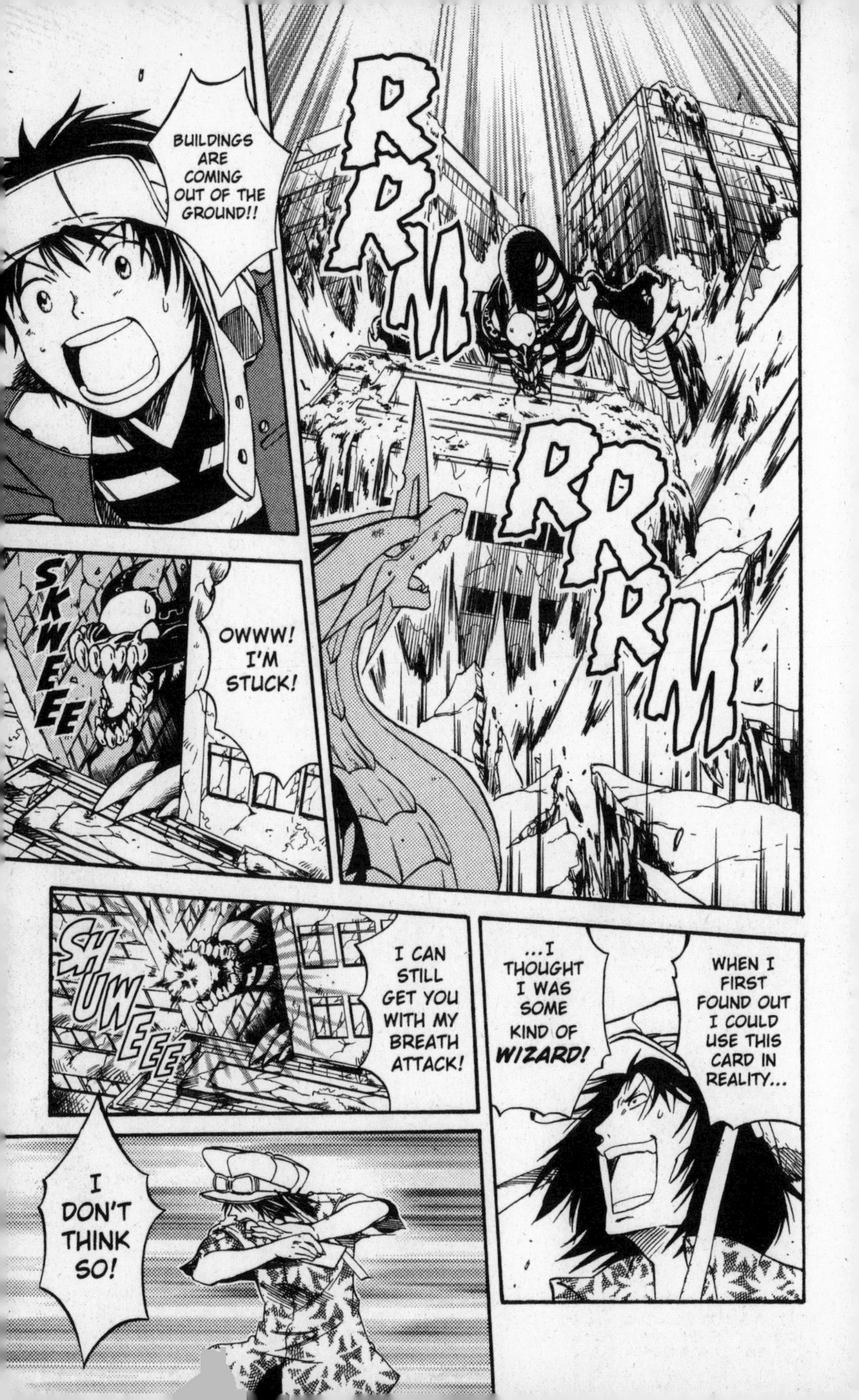
RRM
RRRM
BUILDINGS ARE COMING OUT OF THE GROUND!!
SKWEEE
OWWW! I'M STUCK!
WHEN I FIRST FOUND OUT I COULD USE THIS CARD IN REALITY...
...I THOUGHT I WAS SOME KIND OF *WIZARD!*
SHUWEEE
I CAN STILL GET YOU WITH MY BREATH ATTACK!
I DON'T THINK SO!

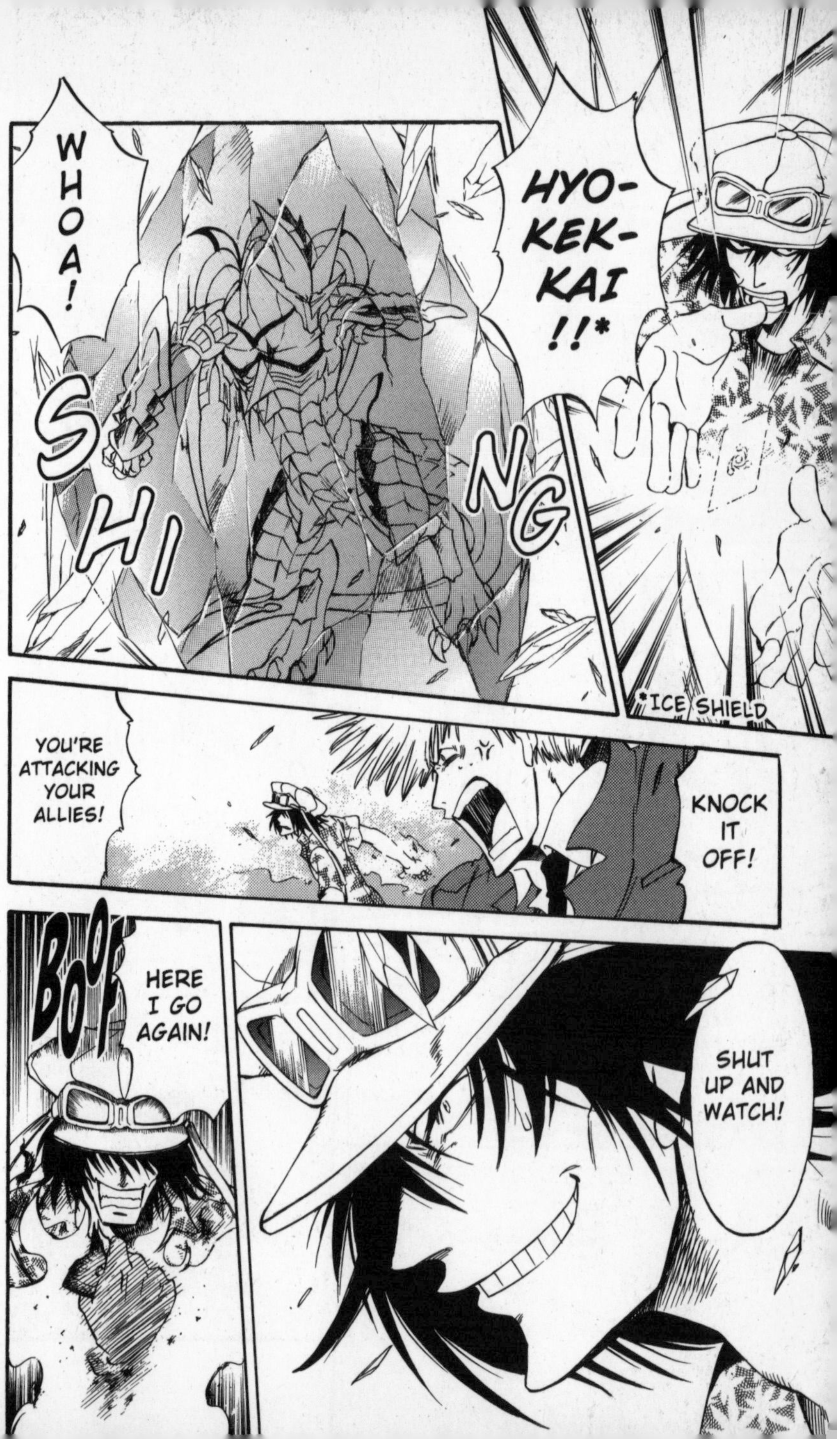
HYO-KEK-KAI!!*
SHING
*ICE SHIELD
WHOA!
KNOCK IT OFF!
YOU'RE ATTACKING YOUR ALLIES!
SHUT UP AND WATCH!
BOOF
HERE I GO AGAIN!

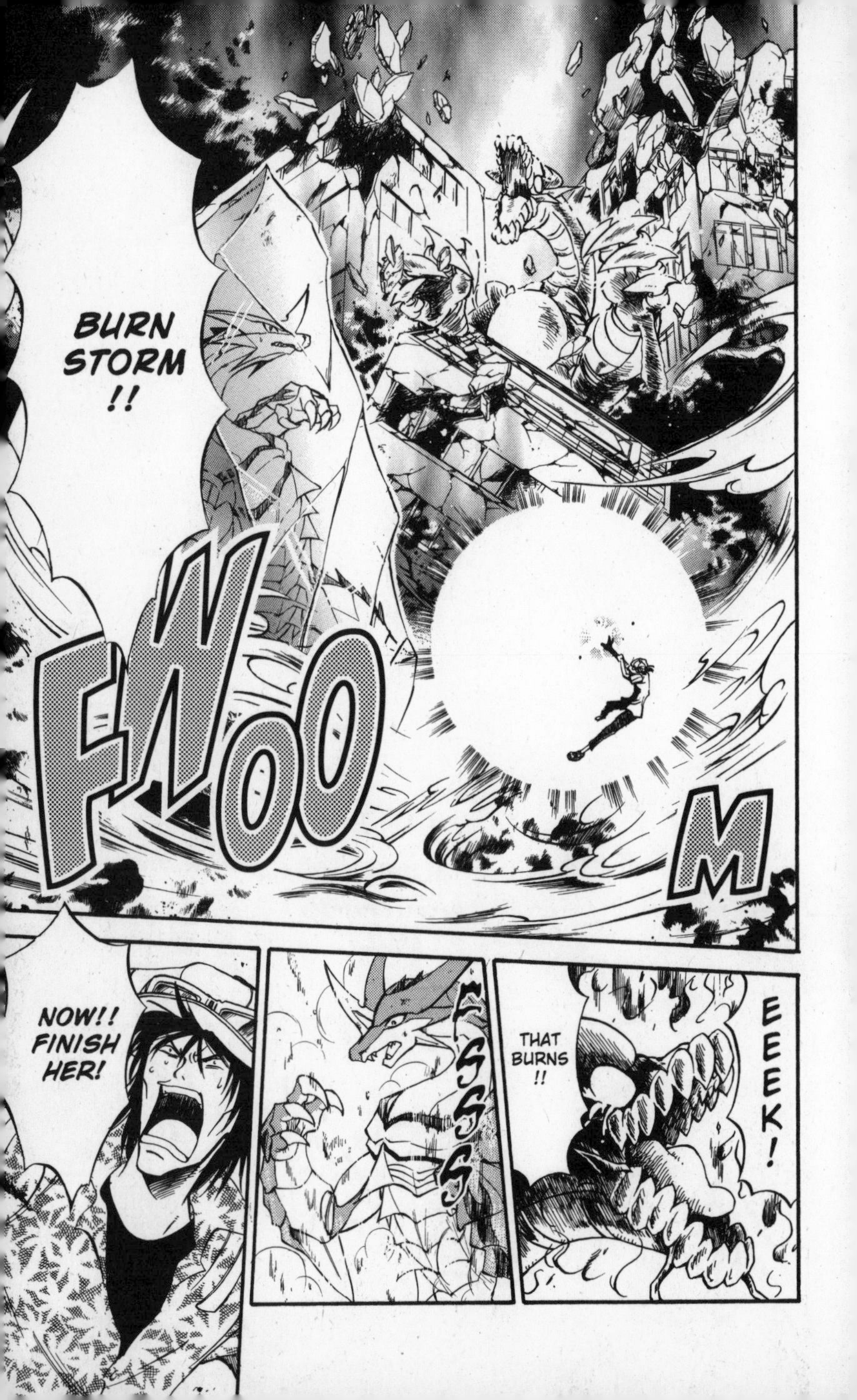
BURN STORM !!
FWOOM
EEEK!
THAT BURNS !!
FSSSS
NOW!! FINISH HER!

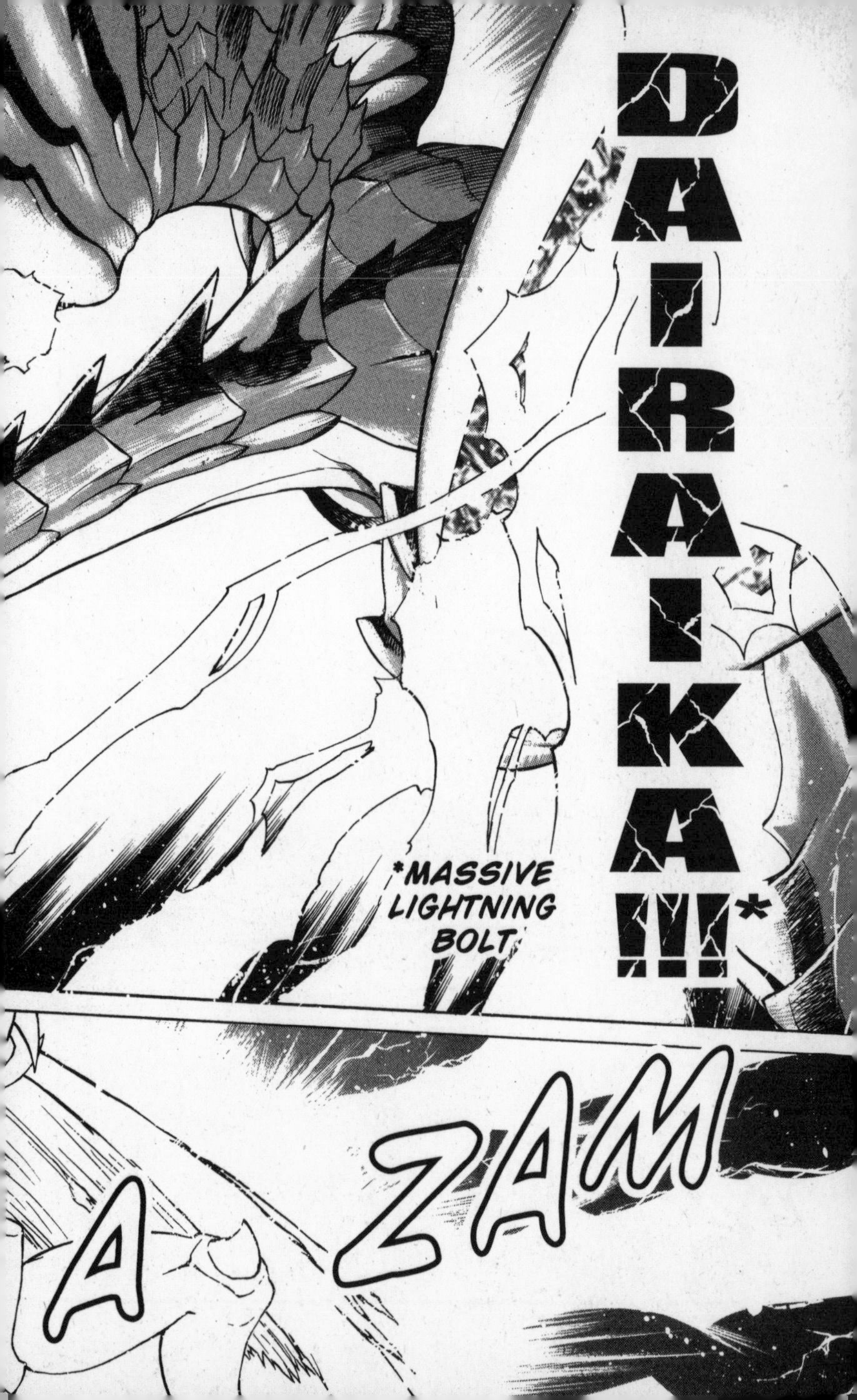
DAIRAKAI!!!*
*MASSIVE LIGHTNING BOLT
A ZAM

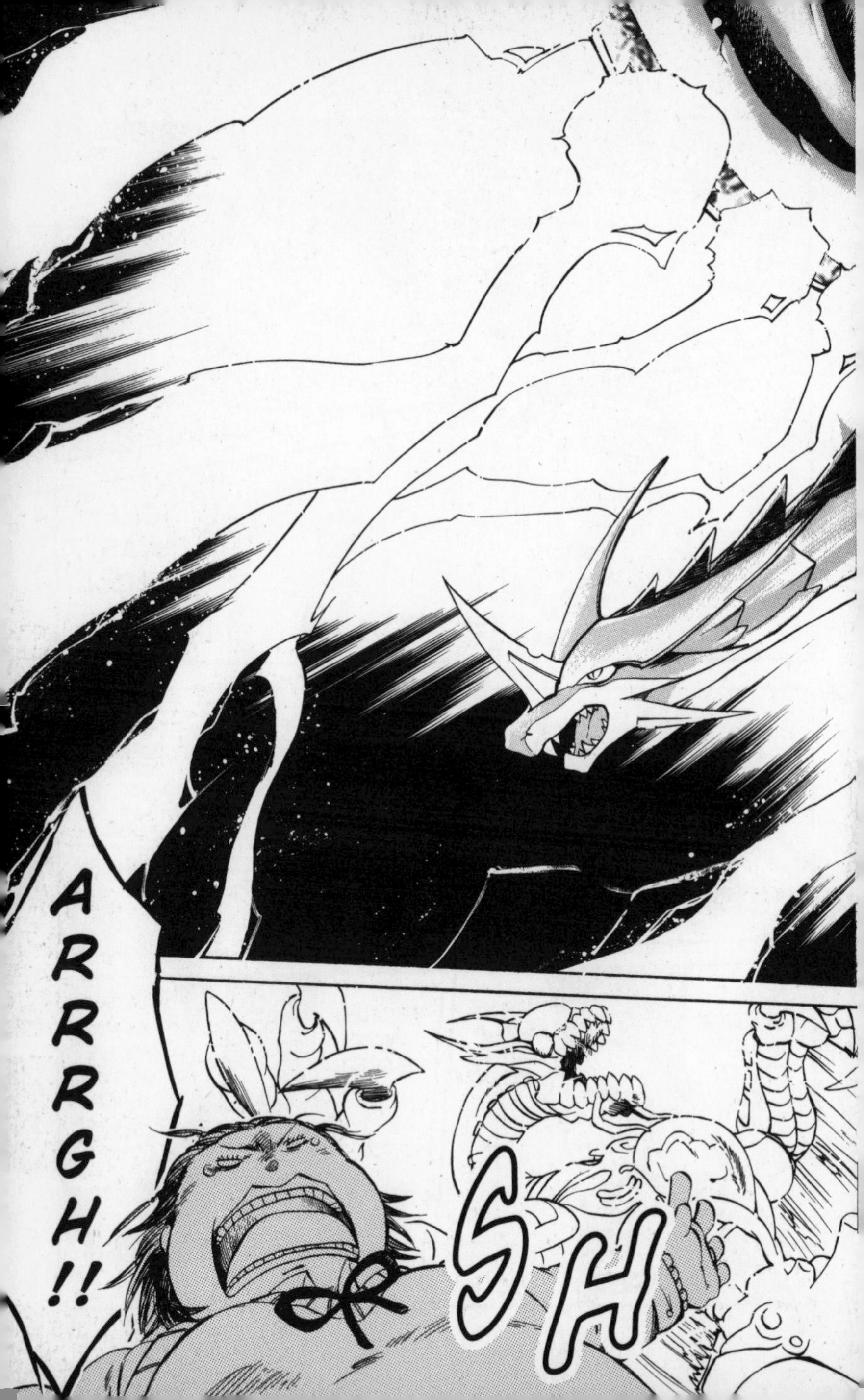
ARRRGH!!
SH

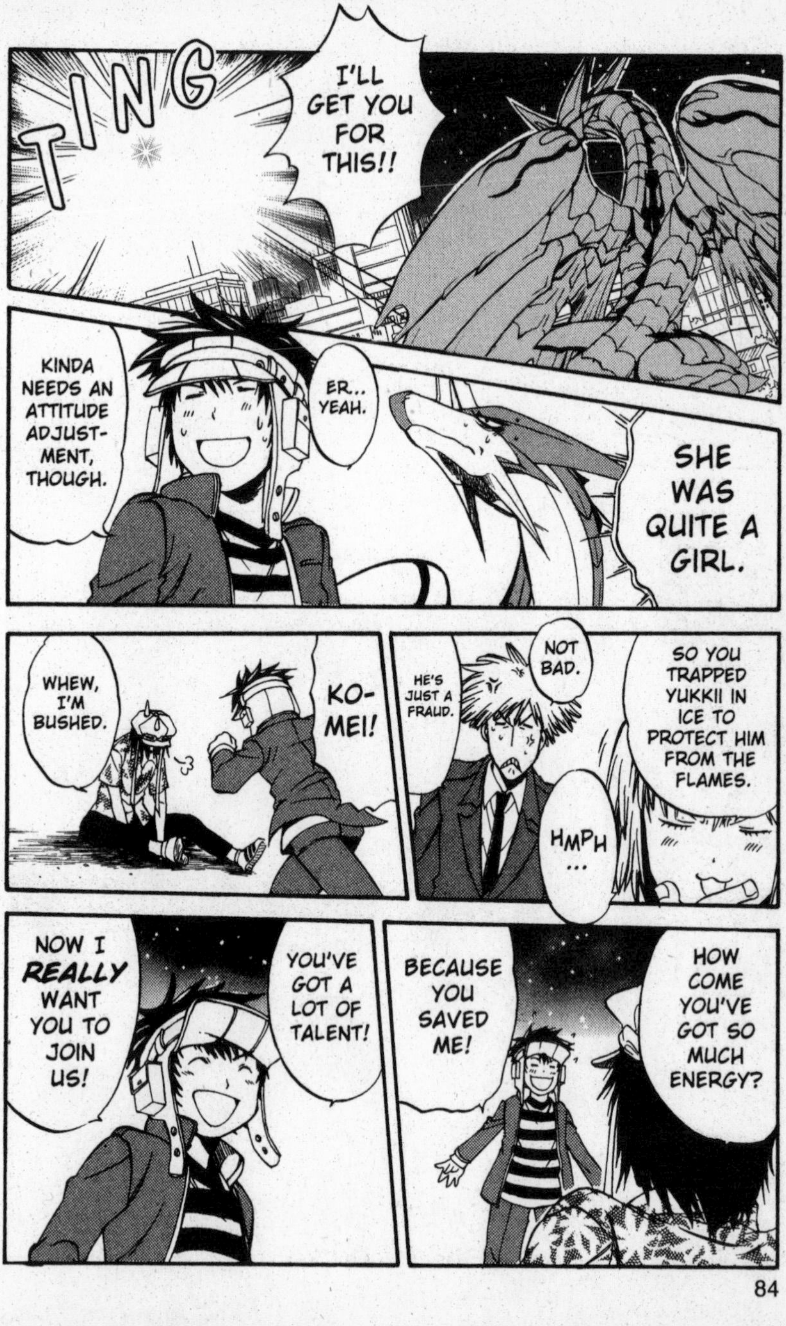
I'LL GET YOU FOR THIS!!
TING
SHE WAS QUITE A GIRL.
ER.. YEAH.
KINDA NEEDS AN ATTITUDE ADJUSTMENT, THOUGH.
SO YOU TRAPPED YUKKII IN ICE TO PROTECT HIM FROM THE FLAMES.
NOT BAD.
HE'S JUST A FRAUD.
HMPH...
KO-MEI!
WHEW, I'M BUSHED.
HOW COME YOU'VE GOT SO MUCH ENERGY?
BECAUSE YOU SAVED ME!
YOU'VE GOT A LOT OF TALENT!
NOW I REALLY WANT YOU TO JOIN US!

READ THIS WAY

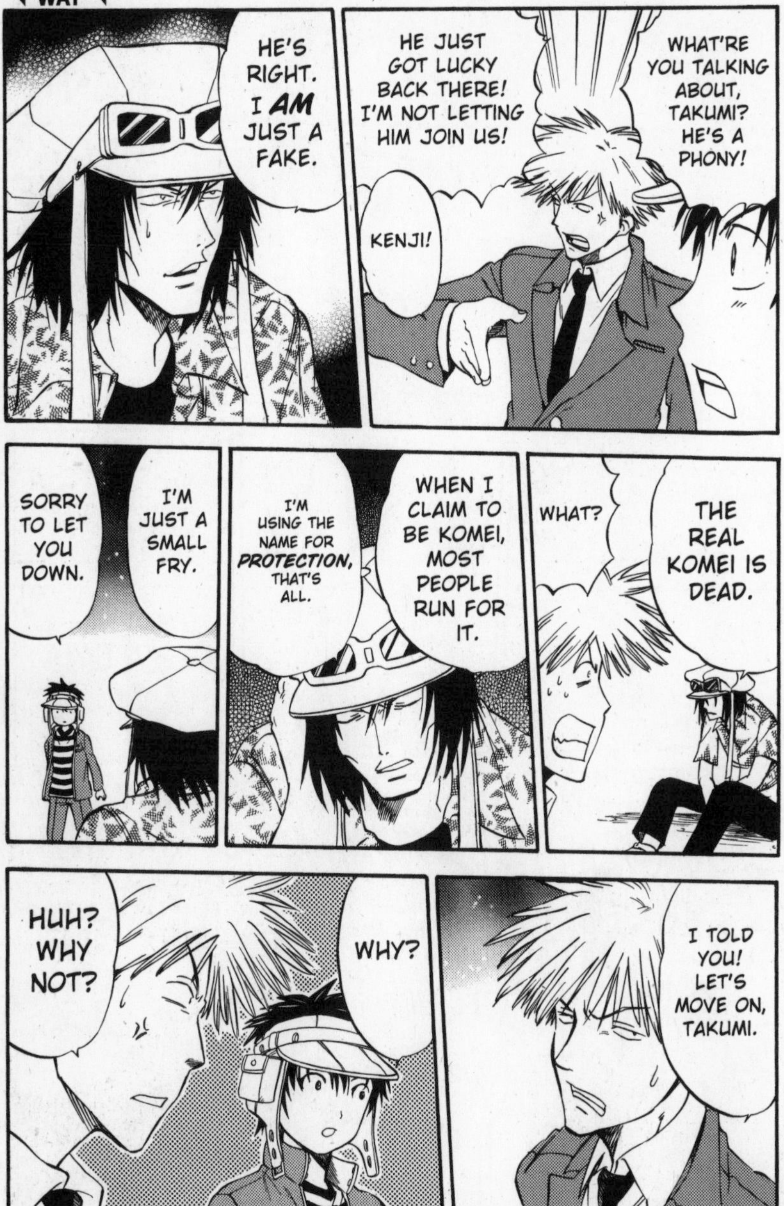
WHAT'RE YOU TALKING ABOUT, TAKUMI? HE'S A PHONY!
HE JUST GOT LUCKY BACK THERE! I'M NOT LETTING HIM JOIN US!
KENJI!
HE'S RIGHT. I **AM** JUST A FAKE.
THE REAL KOMEI IS DEAD.
WHAT?
WHEN I CLAIM TO BE KOMEI, MOST PEOPLE RUN FOR IT.
I'M USING THE NAME FOR **PROTECTION,** THAT'S ALL.
I'M JUST A SMALL FRY.
SORRY TO LET YOU DOWN.
I TOLD YOU! LET'S MOVE ON, TAKUMI.
WHY?
HUH? WHY NOT?

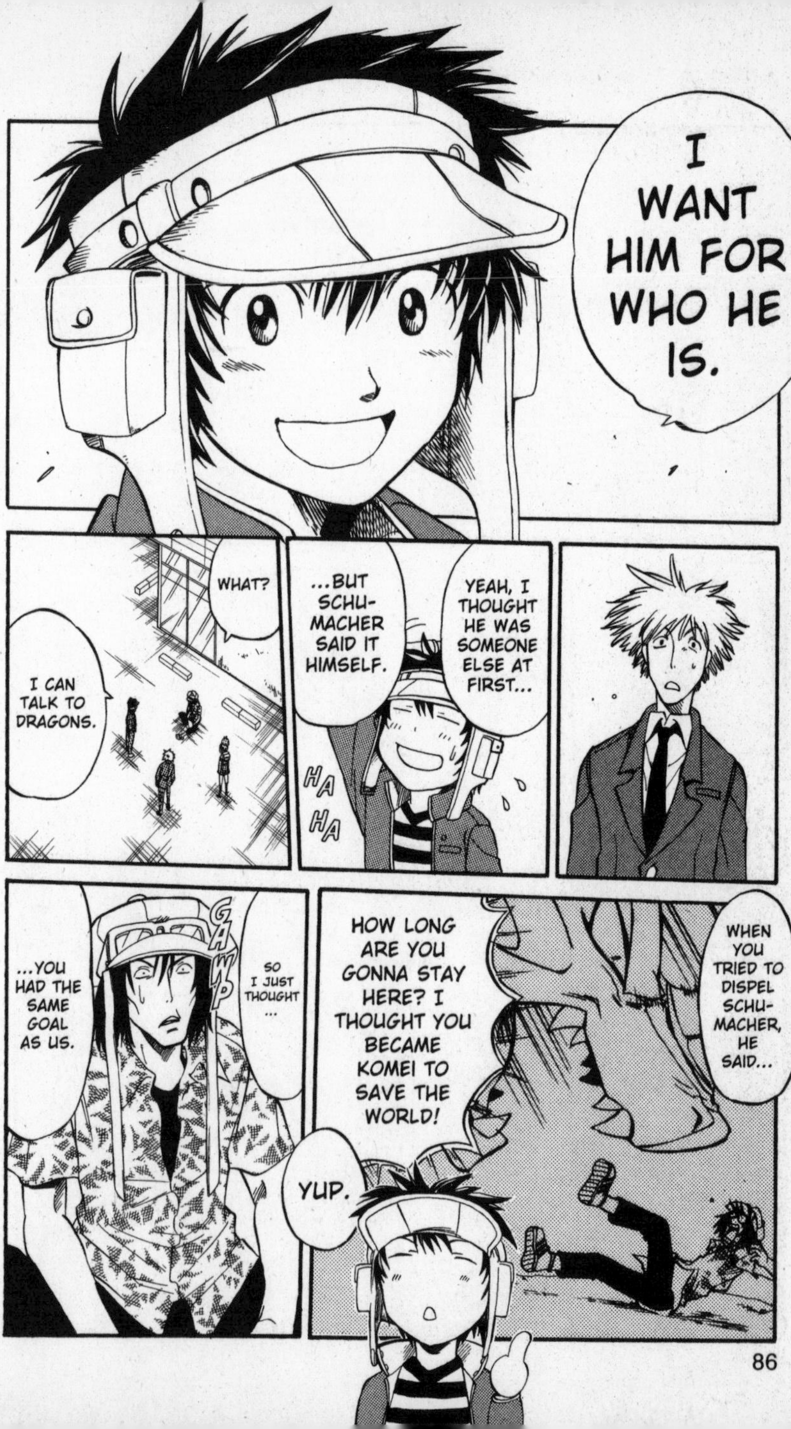

I WANT HIM FOR WHO HE IS.
YEAH, I THOUGHT HE WAS SOMEONE ELSE AT FIRST...
...BUT SCHUMACHER SAID IT HIMSELF.
HA HA
WHAT?
I CAN TALK TO DRAGONS.
WHEN YOU TRIED TO DISPEL SCHUMACHER, HE SAID...
HOW LONG ARE YOU GONNA STAY HERE? I THOUGHT YOU BECAME KOMEI TO SAVE THE WORLD!
YUP.
GAWP
SO I JUST THOUGHT...
...YOU HAD THE SAME GOAL AS US.

READ THIS WAY

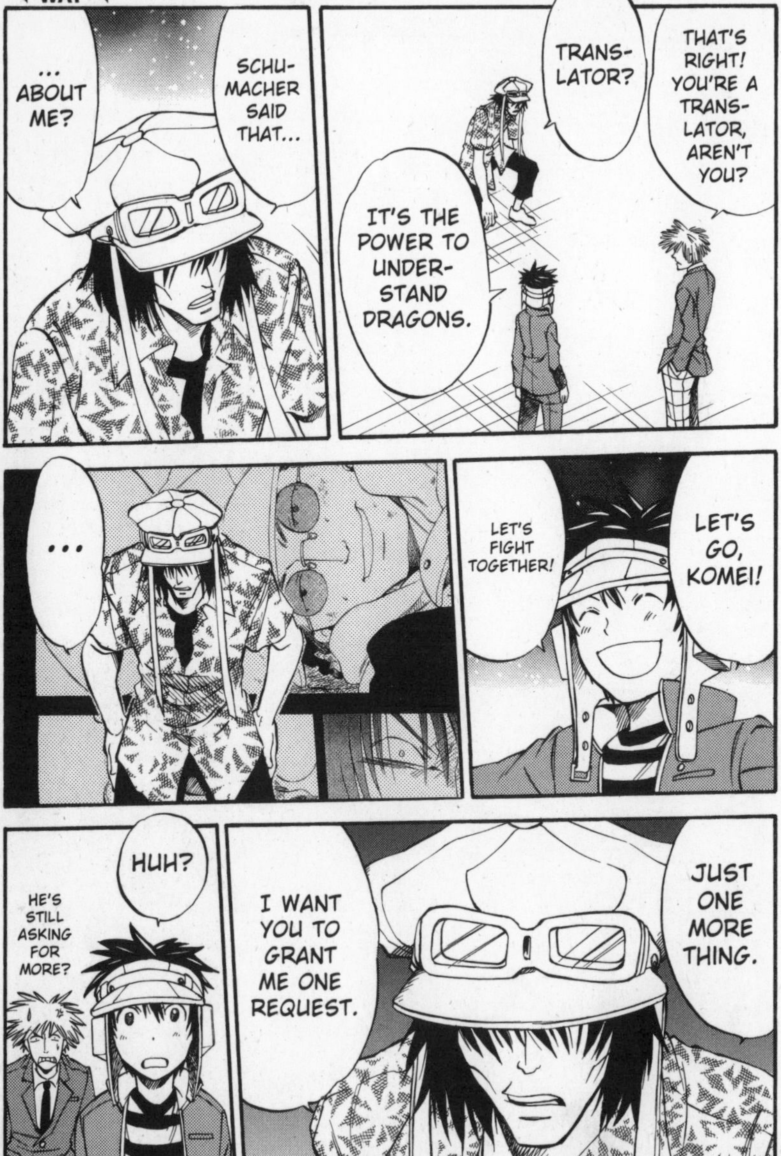
TRANS-LATOR?
THAT'S RIGHT! YOU'RE A TRANS-LATOR, AREN'T YOU?
IT'S THE POWER TO UNDER-STAND DRAGONS.
SCHU-MACHER SAID THAT...
... ABOUT ME?
LET'S GO, KOMEI!
LET'S FIGHT TOGETHER!
...
JUST ONE MORE THING.
I WANT YOU TO GRANT ME ONE REQUEST.
HUH?
HE'S STILL ASKING FOR MORE?

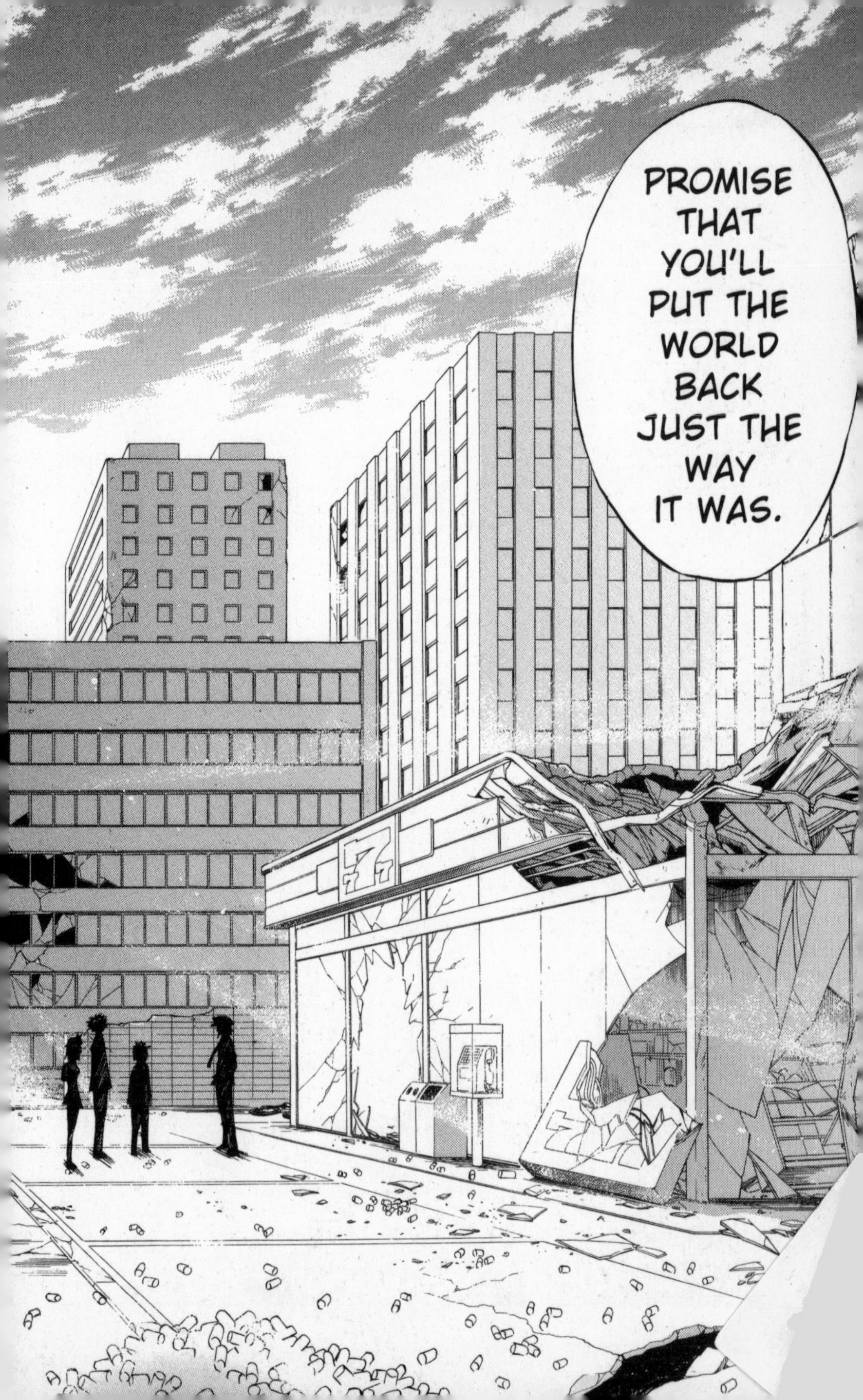
PROMISE THAT YOU'LL PUT THE WORLD BACK JUST THE WAY IT WAS.

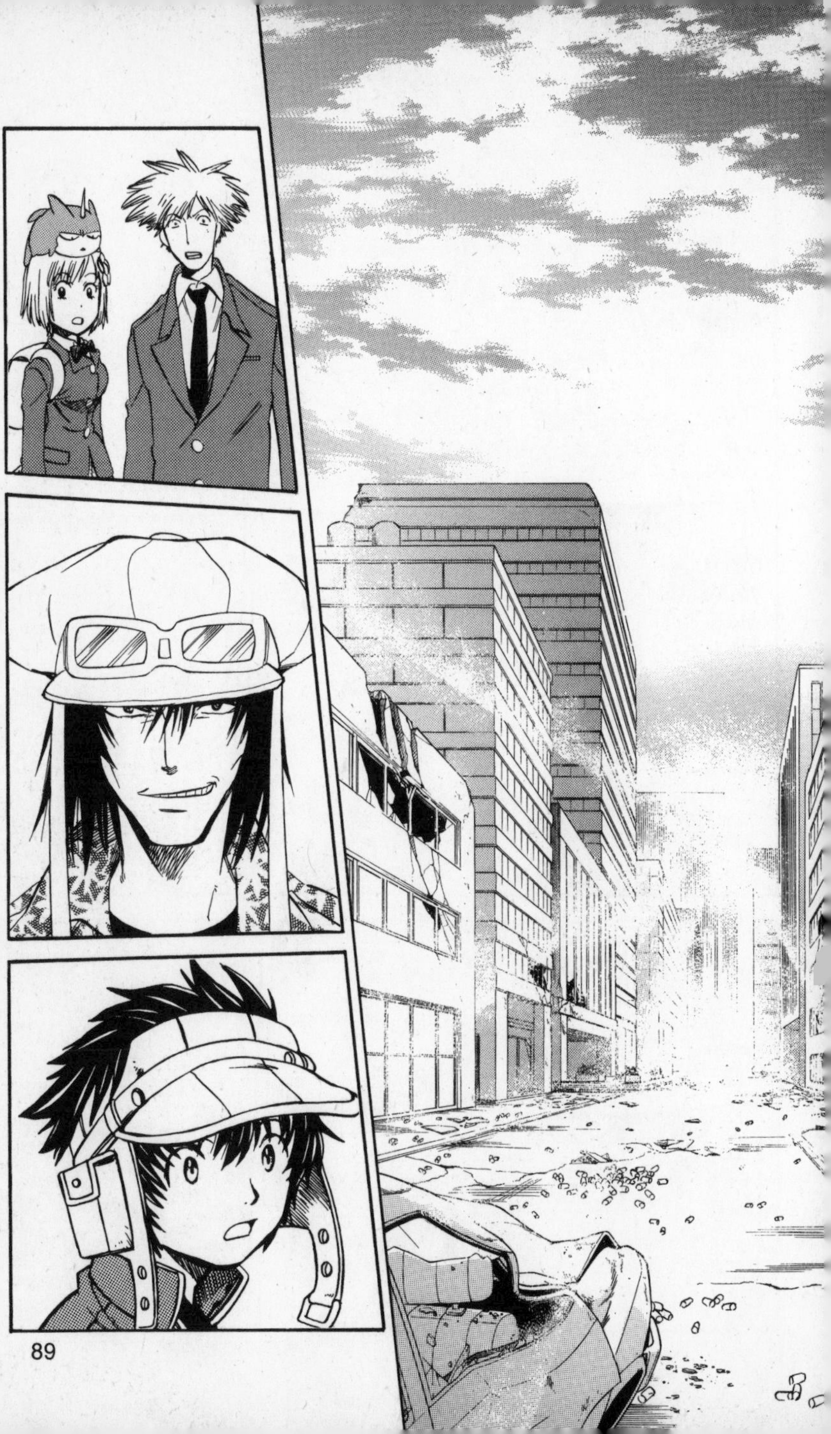

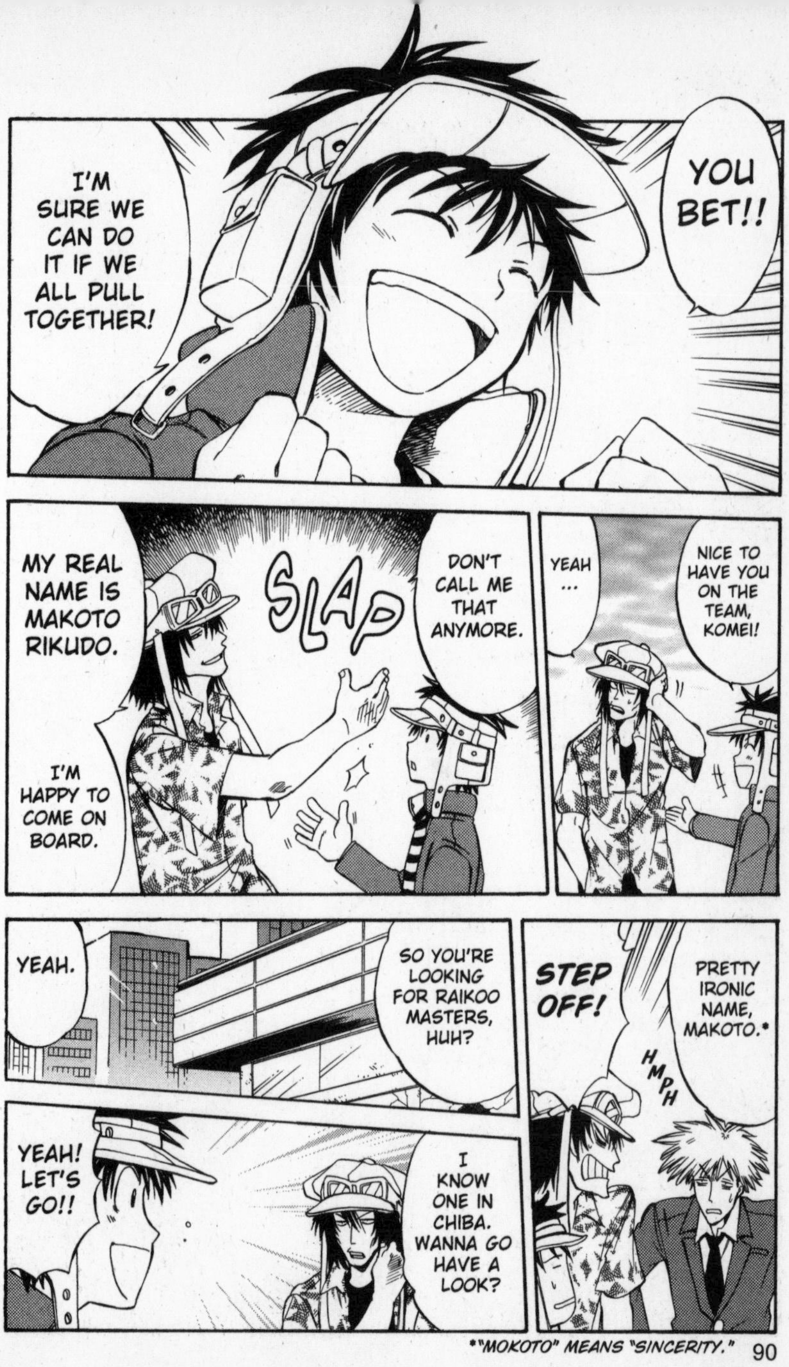
YOU BET!!
I'M SURE WE CAN DO IT IF WE ALL PULL TOGETHER!
NICE TO HAVE YOU ON THE TEAM, KOMEI!
YEAH ...
DON'T CALL ME THAT ANYMORE.
SLAP
MY REAL NAME IS MAKOTO RIKUDO.
I'M HAPPY TO COME ON BOARD.
PRETTY IRONIC NAME, MAKOTO.*
HMPH
STEP OFF!
SO YOU'RE LOOKING FOR RAIKOO MASTERS, HUH?
YEAH.
I KNOW ONE IN CHIBA. WANNA GO HAVE A LOOK?
YEAH! LET'S GO!!

*"MOKOTO" MEANS "SINCERITY."

READ THIS WAY

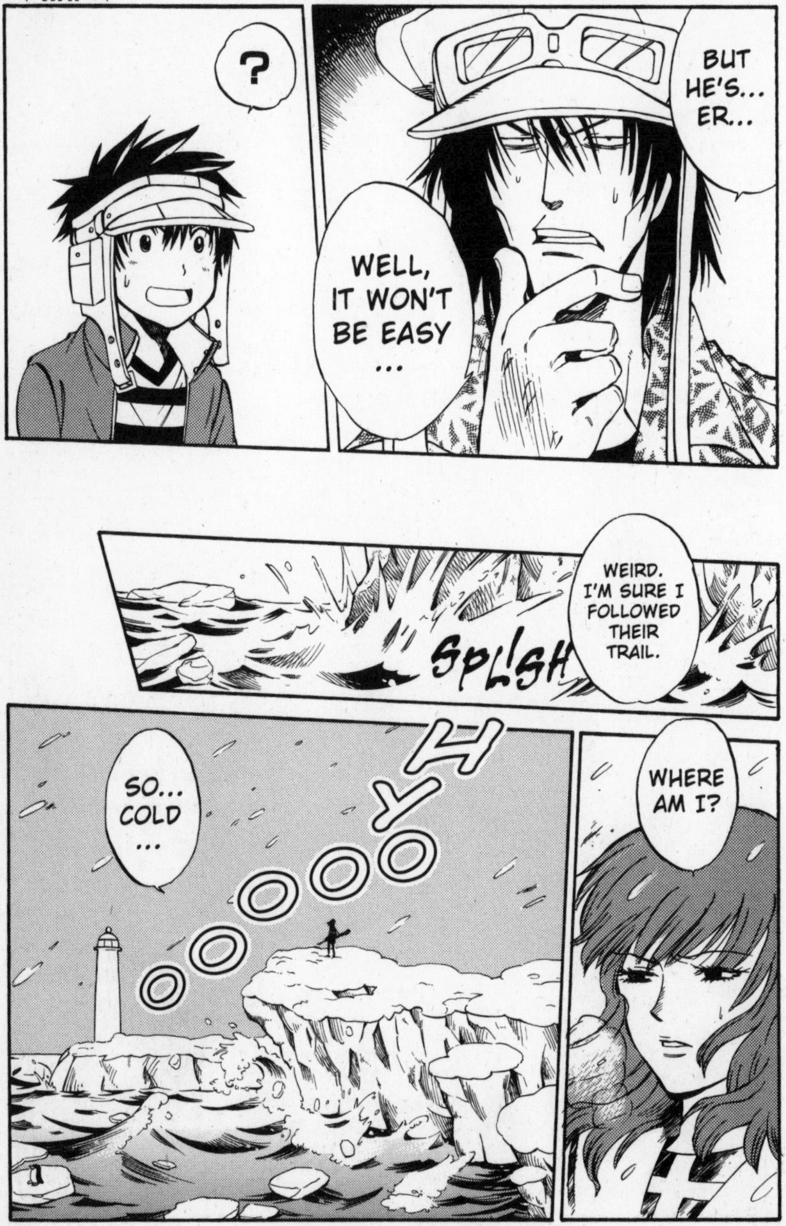
BUT HE'S... ER...
WELL, IT WON'T BE EASY ...
?
WEIRD. I'M SURE I FOLLOWED THEIR TRAIL.
SPL!SH
WHERE AM I?
HYOOOOOO
SO... COLD ...

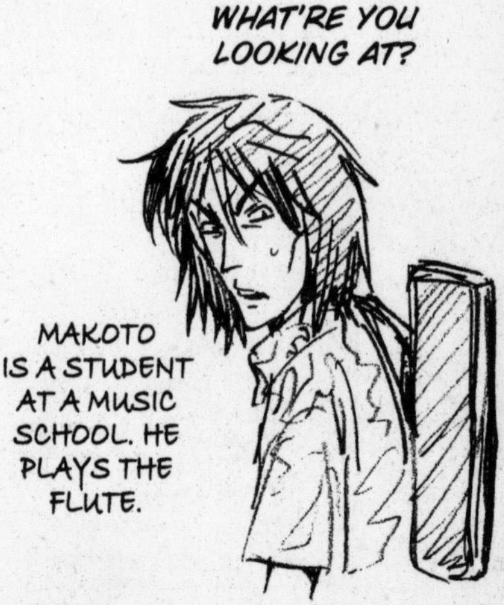
WHAT'RE YOU LOOKING AT?
MAKOTO IS A STUDENT AT A MUSIC SCHOOL. HE PLAYS THE FLUTE.

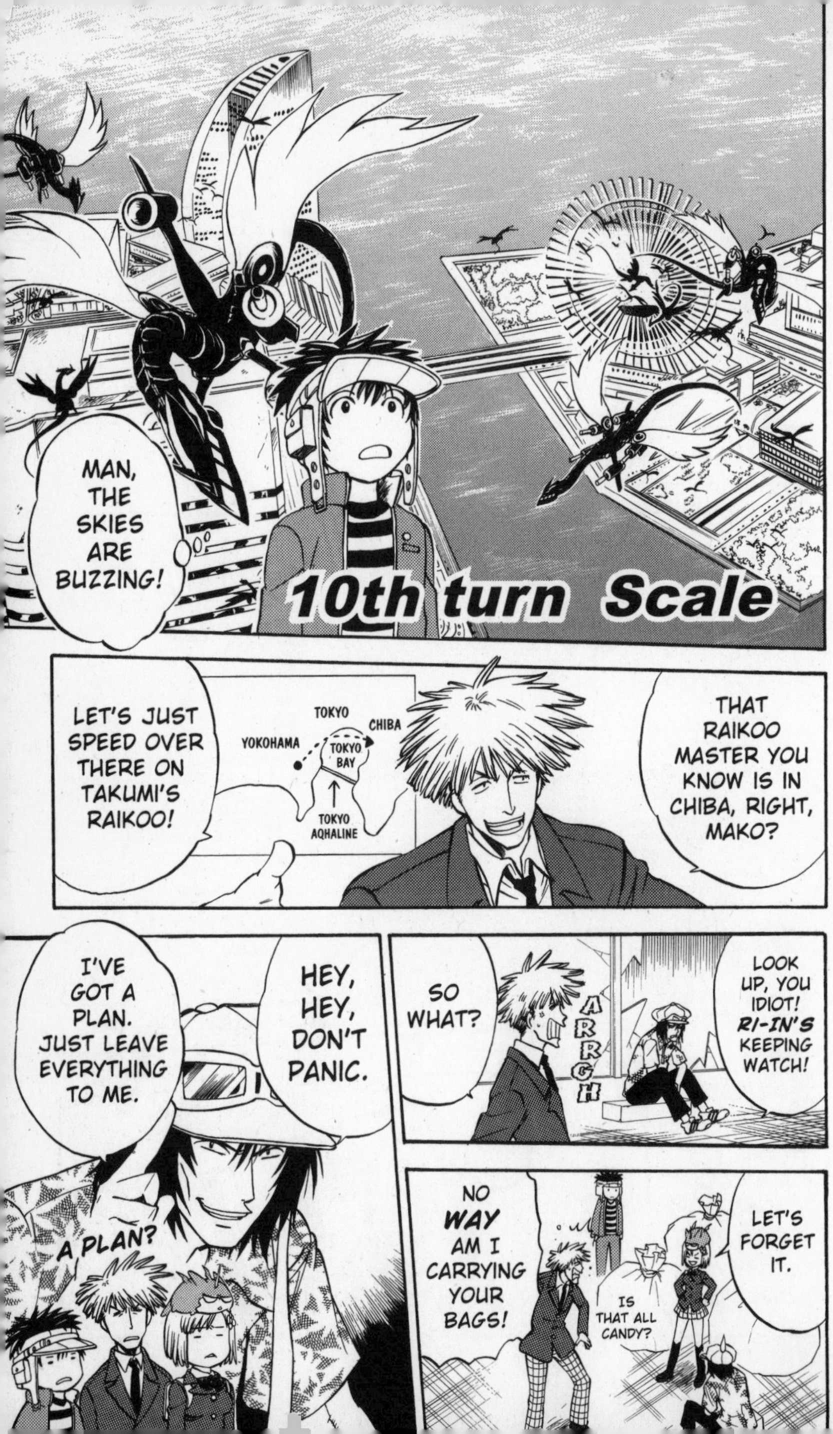
MAN, THE SKIES ARE BUZZING!
10th turn Scale
THAT RAIKOO MASTER YOU KNOW IS IN CHIBA, RIGHT, MAKO?
LET'S JUST SPEED OVER THERE ON TAKUMI'S RAIKOO!
TOKYO
CHIBA
YOKOHAMA
TOKYO BAY
TOKYO AQHALINE
LOOK UP, YOU IDIOT! RI-IN'S KEEPING WATCH!
ARRGH
SO WHAT?
HEY, HEY, DON'T PANIC.
I'VE GOT A PLAN. JUST LEAVE EVERYTHING TO ME.
A PLAN?
LET'S FORGET IT.
IS THAT ALL CANDY?
NO WAY AM I CARRYING YOUR BAGS!

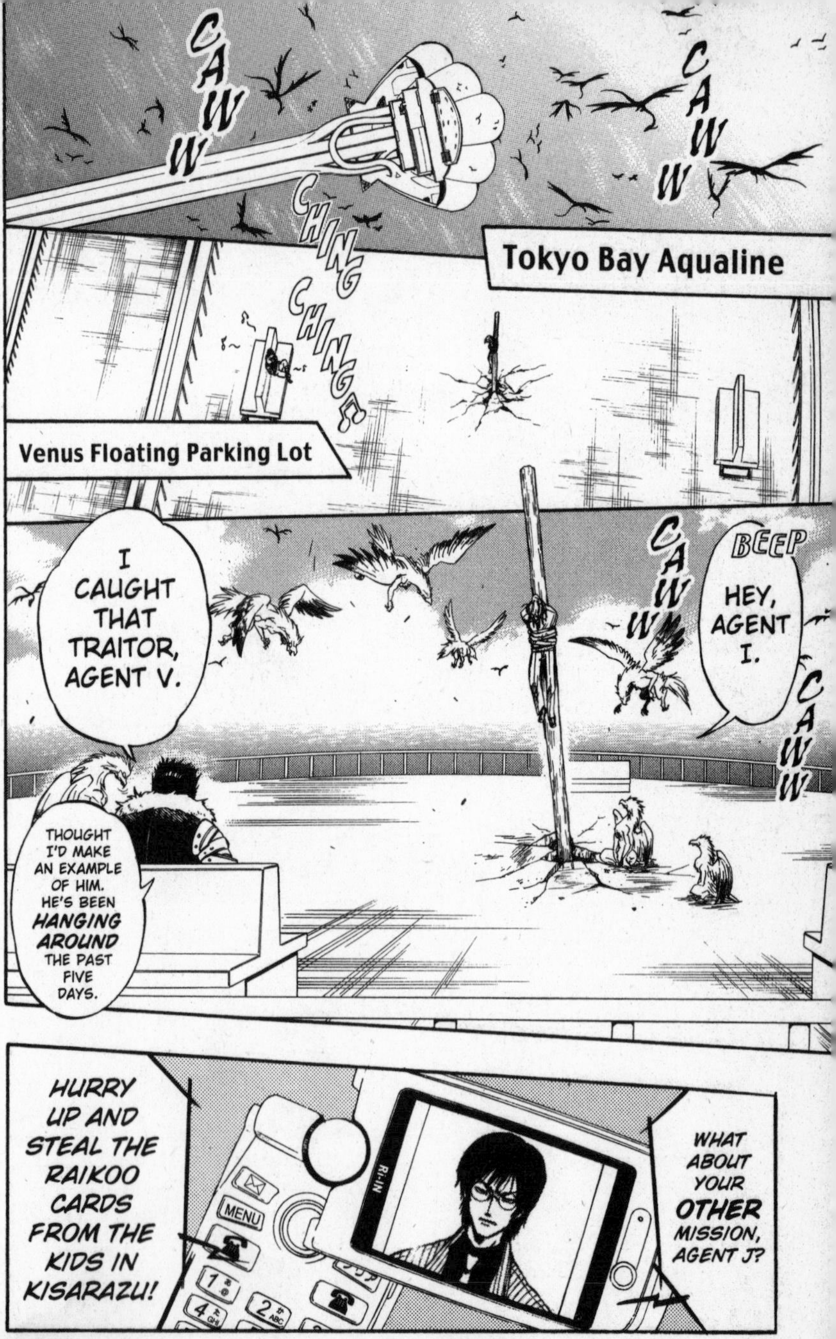
CAWW
CAWW
CHING CHING♫
Tokyo Bay Aqualine
Venus Floating Parking Lot
CAWW
BEEP
HEY, AGENT I.
CAWW
I CAUGHT THAT TRAITOR, AGENT V.
THOUGHT I'D MAKE AN EXAMPLE OF HIM. HE'S BEEN HANGING AROUND THE PAST FIVE DAYS.
WHAT ABOUT YOUR OTHER MISSION, AGENT J?
HURRY UP AND STEAL THE RAIKOO CARDS FROM THE KIDS IN KISARAZU!
MENU

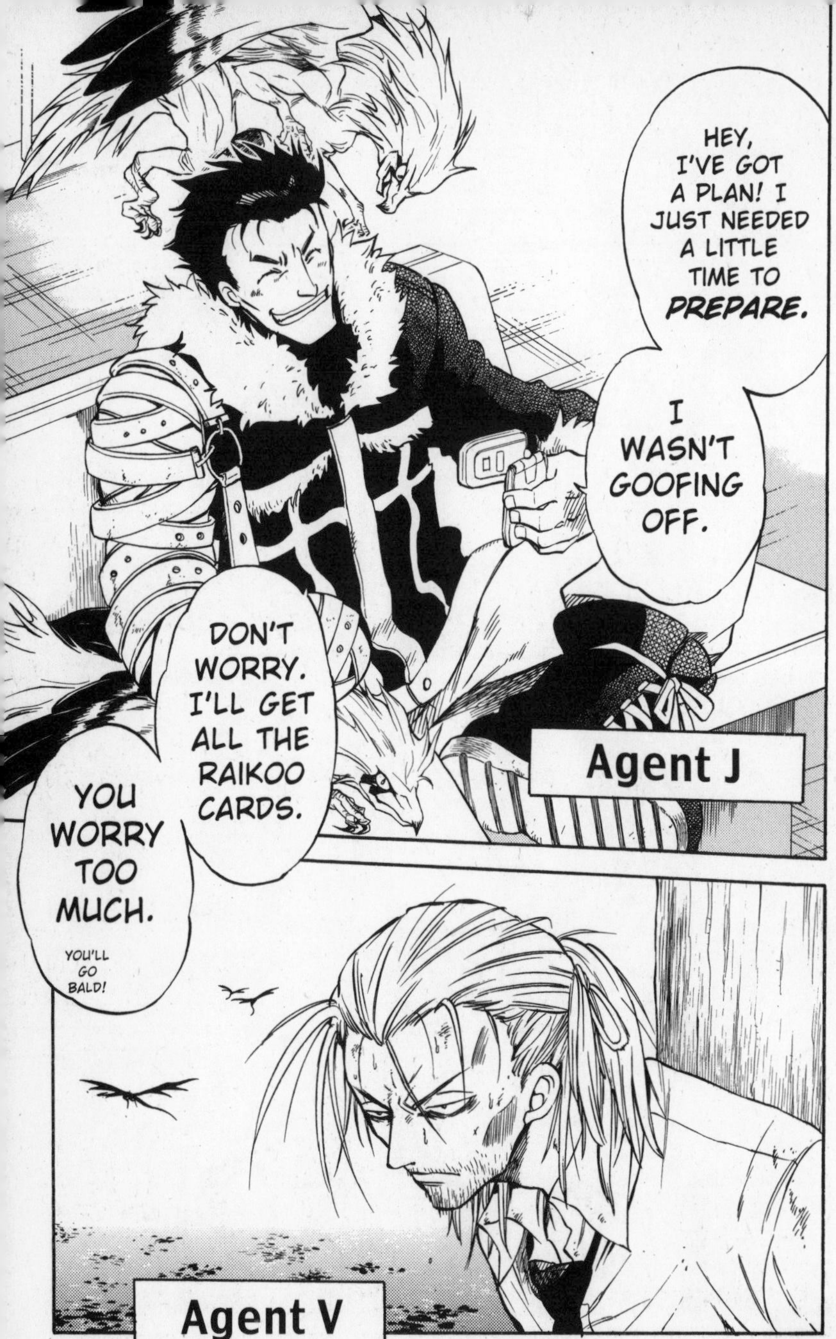
HEY, I'VE GOT A PLAN! I JUST NEEDED A LITTLE TIME TO PREPARE.
I WASN'T GOOFING OFF.
DON'T WORRY. I'LL GET ALL THE RAIKOO CARDS.
YOU WORRY TOO MUCH.
YOU'LL GO BALD!
Agent J
Agent V

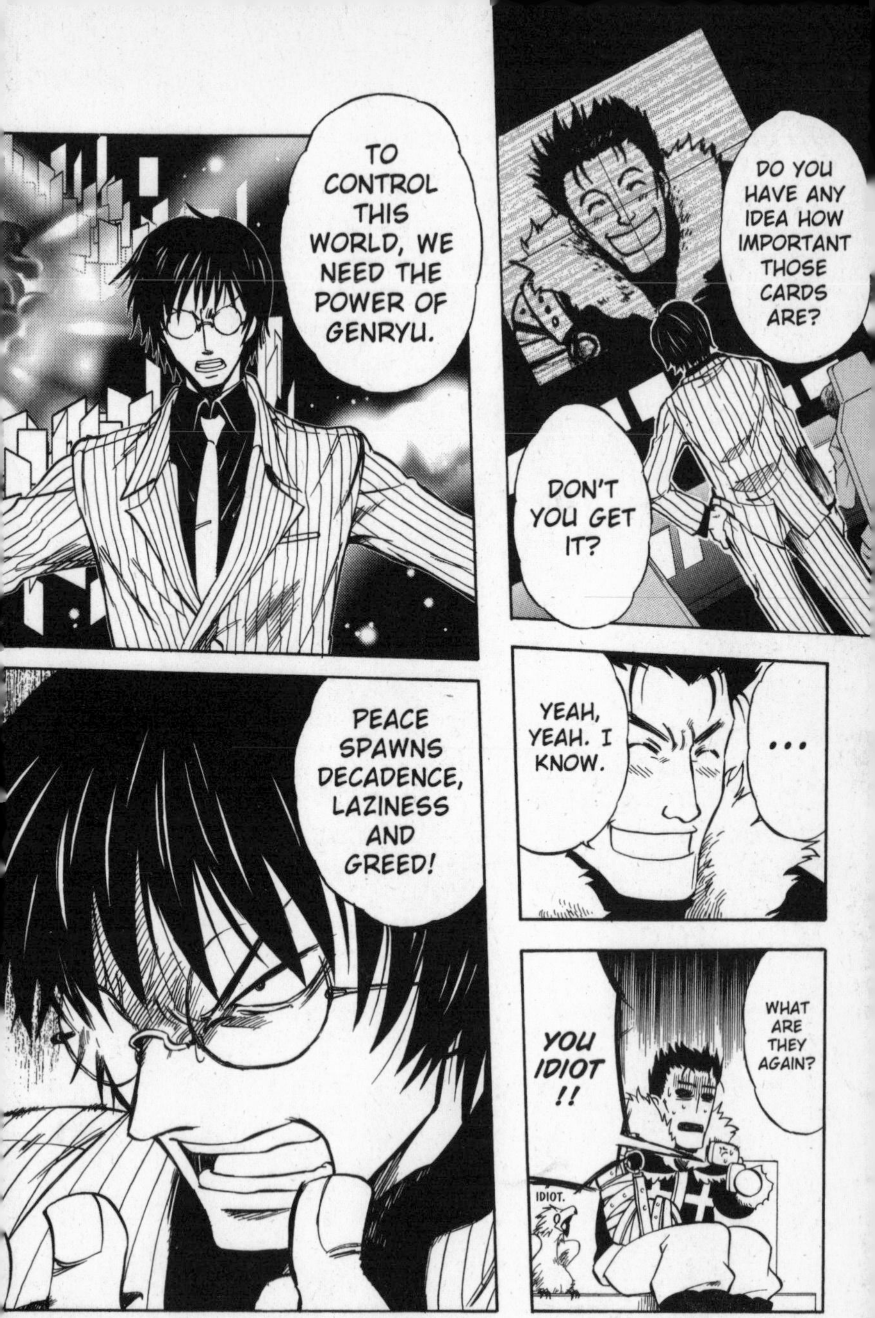
DO YOU HAVE ANY IDEA HOW IMPORTANT THOSE CARDS ARE?
DON'T YOU GET IT?
TO CONTROL THIS WORLD, WE NEED THE POWER OF GENRYU.
...
YEAH, YEAH. I KNOW.
WHAT ARE THEY AGAIN?
YOU IDIOT!!
IDIOT.
PEACE SPAWNS DECADENCE, LAZINESS AND GREED!

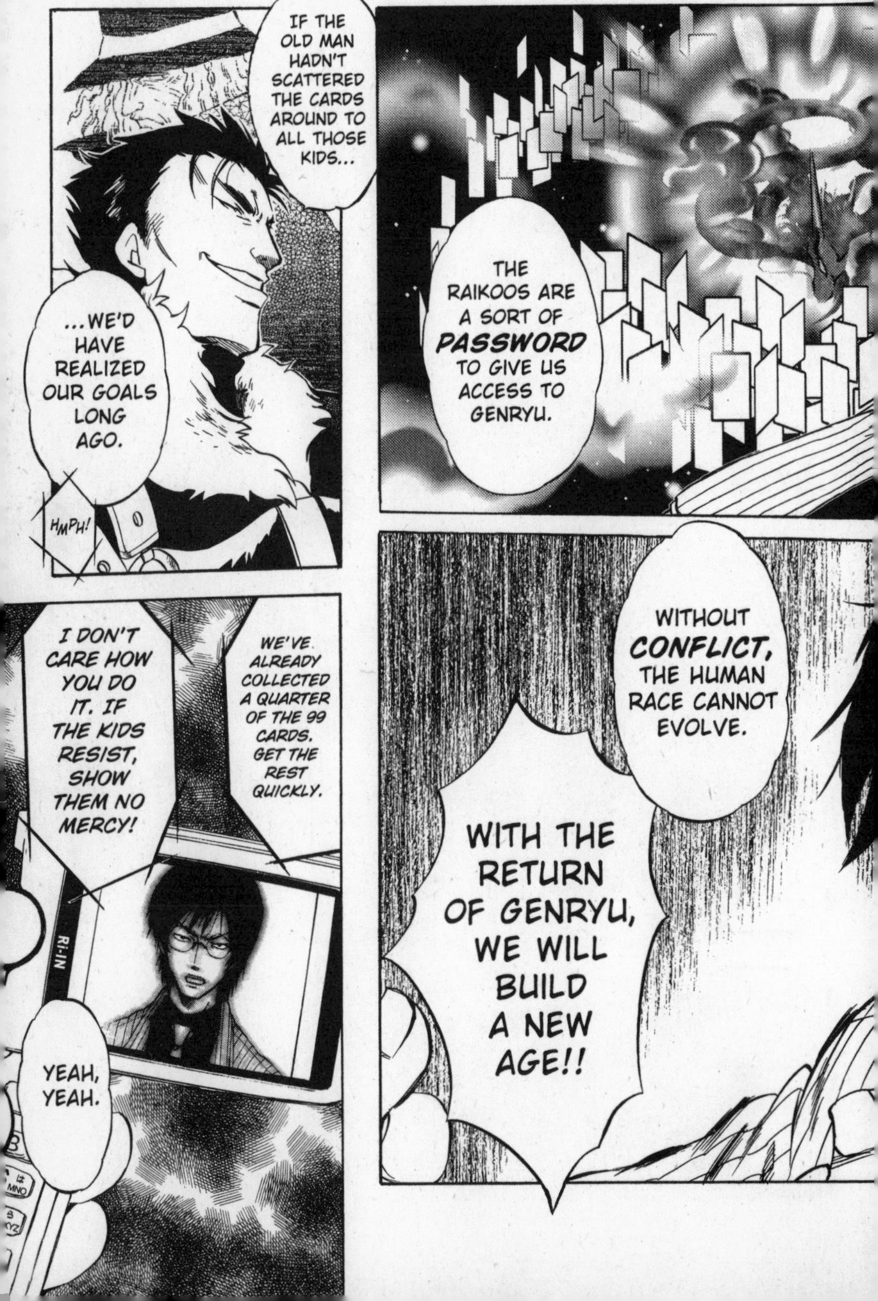
THE RAIKOOS ARE A SORT OF PASSWORD TO GIVE US ACCESS TO GENRYU.
IF THE OLD MAN HADN'T SCATTERED THE CARDS AROUND TO ALL THOSE KIDS...
...WE'D HAVE REALIZED OUR GOALS LONG AGO.
HMPH!
WITHOUT CONFLICT, THE HUMAN RACE CANNOT EVOLVE.
WITH THE RETURN OF GENRYU, WE WILL BUILD A NEW AGE!!
WE'VE ALREADY COLLECTED A QUARTER OF THE 99 CARDS. GET THE REST QUICKLY.
I DON'T CARE HOW YOU DO IT. IF THE KIDS RESIST, SHOW THEM NO MERCY!
Ri-IN
YEAH, YEAH.

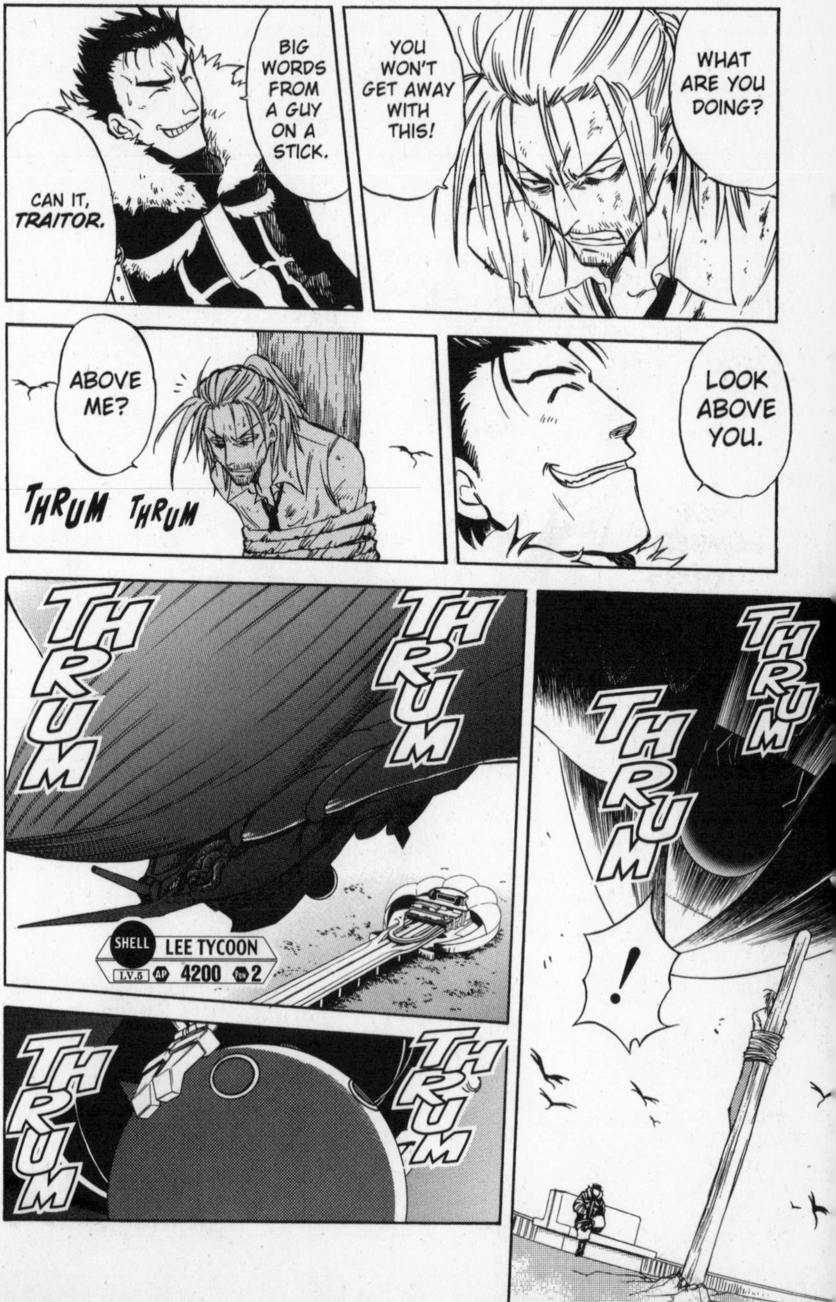
WHAT ARE YOU DOING?
YOU WON'T GET AWAY WITH THIS!
BIG WORDS FROM A GUY ON A STICK.
CAN IT, TRAITOR.
LOOK ABOVE YOU.
ABOVE ME?
THRUM THRUM
THRUM THRUM
!
THRUM THRUM
SHELL LEE TYCOON
LV.5 AP 4200 Pow 2
THRUM THRUM

READ THIS WAY

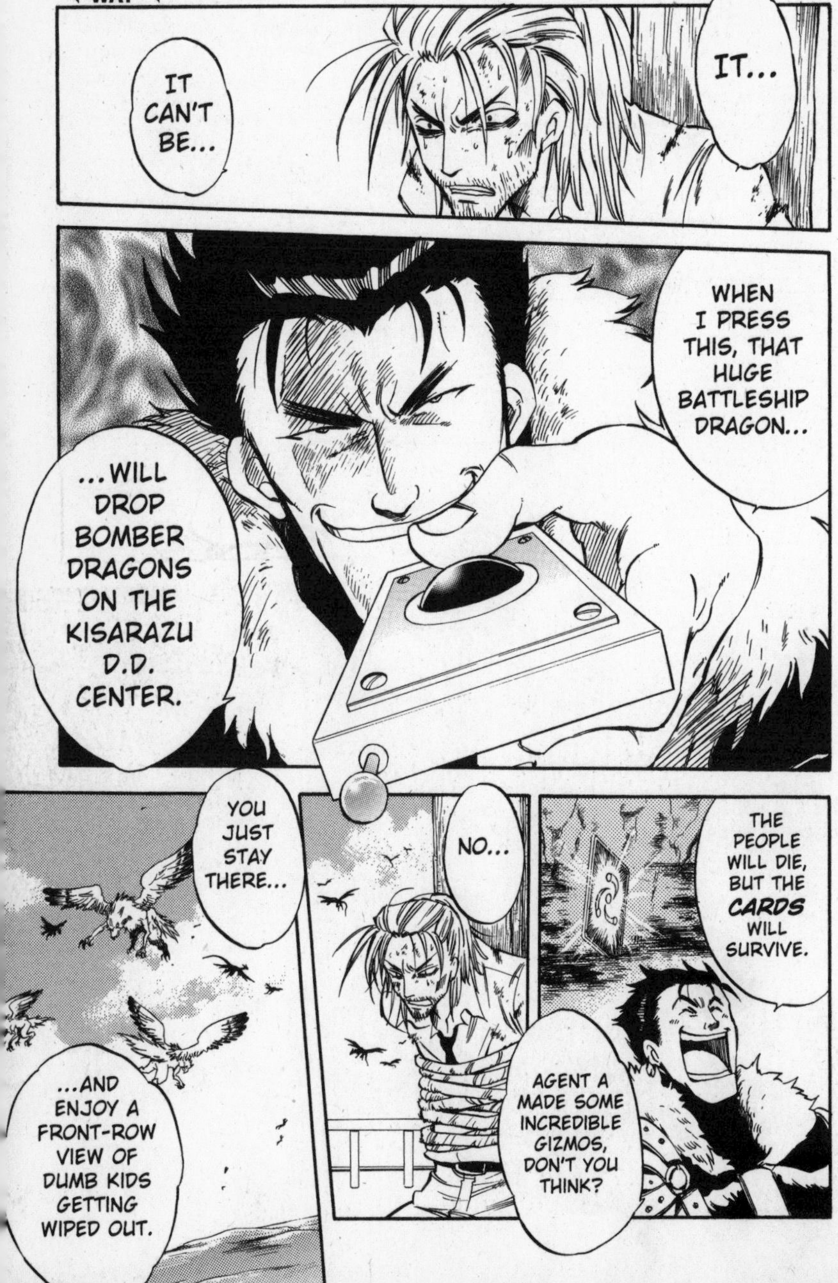
IT...
IT CAN'T BE...
WHEN I PRESS THIS, THAT HUGE BATTLESHIP DRAGON...
...WILL DROP BOMBER DRAGONS ON THE KISARAZU D.D. CENTER.
THE PEOPLE WILL DIE, BUT THE CARDS WILL SURVIVE.
AGENT A MADE SOME INCREDIBLE GIZMOS, DON'T YOU THINK?
NO...
YOU JUST STAY THERE...
...AND ENJOY A FRONT-ROW VIEW OF DUMB KIDS GETTING WIPED OUT.

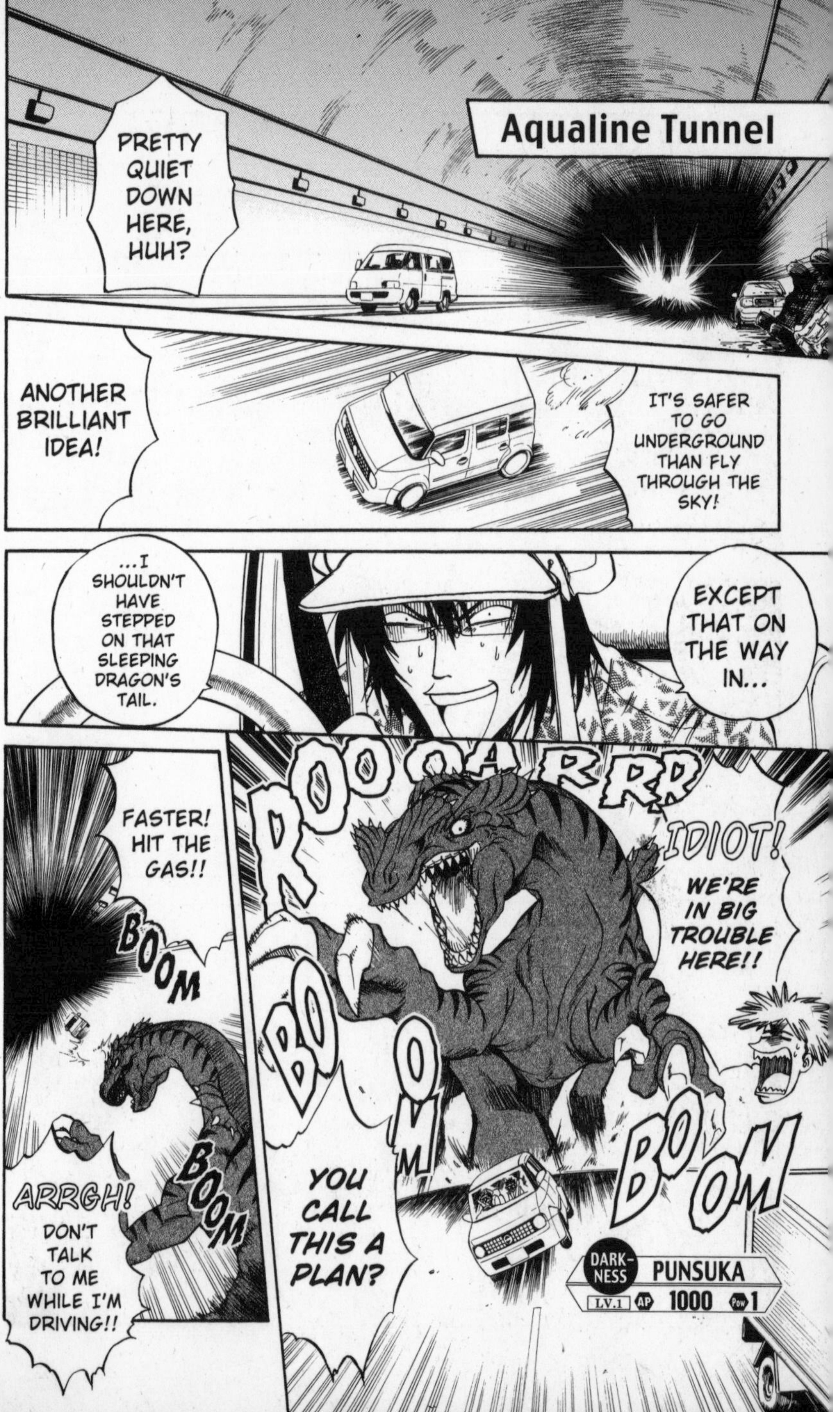
Aqualine Tunnel
PRETTY QUIET DOWN HERE, HUH?
IT'S SAFER TO GO UNDERGROUND THAN FLY THROUGH THE SKY!
ANOTHER BRILLIANT IDEA!
EXCEPT THAT ON THE WAY IN...
...I SHOULDN'T HAVE STEPPED ON THAT SLEEPING DRAGON'S TAIL.
ROOOARRR
IDIOT! WE'RE IN BIG TROUBLE HERE!!
BOOOM
BOOM
YOU CALL THIS A PLAN?
DARKNESS PUNSUKA
LV.1 AP 1000 Pow 1
FASTER! HIT THE GAS!!
BOOM
BOOM
ARRGH! DON'T TALK TO ME WHILE I'M DRIVING!!

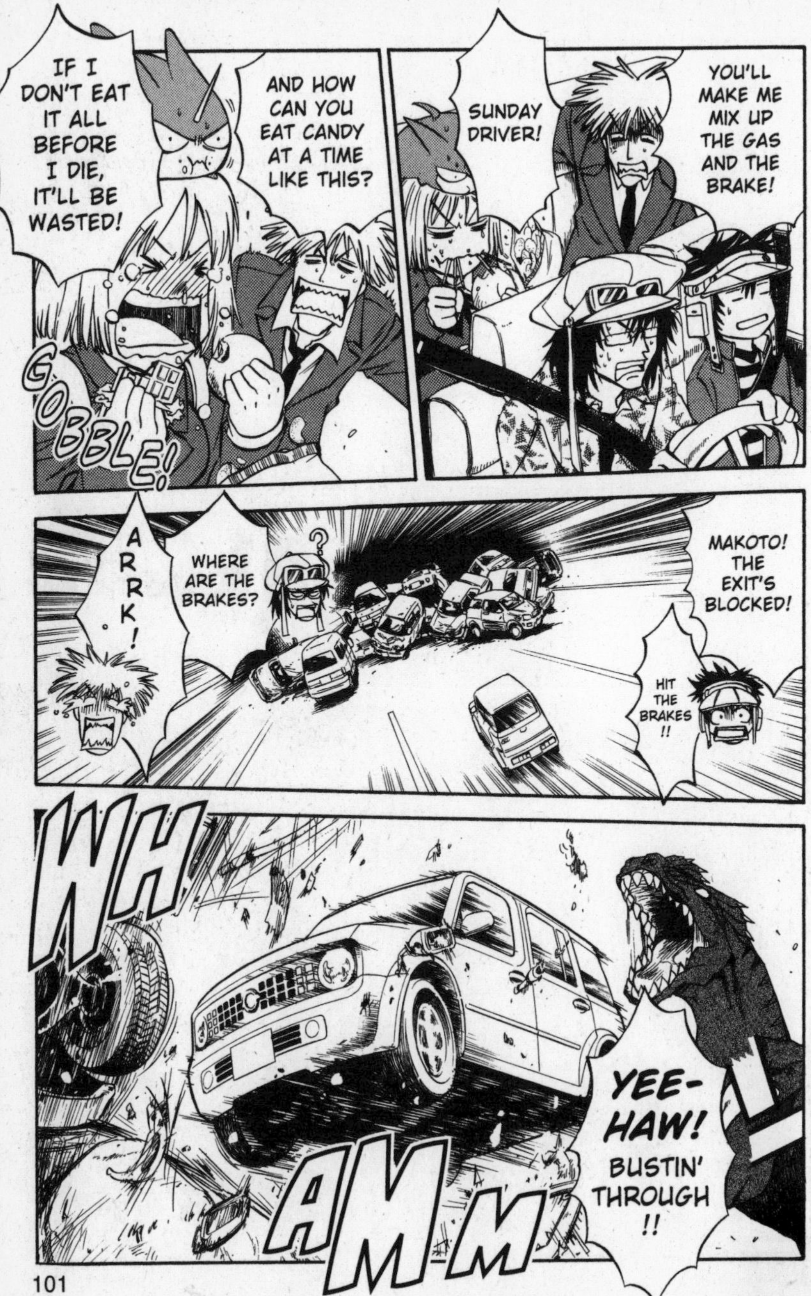
YOU'LL MAKE ME MIX UP THE GAS AND THE BRAKE!
SUNDAY DRIVER!
AND HOW CAN YOU EAT CANDY AT A TIME LIKE THIS?
IF I DON'T EAT IT ALL BEFORE I DIE, IT'LL BE WASTED!
GOBBLE!
MAKOTO! THE EXIT'S BLOCKED!
HIT THE BRAKES!!
WHERE ARE THE BRAKES?
ARRK!
YEE-HAW! BUSTIN' THROUGH!!
WHAMM

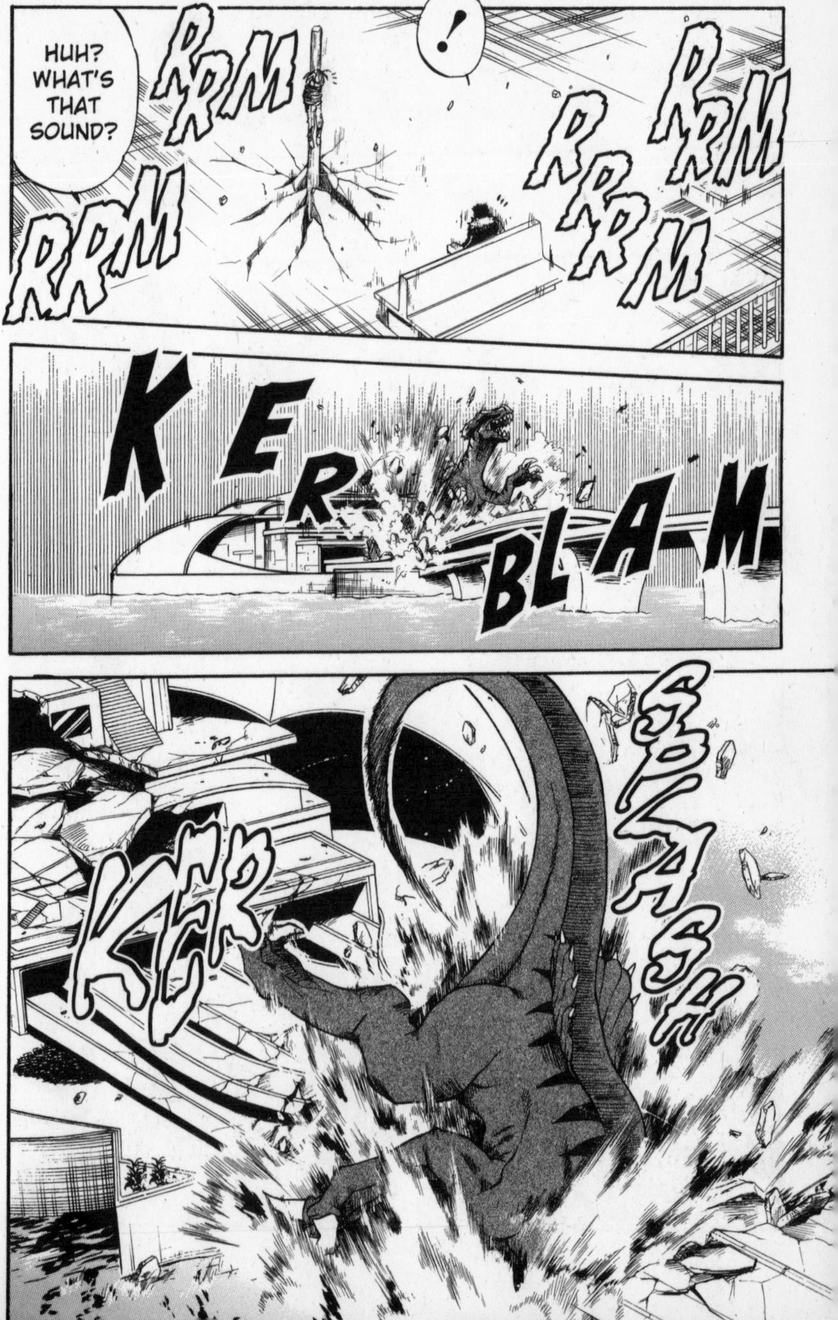
!
RRM
RRRM
RRM
HUH? WHAT'S THAT SOUND?
RRM
KERBLAM
SPLAASH
KRR

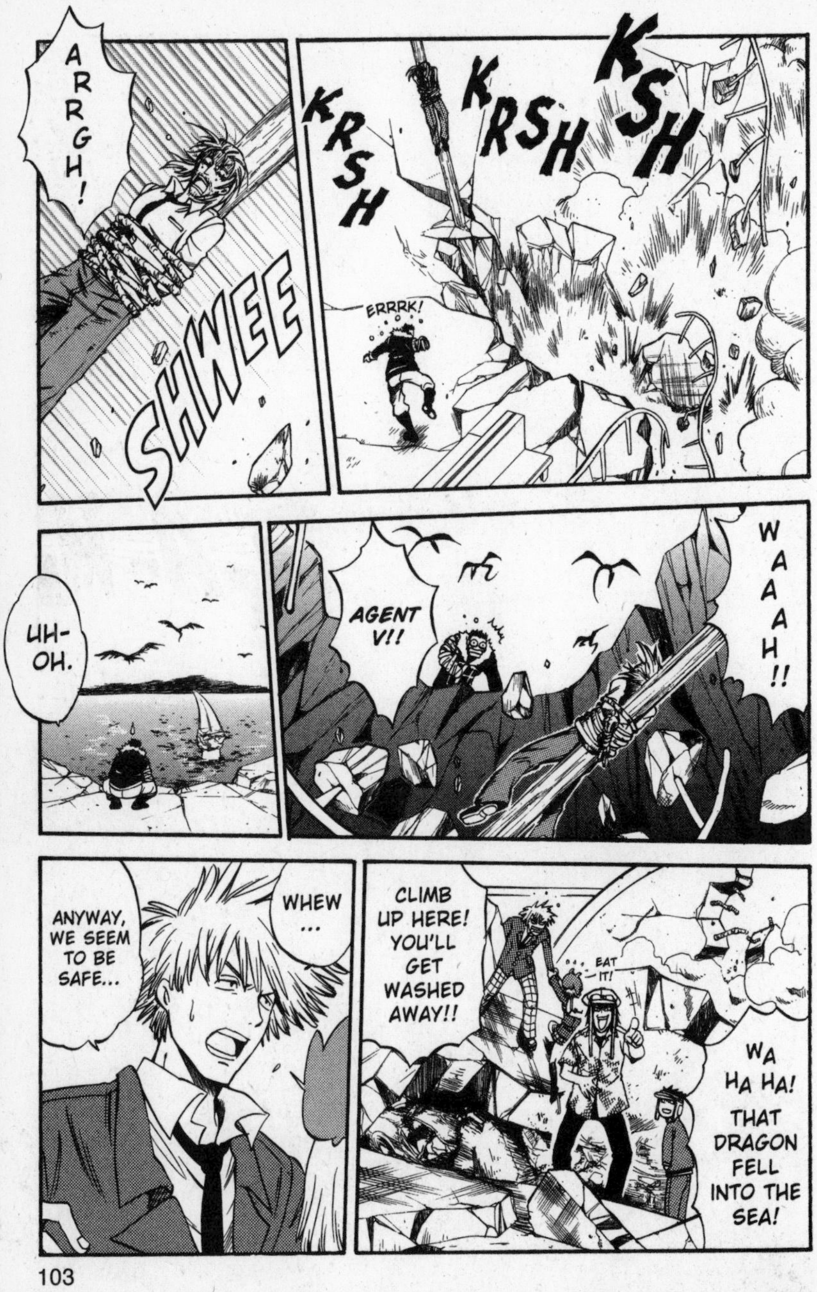
KRSH
KRSH
KSH
ERRRK!
ARRGH!
SHWEE
WAAAAH!!
AGENT V!!
UH-OH.
CLIMB UP HERE! YOU'LL GET WASHED AWAY!!
... EAT IT!
WA HA HA! THAT DRAGON FELL INTO THE SEA!
WHEW ...
ANYWAY, WE SEEM TO BE SAFE...

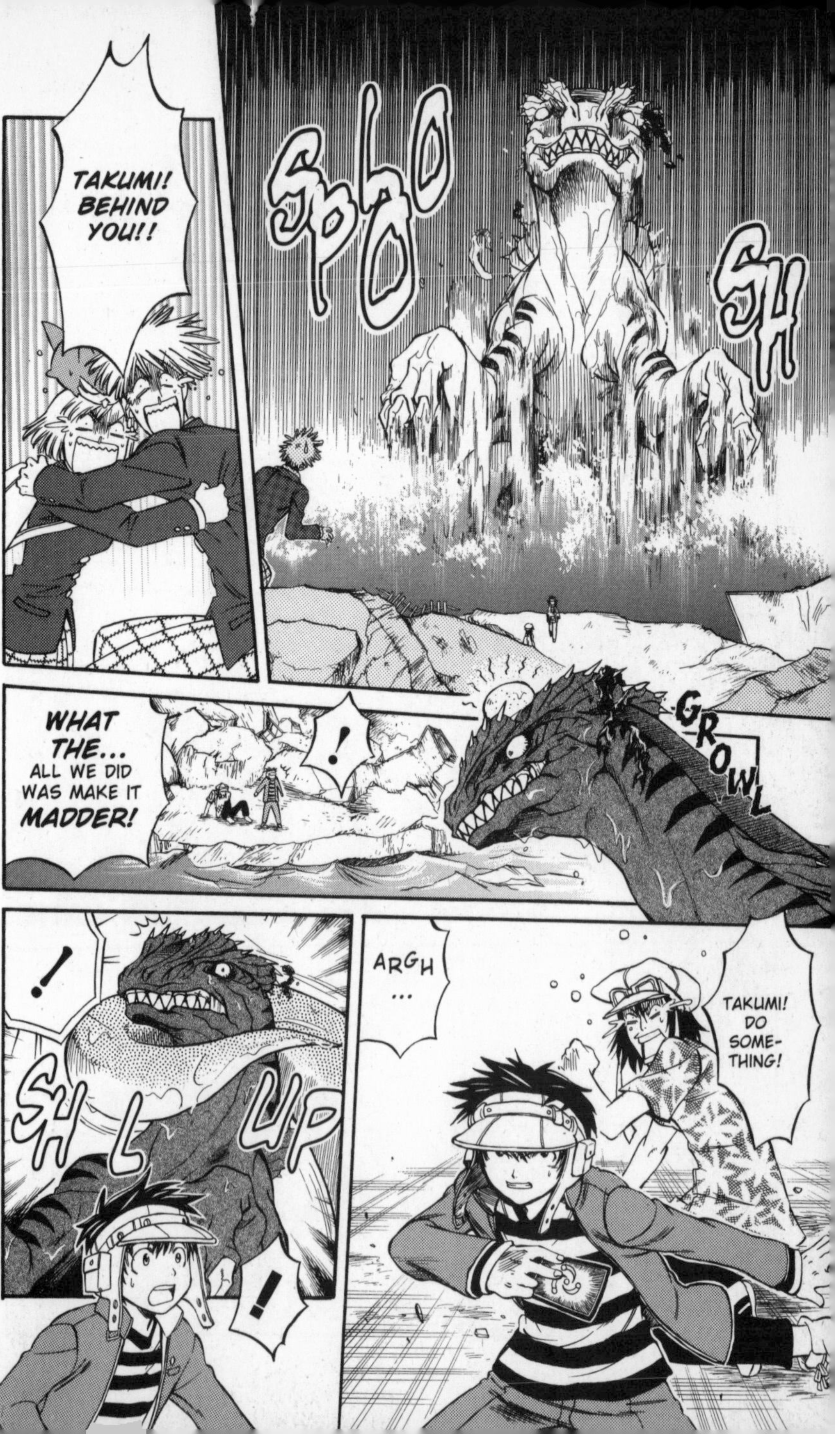
SPLOO
SH
TAKUMI! BEHIND YOU!!
GROWL
!
WHAT THE... ALL WE DID WAS MAKE IT MADDER!
TAKUMI! DO SOME-THING!
ARGH ...
!
SHLUP
!

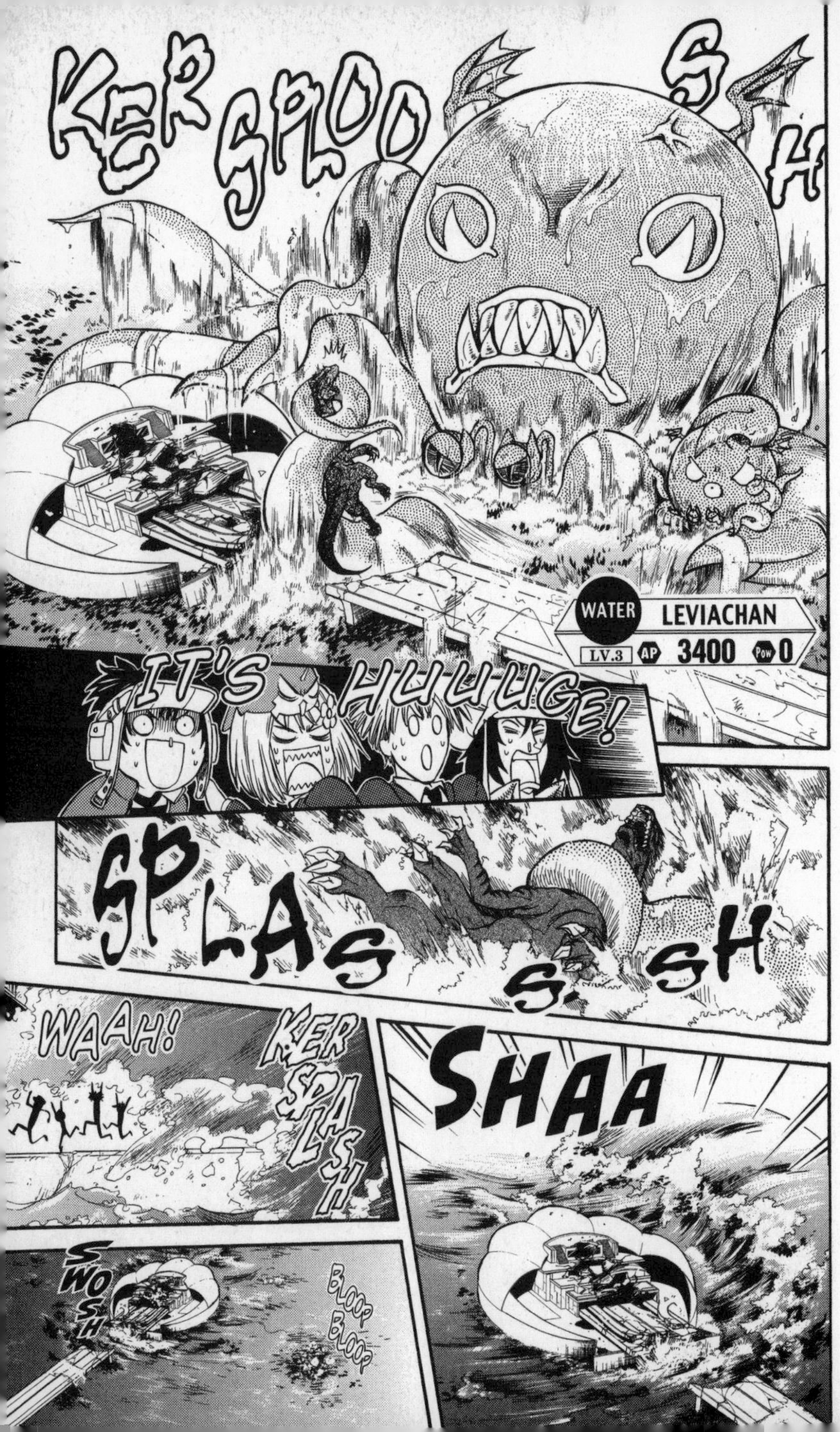
KERSPLOOSH
WATER LEVIACHAN
LV.3 AP 3400 Pow 0
IT'S HUUUGE!
SPLASS SH
SHAA
WAAH!
KERSPLASH
SWOSH
BLOOP BLOOP

UGH...

THROB

SLOSH

SLOSH

HOT SPRINGS

HFF

HFF

CURSE YOU, AGENT J... BRINGING OUT LEE TYCOON...

ARE YOU OKAY?

HEY! KID!

BLUB... YES, PLEASE, WITH EXTRA MUSH-ROOMS...

SPL

OSH

SPLGH

SPLGH

...HUH?

SHOO

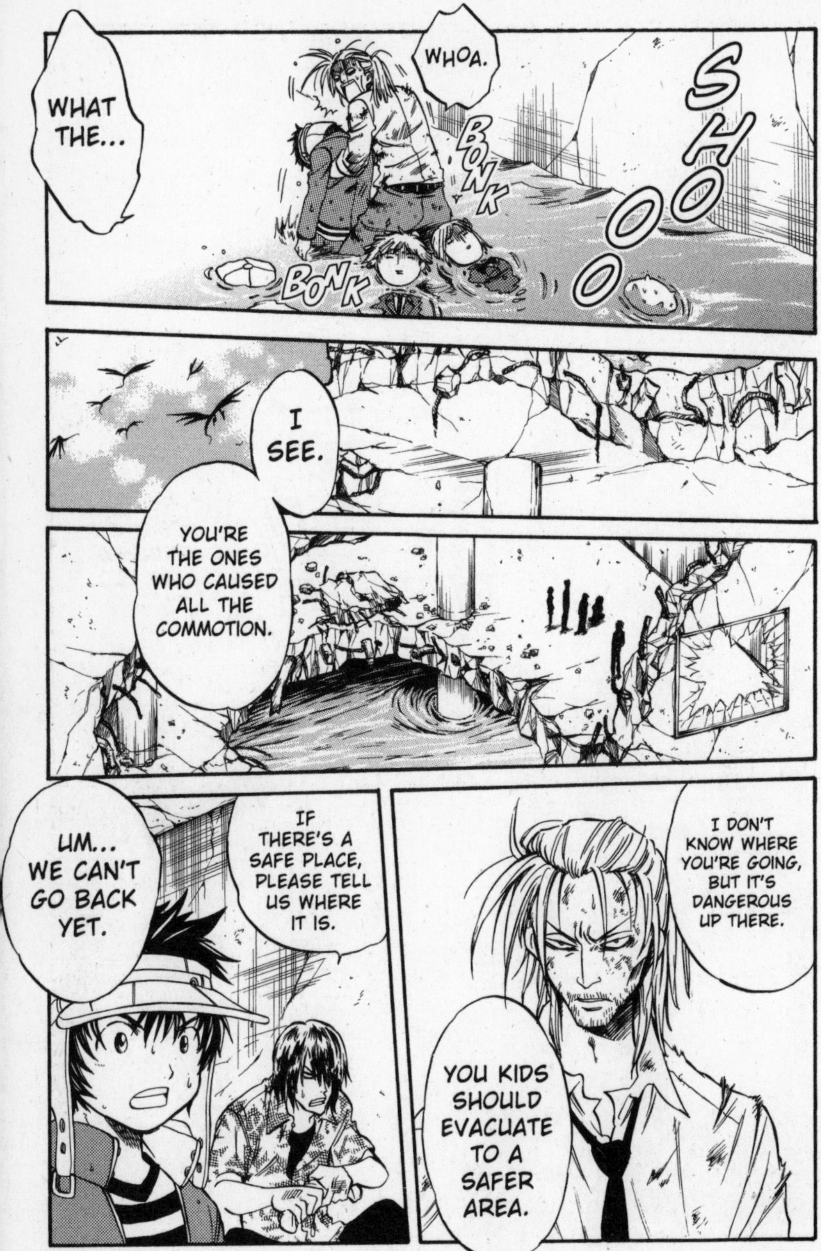
SHOOO
BONK
WHOA.
BONK
WHAT THE...
I SEE.
YOU'RE THE ONES WHO CAUSED ALL THE COMMOTION.
I DON'T KNOW WHERE YOU'RE GOING, BUT IT'S DANGEROUS UP THERE.
YOU KIDS SHOULD EVACUATE TO A SAFER AREA.
IF THERE'S A SAFE PLACE, PLEASE TELL US WHERE IT IS.
UM... WE CAN'T GO BACK YET.

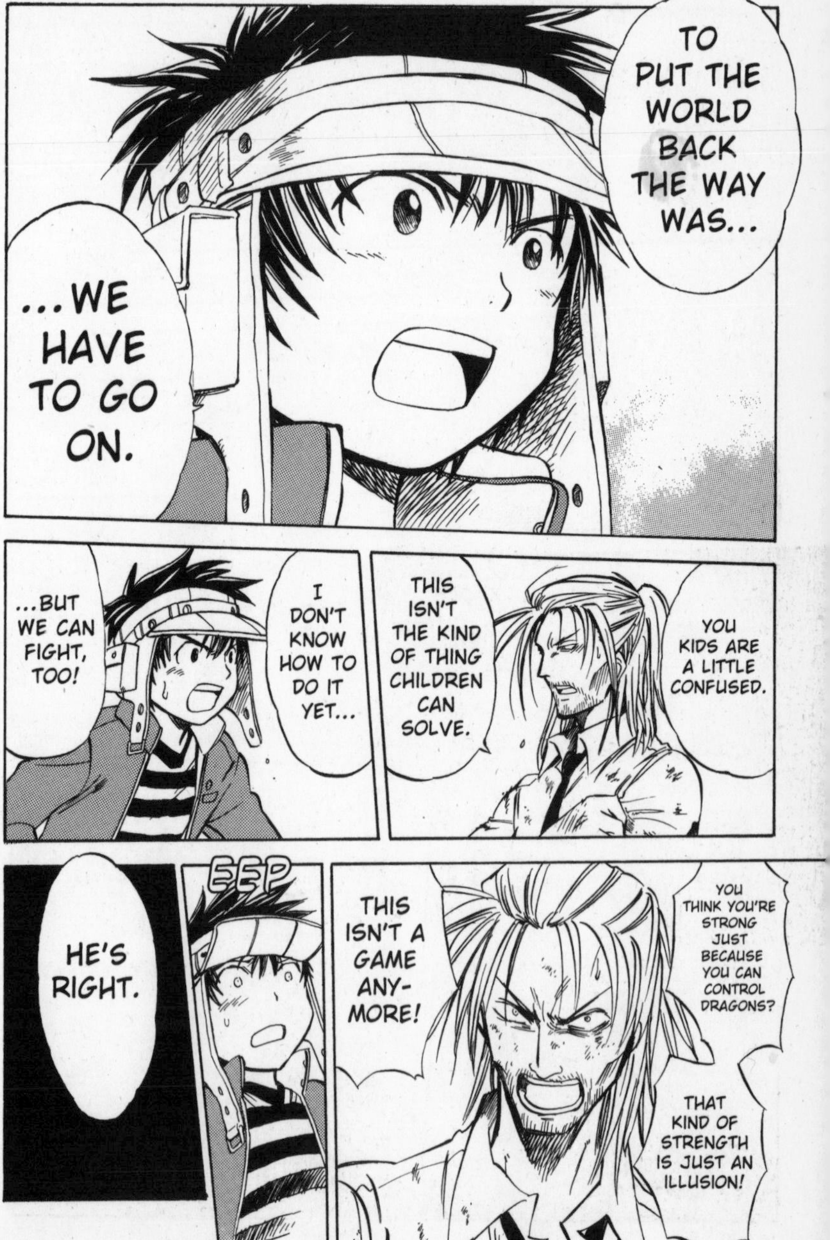
TO PUT THE WORLD BACK THE WAY WAS...
...WE HAVE TO GO ON.
YOU KIDS ARE A LITTLE CONFUSED.
THIS ISN'T THE KIND OF THING CHILDREN CAN SOLVE.
I DON'T KNOW HOW TO DO IT YET...
...BUT WE CAN FIGHT, TOO!
YOU THINK YOU'RE STRONG JUST BECAUSE YOU CAN CONTROL DRAGONS?
THAT KIND OF STRENGTH IS JUST AN ILLUSION!
THIS ISN'T A GAME ANY-MORE!
EEP
HE'S RIGHT.

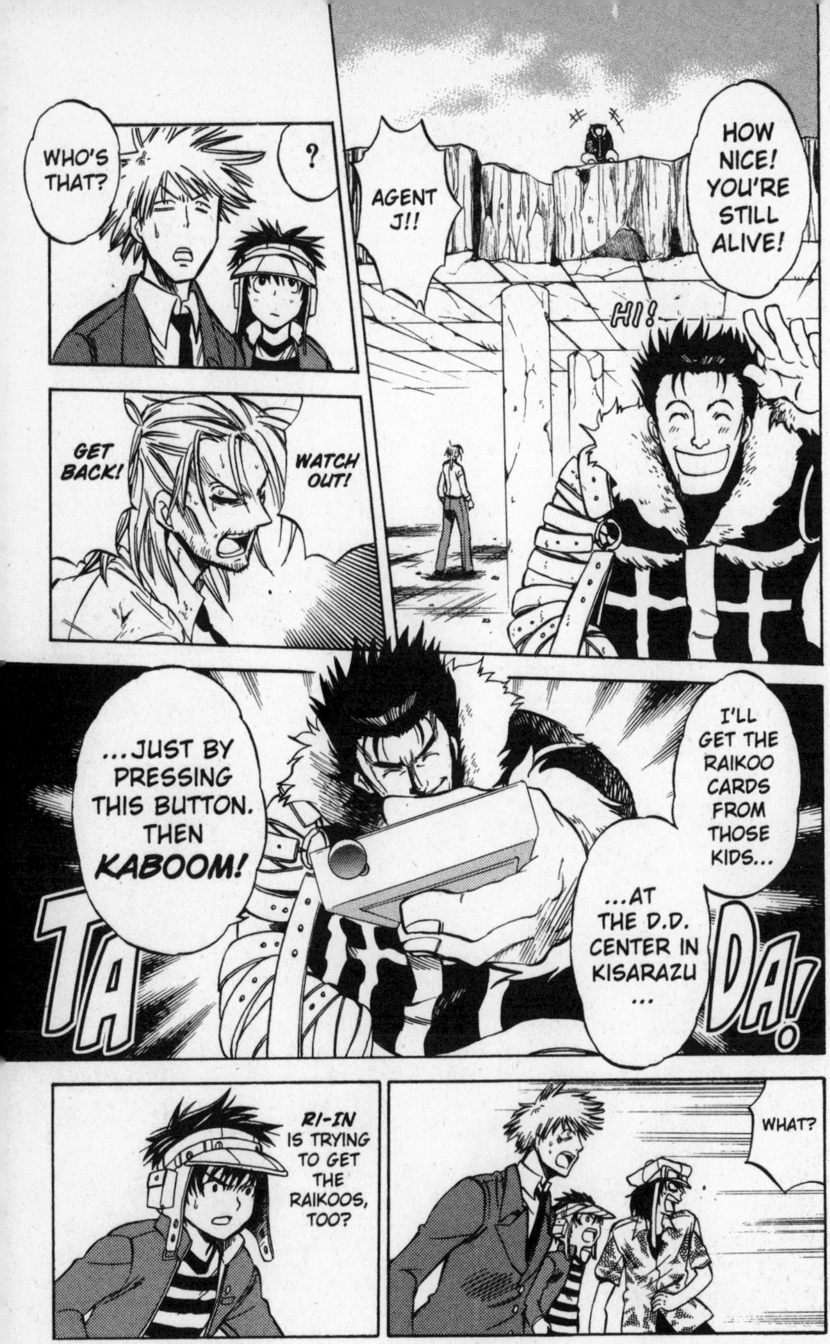
HOW NICE! YOU'RE STILL ALIVE!
AGENT J!!
HI!
?
WHO'S THAT?
WATCH OUT!
GET BACK!
I'LL GET THE RAIKOO CARDS FROM THOSE KIDS...
...AT THE D.D. CENTER IN KISARAZU ...
...JUST BY PRESSING THIS BUTTON. THEN KABOOM!
TA DA!
WHAT?
RI-IN IS TRYING TO GET THE RAIKOOS, TOO?

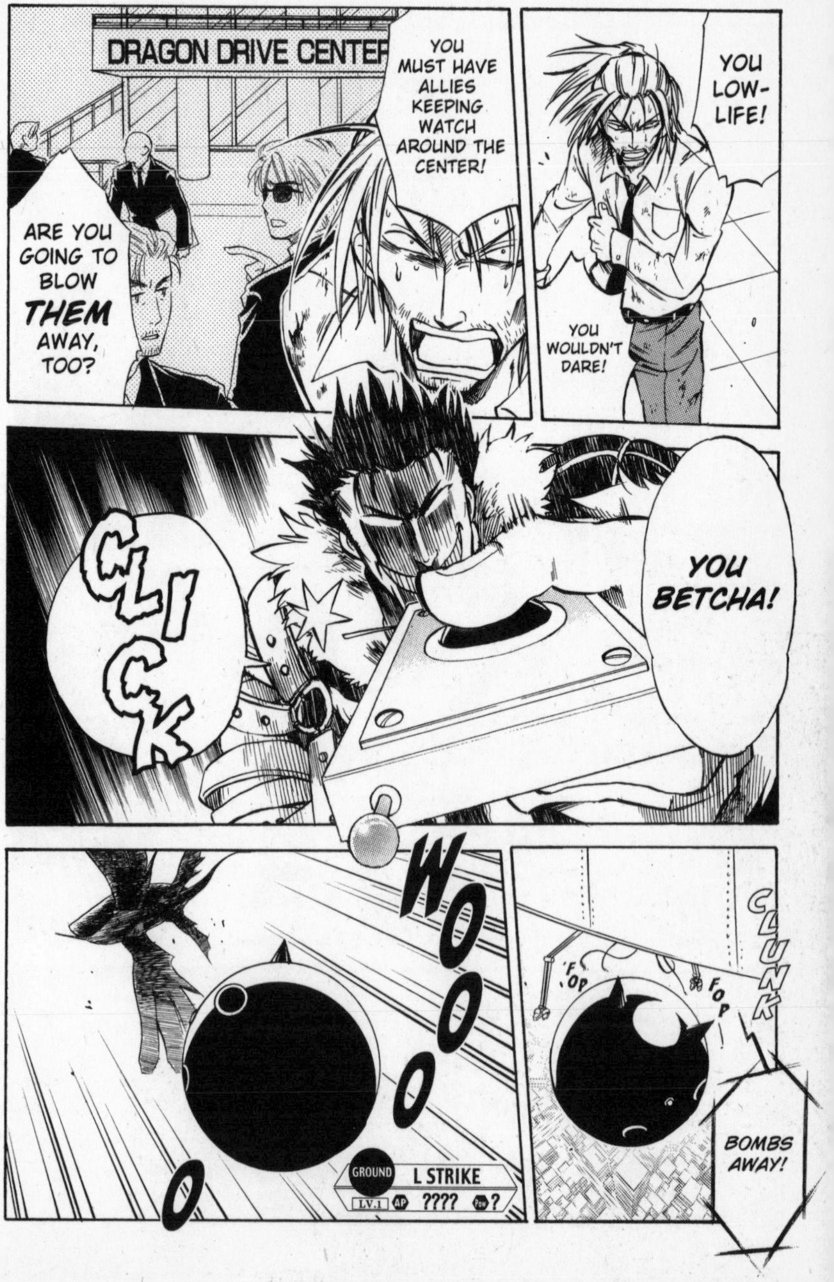
YOU LOW-LIFE!
YOU WOULDN'T DARE!
YOU MUST HAVE ALLIES KEEPING WATCH AROUND THE CENTER!
DRAGON DRIVE CENTER
ARE YOU GOING TO BLOW ***THEM*** AWAY, TOO?
YOU BETCHA!
CLICK
CLUNK
FOP
FOP
BOMBS AWAY!
WOOOOOO
GROUND L STRIKE
LV.1 AP ???? Pow ?

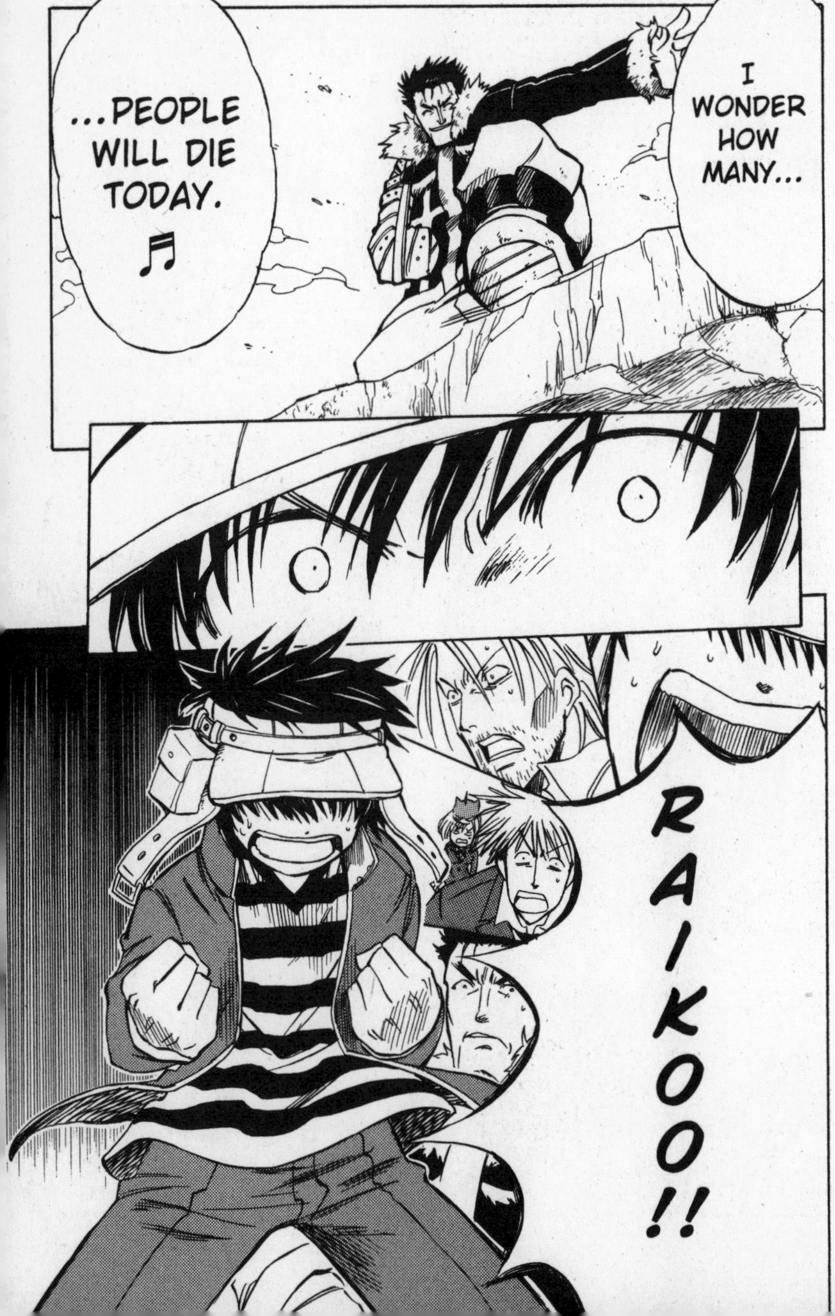
I WONDER HOW MANY...
...PEOPLE WILL DIE TODAY. ♬
RAIKOO!!

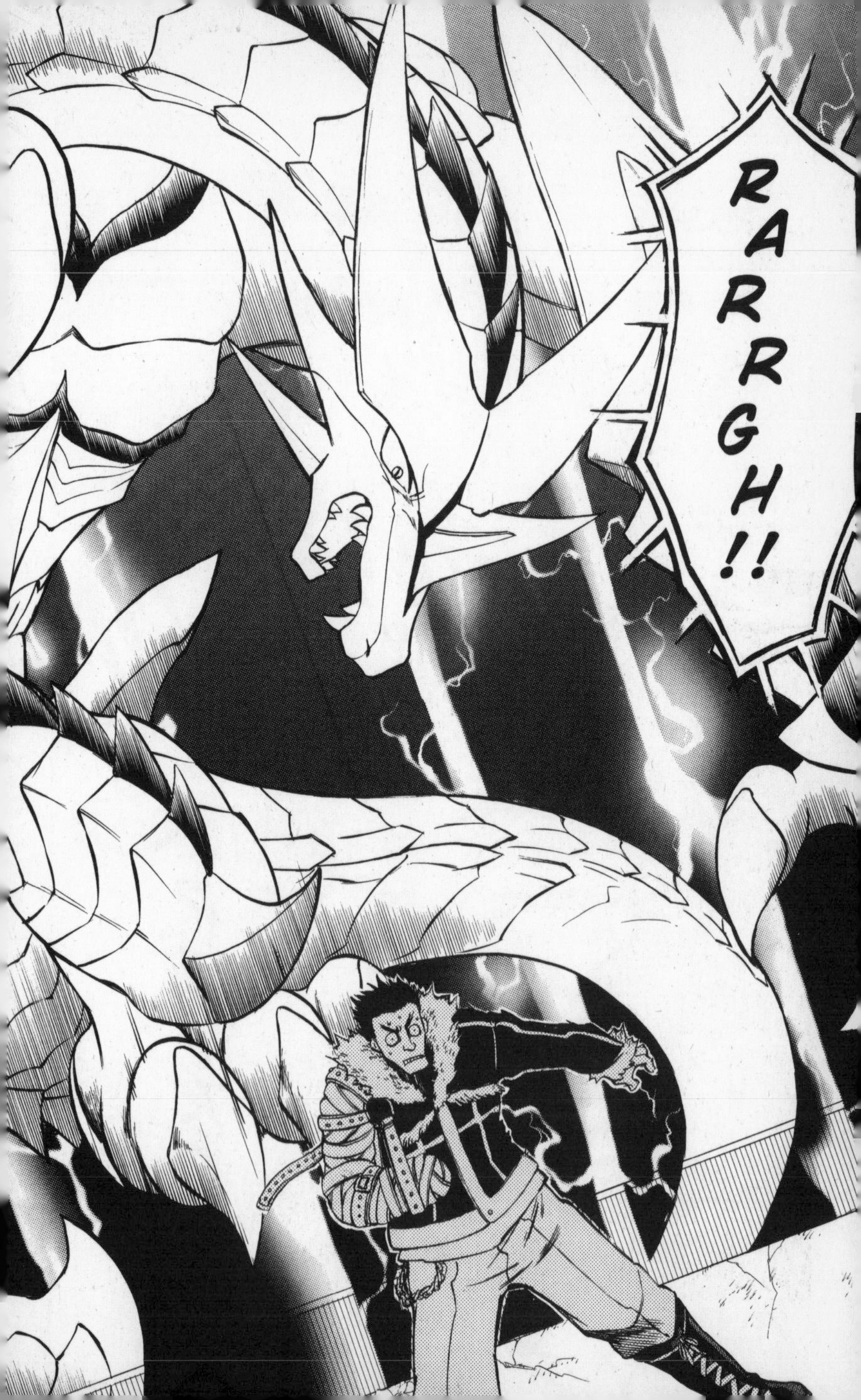
RARRGH!!

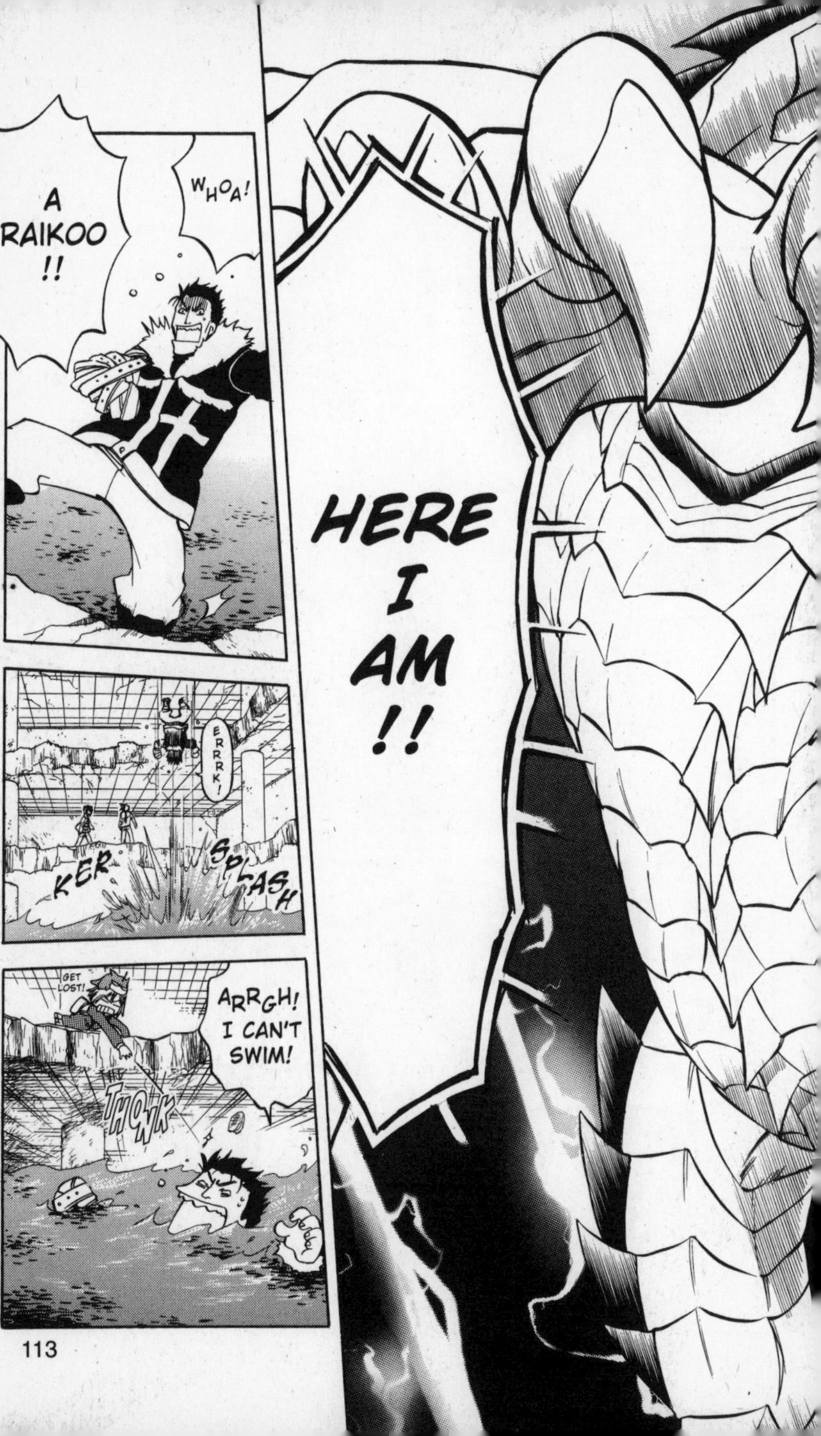
HERE I AM!!
A RAIKOO!!
WHOA!
ERRRK!
KER SPLASH
GET LOST!
ARRGH! I CAN'T SWIM!
THONK

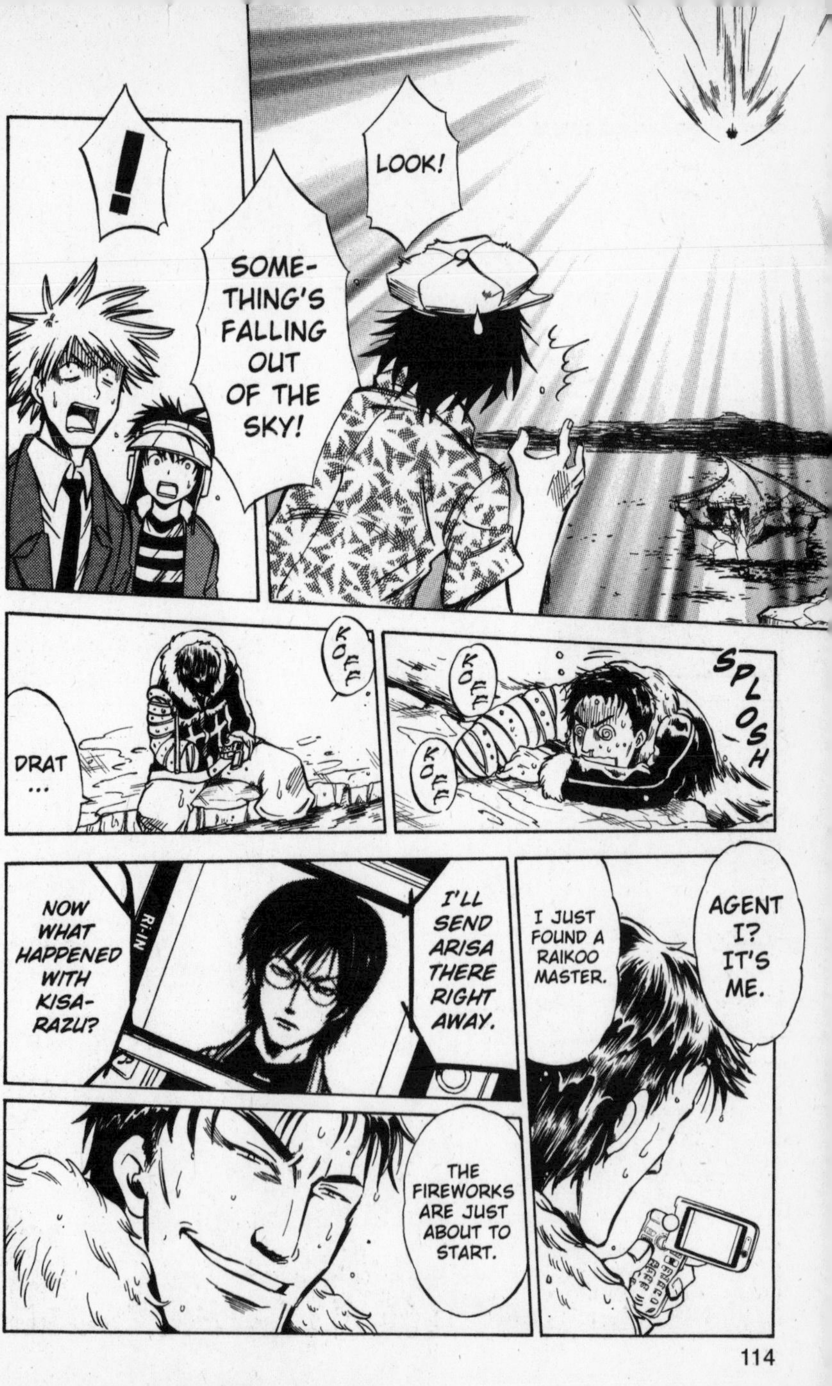
LOOK!
!
SOME-THING'S FALLING OUT OF THE SKY!
SPLOSH
KOFF
KOFF
KOFF
DRAT ...
AGENT I? IT'S ME.
I JUST FOUND A RAIKOO MASTER.
I'LL SEND ARISA THERE RIGHT AWAY.
NOW WHAT HAPPENED WITH KISA-RAZU?
RI-IN
THE FIREWORKS ARE JUST ABOUT TO START.

READ THIS WAY

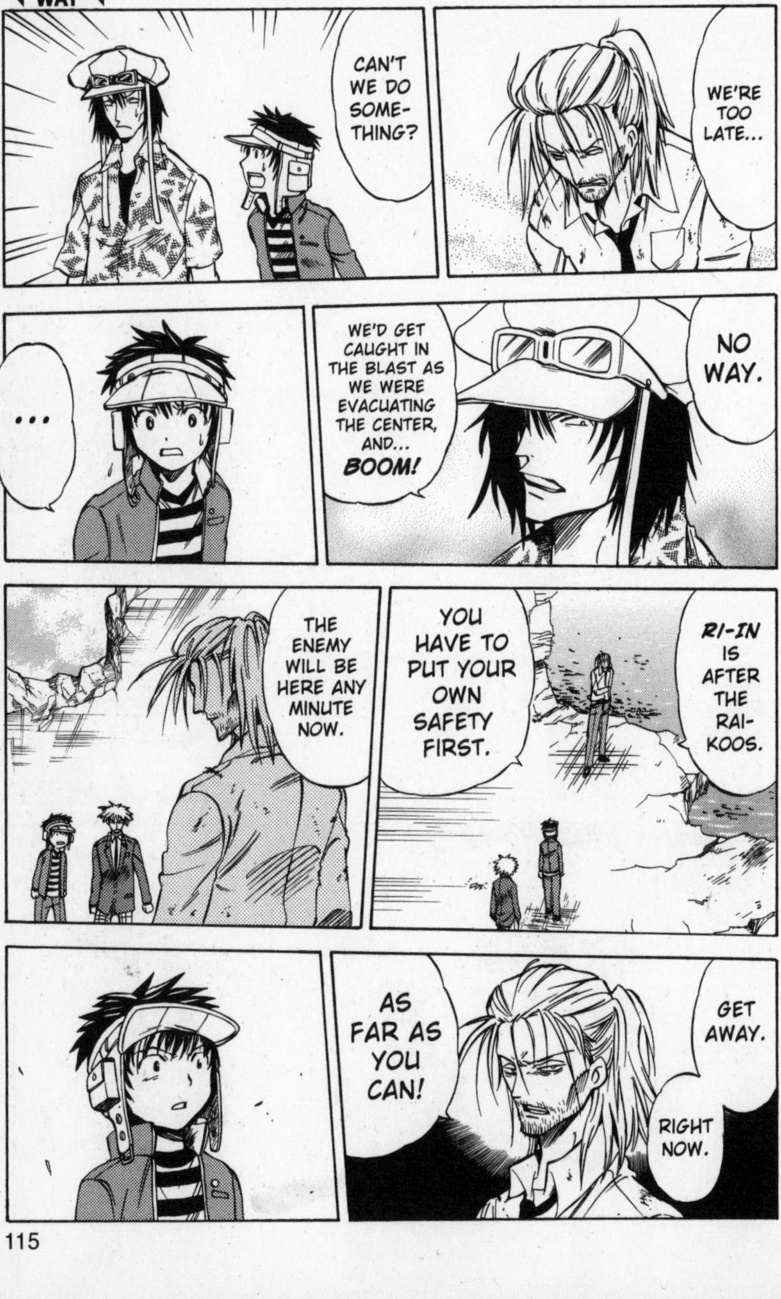
WE'RE TOO LATE...
CAN'T WE DO SOME-THING?
NO WAY.
WE'D GET CAUGHT IN THE BLAST AS WE WERE EVACUATING THE CENTER, AND... BOOM!
...
RI-IN IS AFTER THE RAI-KOOS.
YOU HAVE TO PUT YOUR OWN SAFETY FIRST.
THE ENEMY WILL BE HERE ANY MINUTE NOW.
GET AWAY.
AS FAR AS YOU CAN!
RIGHT NOW.

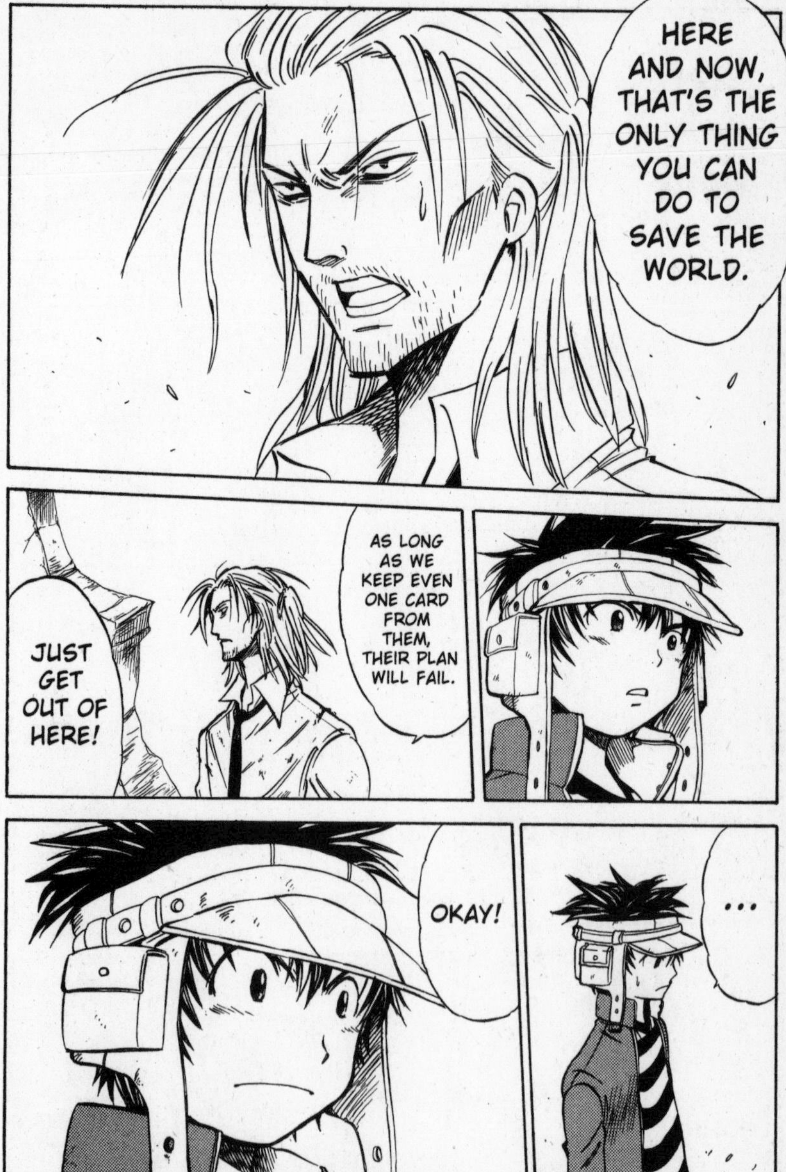
HERE AND NOW, THAT'S THE ONLY THING YOU CAN DO TO SAVE THE WORLD.
AS LONG AS WE KEEP EVEN ONE CARD FROM THEM, THEIR PLAN WILL FAIL.
JUST GET OUT OF HERE!
...
OKAY!

ER...
YEAH!

BAM

LET'S
GO,
GUYS!

I'M
SORRY
...

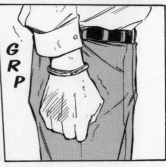

GRP

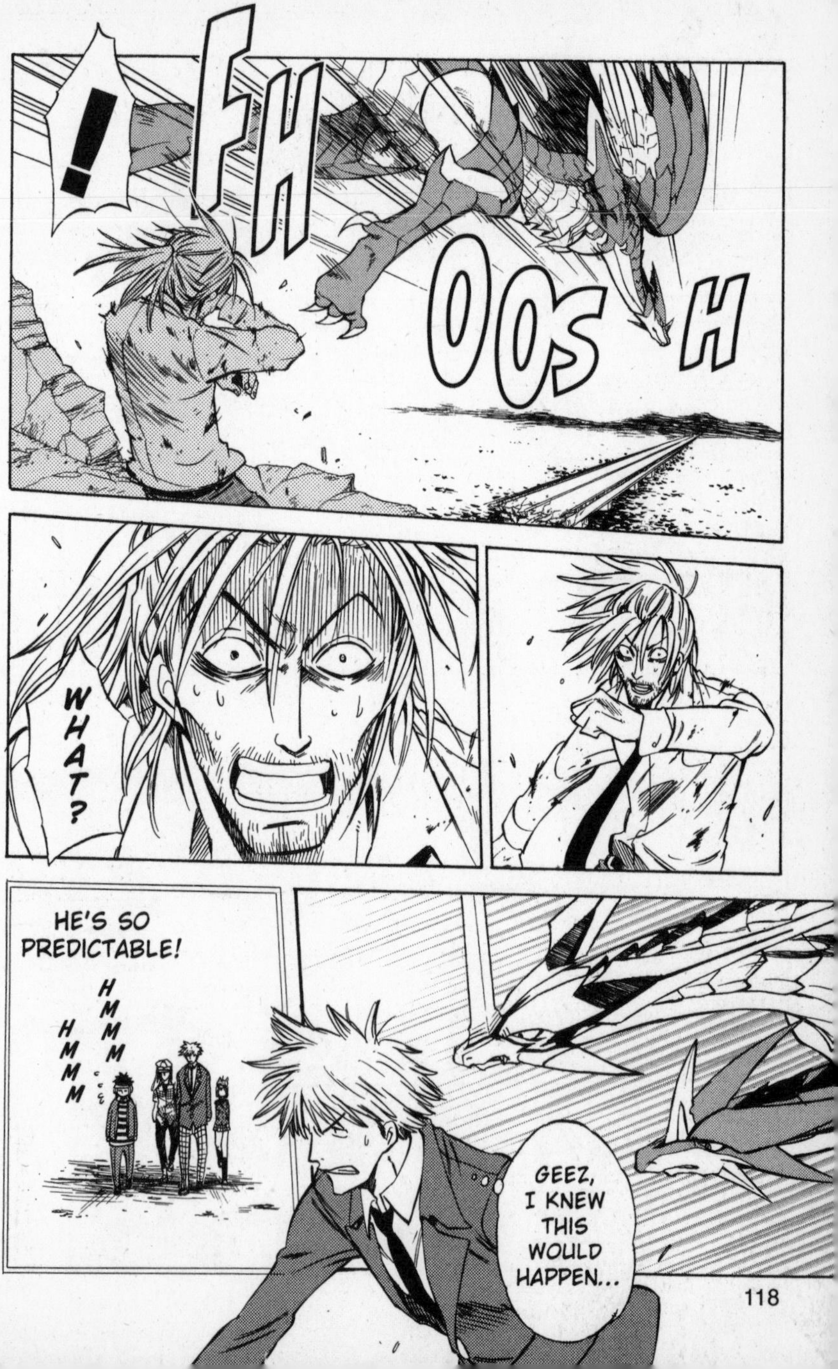
!
FHOOSH
WHAT?
GEEZ, I KNEW THIS WOULD HAPPEN...
HE'S SO PREDICTABLE!
HMMM HMMM

READ THIS WAY

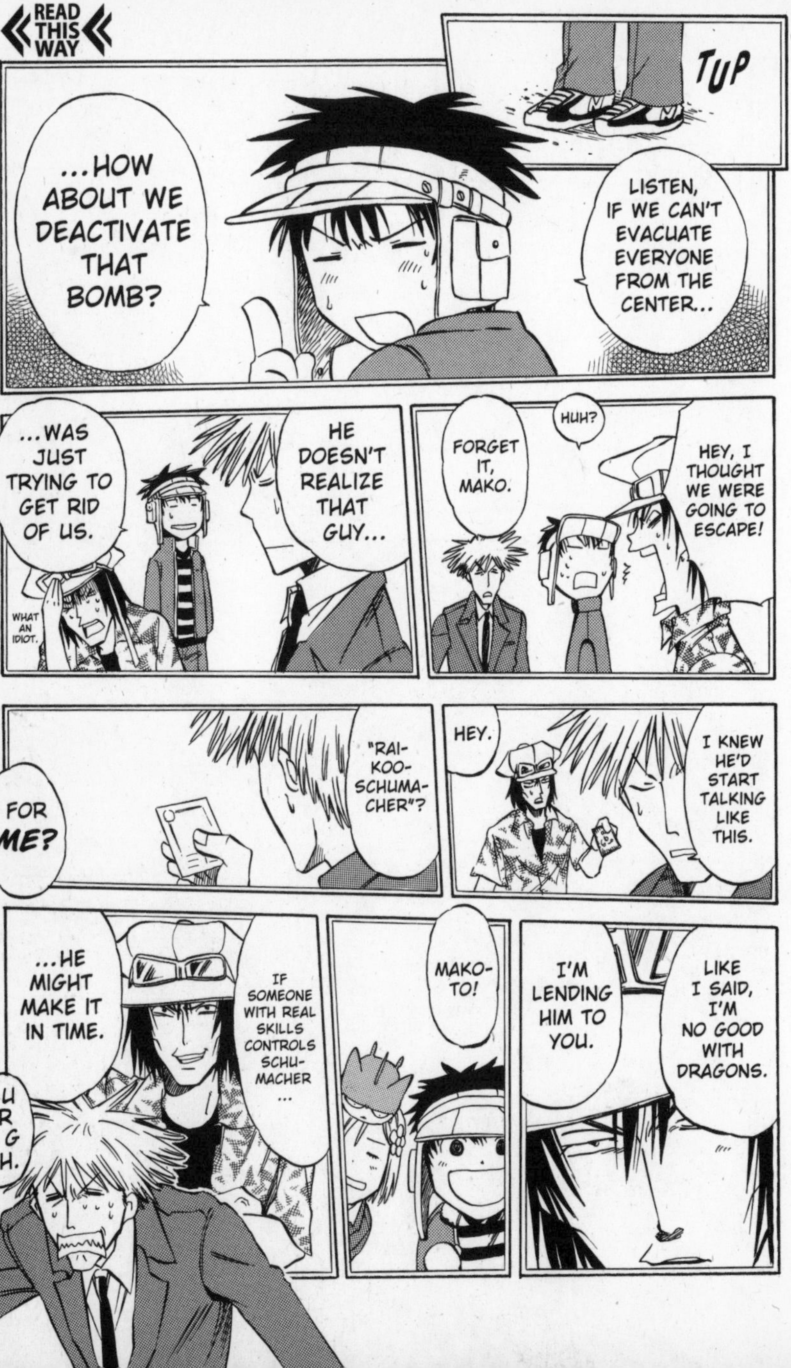
TUP
LISTEN, IF WE CAN'T EVACUATE EVERYONE FROM THE CENTER...
...HOW ABOUT WE DEACTIVATE THAT BOMB?
HEY, I THOUGHT WE WERE GOING TO ESCAPE!
HUH?
FORGET IT, MAKO.
HE DOESN'T REALIZE THAT GUY...
...WAS JUST TRYING TO GET RID OF US.
WHAT AN IDIOT.
I KNEW HE'D START TALKING LIKE THIS.
HEY.
"RAI-KOO-SCHUMACHER"?
FOR **ME?**
LIKE I SAID, I'M NO GOOD WITH DRAGONS.
I'M LENDING HIM TO YOU.
MAKO-TO!
IF SOMEONE WITH REAL SKILLS CONTROLS SCHU-MACHER...
...HE MIGHT MAKE IT IN TIME.
URGH.

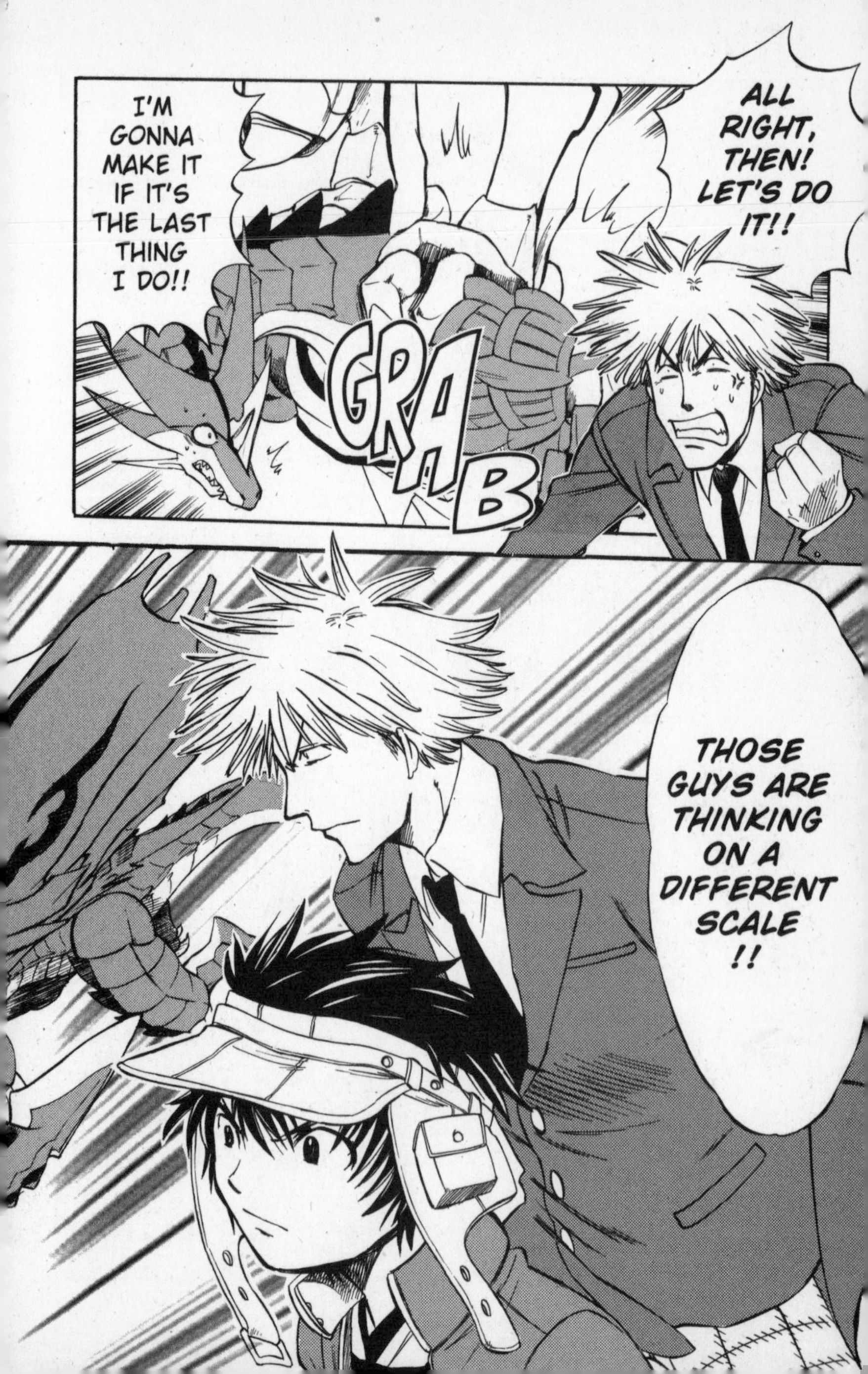
ALL RIGHT, THEN! LET'S DO IT!!
I'M GONNA MAKE IT IF IT'S THE LAST THING I DO!!
GRAB
THOSE GUYS ARE THINKING ON A DIFFERENT SCALE!!

READ THIS WAY

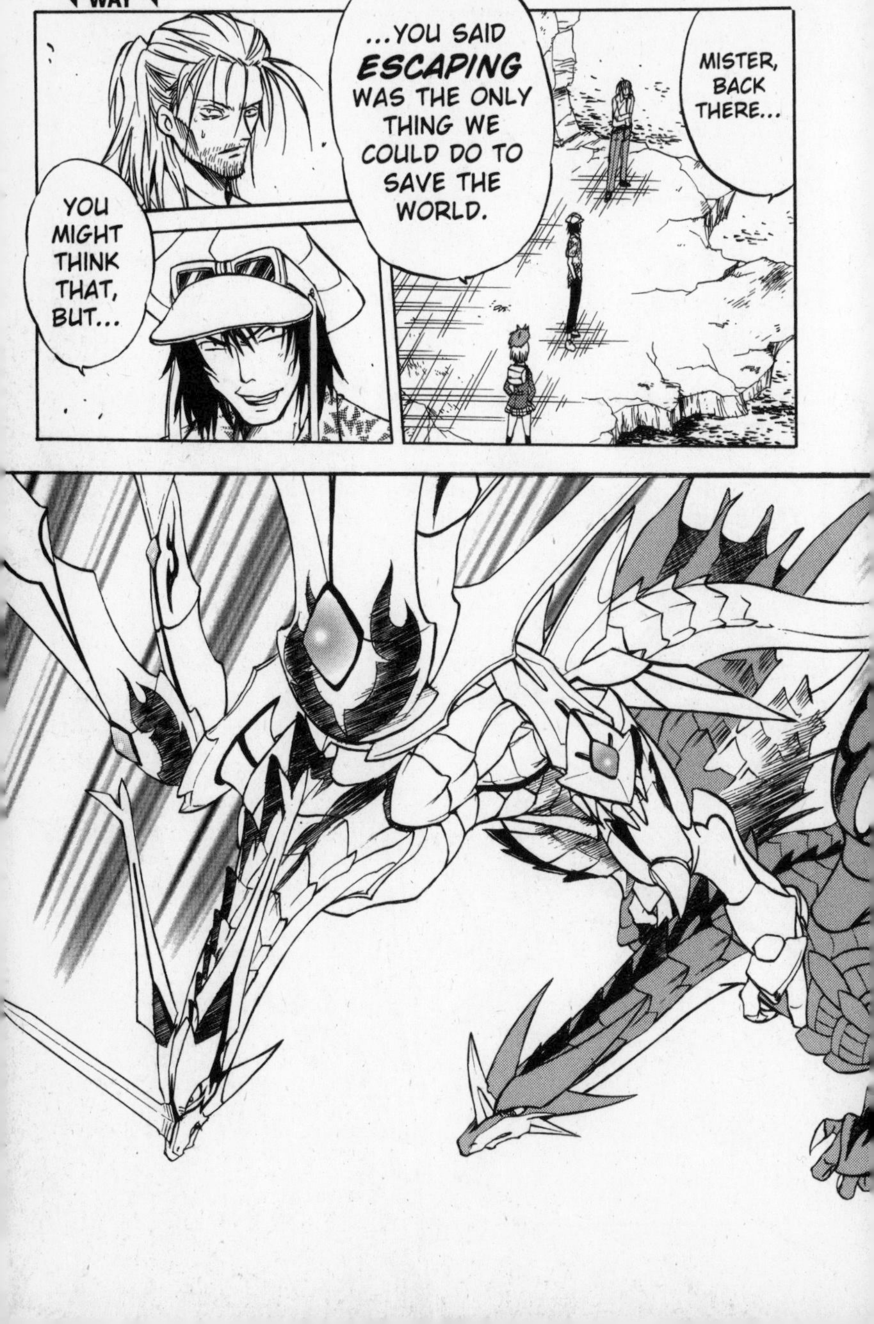

MISTER, BACK THERE...
...YOU SAID *ESCAPING* WAS THE ONLY THING WE COULD DO TO SAVE THE WORLD.
YOU MIGHT THINK THAT, BUT...

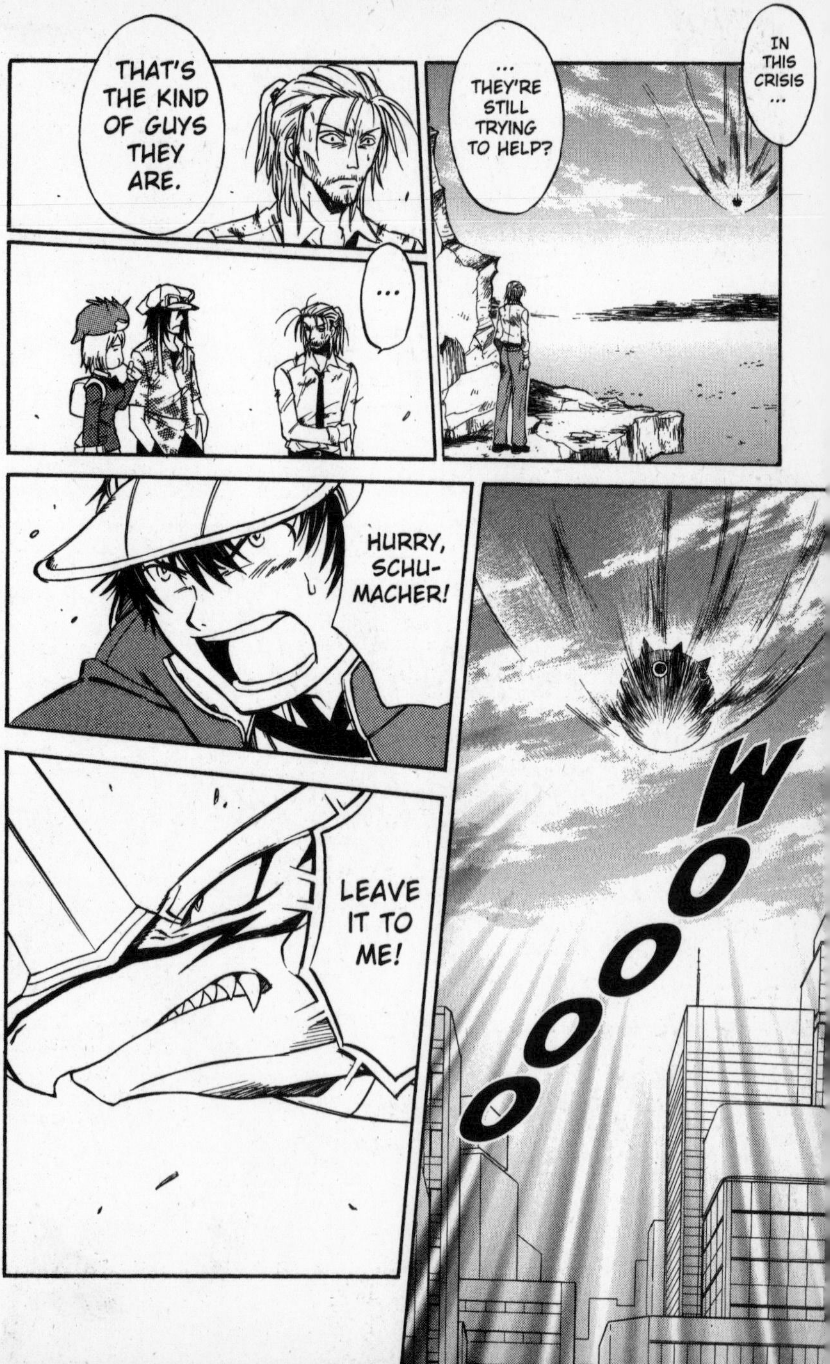
IN THIS CRISIS ...
... THEY'RE STILL TRYING TO HELP?
THAT'S THE KIND OF GUYS THEY ARE.
...
WOOOO
HURRY, SCHU-MACHER!
LEAVE IT TO ME!

READ THIS WAY

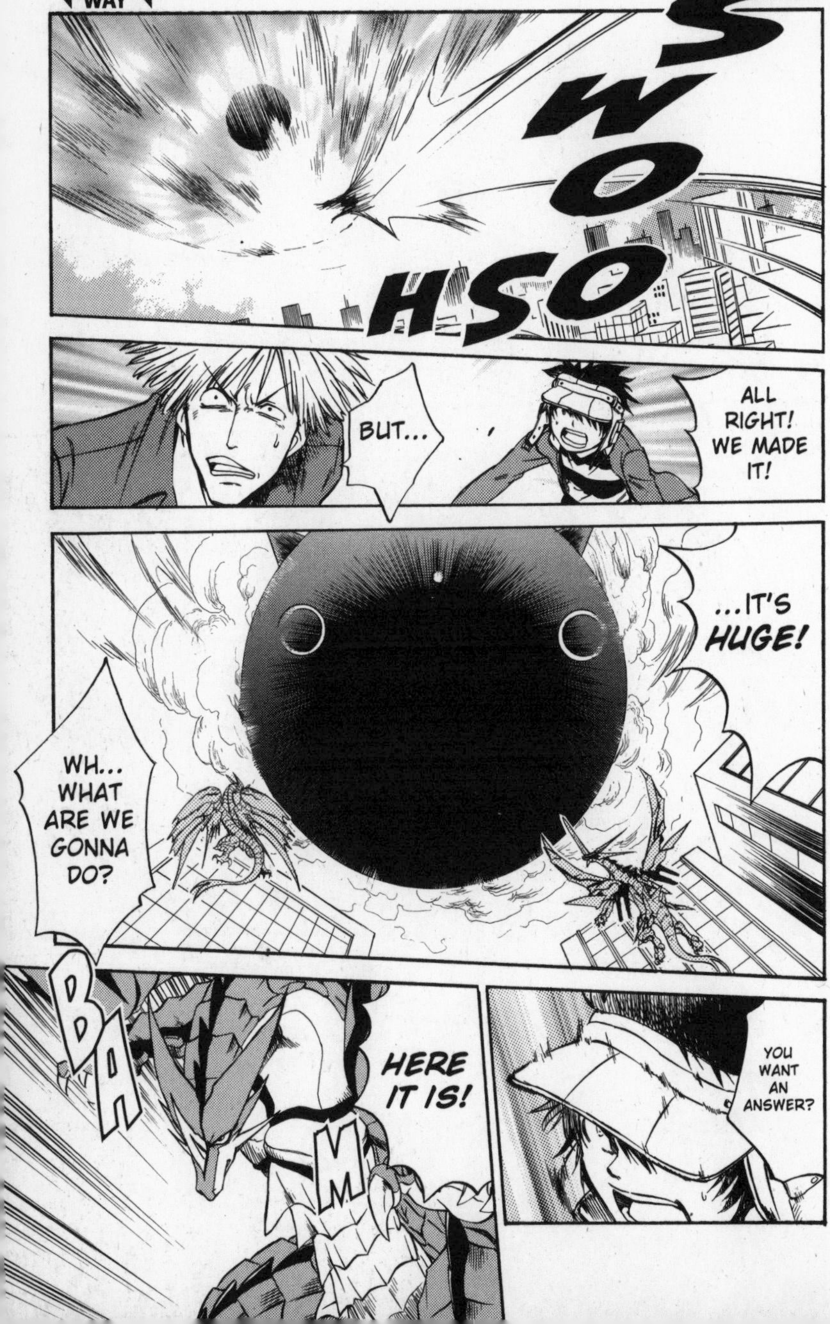
SWOOSH
ALL RIGHT! WE MADE IT!
BUT...
...IT'S HUGE!
WH... WHAT ARE WE GONNA DO?
YOU WANT AN ANSWER?
HERE IT IS!
BAM

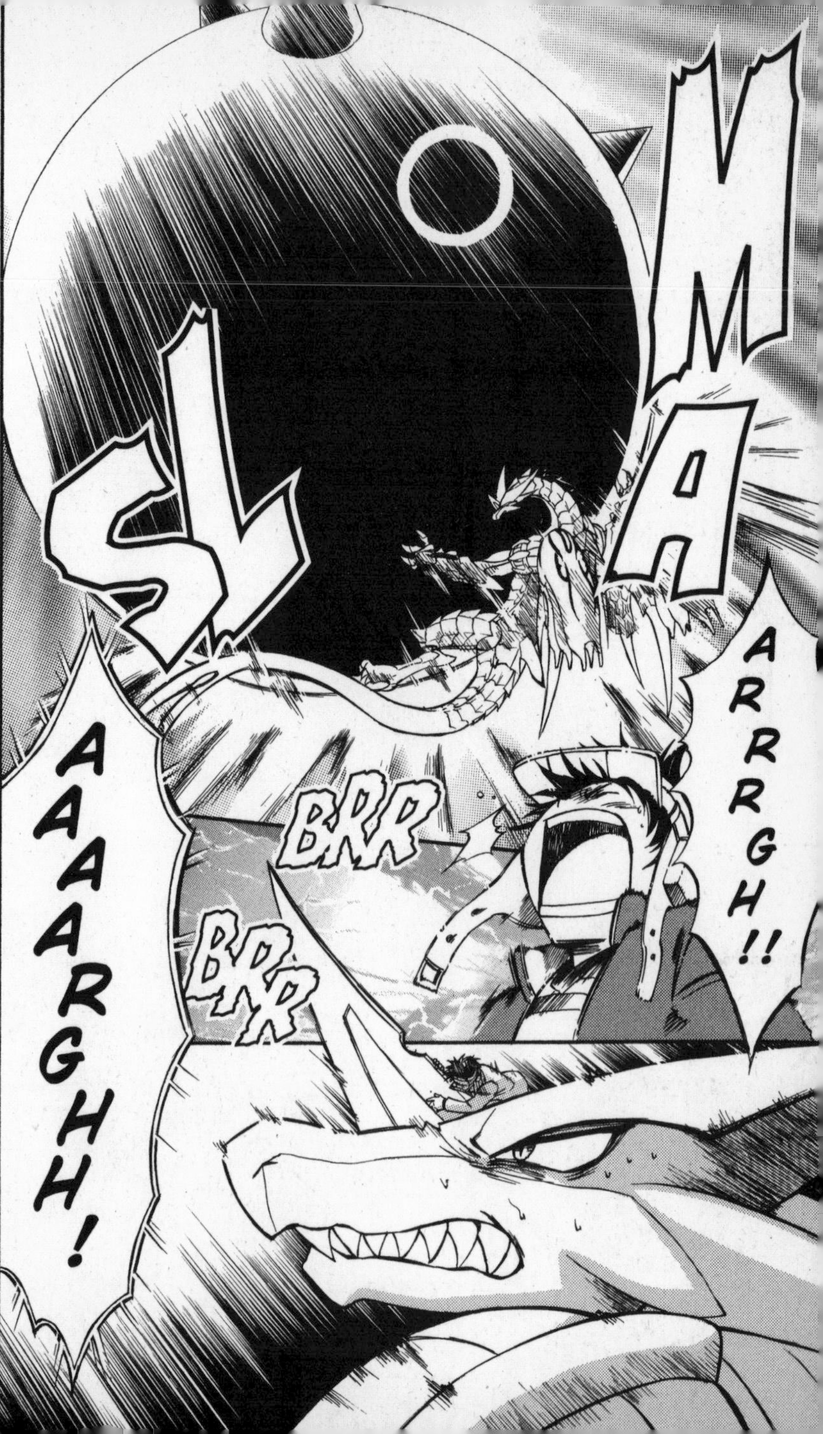
SLAM
ARRRGH!!
BRR
BRR
AAAARGHH!

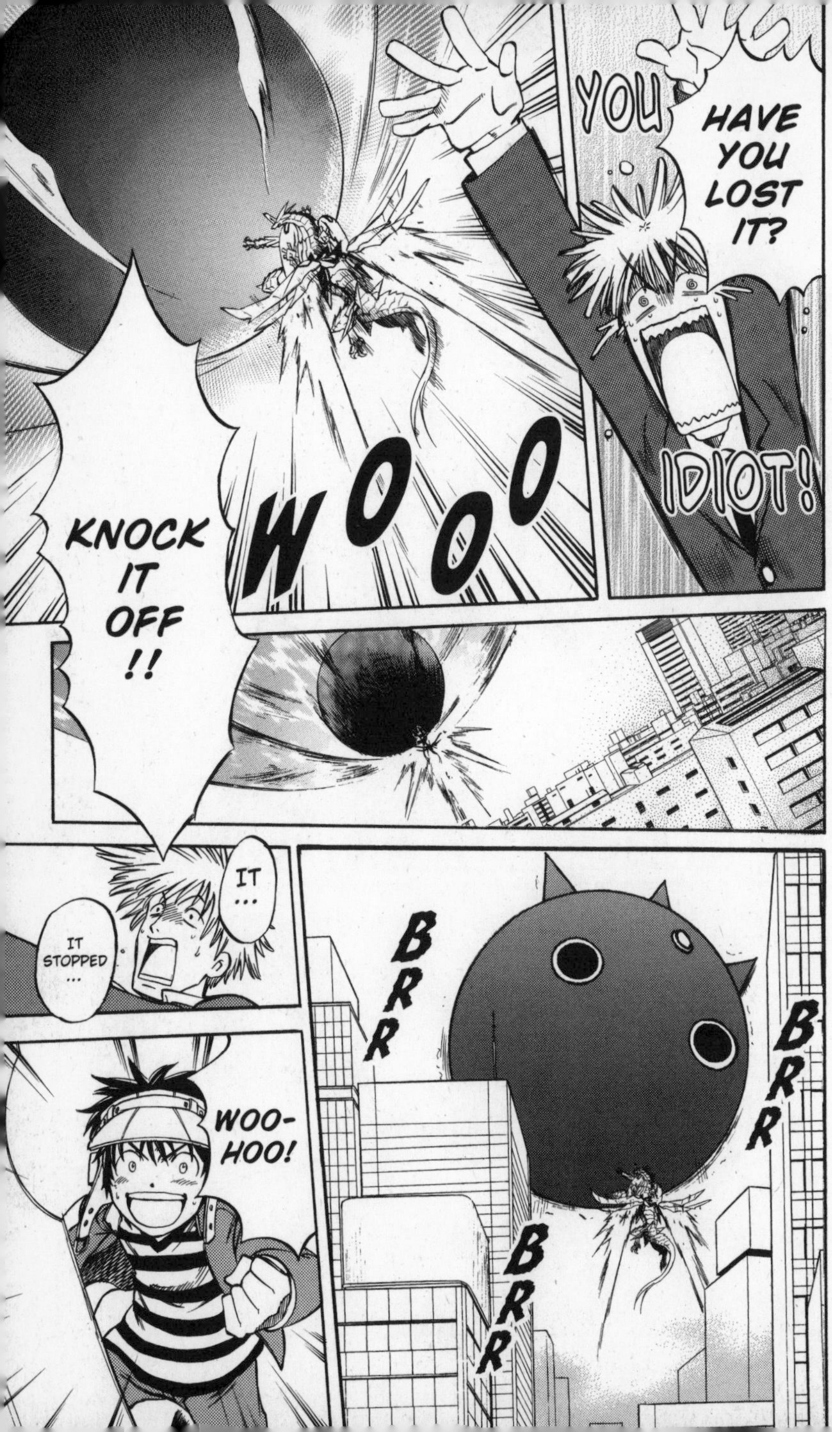
YOU
HAVE YOU LOST IT?
IDIOT!
WOOO
KNOCK IT OFF!!
BRRR
BRRR
BRRR
IT...
IT STOPPED...
WOO-HOO!

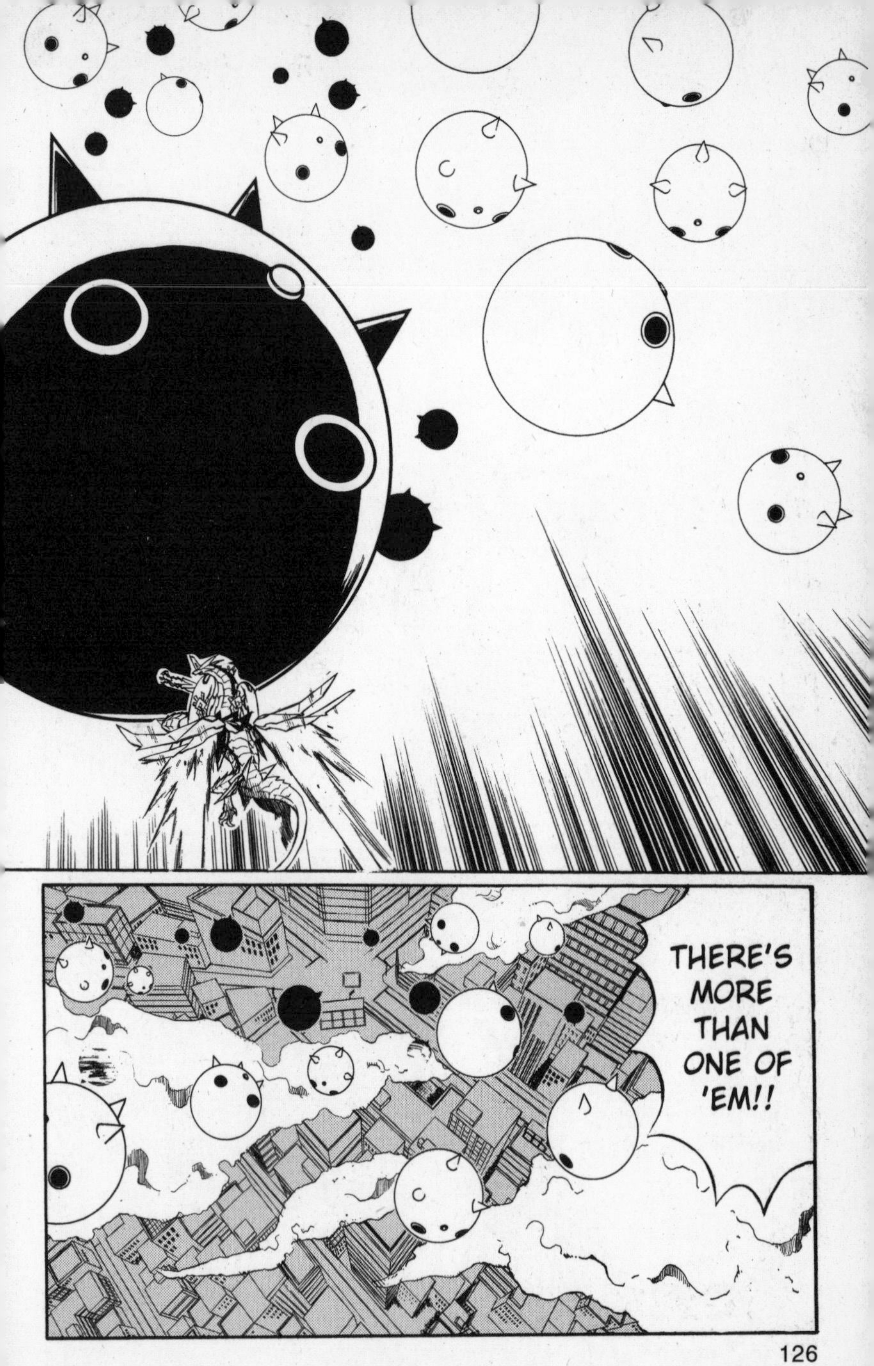
THERE'S MORE THAN ONE OF 'EM!!

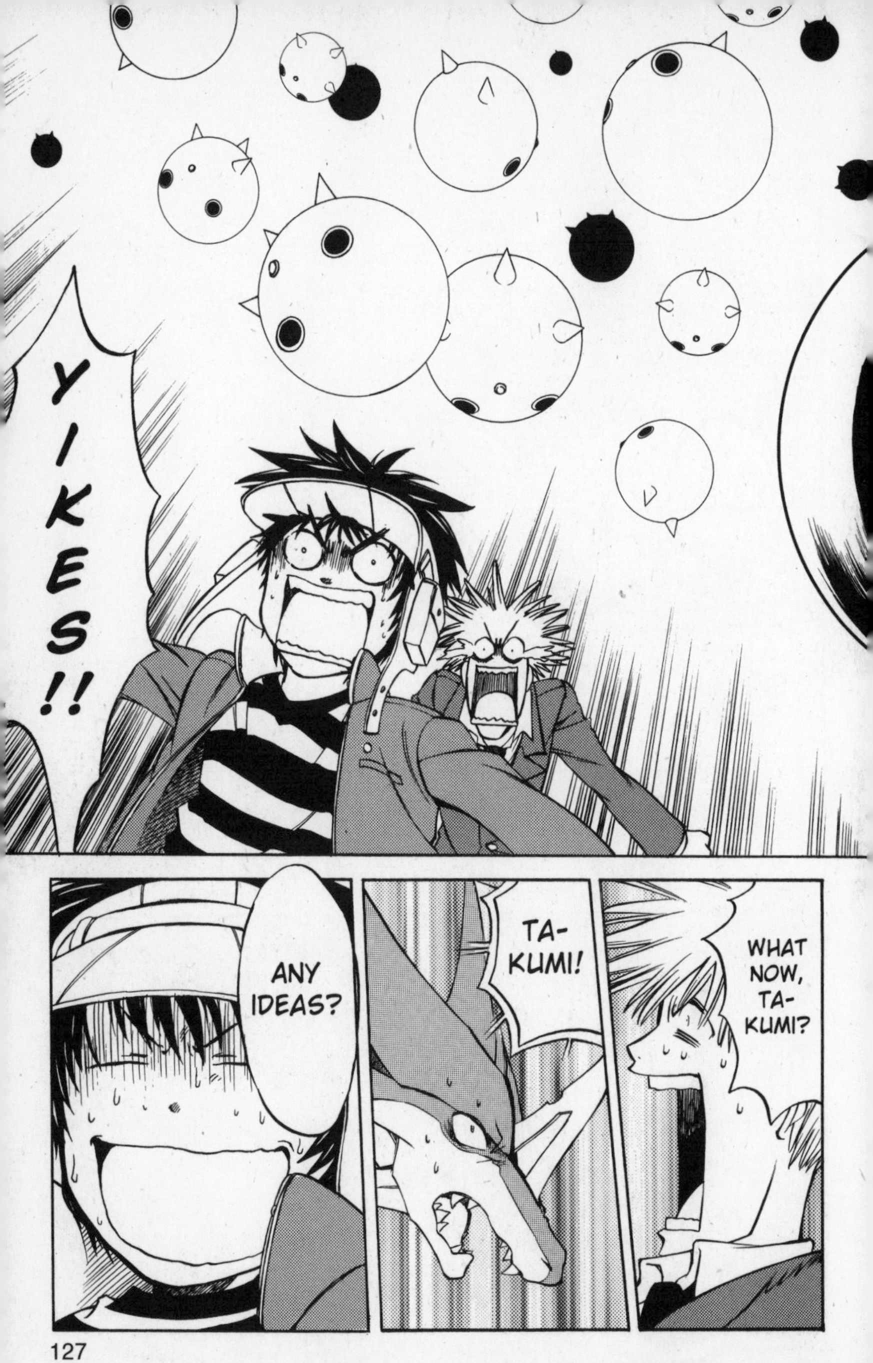
YIKES!!
WHAT NOW, TA-KUMI?
TA-KUMI!
ANY IDEAS?

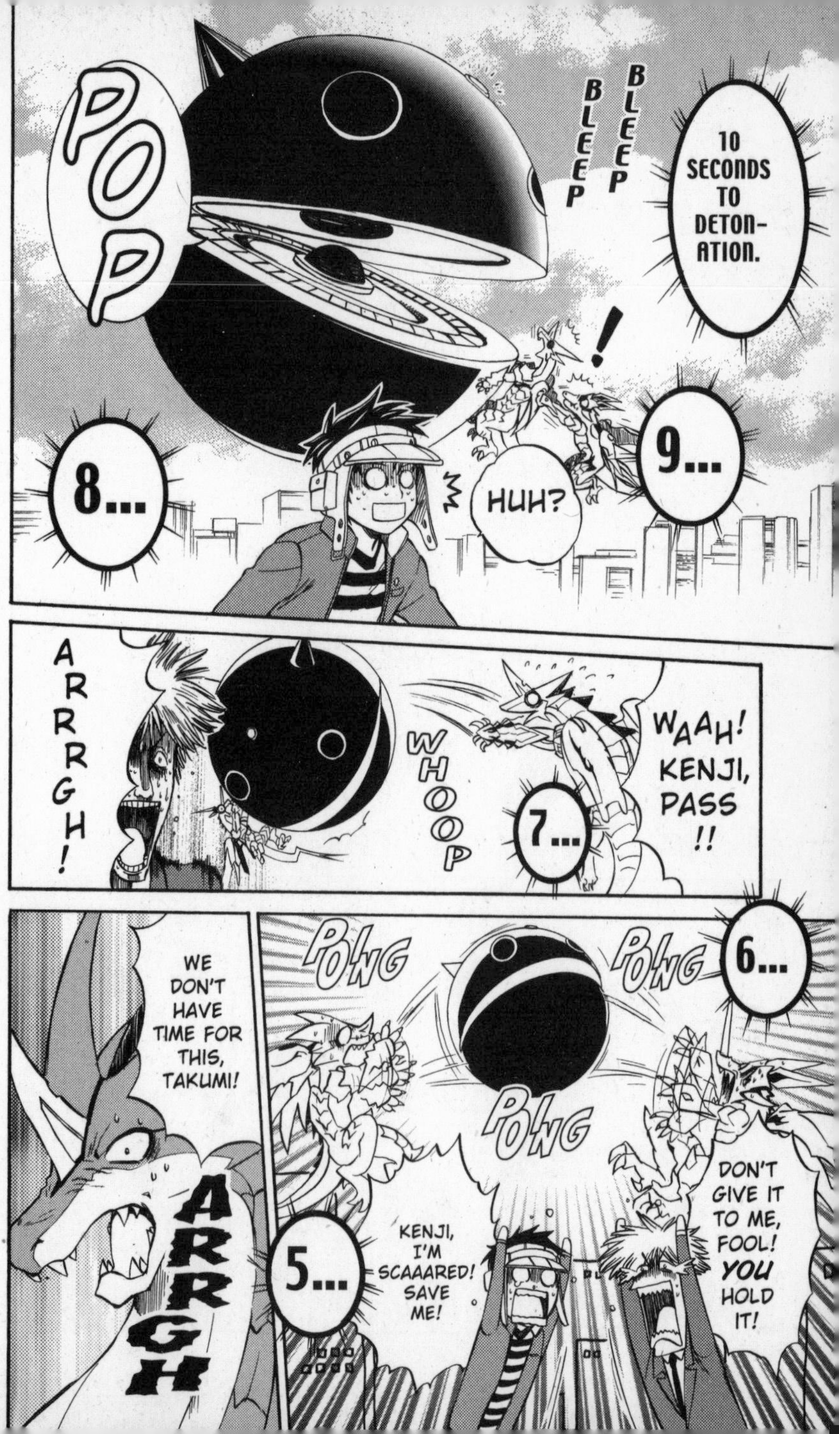
10 SECONDS TO DETON-ATION.
BLEEP BLEEP
POP
!
9...
HUH?
8...
WAAH! KENJI, PASS!!
7...
WHOOOP
ARRRGH!
6...
PONG
PONG
PONG
DON'T GIVE IT TO ME, FOOL! YOU HOLD IT!
KENJI, I'M SCAAARED! SAVE ME!
5...
WE DON'T HAVE TIME FOR THIS, TAKUMI!
ARRGH

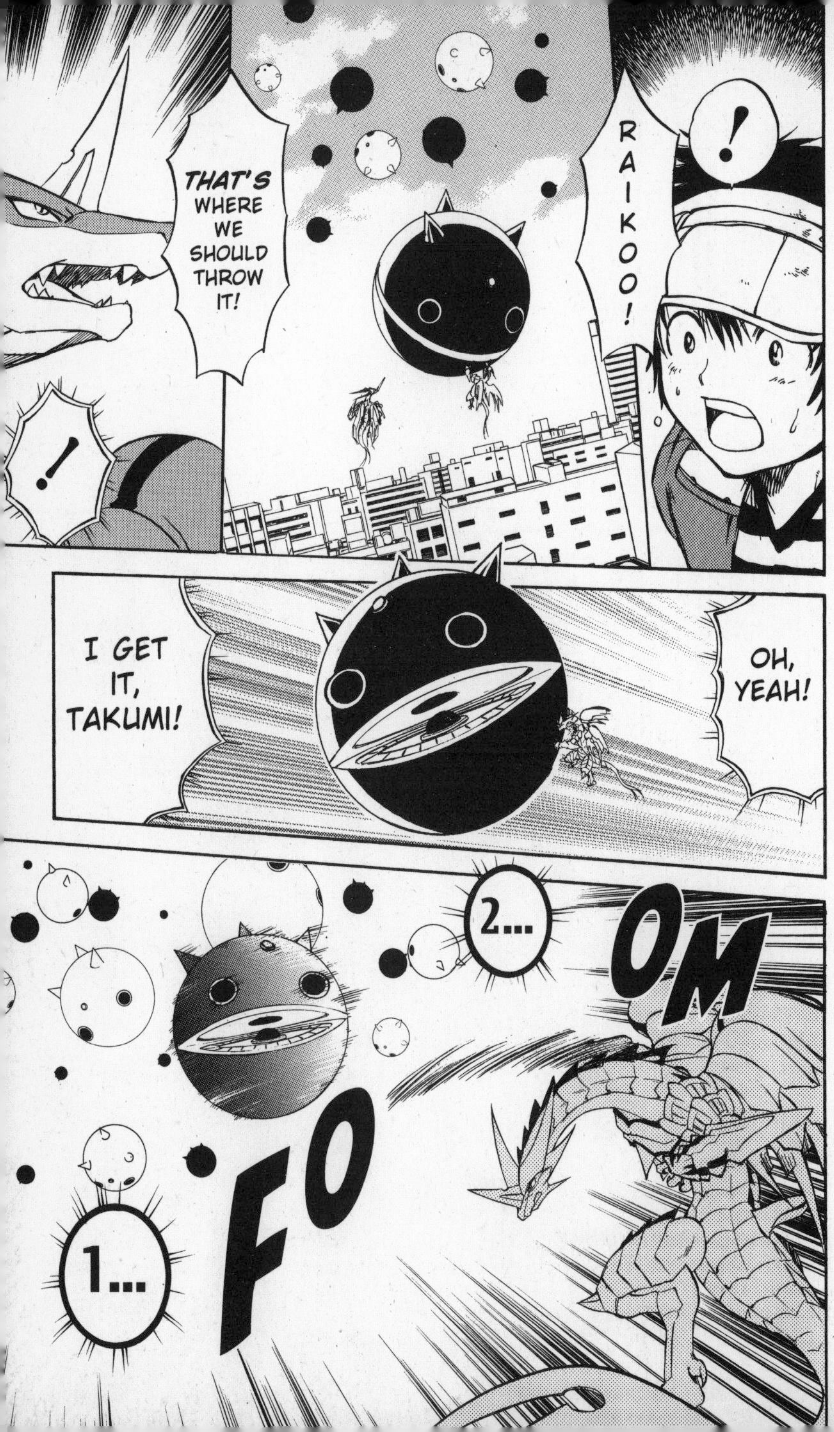
!
RAIKOO!
THAT'S WHERE WE SHOULD THROW IT!
!
OH, YEAH!
I GET IT, TAKUMI!
2...
OM
FO
1...

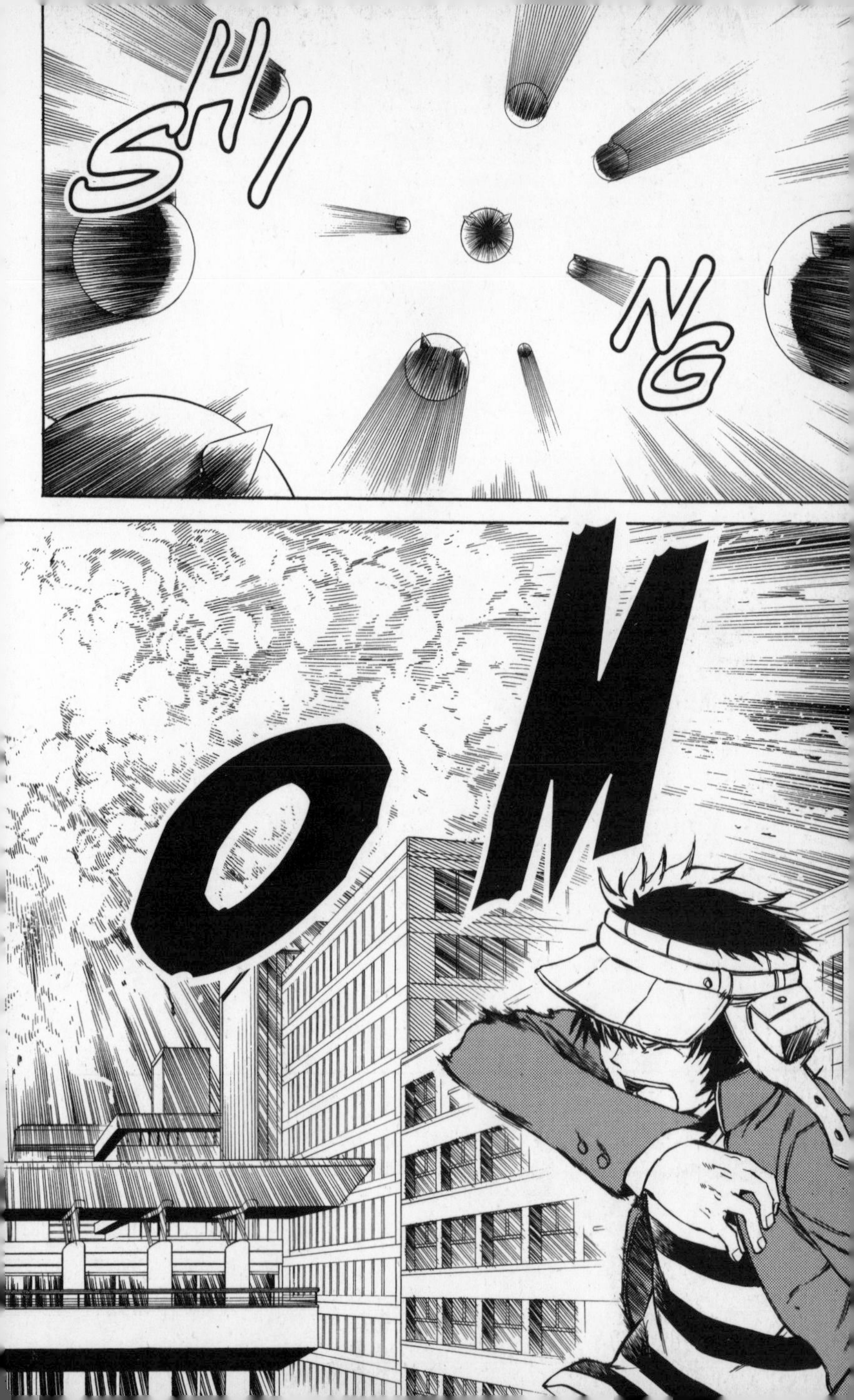
SHING
OM

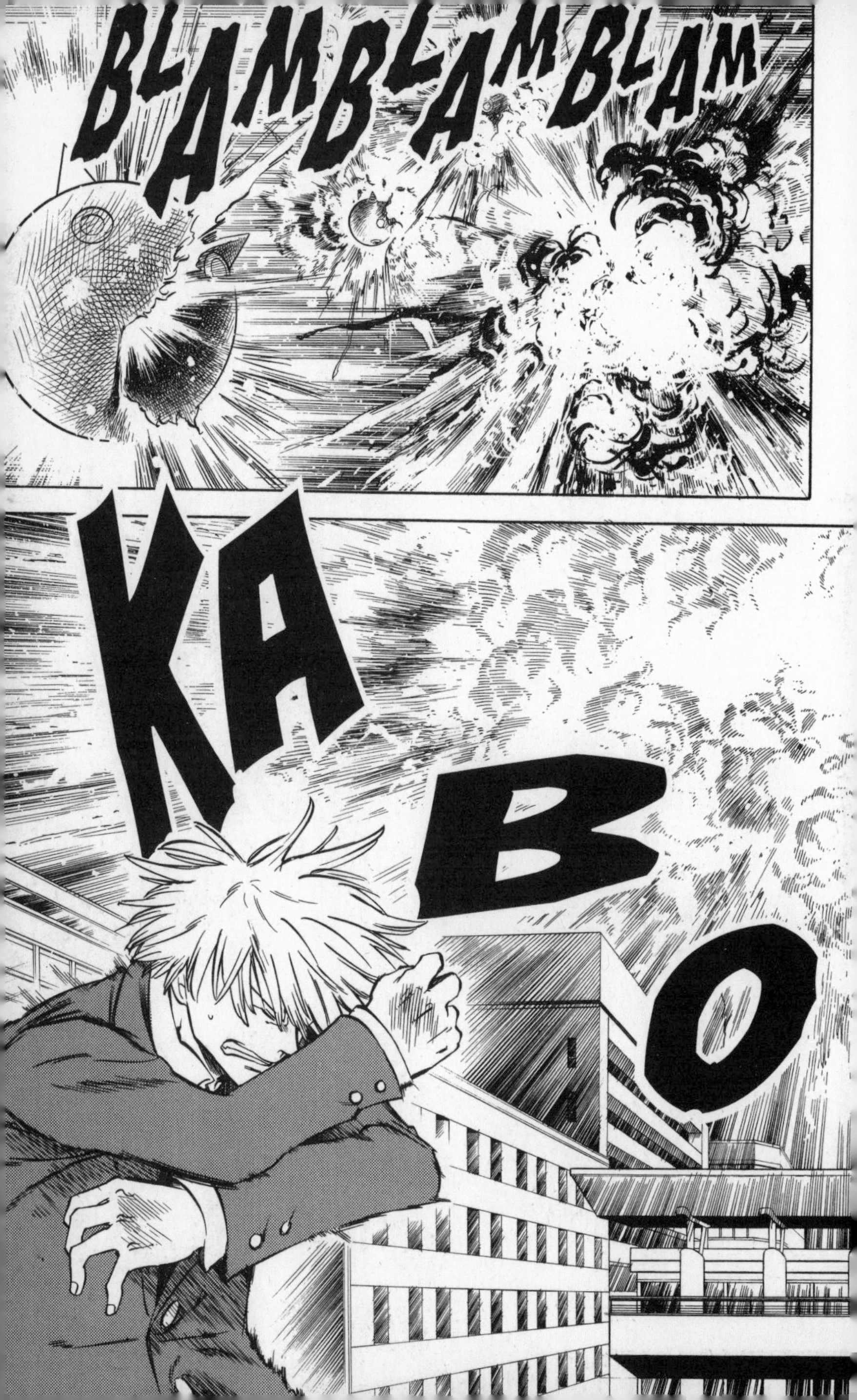
BLAMBLAMBLAM
KABOOM

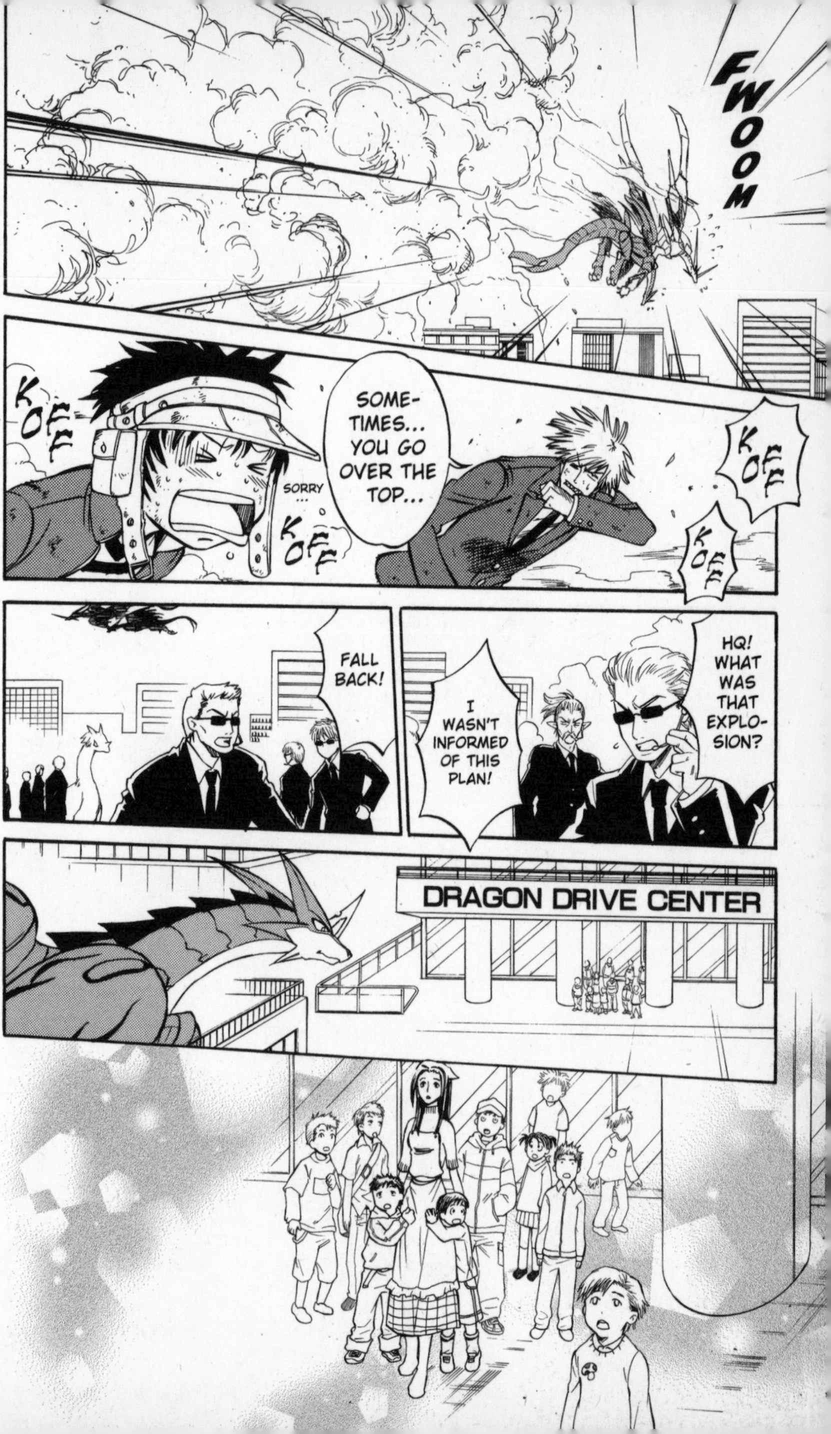
FWOOM
KOFF
KOFF
SOME-TIMES... YOU GO OVER THE TOP...
SORRY...
KOFF
KOFF
HQ! WHAT WAS THAT EXPLO-SION?
I WASN'T INFORMED OF THIS PLAN!
FALL BACK!
DRAGON DRIVE CENTER

READ THIS WAY

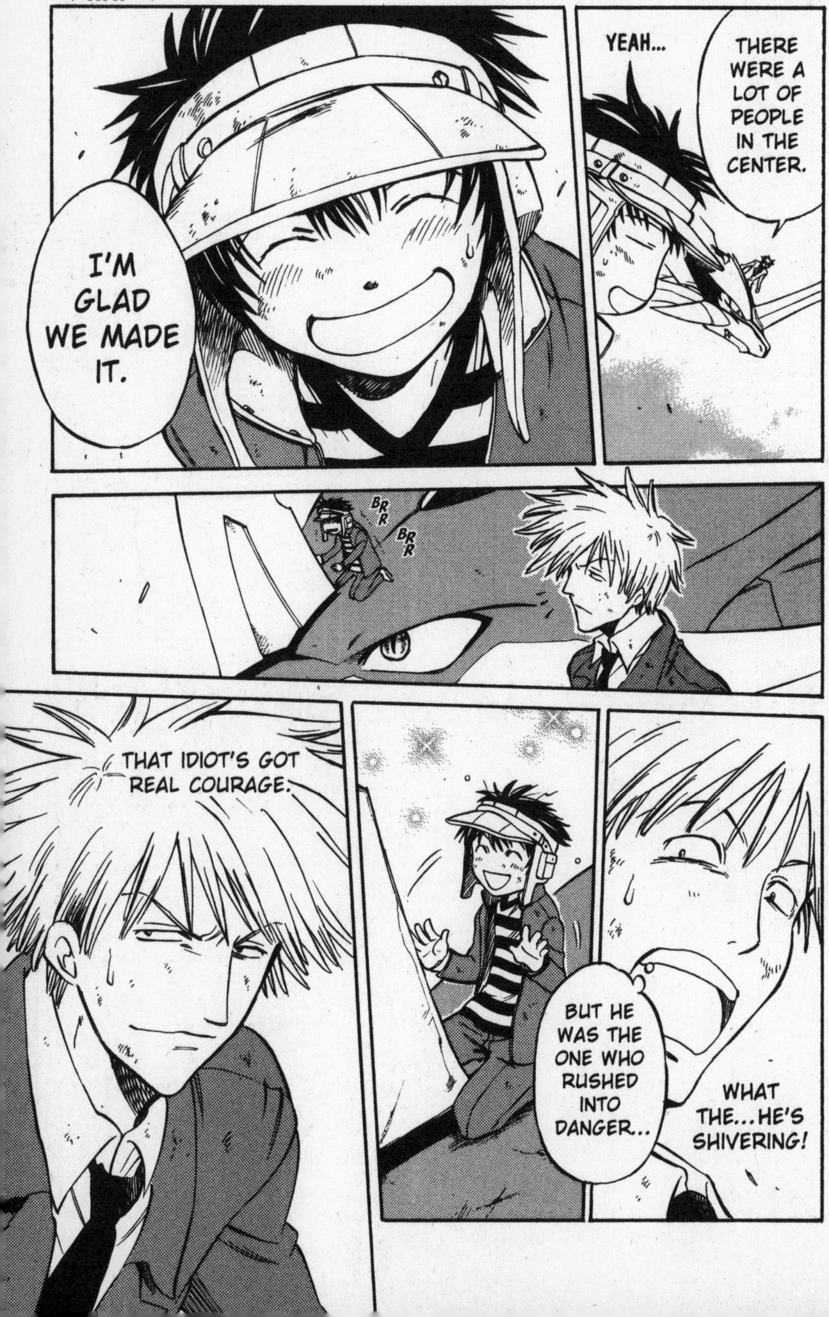
THERE WERE A LOT OF PEOPLE IN THE CENTER.
YEAH...
I'M GLAD WE MADE IT.
BRR
BRR
WHAT THE...HE'S SHIVERING!
BUT HE WAS THE ONE WHO RUSHED INTO DANGER...
THAT IDIOT'S GOT REAL COURAGE.

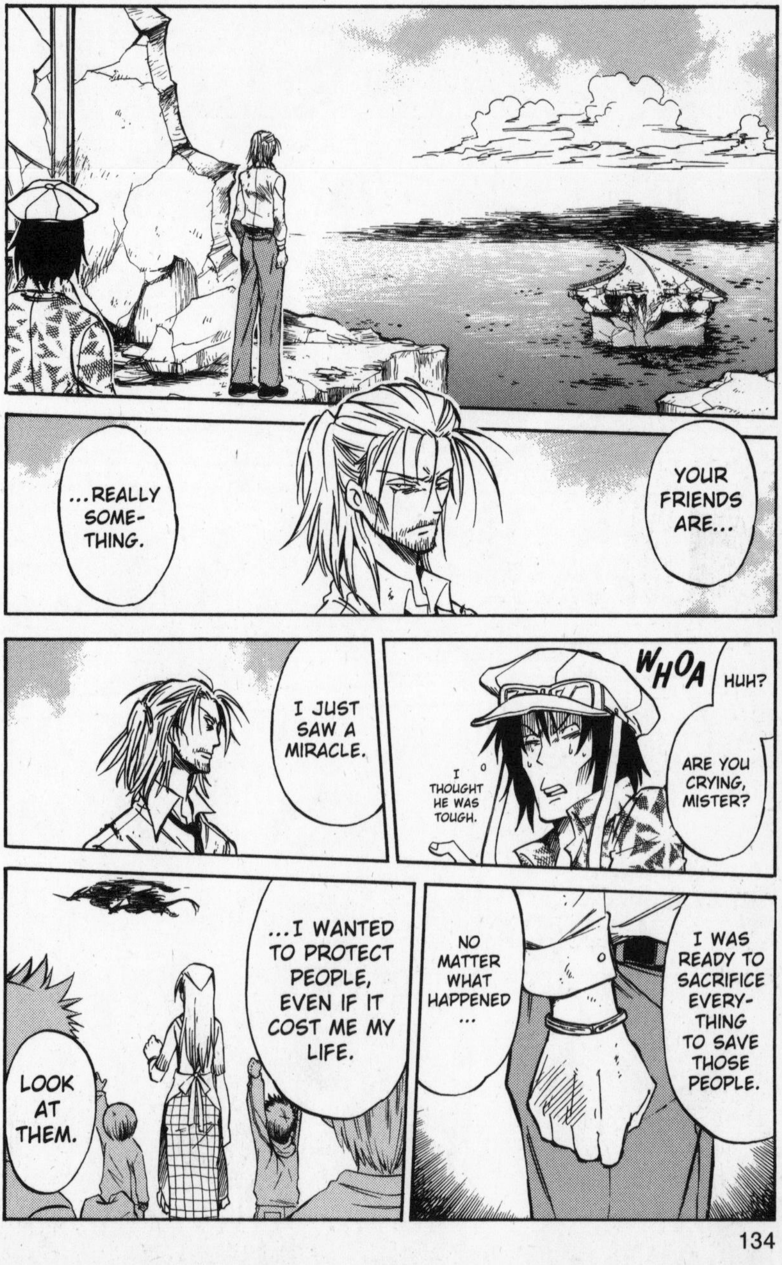
YOUR FRIENDS ARE...
...REALLY SOME-THING.
HUH?
WHOA
ARE YOU CRYING, MISTER?
I THOUGHT HE WAS TOUGH.
I JUST SAW A MIRACLE.
I WAS READY TO SACRIFICE EVERY-THING TO SAVE THOSE PEOPLE.
NO MATTER WHAT HAPPENED...
...I WANTED TO PROTECT PEOPLE, EVEN IF IT COST ME MY LIFE.
LOOK AT THEM.

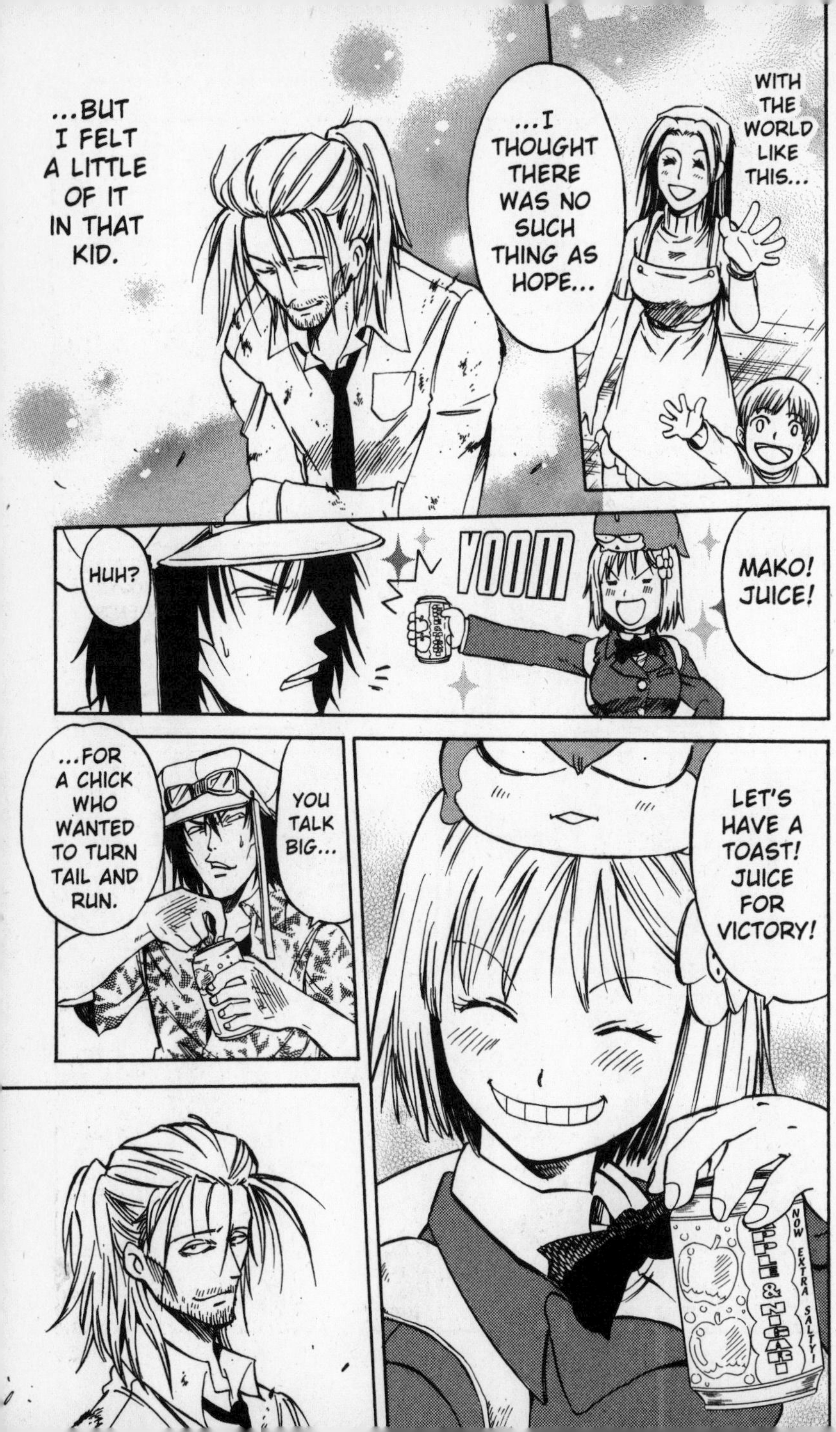
WITH THE WORLD LIKE THIS...
...I THOUGHT THERE WAS NO SUCH THING AS HOPE...
...BUT I FELT A LITTLE OF IT IN THAT KID.
MAKO! JUICE!
VOOM
HUH?
LET'S HAVE A TOAST! JUICE FOR VICTORY!
APPLE & NIGARI
NOW EXTRA SALTY!
YOU TALK BIG...
...FOR A CHICK WHO WANTED TO TURN TAIL AND RUN.

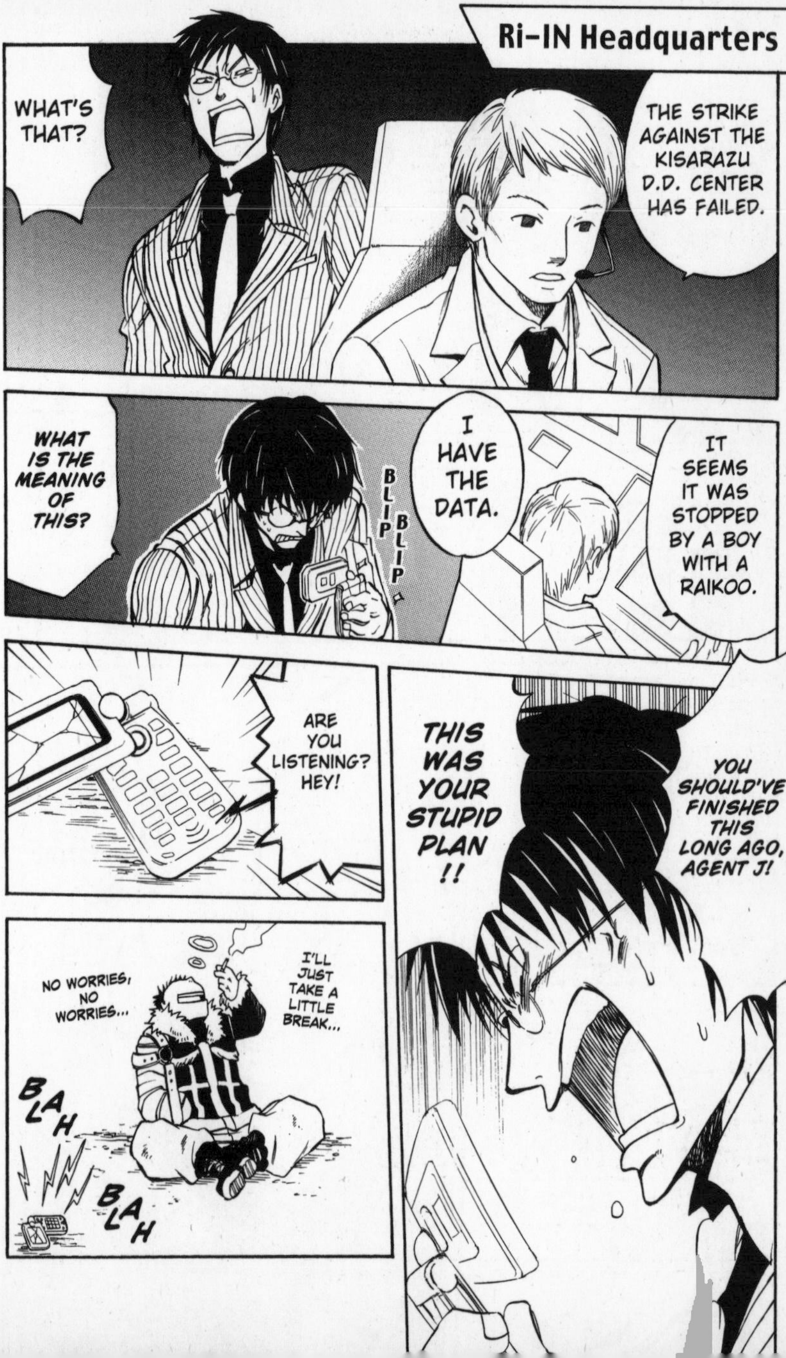
Ri-IN Headquarters
THE STRIKE AGAINST THE KISARAZU D.D. CENTER HAS FAILED.
WHAT'S THAT?
IT SEEMS IT WAS STOPPED BY A BOY WITH A RAIKOO.
I HAVE THE DATA.
BLIP BLIP
WHAT IS THE MEANING OF THIS?
YOU SHOULD'VE FINISHED THIS LONG AGO, AGENT J!
THIS WAS YOUR STUPID PLAN!!
ARE YOU LISTENING? HEY!
I'LL JUST TAKE A LITTLE BREAK...
NO WORRIES, NO WORRIES...
BLAH
BLAH

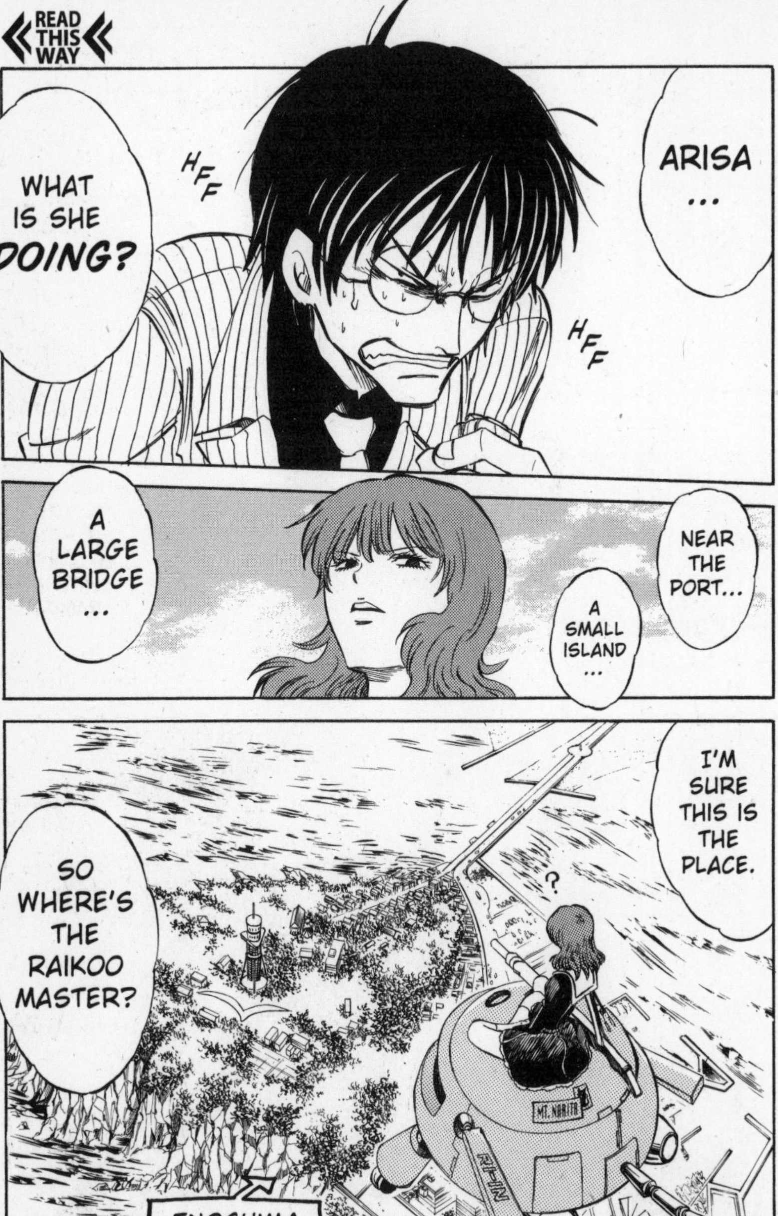
READ THIS WAY
ARISA...
HFF
HFF
WHAT IS SHE DOING?
NEAR THE PORT...
A SMALL ISLAND...
A LARGE BRIDGE...
I'M SURE THIS IS THE PLACE.
?
SO WHERE'S THE RAIKOO MASTER?
MT. NORITA
ENOSHIMA

*SHE'S ON THE WRONG SIDE OF TOKYO BAY.

WHERE AM I?

TOTALLY LOST AS USUAL.

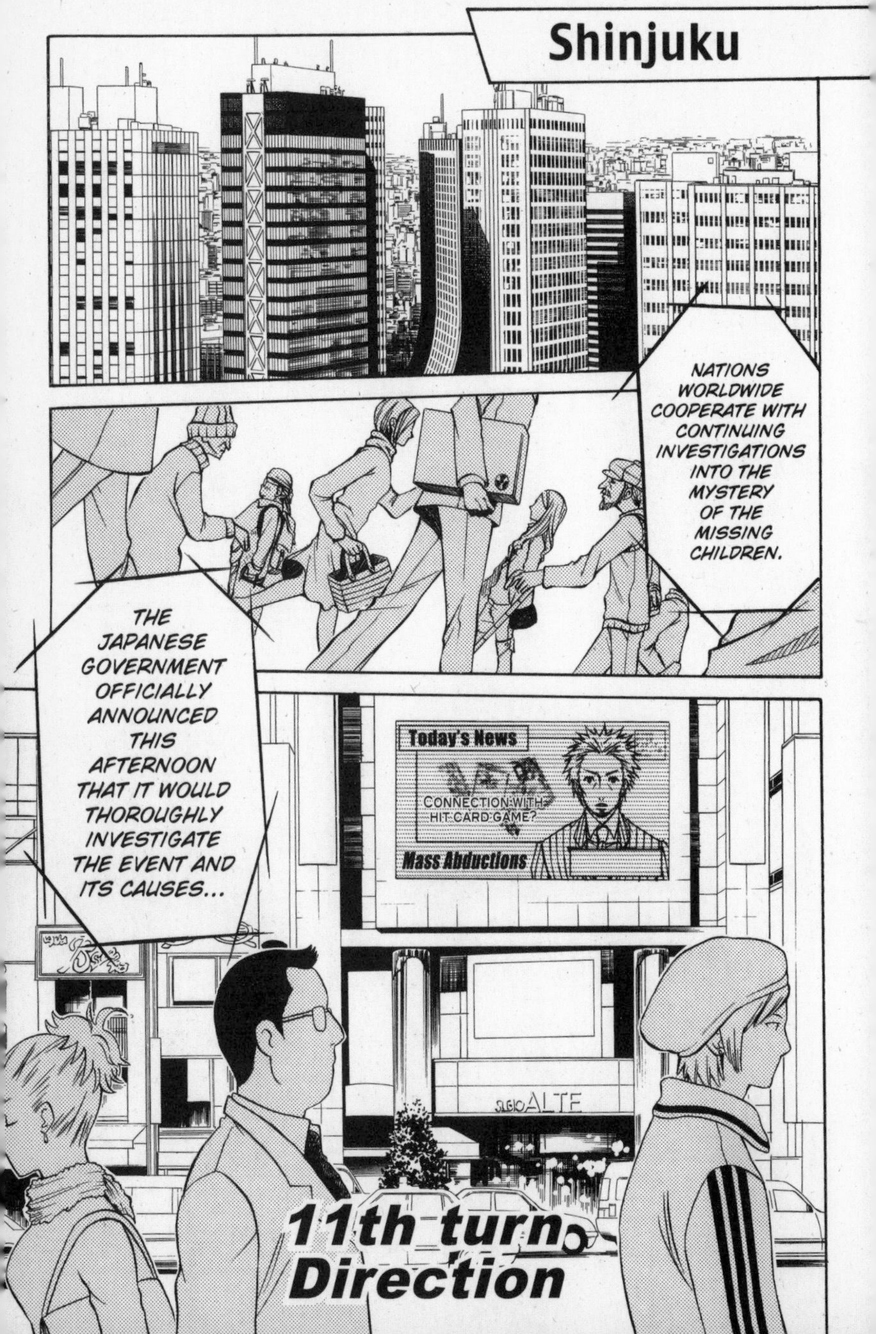
Shinjuku
NATIONS WORLDWIDE COOPERATE WITH CONTINUING INVESTIGATIONS INTO THE MYSTERY OF THE MISSING CHILDREN.
THE JAPANESE GOVERNMENT OFFICIALLY ANNOUNCED THIS AFTERNOON THAT IT WOULD THOROUGHLY INVESTIGATE THE EVENT AND ITS CAUSES...
Today's News
CONNECTION WITH HIT CARD GAME?
Mass Abductions
11th turn
Direction

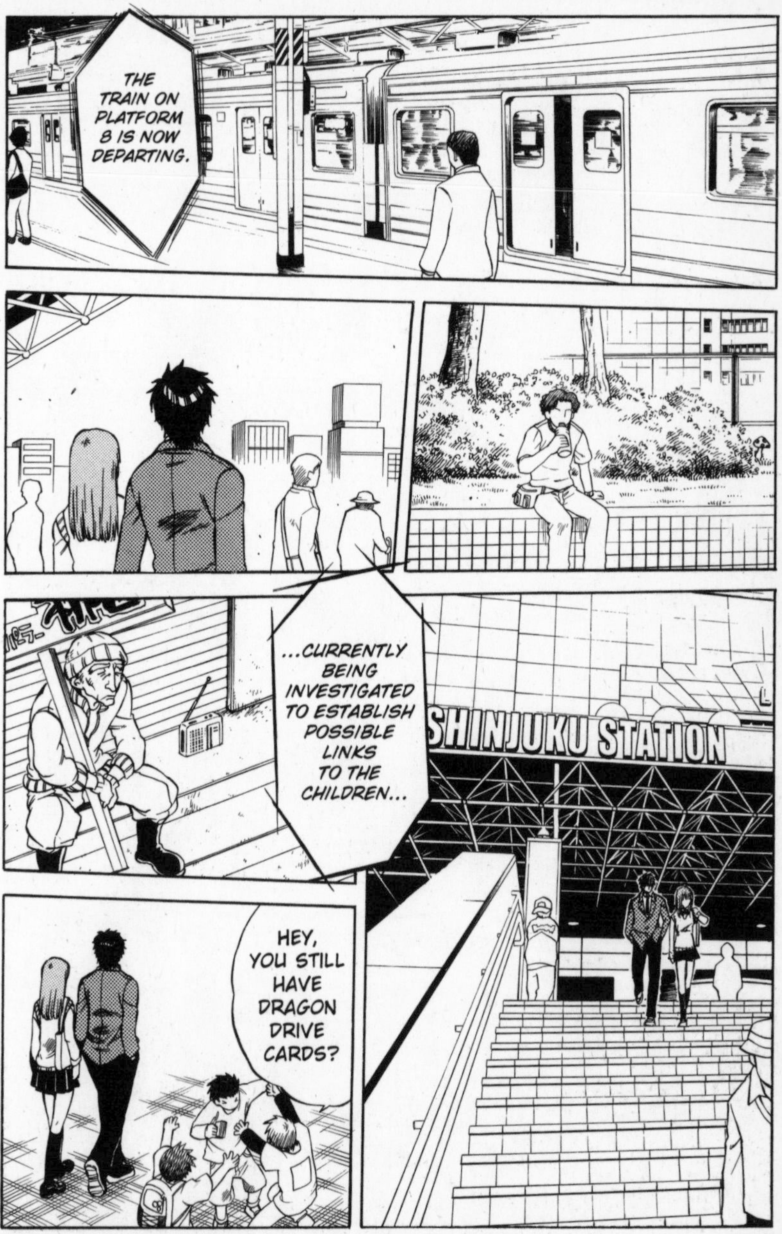
THE TRAIN ON PLATFORM 8 IS NOW DEPARTING.
SHINJUKU STATION
...CURRENTLY BEING INVESTIGATED TO ESTABLISH POSSIBLE LINKS TO THE CHILDREN...
HEY, YOU STILL HAVE DRAGON DRIVE CARDS?

READ THIS WAY

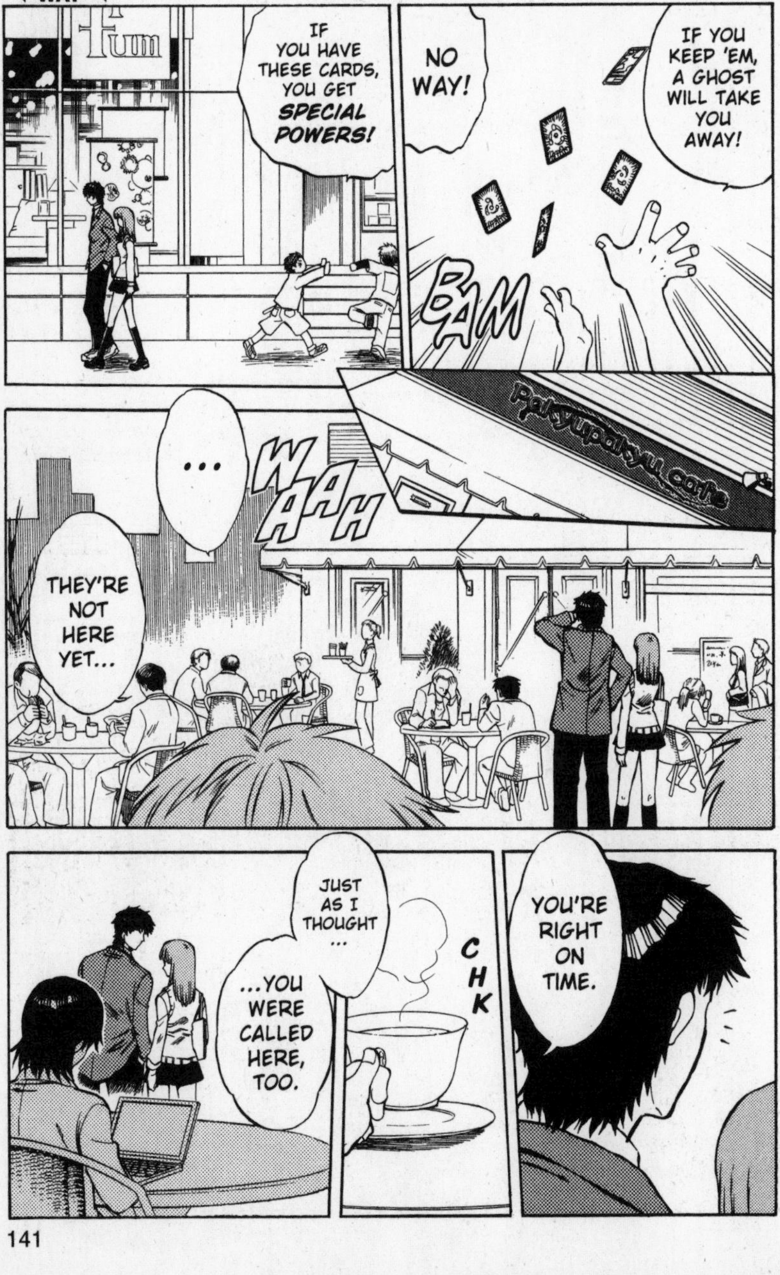
IF YOU KEEP 'EM, A GHOST WILL TAKE YOU AWAY!
NO WAY!
BAM
IF YOU HAVE THESE CARDS, YOU GET SPECIAL POWERS!
Pakyupakyu cafe
...
WAAH
THEY'RE NOT HERE YET...
YOU'RE RIGHT ON TIME.
CHK
JUST AS I THOUGHT...
...YOU WERE CALLED HERE, TOO.

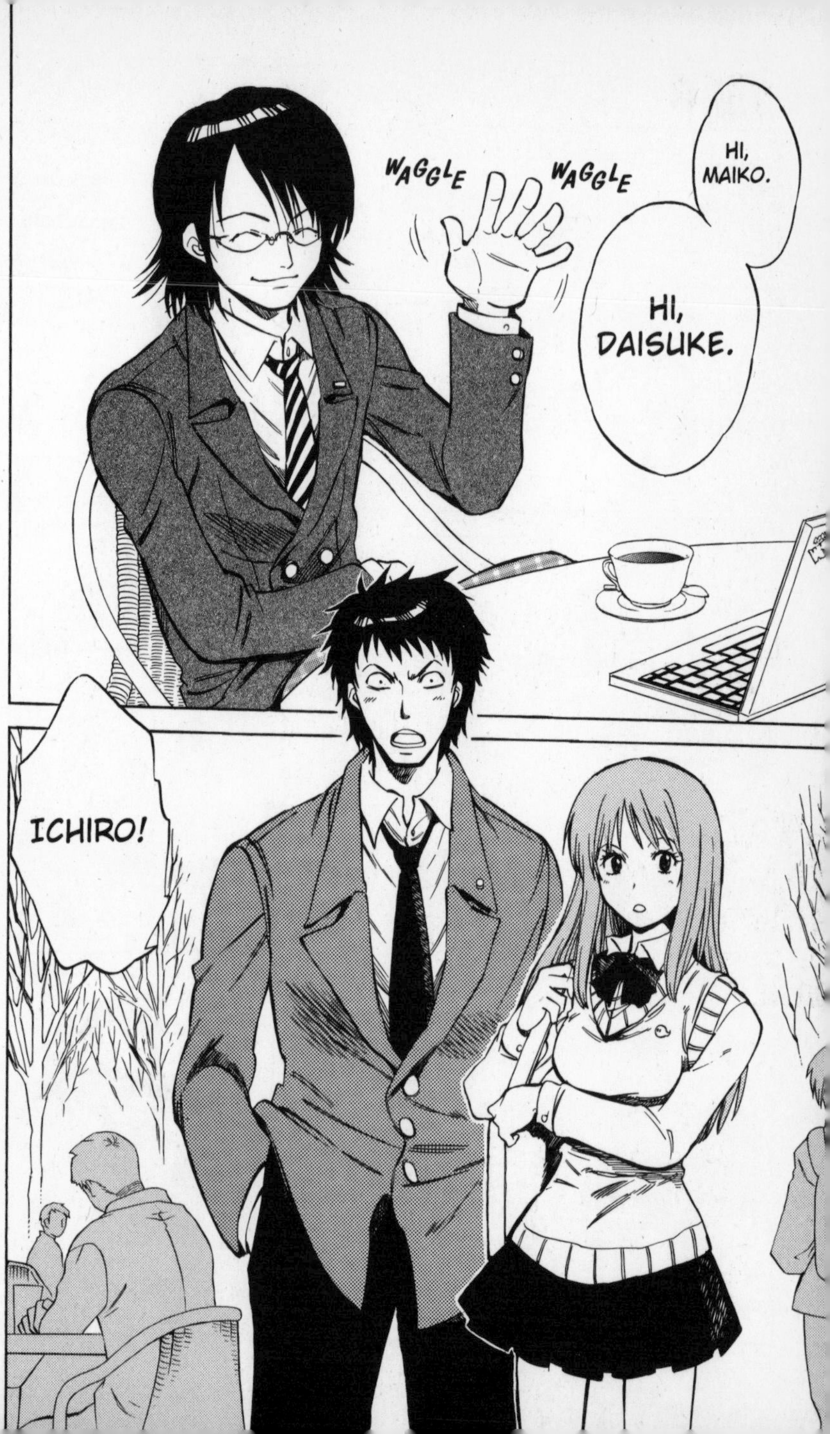
HI, MAIKO.
HI, DAISUKE.
WAGGLE
WAGGLE
ICHIRO!

READ THIS WAY

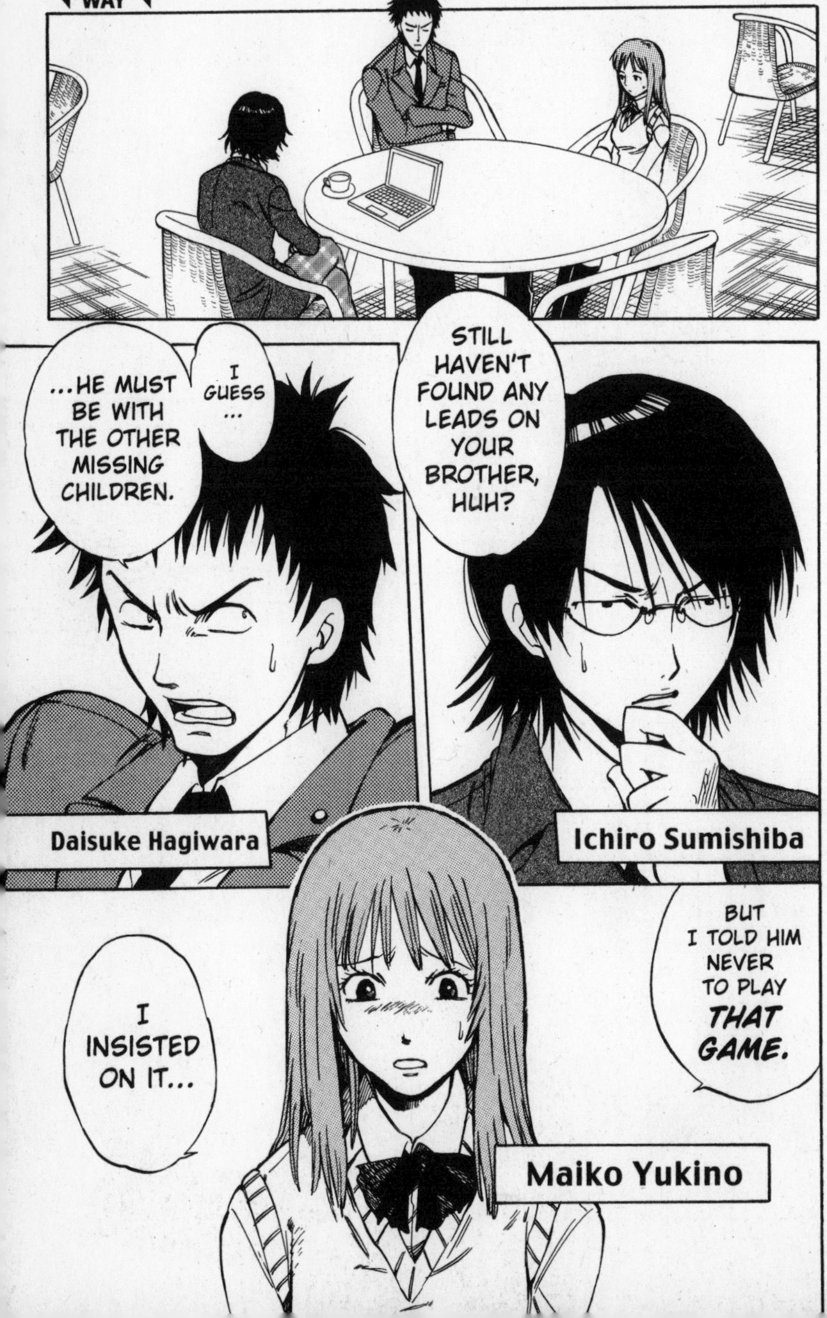
STILL HAVEN'T FOUND ANY LEADS ON YOUR BROTHER, HUH?
Ichiro Sumishiba
I GUESS...
...HE MUST BE WITH THE OTHER MISSING CHILDREN.
Daisuke Hagiwara
BUT I TOLD HIM NEVER TO PLAY *THAT GAME.*
I INSISTED ON IT...
Maiko Yukino

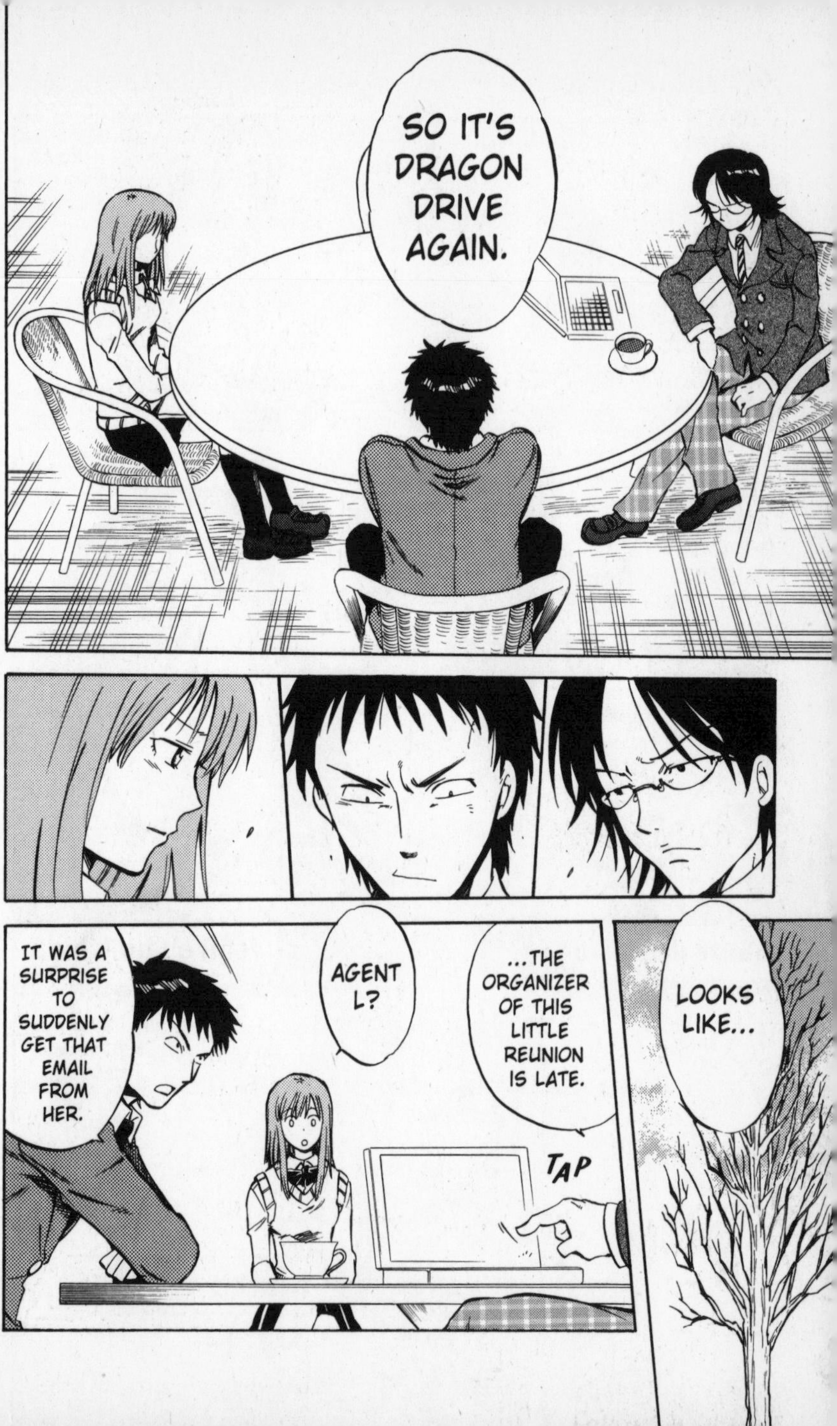
SO IT'S DRAGON DRIVE AGAIN.
LOOKS LIKE...
...THE ORGANIZER OF THIS LITTLE REUNION IS LATE.
TAP
AGENT L?
IT WAS A SURPRISE TO SUDDENLY GET THAT EMAIL FROM HER.

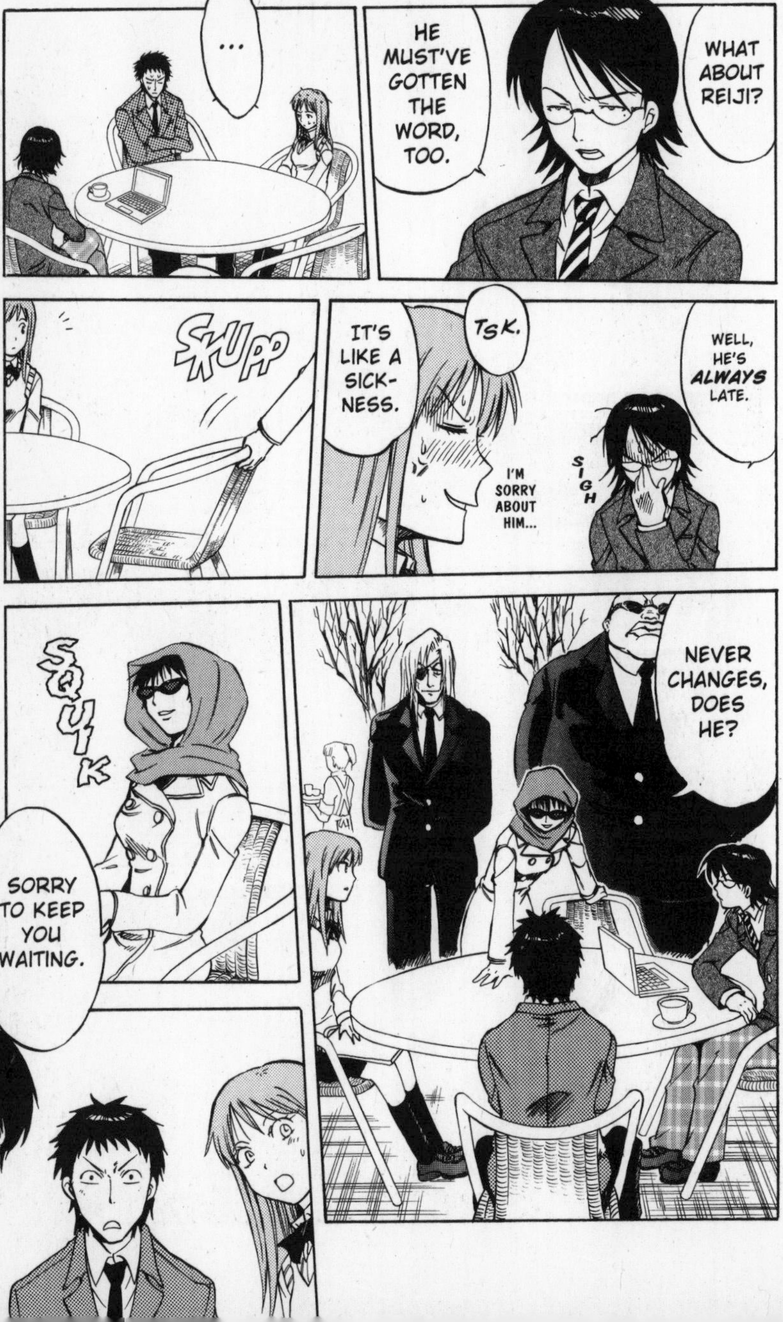
WHAT ABOUT REIJI?
HE MUST'VE GOTTEN THE WORD, TOO.
...
WELL, HE'S ALWAYS LATE.
SIGH
I'M SORRY ABOUT HIM...
TSK.
IT'S LIKE A SICKNESS.
SKUPP
NEVER CHANGES, DOES HE?
SQUIK
SORRY TO KEEP YOU WAITING.

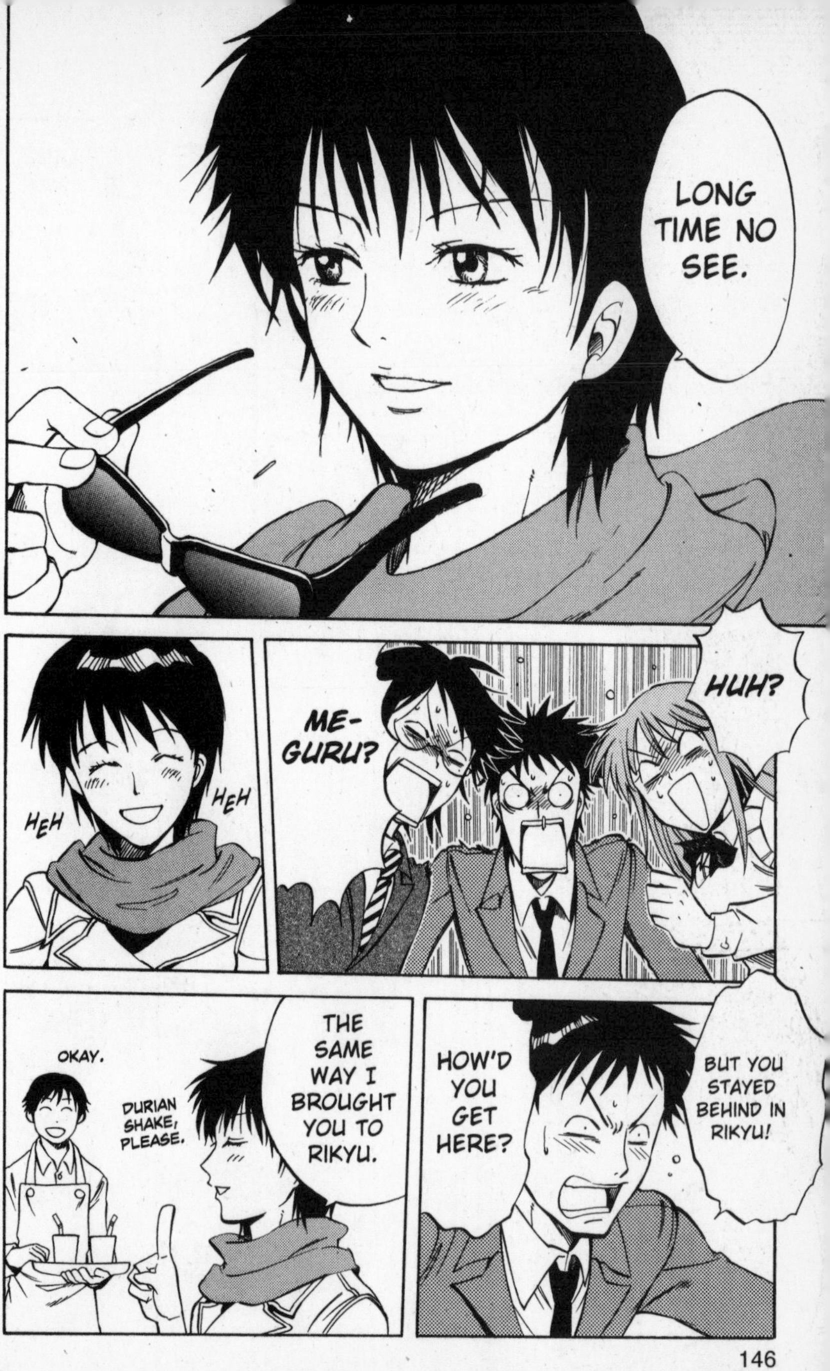
LONG TIME NO SEE.
HUH?
ME-GURU?
HEH HEH
BUT YOU STAYED BEHIND IN RIKYU!
HOW'D YOU GET HERE?
THE SAME WAY I BROUGHT YOU TO RIKYU.
DURIAN SHAKE, PLEASE.
OKAY.

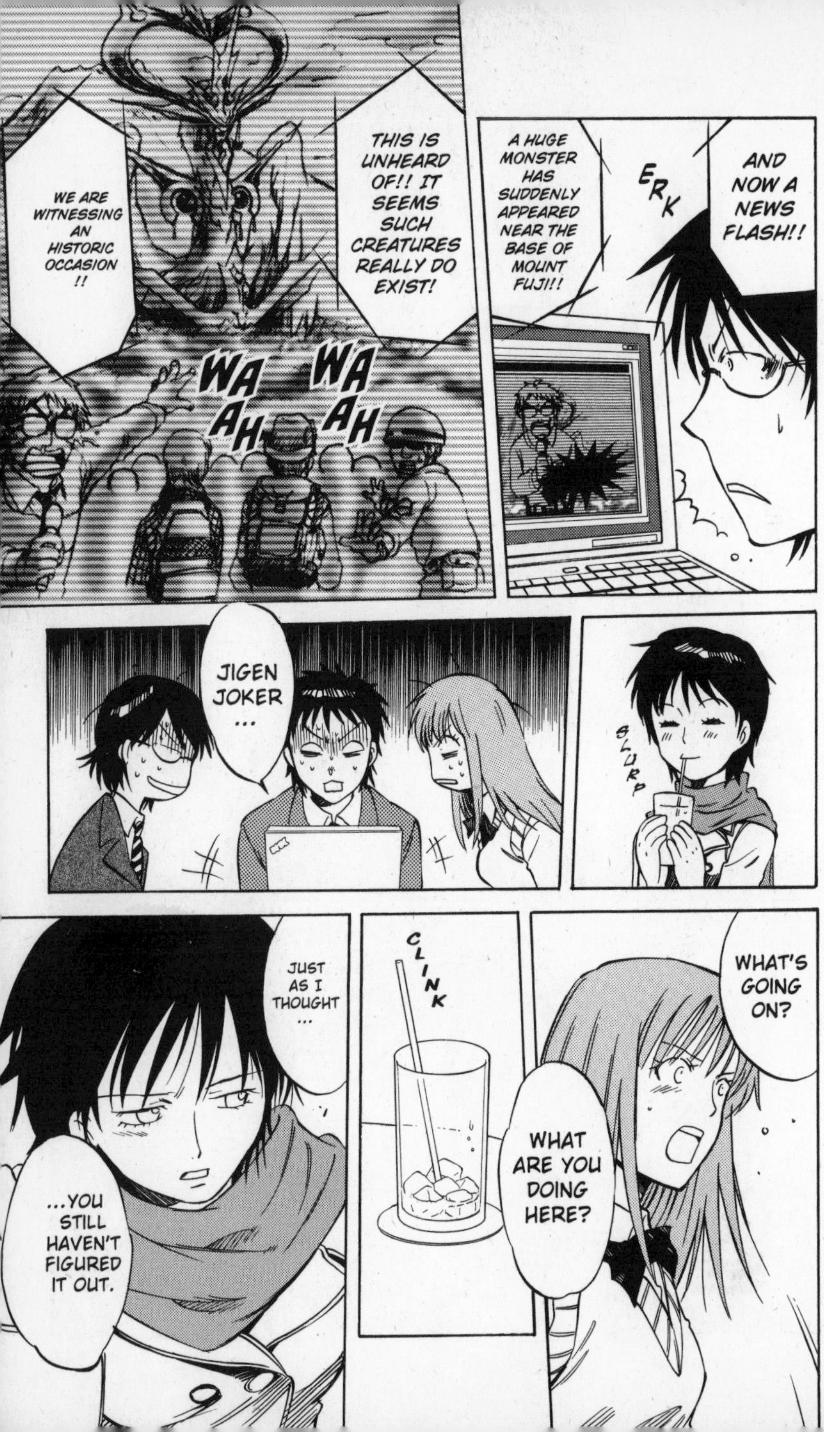
AND NOW A NEWS FLASH!!
ERK
A HUGE MONSTER HAS SUDDENLY APPEARED NEAR THE BASE OF MOUNT FUJI!!
THIS IS UNHEARD OF!! IT SEEMS SUCH CREATURES REALLY DO EXIST!
WE ARE WITNESSING AN HISTORIC OCCASION!!
WAAAH
WAAAH
SLURP
JIGEN JOKER...
WHAT'S GOING ON?
WHAT ARE YOU DOING HERE?
CLINK
JUST AS I THOUGHT...
...YOU STILL HAVEN'T FIGURED IT OUT.

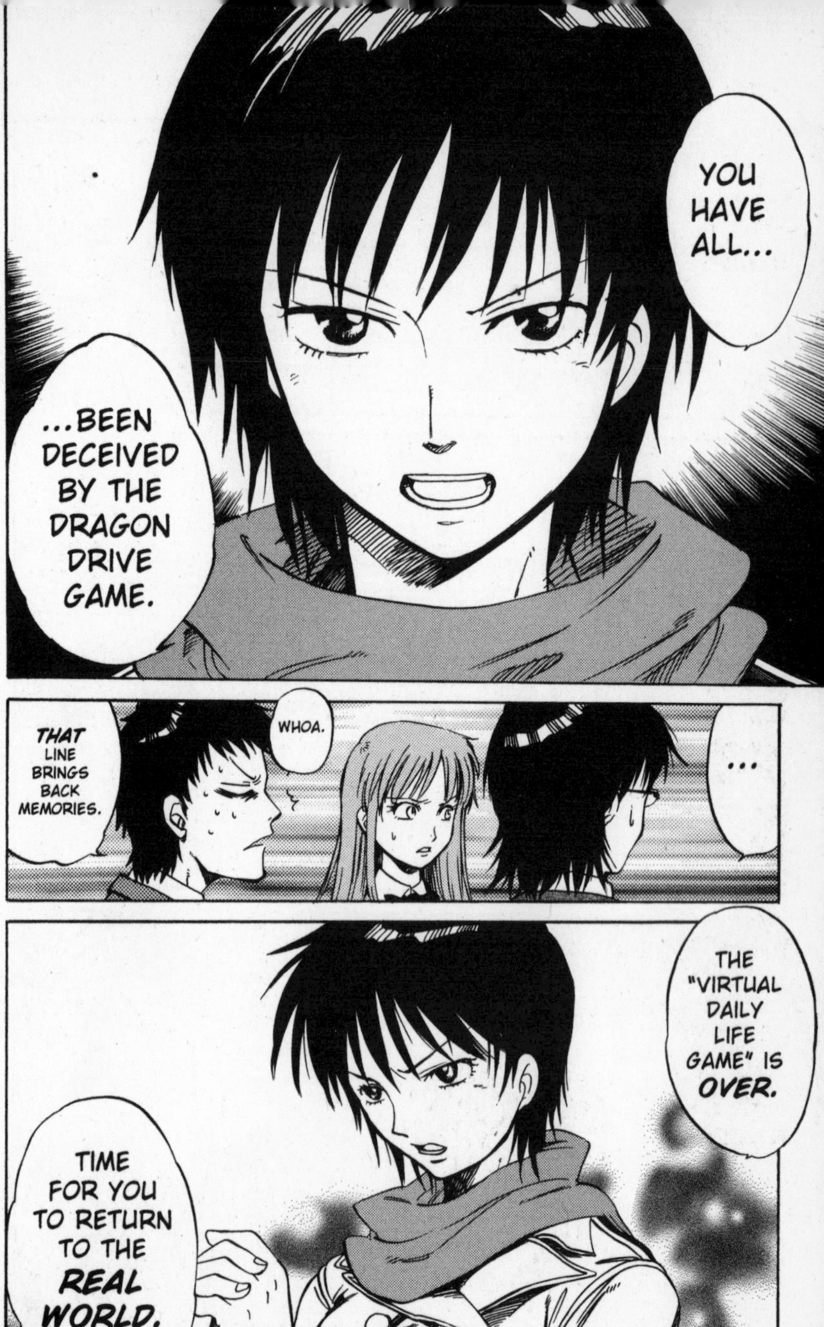
YOU HAVE ALL...
...BEEN DECEIVED BY THE DRAGON DRIVE GAME.
...
WHOA.
THAT LINE BRINGS BACK MEMORIES.
THE "VIRTUAL DAILY LIFE GAME" IS OVER.
TIME FOR YOU TO RETURN TO THE REAL WORLD.

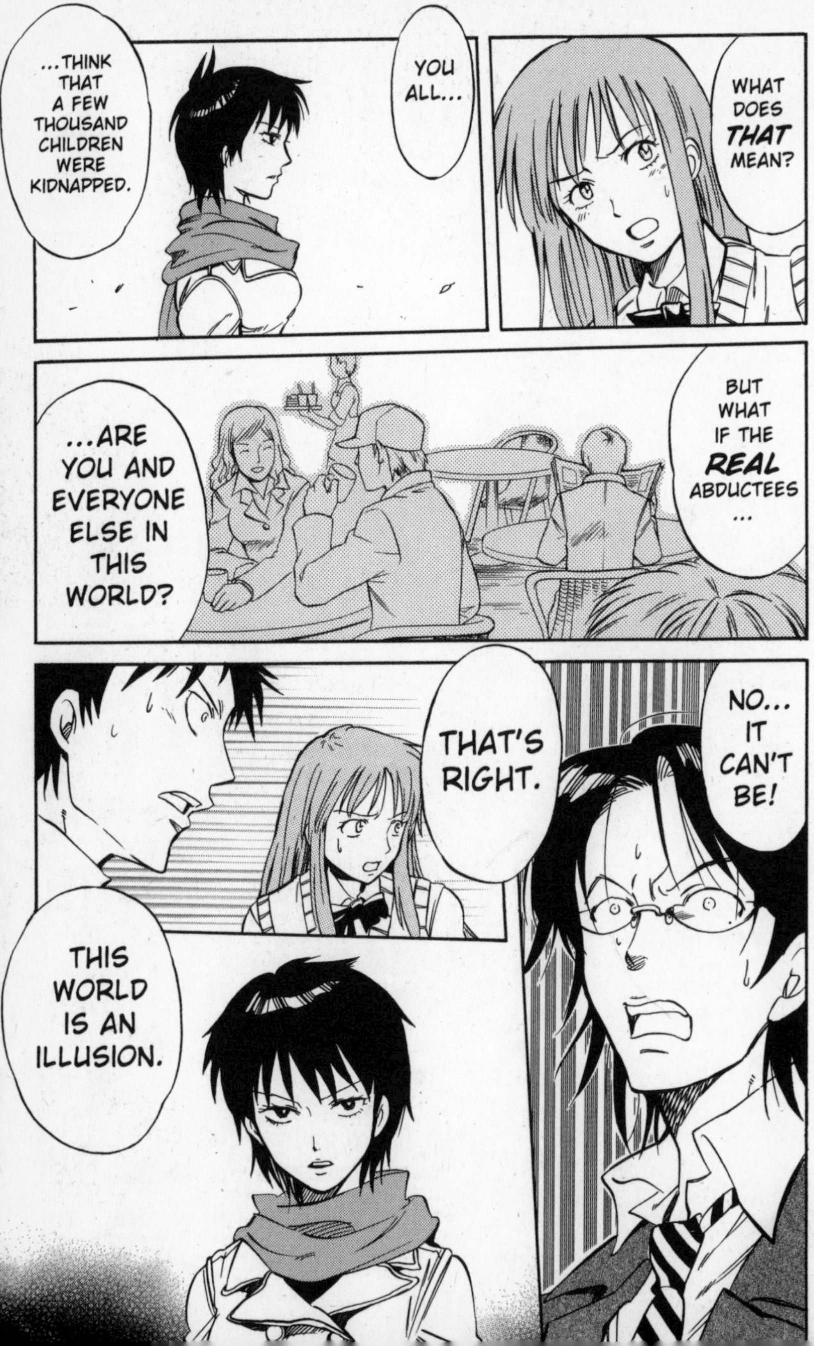
WHAT DOES THAT MEAN?
YOU ALL...
...THINK THAT A FEW THOUSAND CHILDREN WERE KIDNAPPED.
BUT WHAT IF THE REAL ABDUCTEES ...
...ARE YOU AND EVERYONE ELSE IN THIS WORLD?
NO... IT CAN'T BE!
THAT'S RIGHT.
THIS WORLD IS AN ILLUSION.

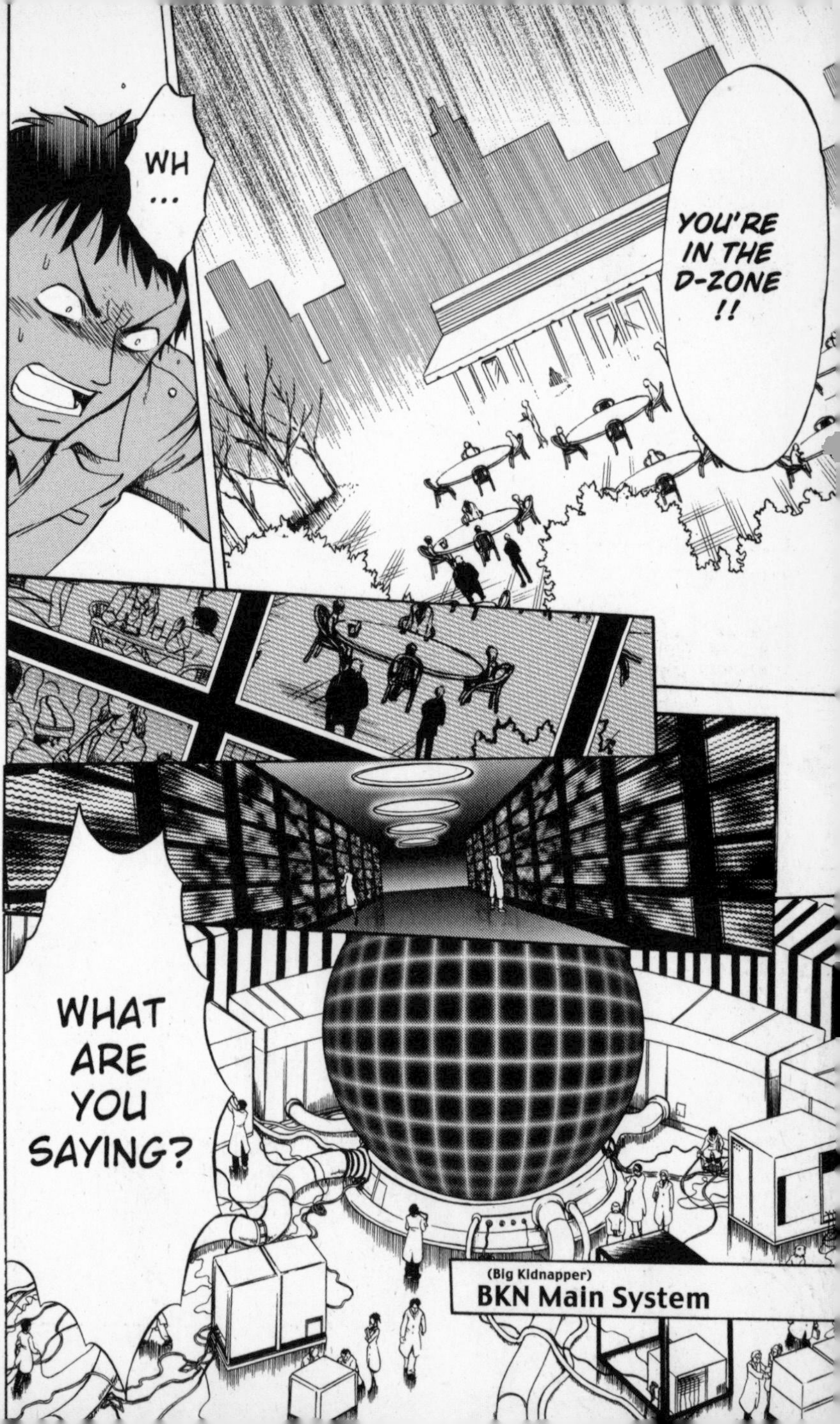
YOU'RE IN THE D-ZONE !!
WH ...
WHAT ARE YOU SAYING?
(Big Kidnapper)
BKN Main System

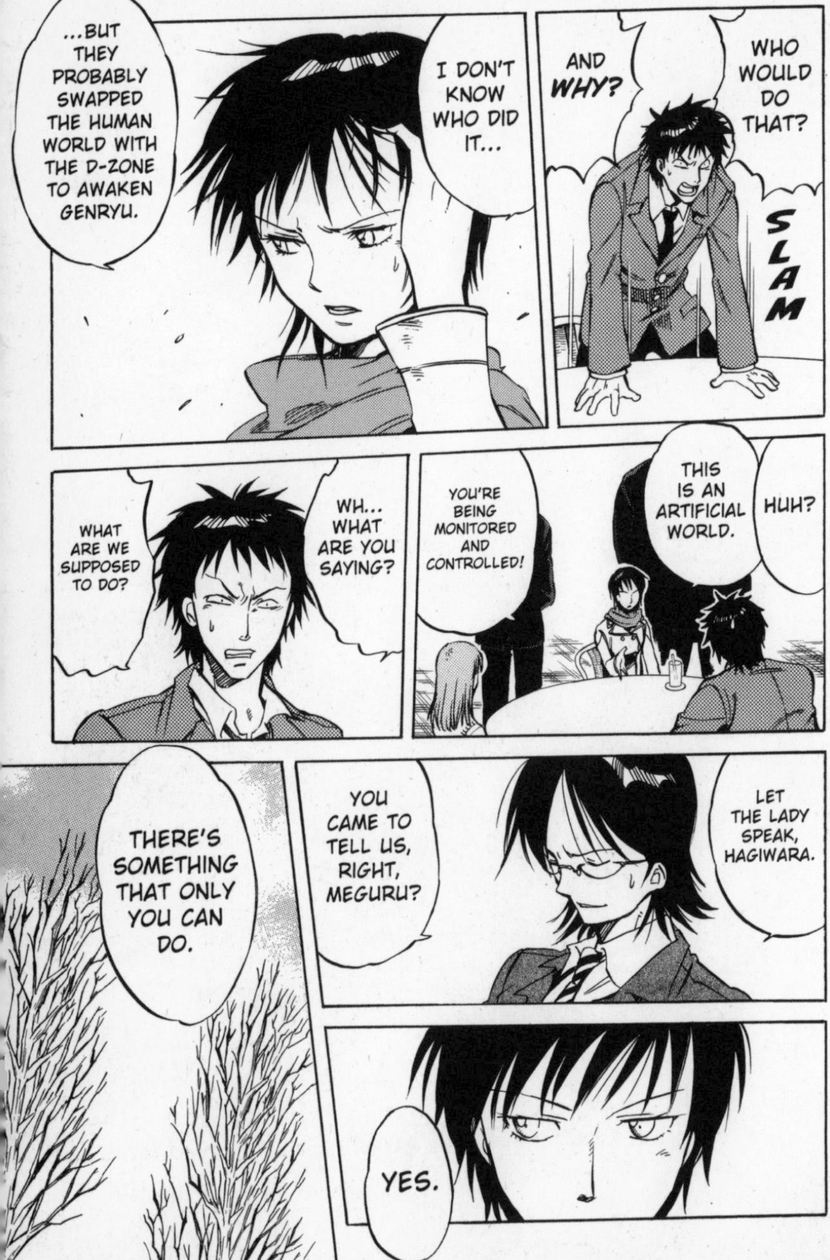
WHO WOULD DO THAT?
AND WHY?
SLAM
I DON'T KNOW WHO DID IT...
...BUT THEY PROBABLY SWAPPED THE HUMAN WORLD WITH THE D-ZONE TO AWAKEN GENRYU.
HUH?
THIS IS AN ARTIFICIAL WORLD.
YOU'RE BEING MONITORED AND CONTROLLED!
WH... WHAT ARE YOU SAYING?
WHAT ARE WE SUPPOSED TO DO?
LET THE LADY SPEAK, HAGIWARA.
YOU CAME TO TELL US, RIGHT, MEGURU?
YES.
THERE'S SOMETHING THAT ONLY YOU CAN DO.

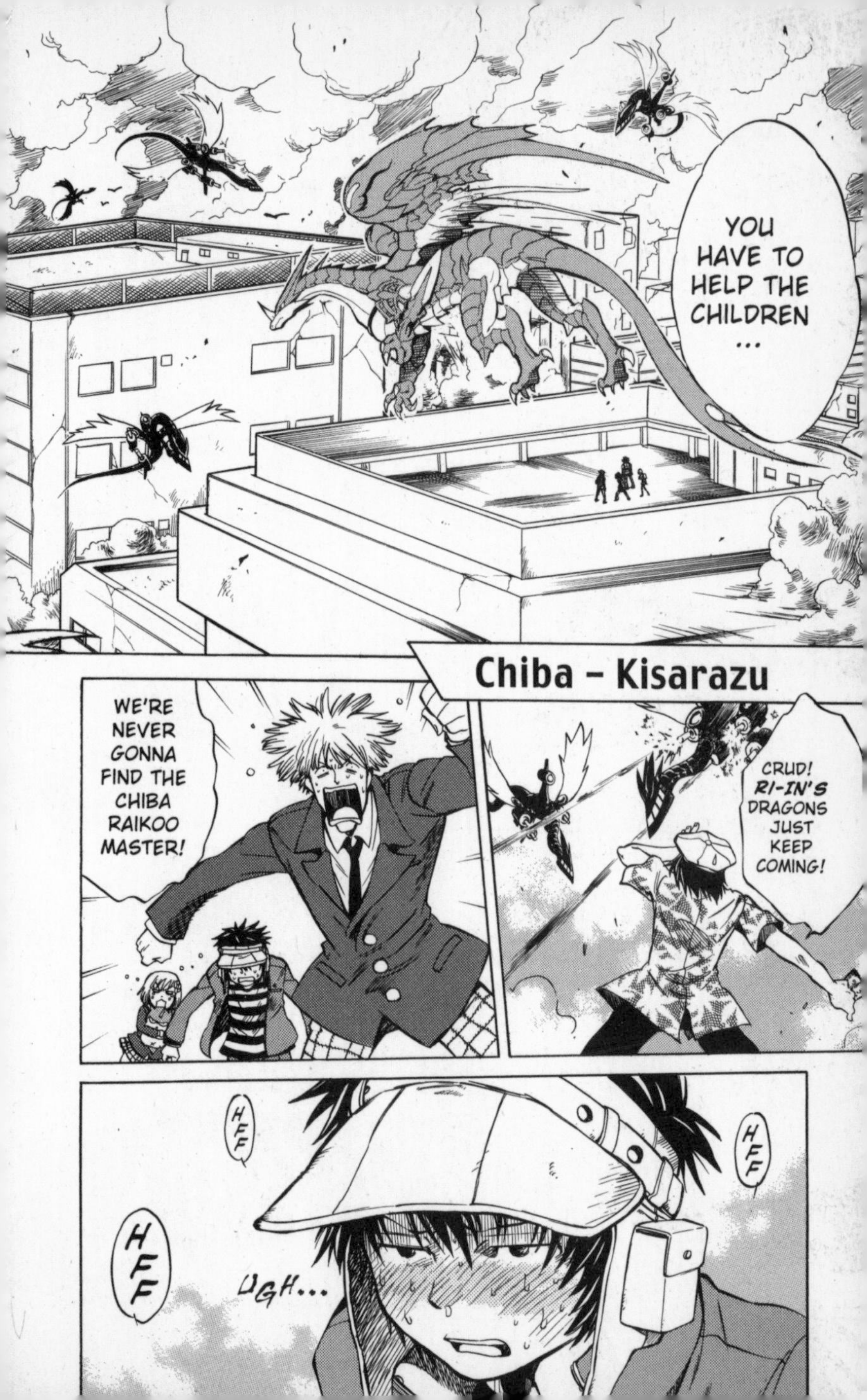
YOU HAVE TO HELP THE CHILDREN ...
Chiba - Kisarazu
CRUD! RI-IN'S DRAGONS JUST KEEP COMING!
WE'RE NEVER GONNA FIND THE CHIBA RAIKOO MASTER!
HFF
HFF
HFF
UGH...

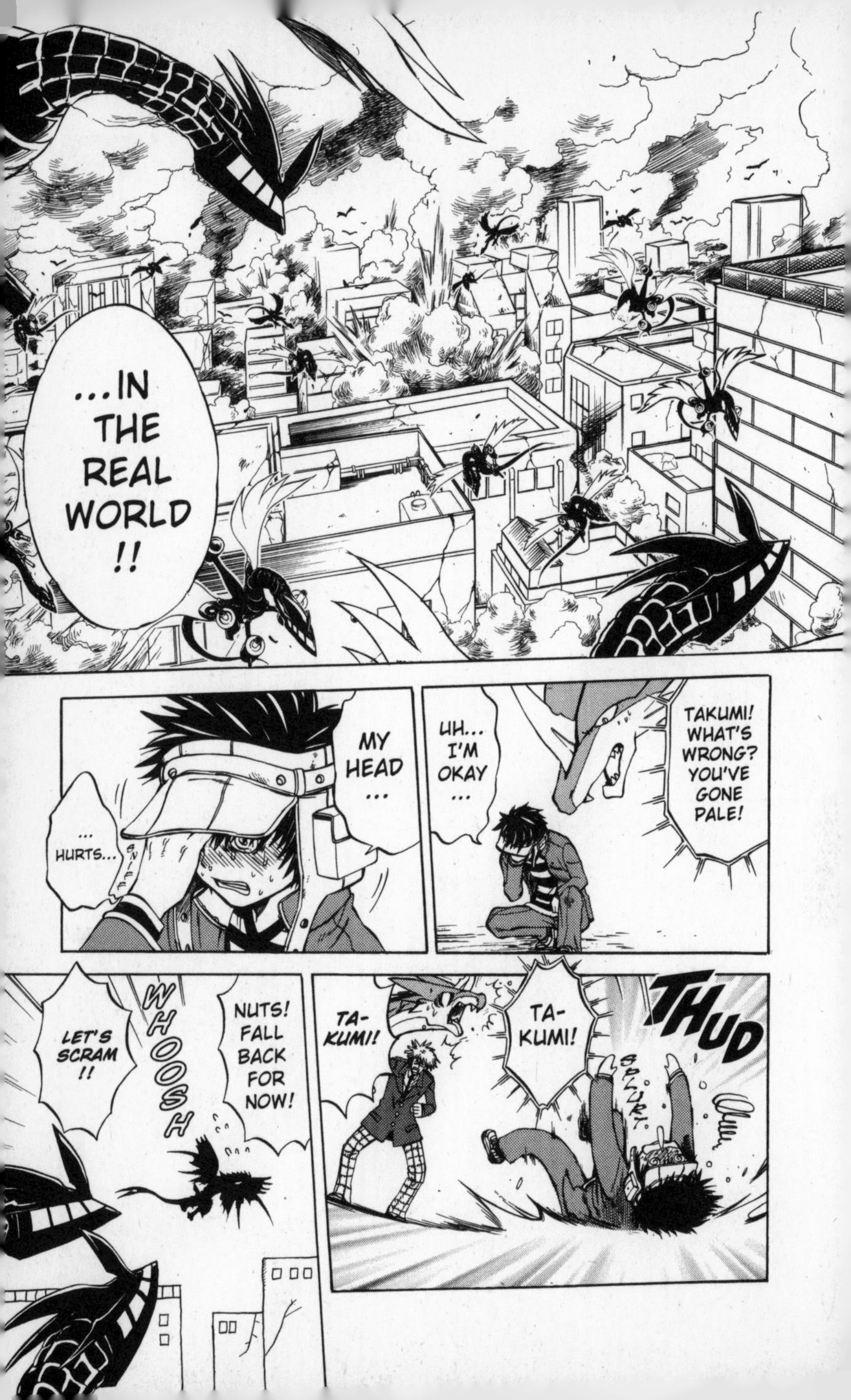
...IN THE REAL WORLD !!
TAKUMI! WHAT'S WRONG? YOU'VE GONE PALE!
UH... I'M OKAY ...
MY HEAD ...
... HURTS...
SNIFF
THUD
TA-KUMI!
TA-KUMI!
SPLURT
NUTS! FALL BACK FOR NOW!
WHOOSH
LET'S SCRAM !!

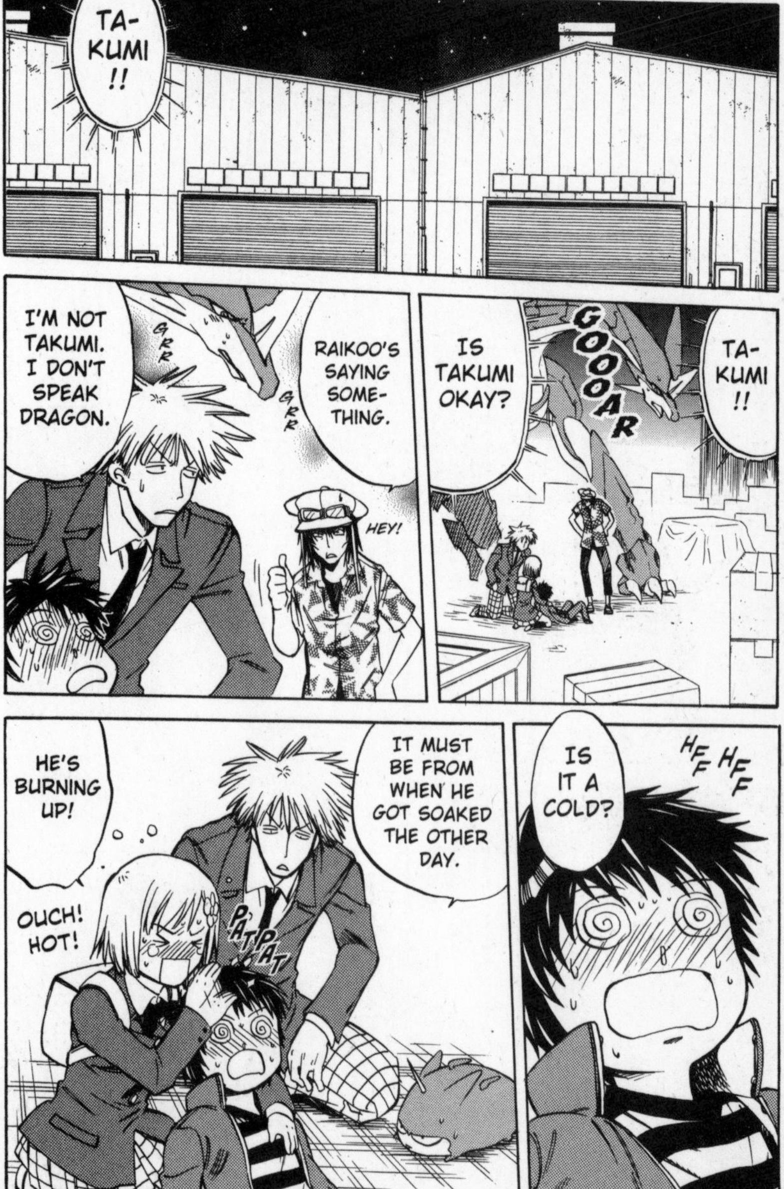
TA-KUMI!!
TA-KUMI!!
GOOOAR
IS TAKUMI OKAY?
RAIKOO'S SAYING SOME-THING.
GRR
GRR
I'M NOT TAKUMI. I DON'T SPEAK DRAGON.
HEY!
HFF HFF
IS IT A COLD?
IT MUST BE FROM WHEN HE GOT SOAKED THE OTHER DAY.
HE'S BURNING UP!
PAT PAT
OUCH! HOT!

READ THIS WAY

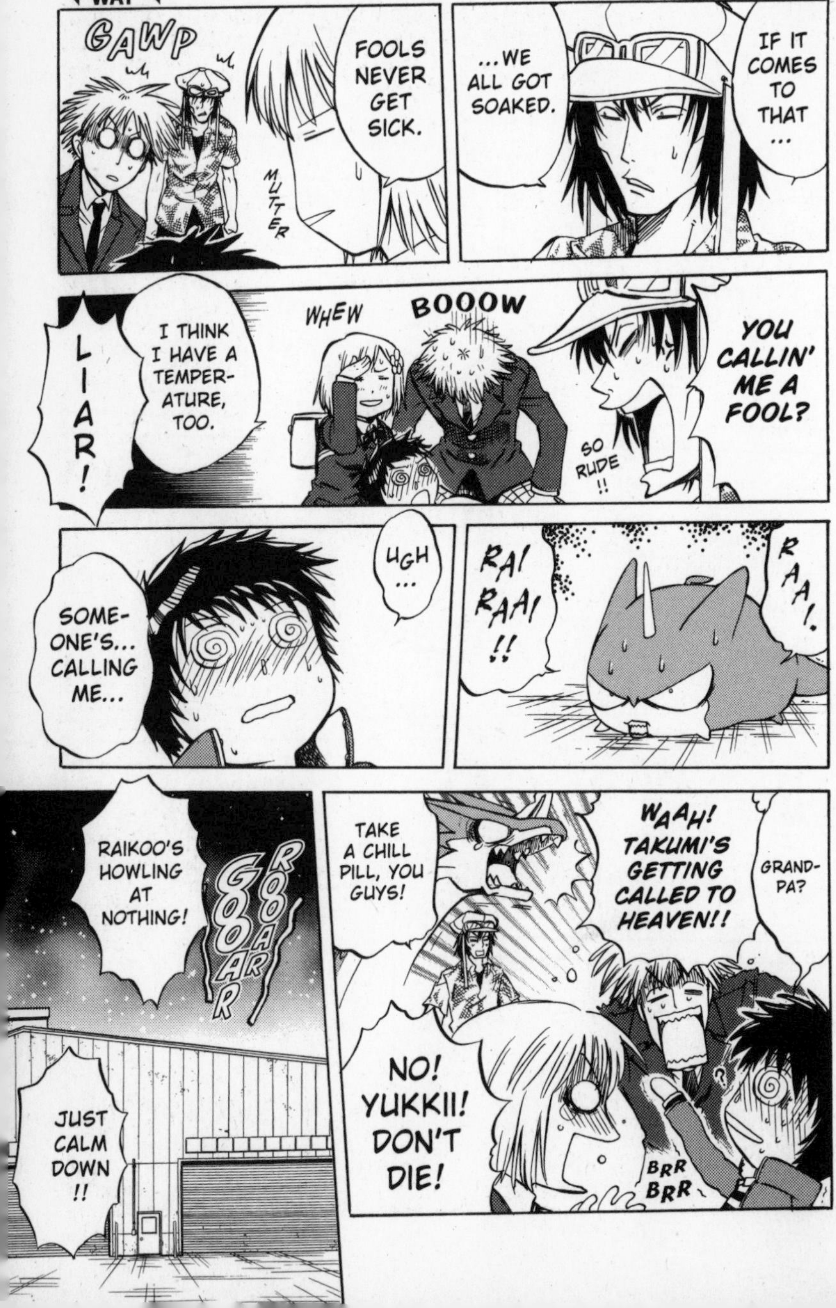
IF IT COMES TO THAT ...
...WE ALL GOT SOAKED.
FOOLS NEVER GET SICK.
MUTTER
GAWP
YOU CALLIN' ME A FOOL?
SO RUDE !!
BOOOW
WHEW
I THINK I HAVE A TEMPER-ATURE, TOO.
LIAR!
RAAA!
RAI RAAI !!
UGH ...
SOME-ONE'S... CALLING ME...
GRAND-PA?
WAAH! TAKUMI'S GETTING CALLED TO HEAVEN!!
TAKE A CHILL PILL, YOU GUYS!
NO! YUKKII! DON'T DIE!
BRR BRR
RAIKOO'S HOWLING AT NOTHING!
JUST CALM DOWN !!

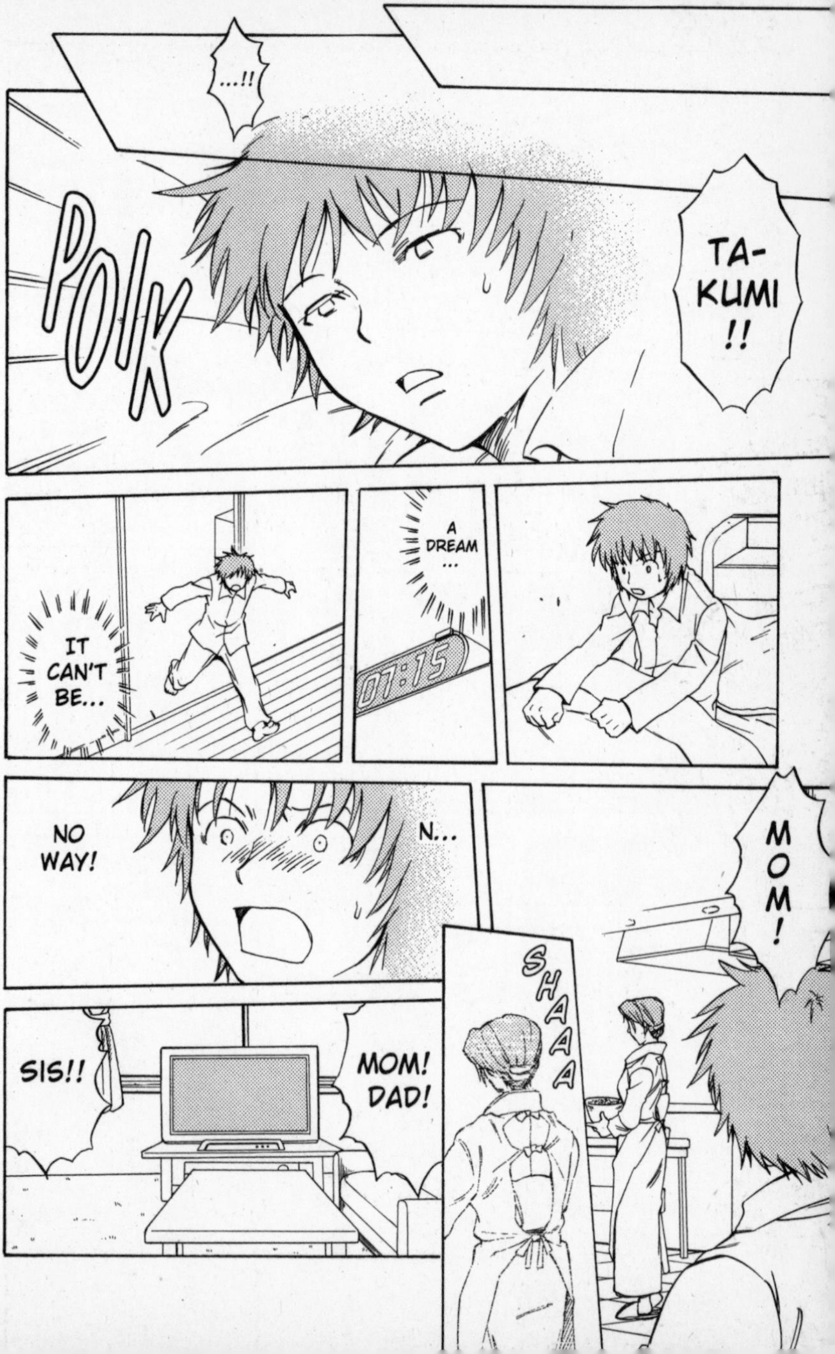
TA-KUMI!!
POLK
...!!
A DREAM...
07:15
IT CAN'T BE...
MOM!
SHAAA
N...
NO WAY!
MOM! DAD!
SIS!!

READ THIS WAY

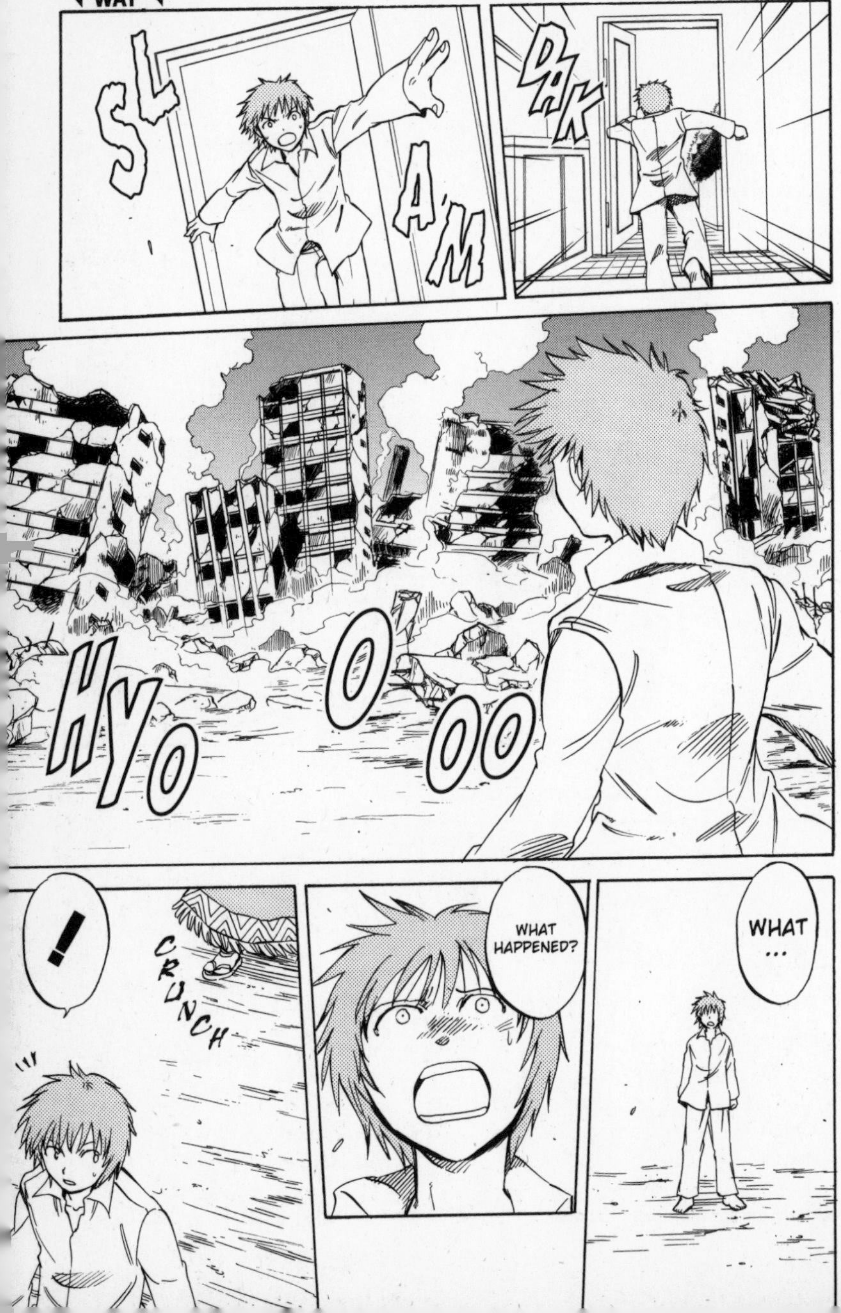
DAK
SLAM
HYOOOOO
WHAT ...
WHAT HAPPENED?
!
CRUNCH

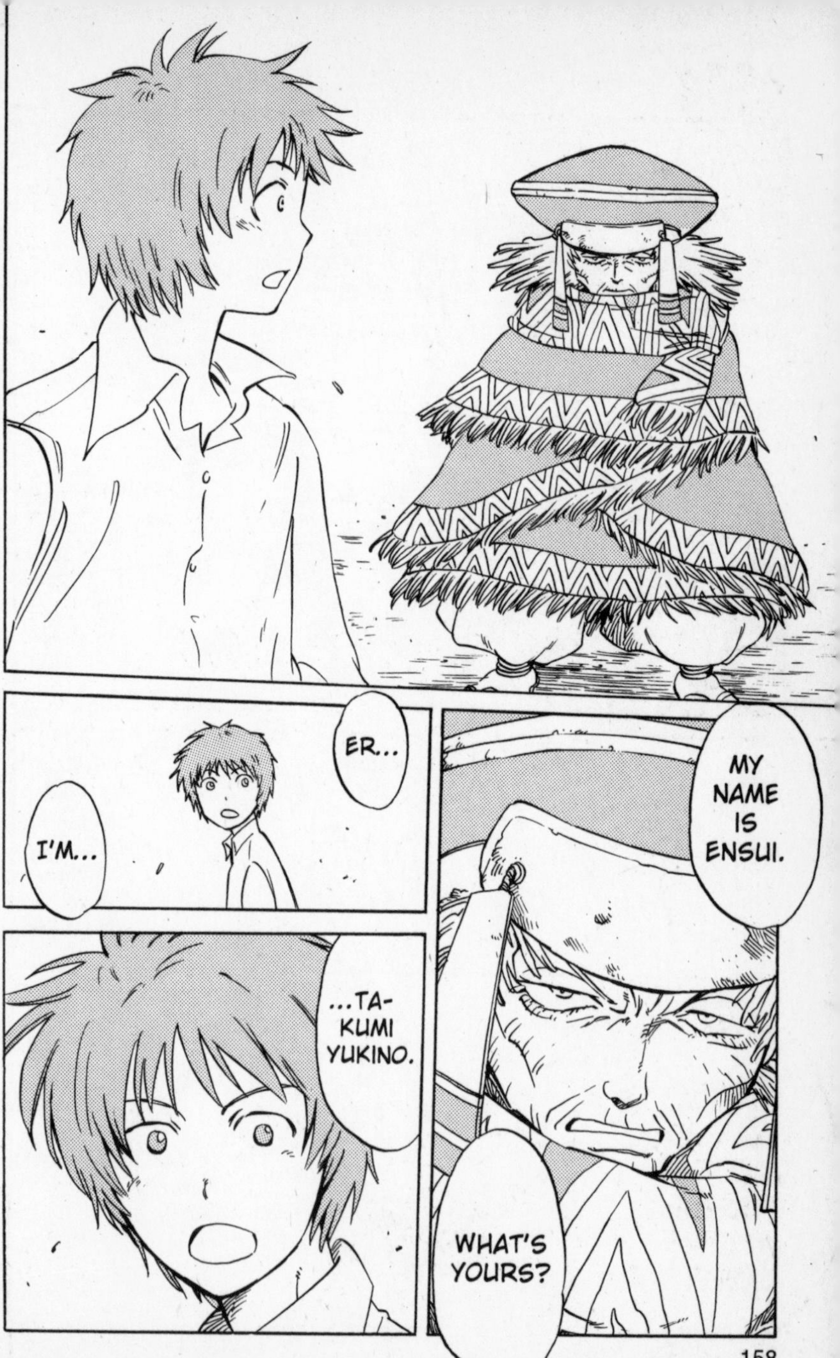
MY NAME IS ENSUI.
WHAT'S YOURS?
ER...
I'M...
...TA-KUMI YUKINO.

READ THIS WAY

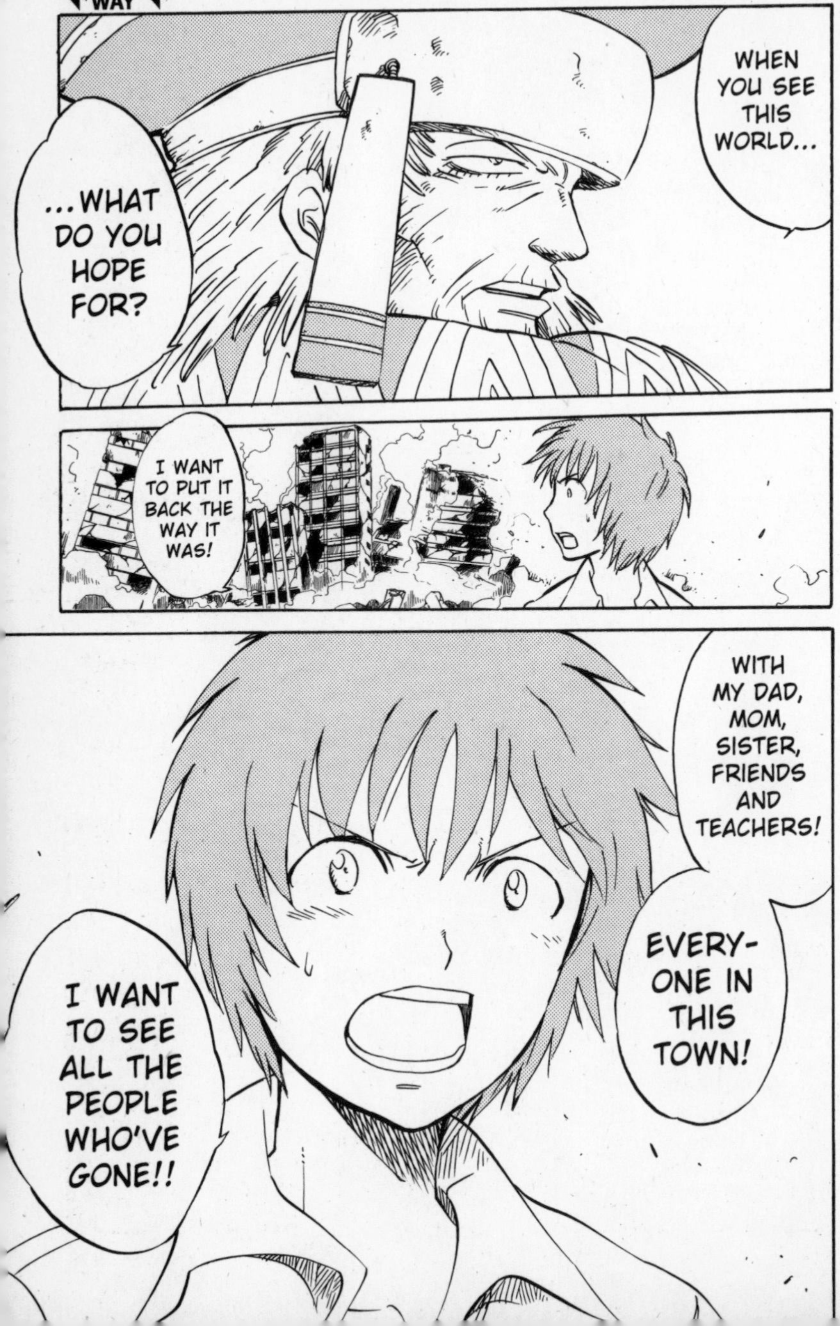
WHEN YOU SEE THIS WORLD...
...WHAT DO YOU HOPE FOR?
I WANT TO PUT IT BACK THE WAY IT WAS!
WITH MY DAD, MOM, SISTER, FRIENDS AND TEACHERS!
EVERY-ONE IN THIS TOWN!
I WANT TO SEE ALL THE PEOPLE WHO'VE GONE!!

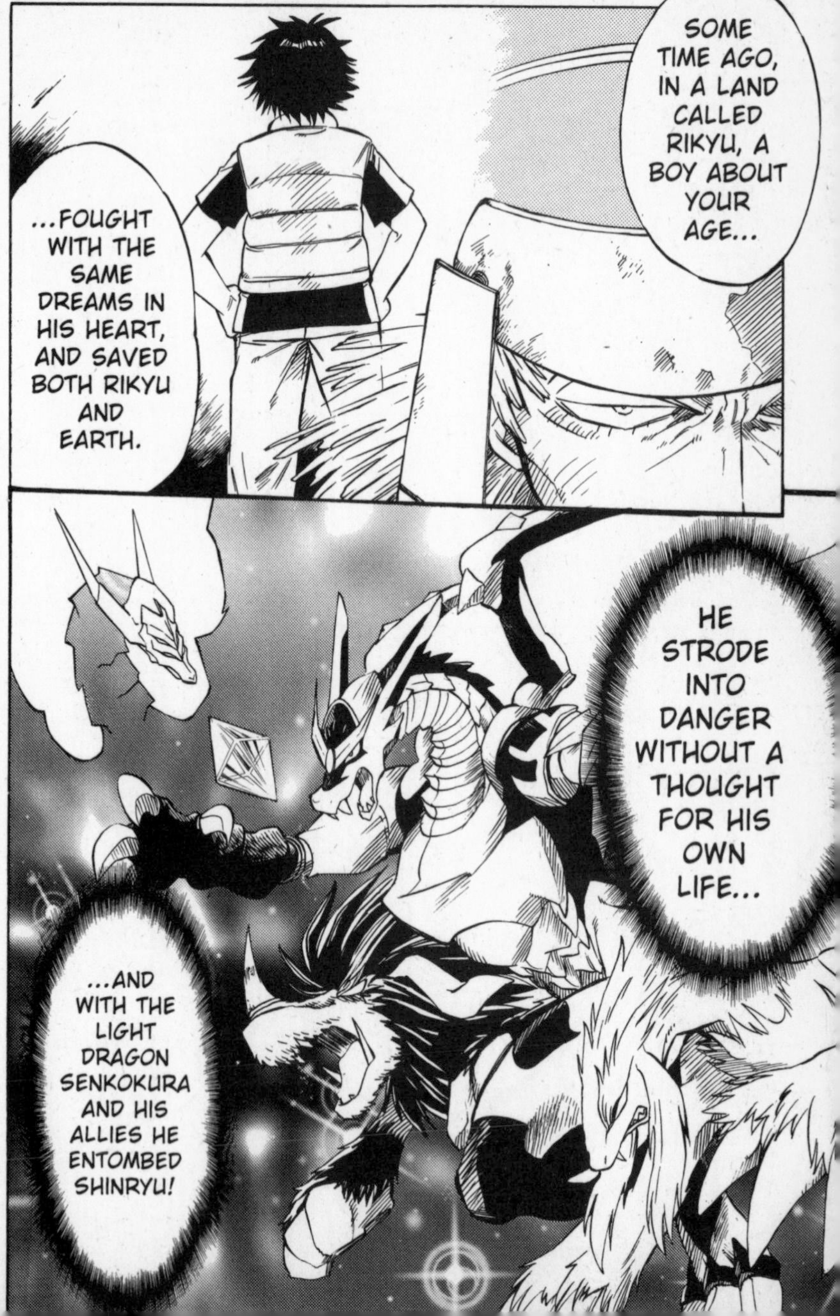
SOME TIME AGO, IN A LAND CALLED RIKYU, A BOY ABOUT YOUR AGE...
...FOUGHT WITH THE SAME DREAMS IN HIS HEART, AND SAVED BOTH RIKYU AND EARTH.
HE STRODE INTO DANGER WITHOUT A THOUGHT FOR HIS OWN LIFE...
...AND WITH THE LIGHT DRAGON SENKOKURA AND HIS ALLIES HE ENTOMBED SHINRYU!

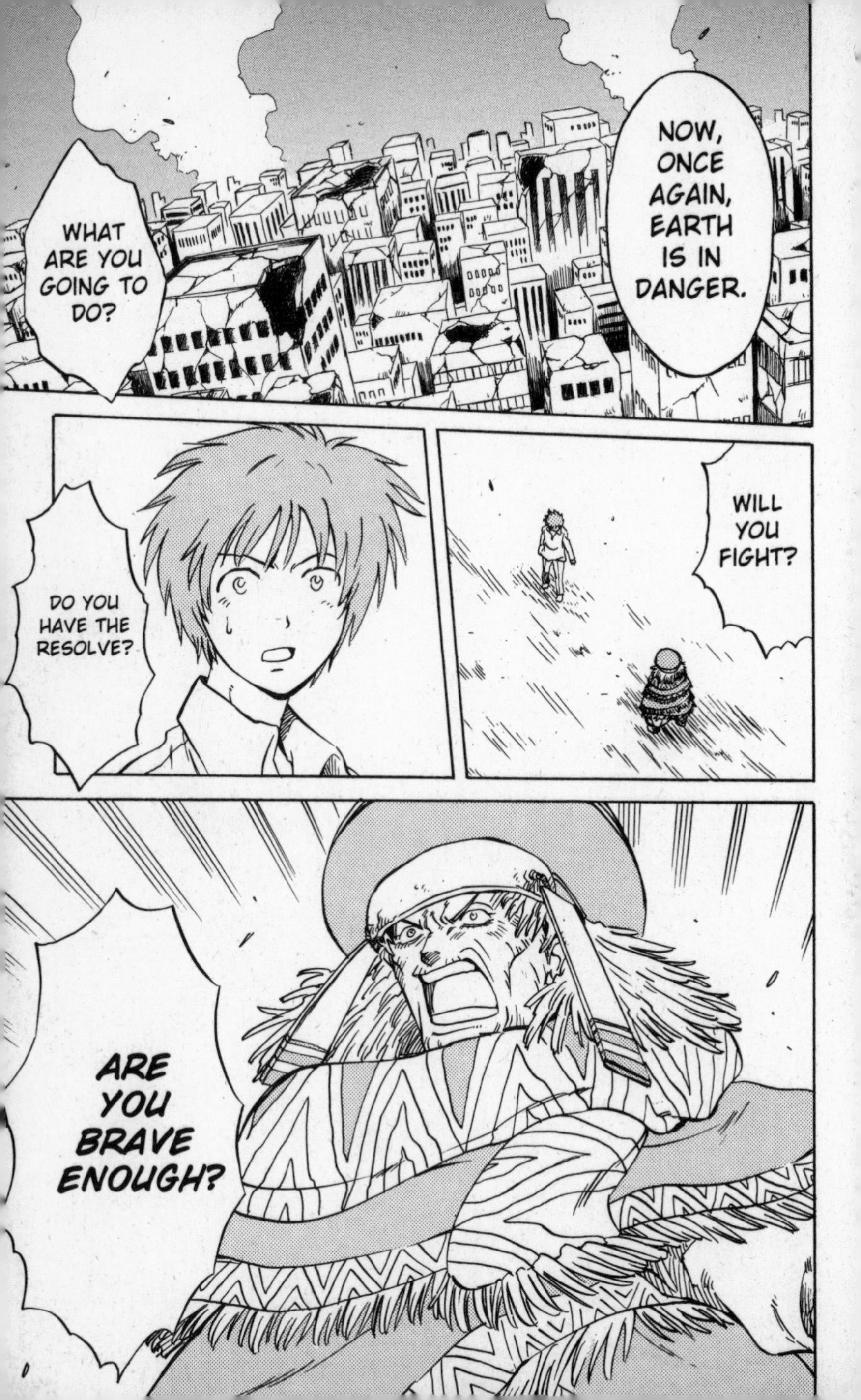
NOW, ONCE AGAIN, EARTH IS IN DANGER.
WHAT ARE YOU GOING TO DO?
WILL YOU FIGHT?
DO YOU HAVE THE RESOLVE?
ARE YOU BRAVE ENOUGH?

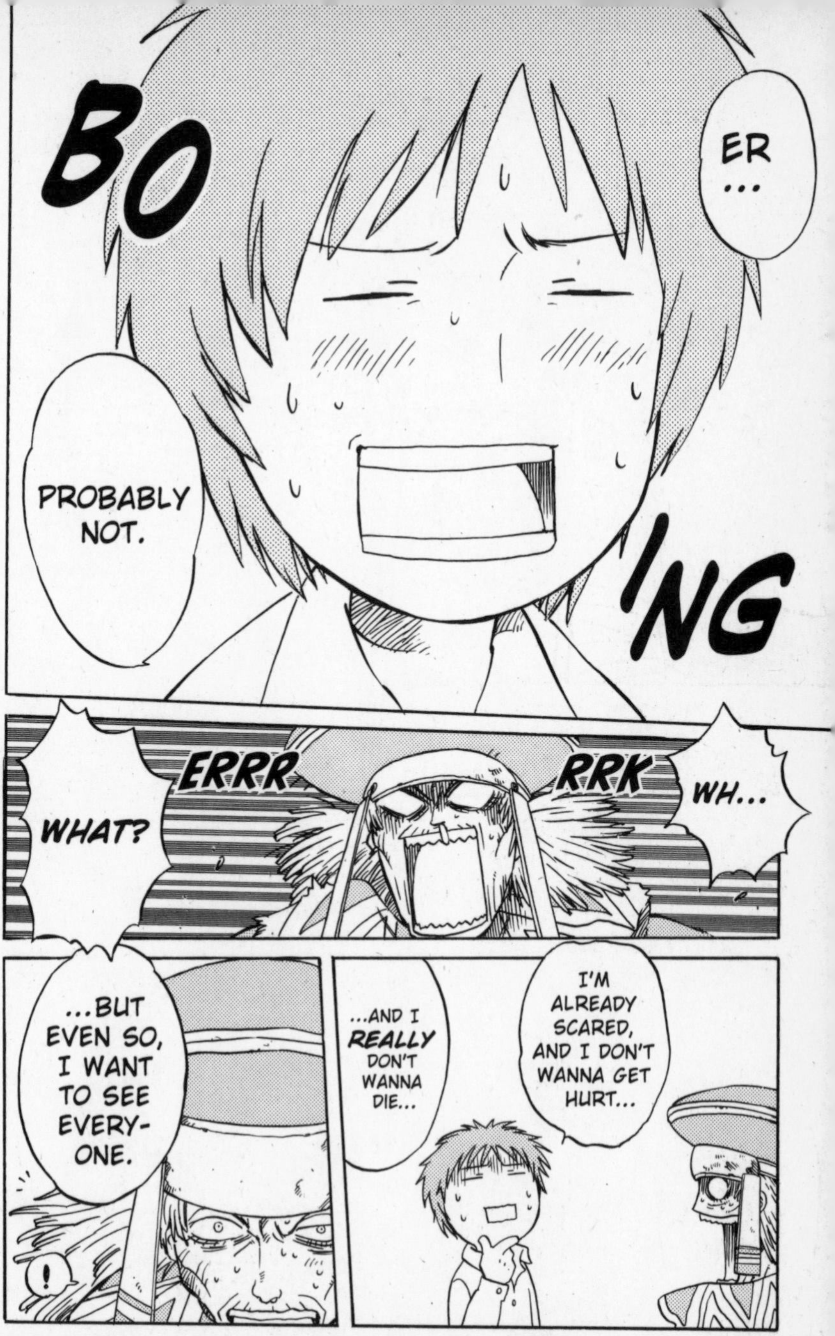
ER...
BO
ING
PROBABLY NOT.
WH...
ERRR
RRK
WHAT?
I'M ALREADY SCARED, AND I DON'T WANNA GET HURT...
...AND I **REALLY** DON'T WANNA DIE...
...BUT EVEN SO, I WANT TO SEE EVERY-ONE.
!

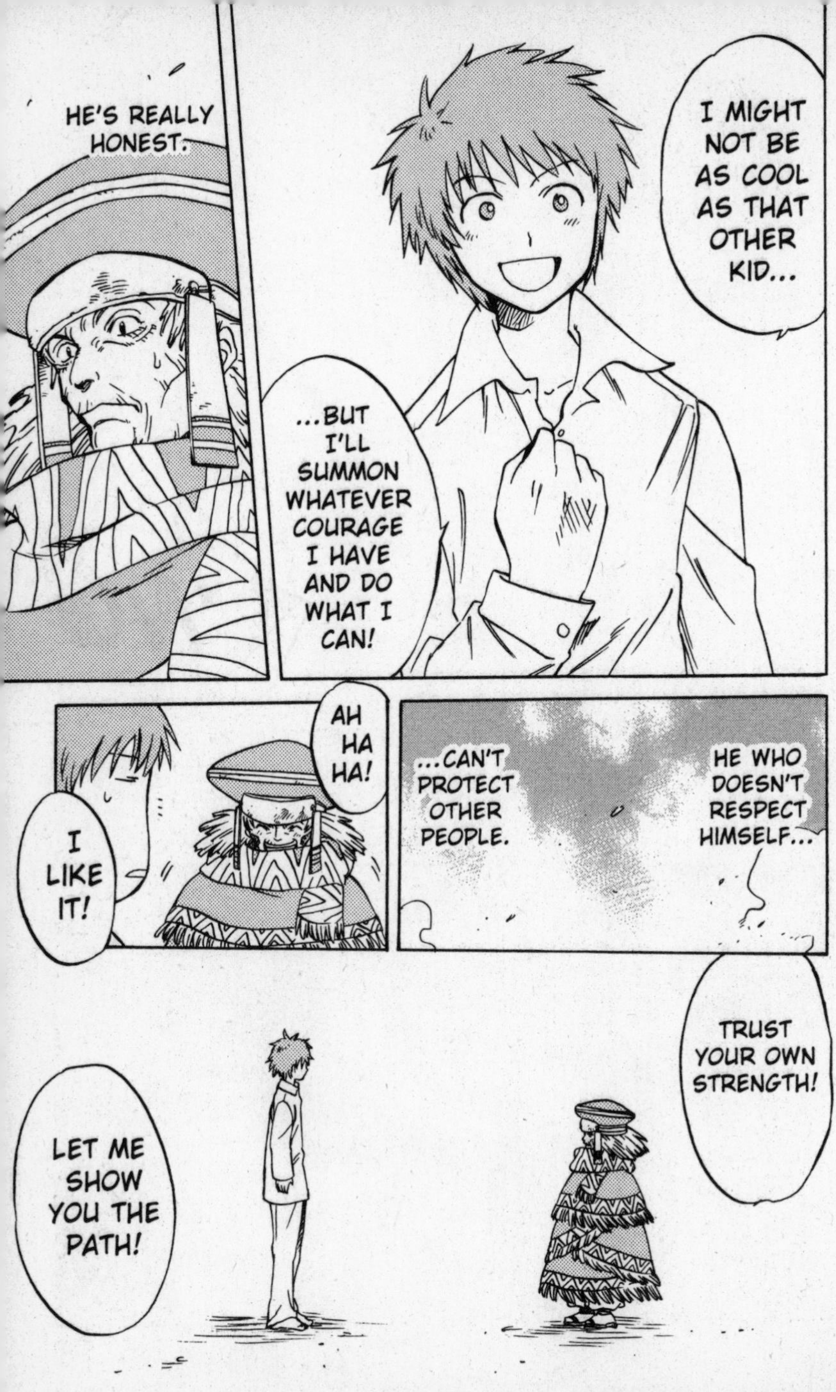
I MIGHT NOT BE AS COOL AS THAT OTHER KID...
...BUT I'LL SUMMON WHATEVER COURAGE I HAVE AND DO WHAT I CAN!
HE'S REALLY HONEST.
HE WHO DOESN'T RESPECT HIMSELF...
...CAN'T PROTECT OTHER PEOPLE.
AH HA HA!
I LIKE IT!
TRUST YOUR OWN STRENGTH!
LET ME SHOW YOU THE PATH!

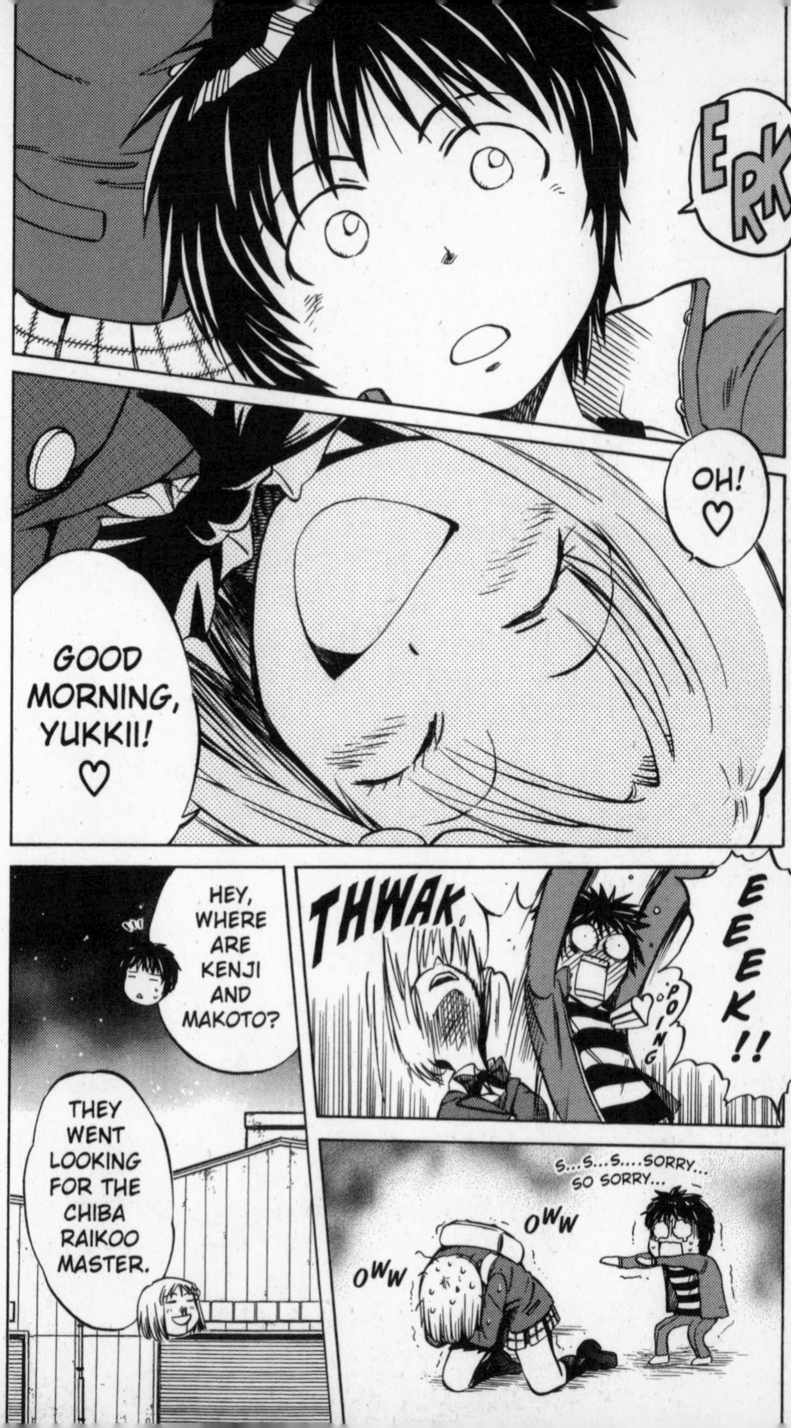
ERK
OH! ♥
GOOD MORNING, YUKKII! ♥
EEEEK!!
POING
THWAK
S...S...S....SORRY... SO SORRY...
OWW
OWW
HEY, WHERE ARE KENJI AND MAKOTO?
THEY WENT LOOKING FOR THE CHIBA RAIKOO MASTER.

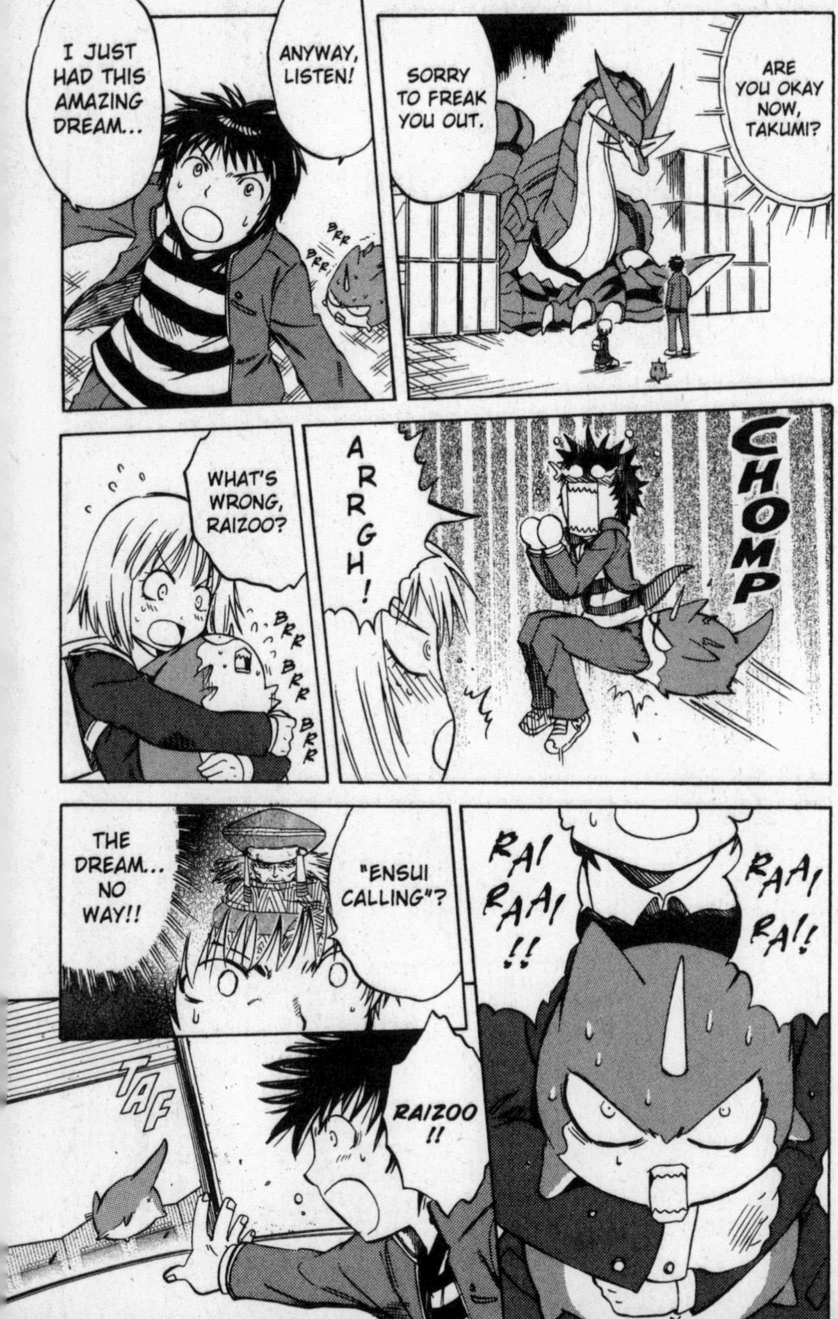
ARE YOU OKAY NOW, TAKUMI?
SORRY TO FREAK YOU OUT.
ANYWAY, LISTEN!
I JUST HAD THIS AMAZING DREAM...
BRR BRR
CHOMP
ARRGH!
WHAT'S WRONG, RAIZOO?
BRR BRR BRR
RAAI RAI!!
RAI RAAI!!
RAIZOO!!
TAF
"ENSUI CALLING"?
THE DREAM... NO WAY!!

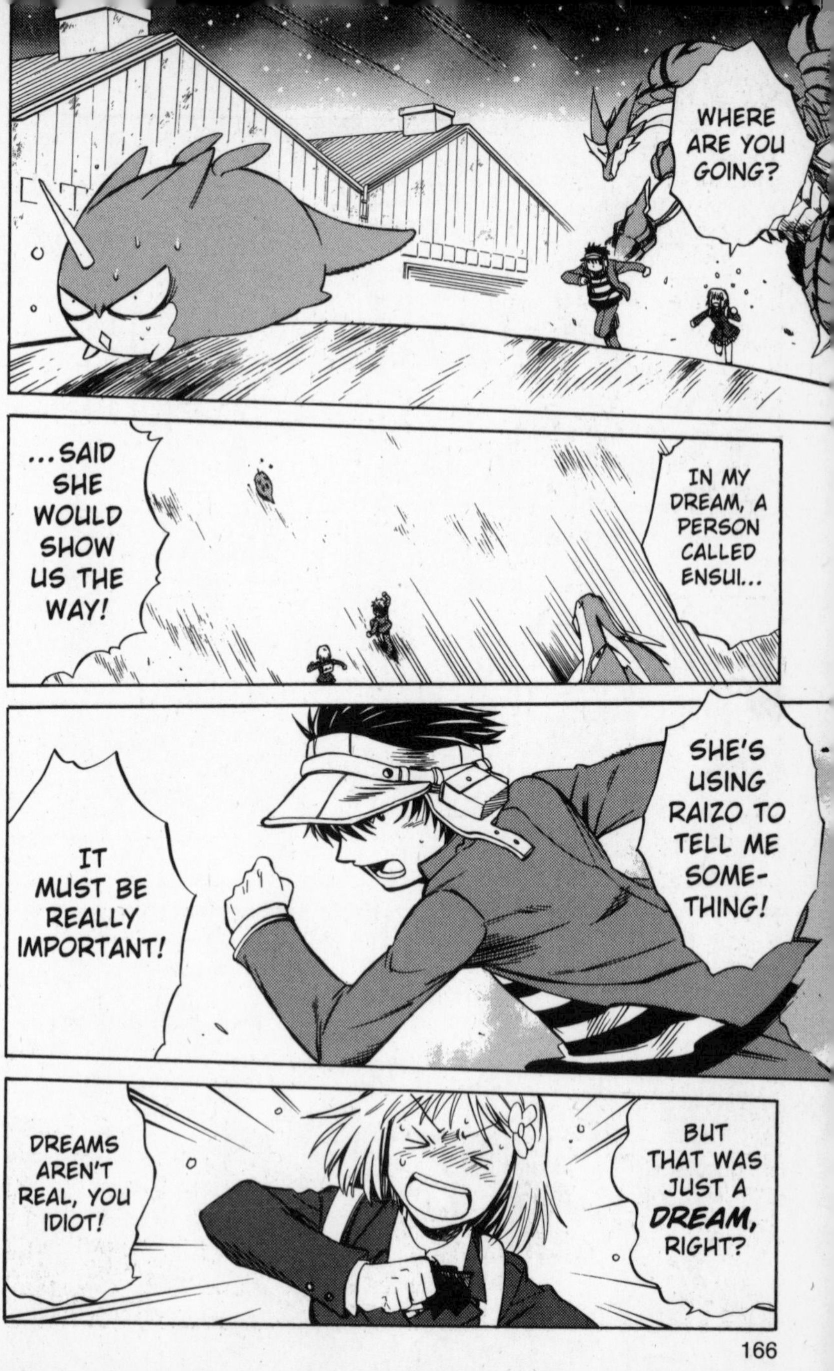
WHERE ARE YOU GOING?
IN MY DREAM, A PERSON CALLED ENSUI...
...SAID SHE WOULD SHOW US THE WAY!
SHE'S USING RAIZO TO TELL ME SOME-THING!
IT MUST BE REALLY IMPORTANT!
BUT THAT WAS JUST A DREAM, RIGHT?
DREAMS AREN'T REAL, YOU IDIOT!

READ THIS WAY

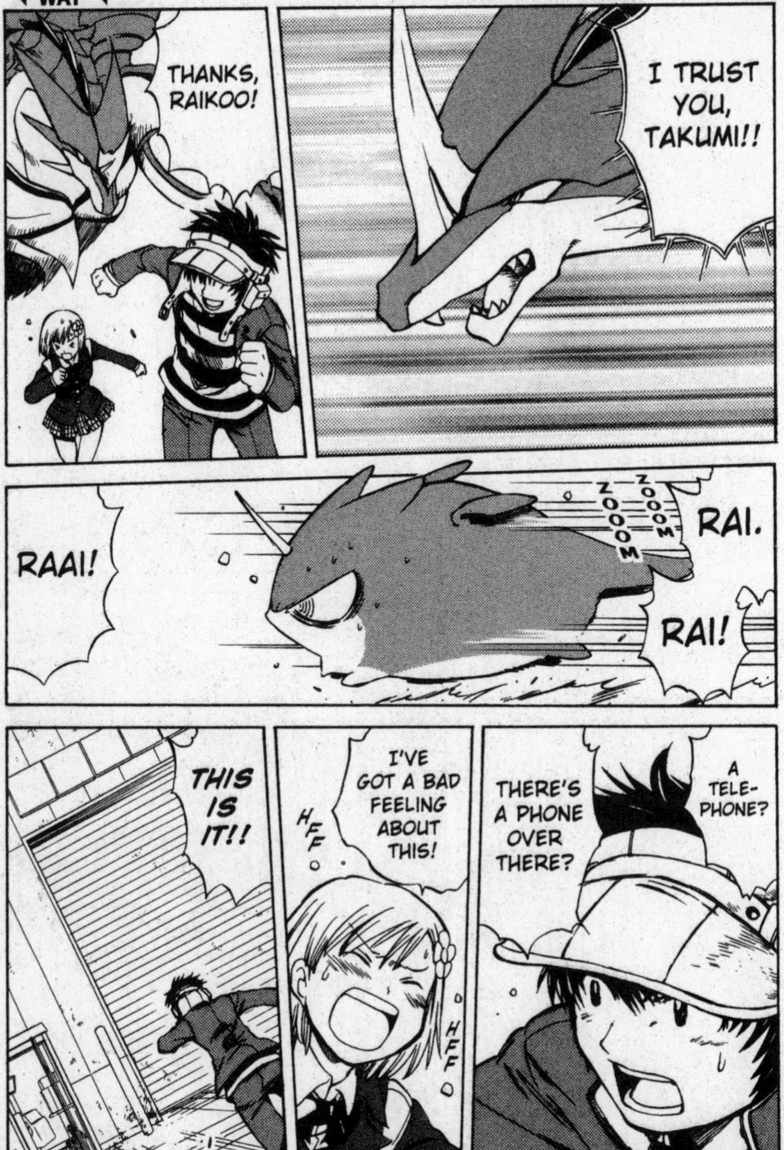

I TRUST YOU, TAKUMI!!
THANKS, RAIKOO!
RAI.
ZOOOOM
ZOOOOM
RAI!
RAAI!
A TELE-PHONE?
THERE'S A PHONE OVER THERE?
I'VE GOT A BAD FEELING ABOUT THIS!
HFF
HFF
THIS IS IT!!

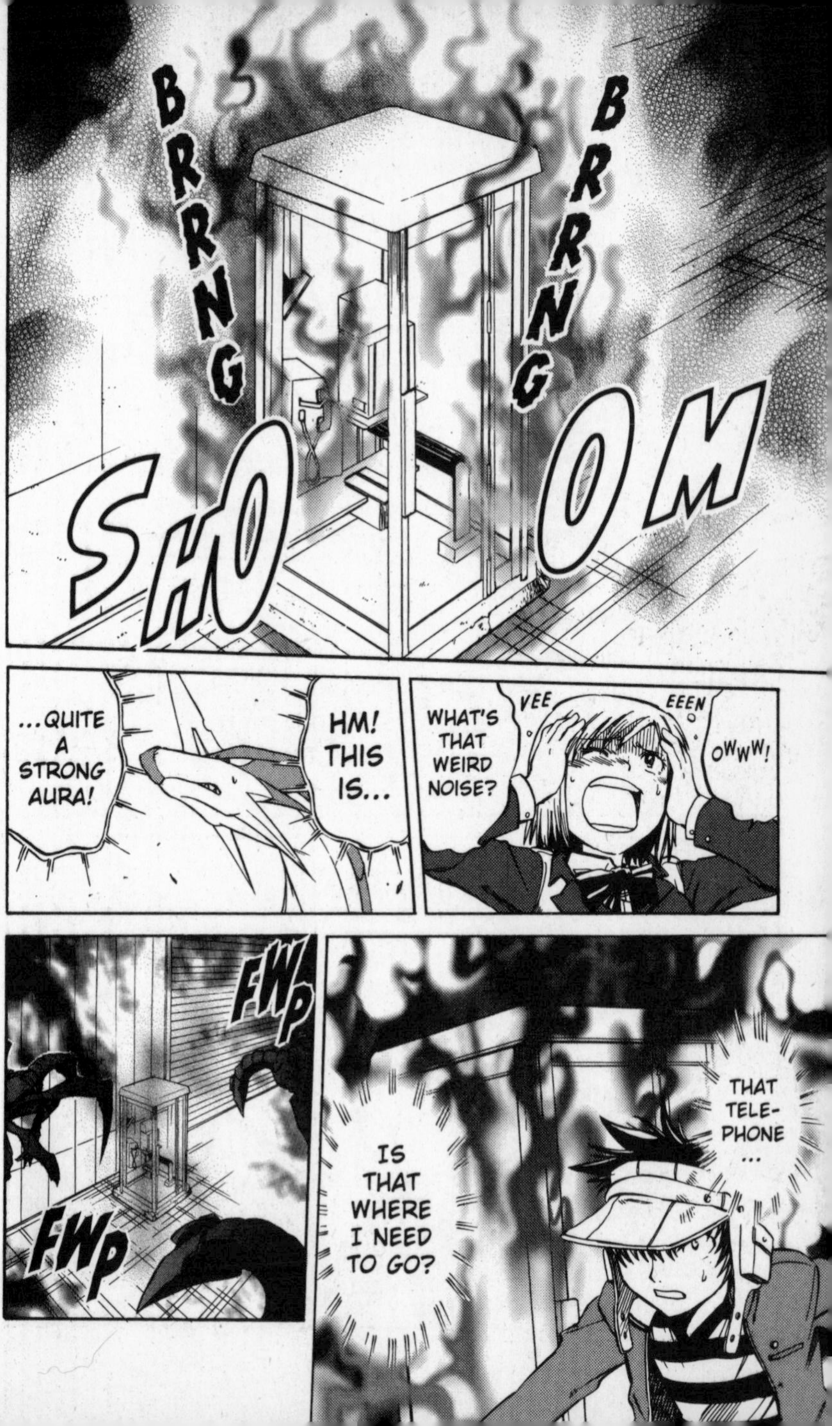
BRRNG
BRRNG
SHOOM
VEE
EEEN
WHAT'S THAT WEIRD NOISE?
OWWW!
HM! THIS IS...
...QUITE A STRONG AURA!
THAT TELE-PHONE ...
IS THAT WHERE I NEED TO GO?
FWP
FWP

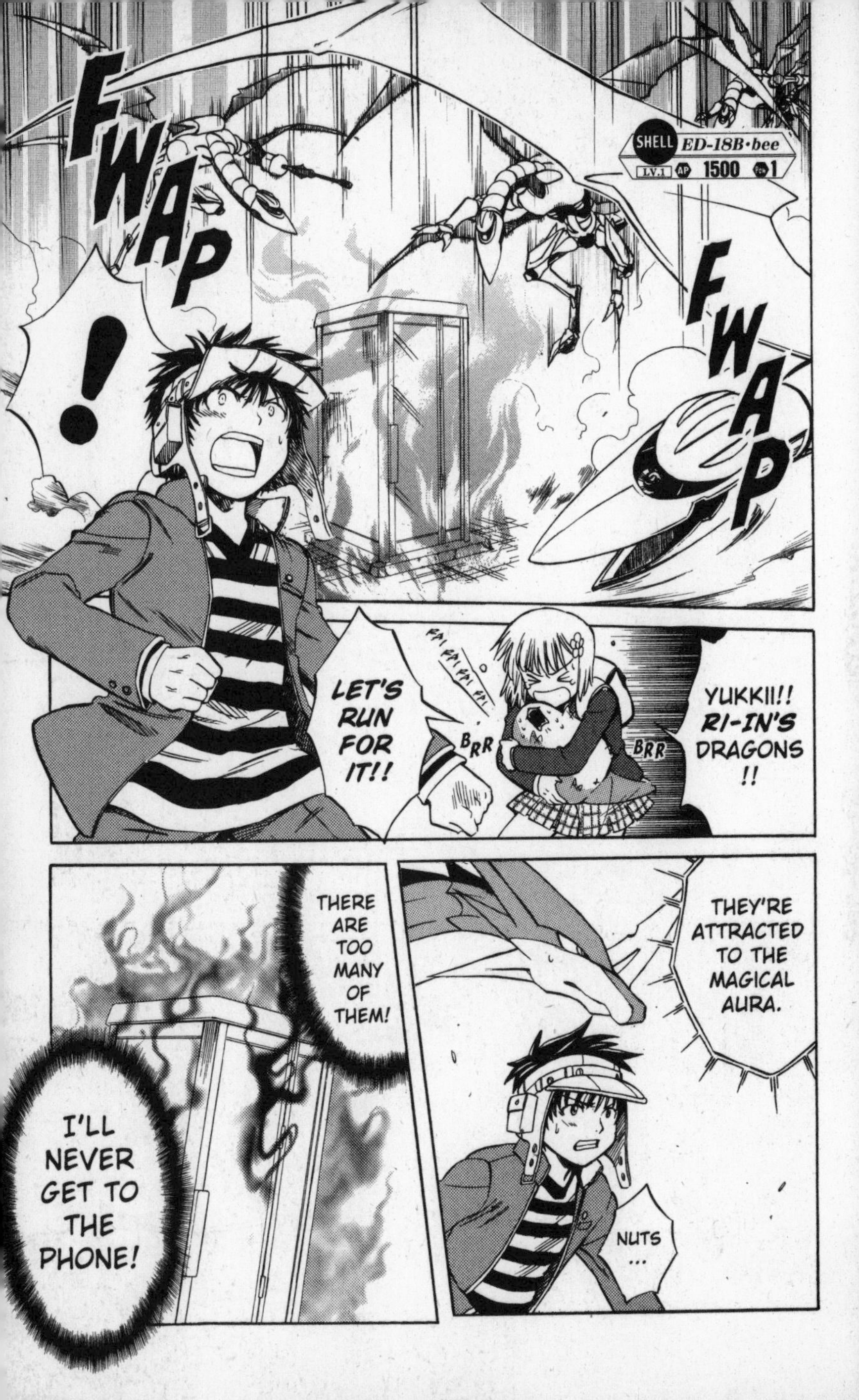
SHELL ED-18B·bee
LV.1 AP 1500 1
FWAP
FWAP
!
YUKKI!! RI-IN'S DRAGONS!!
BRR
BRR
LET'S RUN FOR IT!!
THEY'RE ATTRACTED TO THE MAGICAL AURA.
NUTS...
THERE ARE TOO MANY OF THEM!
I'LL NEVER GET TO THE PHONE!

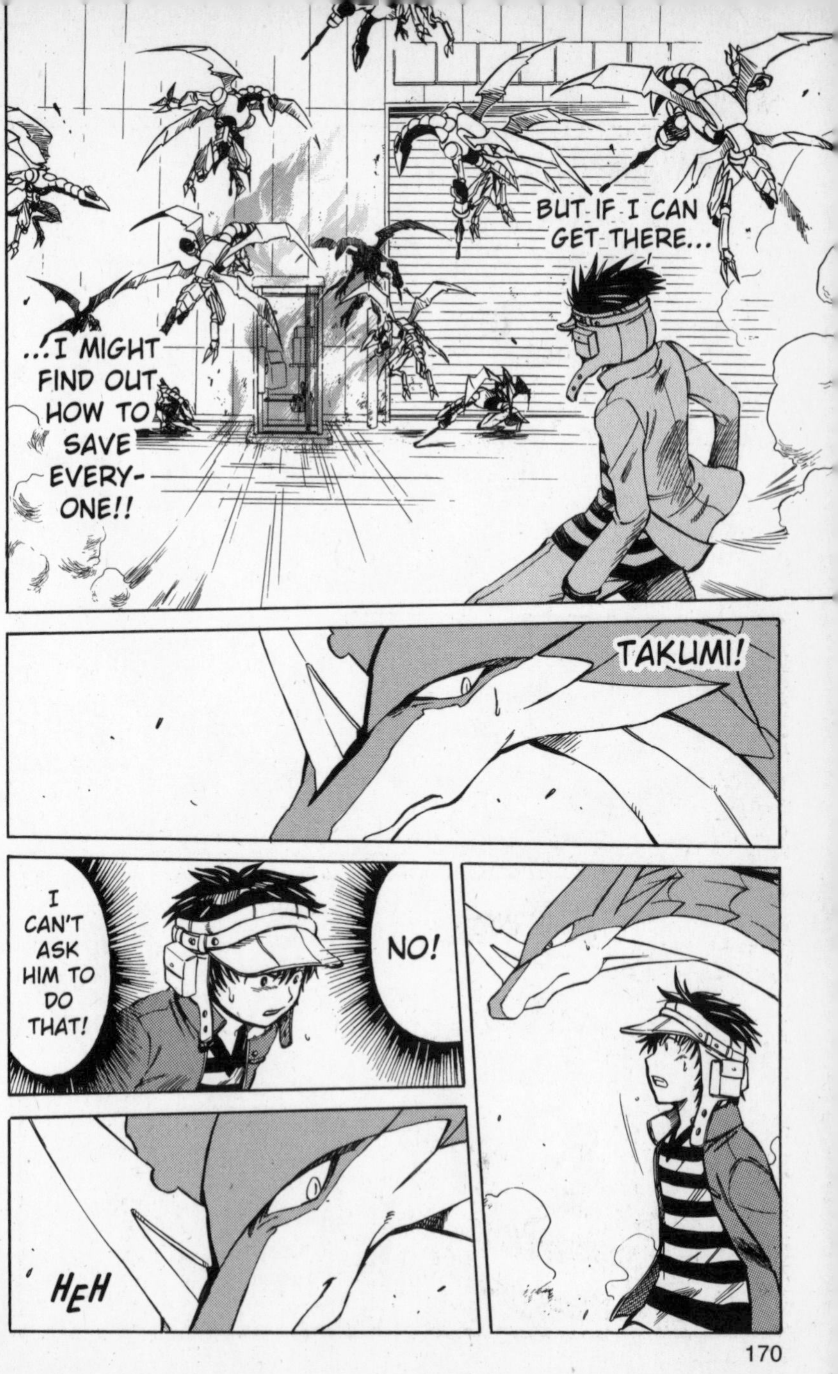
BUT IF I CAN GET THERE...
...I MIGHT FIND OUT HOW TO SAVE EVERY-ONE!!
TAKUMI!
NO!
I CAN'T ASK HIM TO DO THAT!
HEH

READ THIS WAY

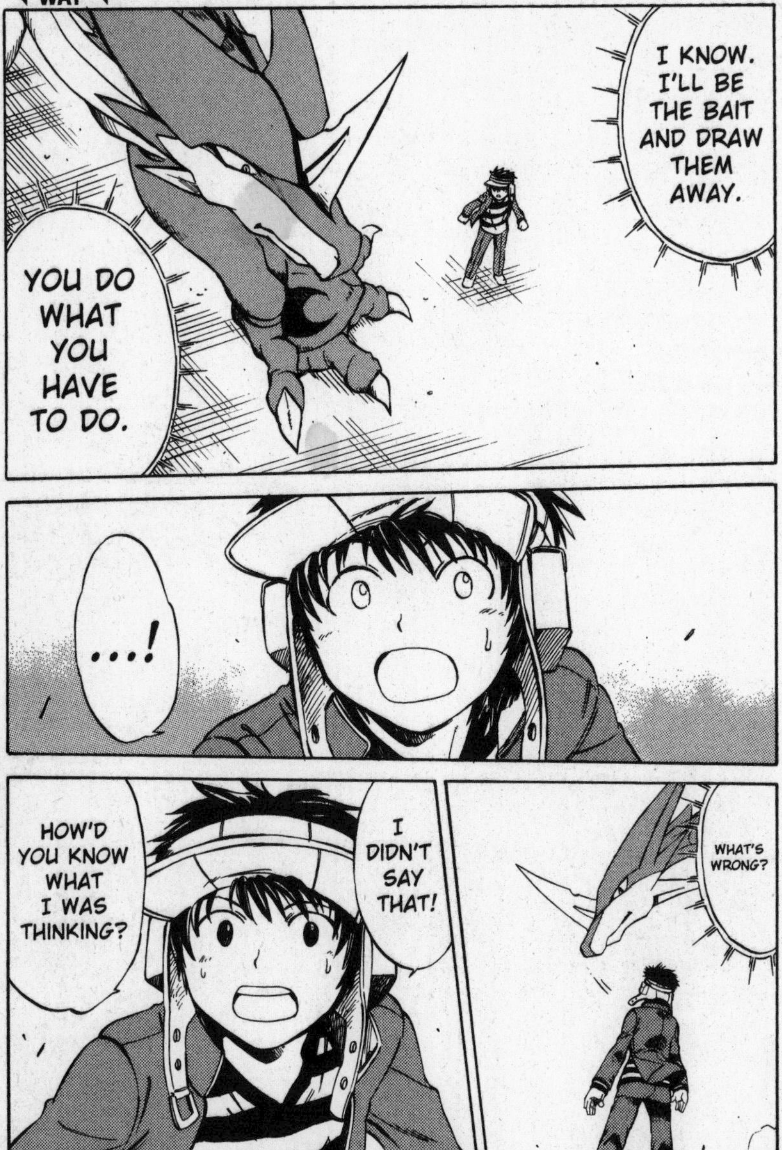
I KNOW. I'LL BE THE BAIT AND DRAW THEM AWAY.
YOU DO WHAT YOU HAVE TO DO.
...!
WHAT'S WRONG?
I DIDN'T SAY THAT!
HOW'D YOU KNOW WHAT I WAS THINKING?

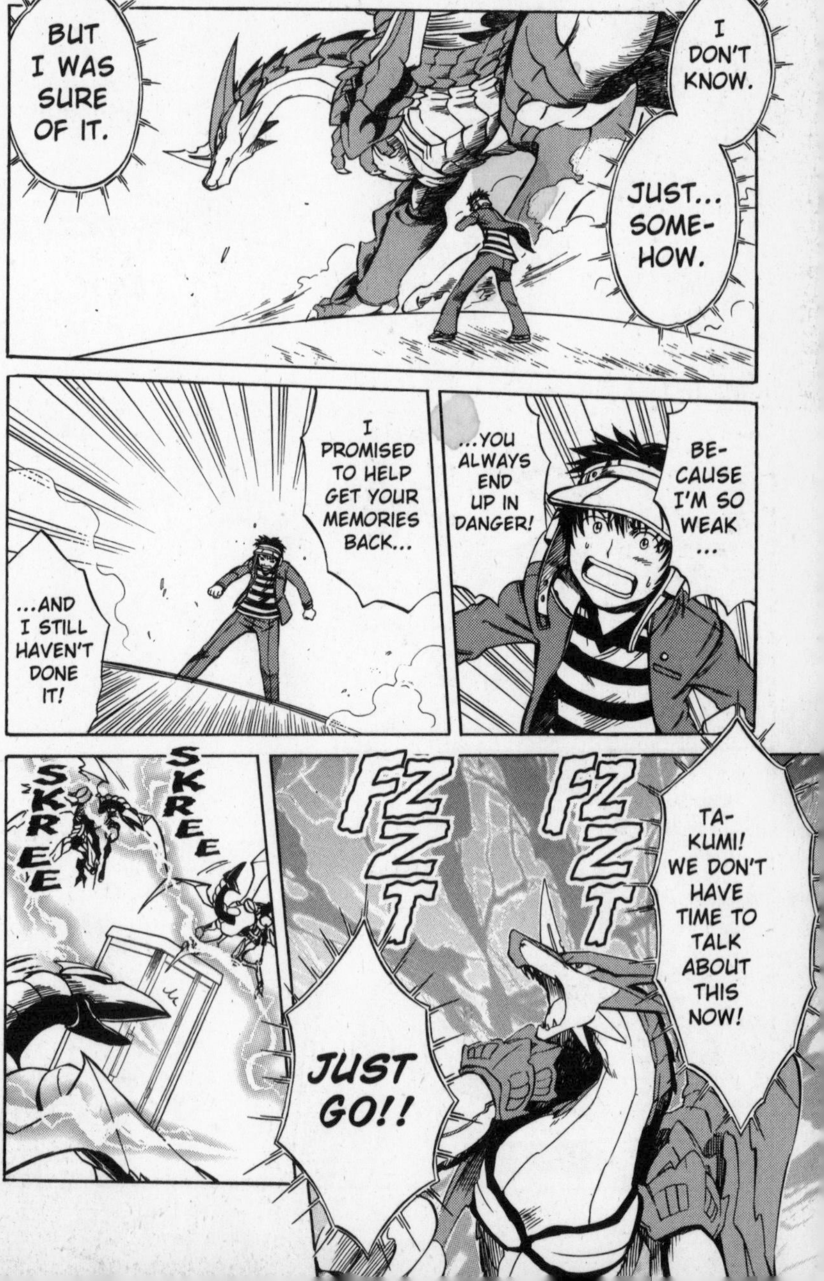
I DON'T KNOW.
JUST... SOME-HOW.
BUT I WAS SURE OF IT.
BE-CAUSE I'M SO WEAK...
...YOU ALWAYS END UP IN DANGER!
I PROMISED TO HELP GET YOUR MEMORIES BACK...
...AND I STILL HAVEN'T DONE IT!
TA-KUMI! WE DON'T HAVE TIME TO TALK ABOUT THIS NOW!
FZZT
FZZT
JUST GO!!
SKREE
SKREE

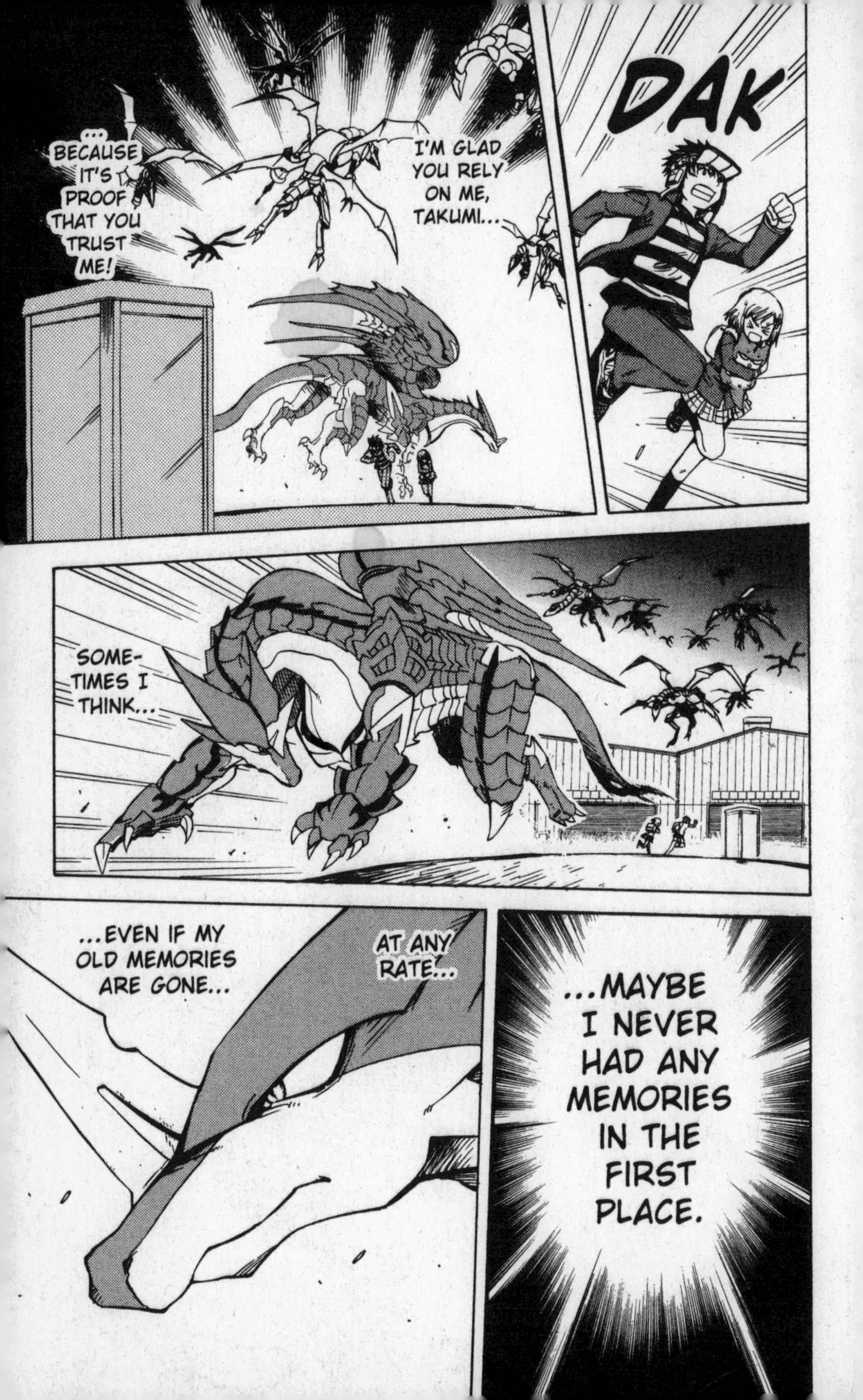
DAK
I'M GLAD YOU RELY ON ME, TAKUMI...
...BECAUSE IT'S PROOF THAT YOU TRUST ME!
SOME-TIMES I THINK...
...MAYBE I NEVER HAD ANY MEMORIES IN THE FIRST PLACE.
AT ANY RATE...
...EVEN IF MY OLD MEMORIES ARE GONE...

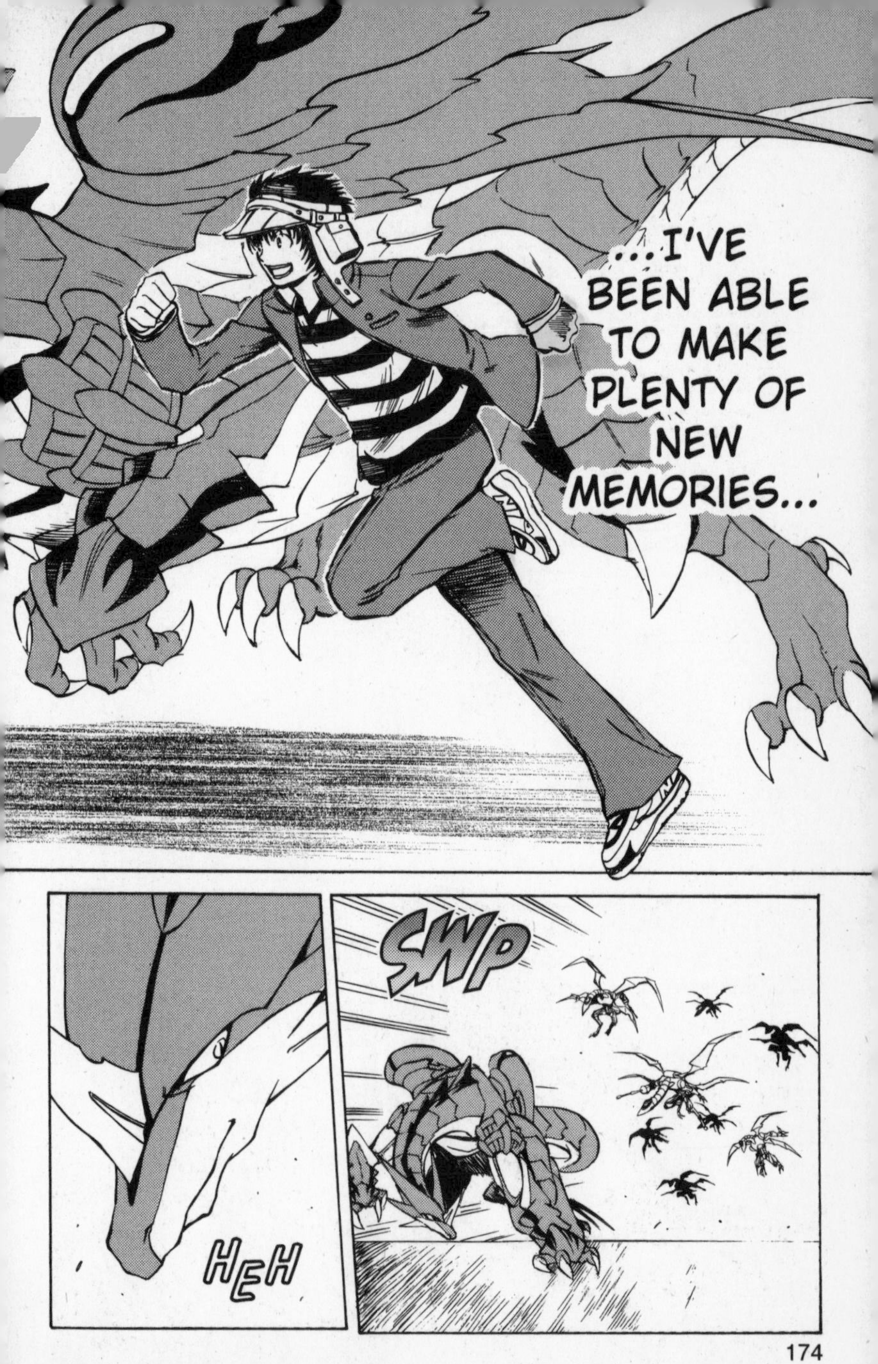
...I'VE BEEN ABLE TO MAKE PLENTY OF NEW MEMORIES...
SWP
HEH

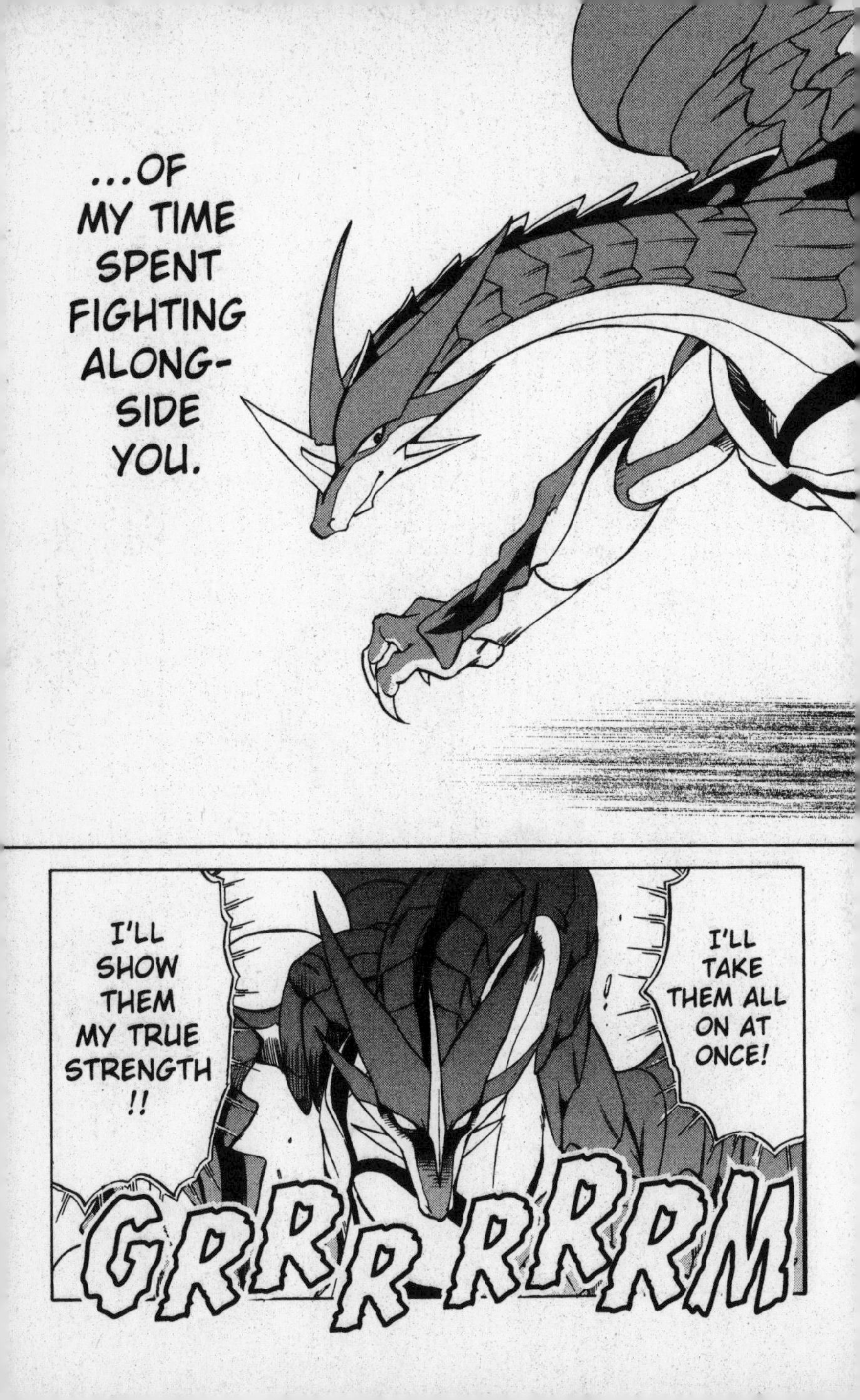
...OF MY TIME SPENT FIGHTING ALONG-SIDE YOU.
I'LL TAKE THEM ALL ON AT ONCE!
I'LL SHOW THEM MY TRUE STRENGTH!!
GRRR-RRRM

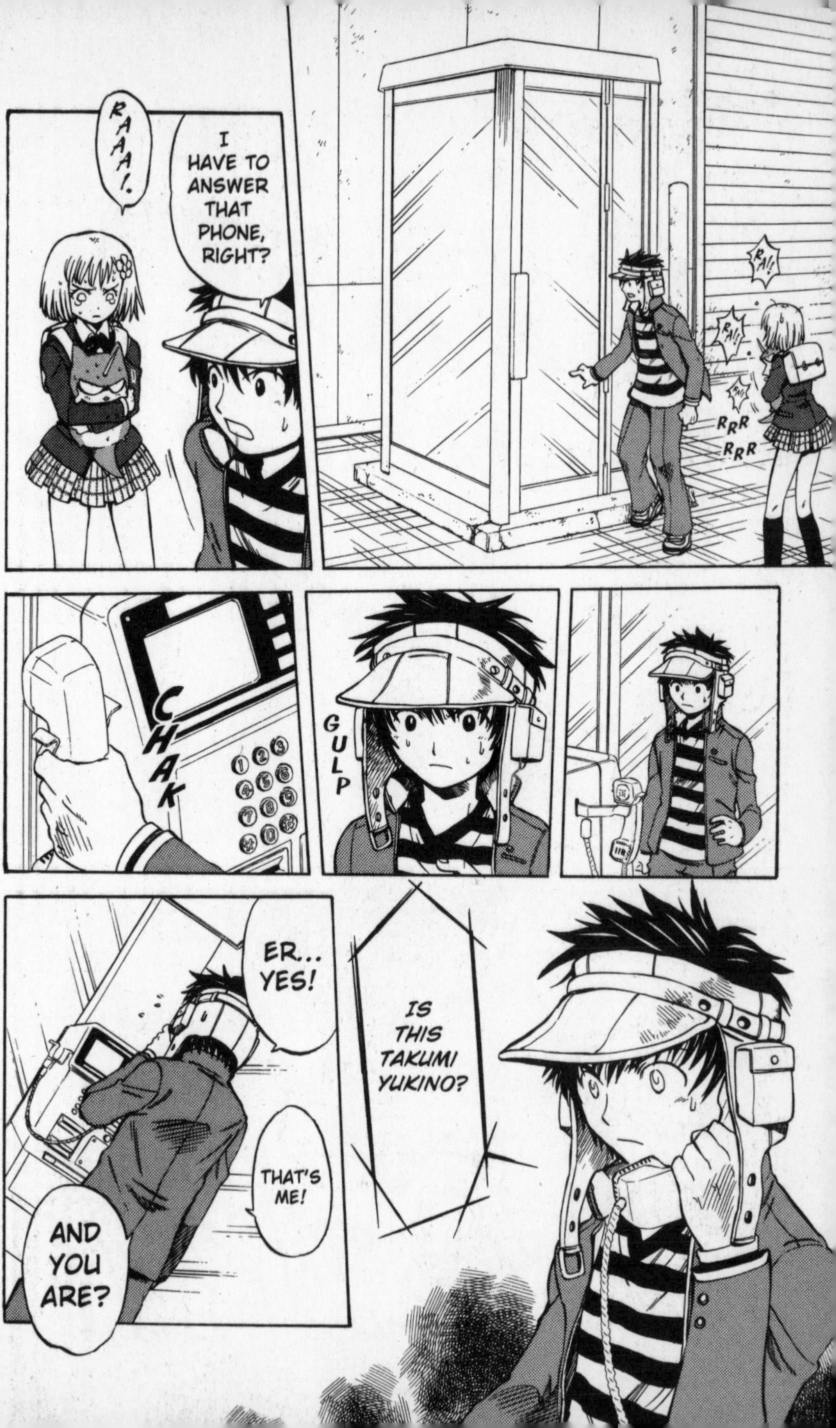
RA!!
RA!!
RA!!
RRR
RRR
I HAVE TO ANSWER THAT PHONE, RIGHT?
RAAA!
GULP
CHAK
IS THIS TAKUMI YUKINO?
ER... YES!
THAT'S ME!
AND YOU ARE?

READ THIS WAY

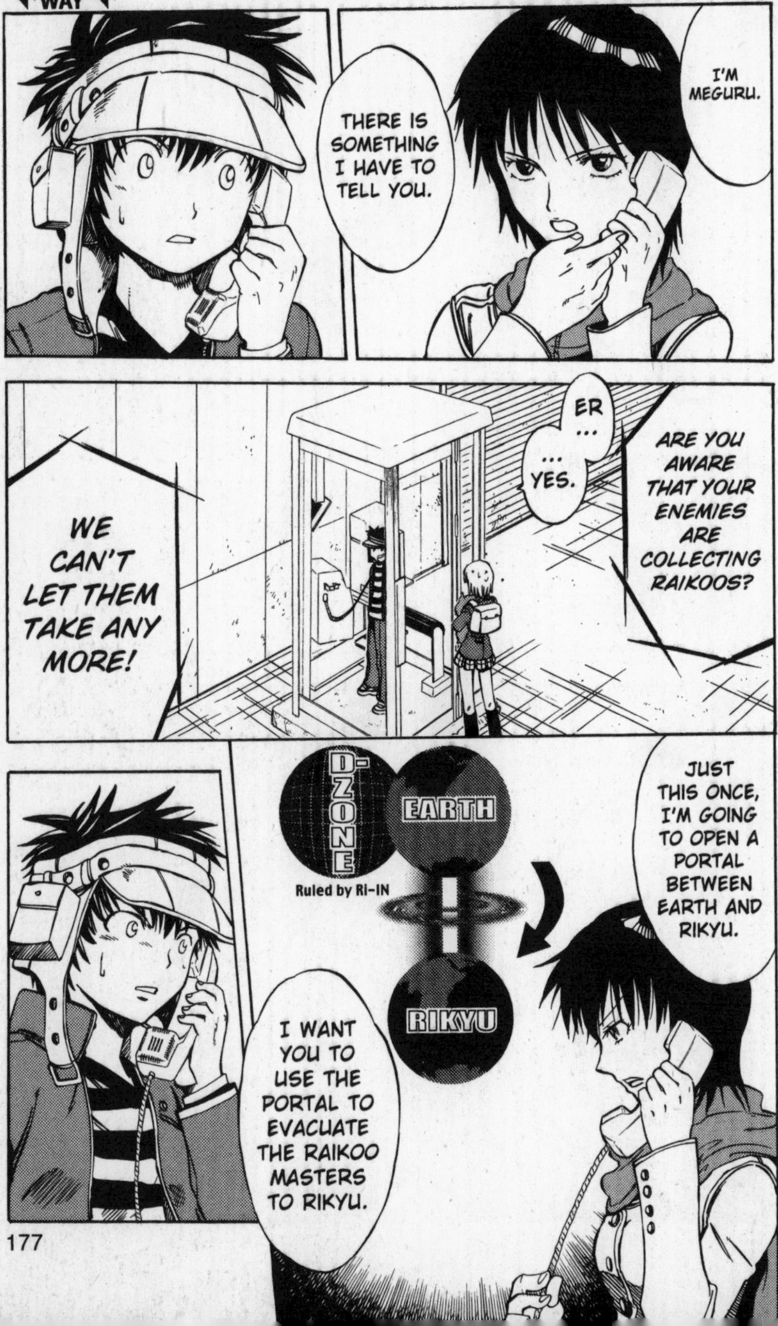
I'M MEGURU.
THERE IS SOMETHING I HAVE TO TELL YOU.
ARE YOU AWARE THAT YOUR ENEMIES ARE COLLECTING RAIKOOS?
ER ...
... YES.
WE CAN'T LET THEM TAKE ANY MORE!
JUST THIS ONCE, I'M GOING TO OPEN A PORTAL BETWEEN EARTH AND RIKYU.
D-ZONE
Ruled by RI-IN
EARTH
RIKYU
I WANT YOU TO USE THE PORTAL TO EVACUATE THE RAIKOO MASTERS TO RIKYU.

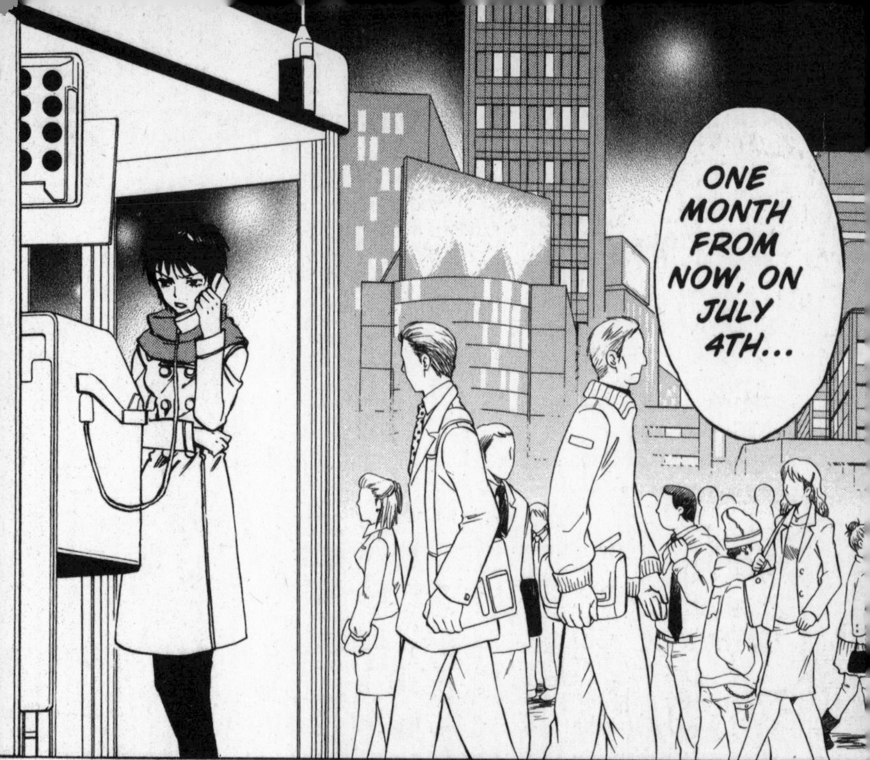
ONE MONTH FROM NOW, ON JULY 4TH...

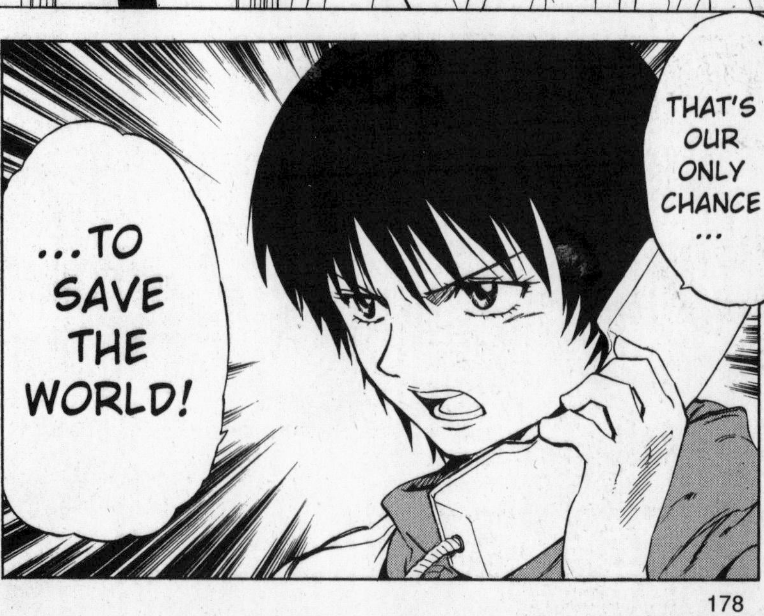
THAT'S OUR ONLY CHANCE...
...TO SAVE THE WORLD!

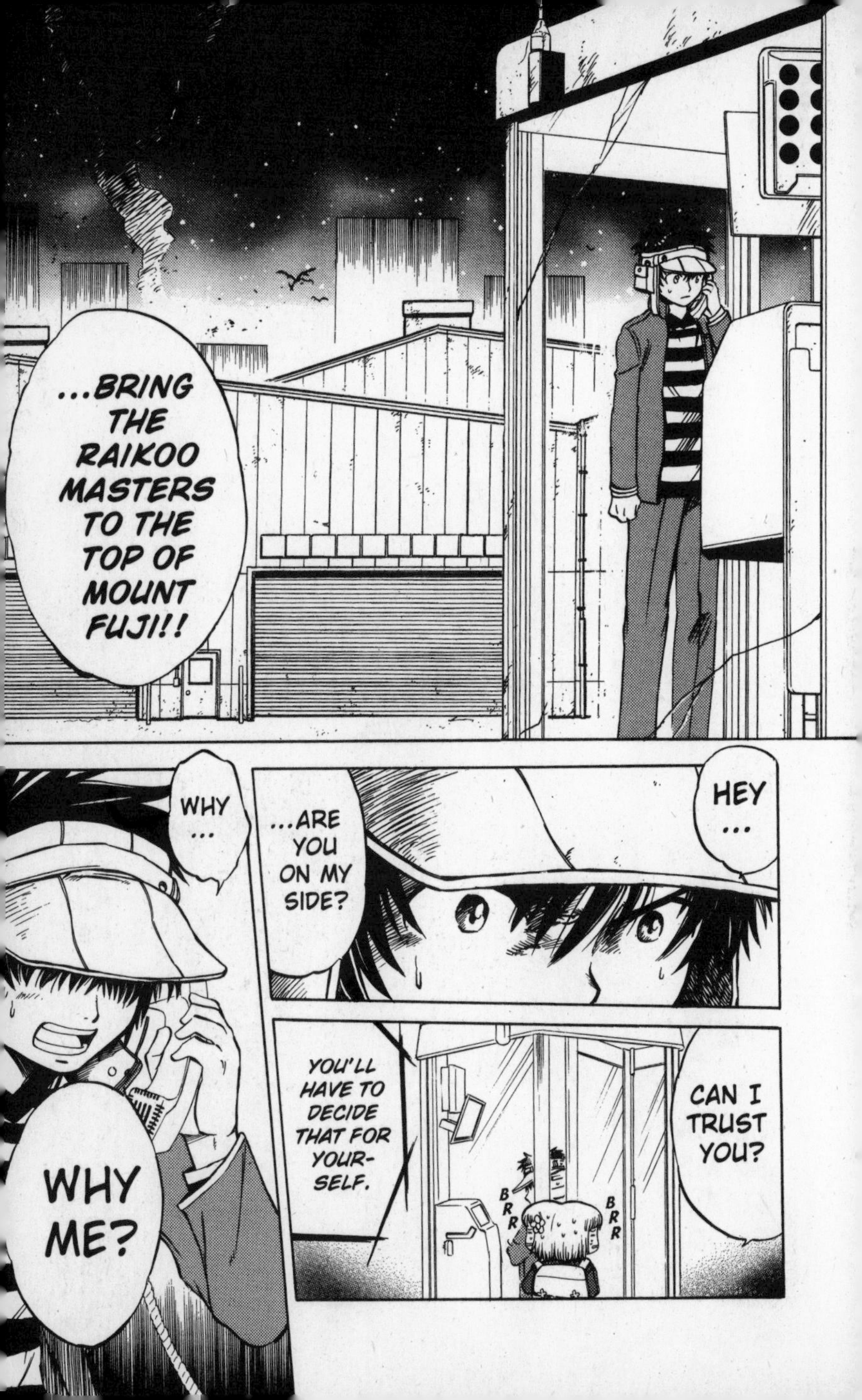
...BRING THE RAIKOO MASTERS TO THE TOP OF MOUNT FUJI!!
HEY ...
WHY ...
...ARE YOU ON MY SIDE?
CAN I TRUST YOU?
YOU'LL HAVE TO DECIDE THAT FOR YOUR-SELF.
BRR
BRR
WHY ME?

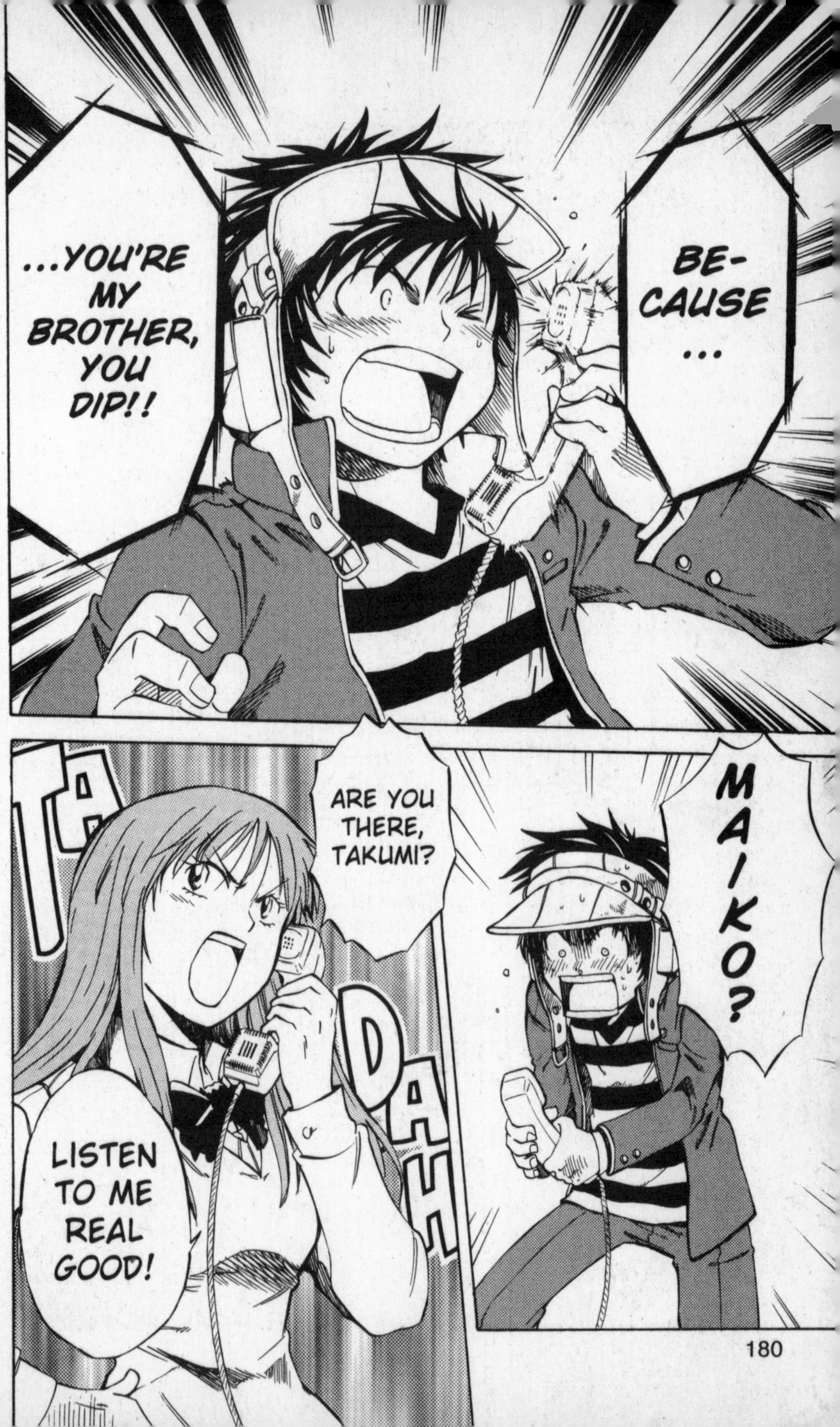
BE-CAUSE...
...YOU'RE MY BROTHER, YOU DIP!!
MAIKO?
ARE YOU THERE, TAKUMI?
LISTEN TO ME REAL GOOD!

READ THIS WAY

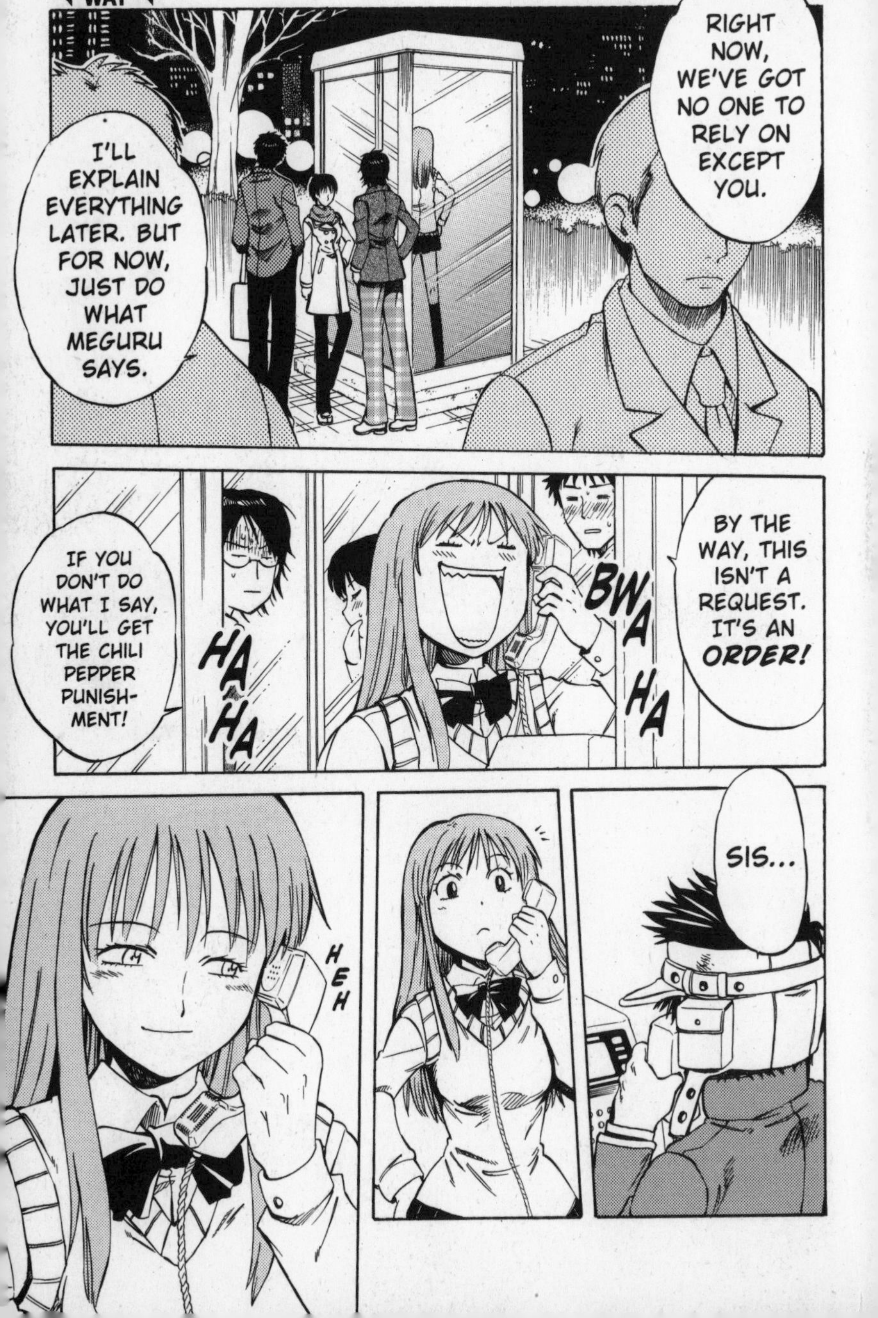

RIGHT NOW, WE'VE GOT NO ONE TO RELY ON EXCEPT YOU.
I'LL EXPLAIN EVERYTHING LATER. BUT FOR NOW, JUST DO WHAT MEGURU SAYS.
BY THE WAY, THIS ISN'T A REQUEST. IT'S AN ORDER!
BWA HA HA
IF YOU DON'T DO WHAT I SAY, YOU'LL GET THE CHILI PEPPER PUNISH-MENT!
HA HA HA
SIS...
HEH

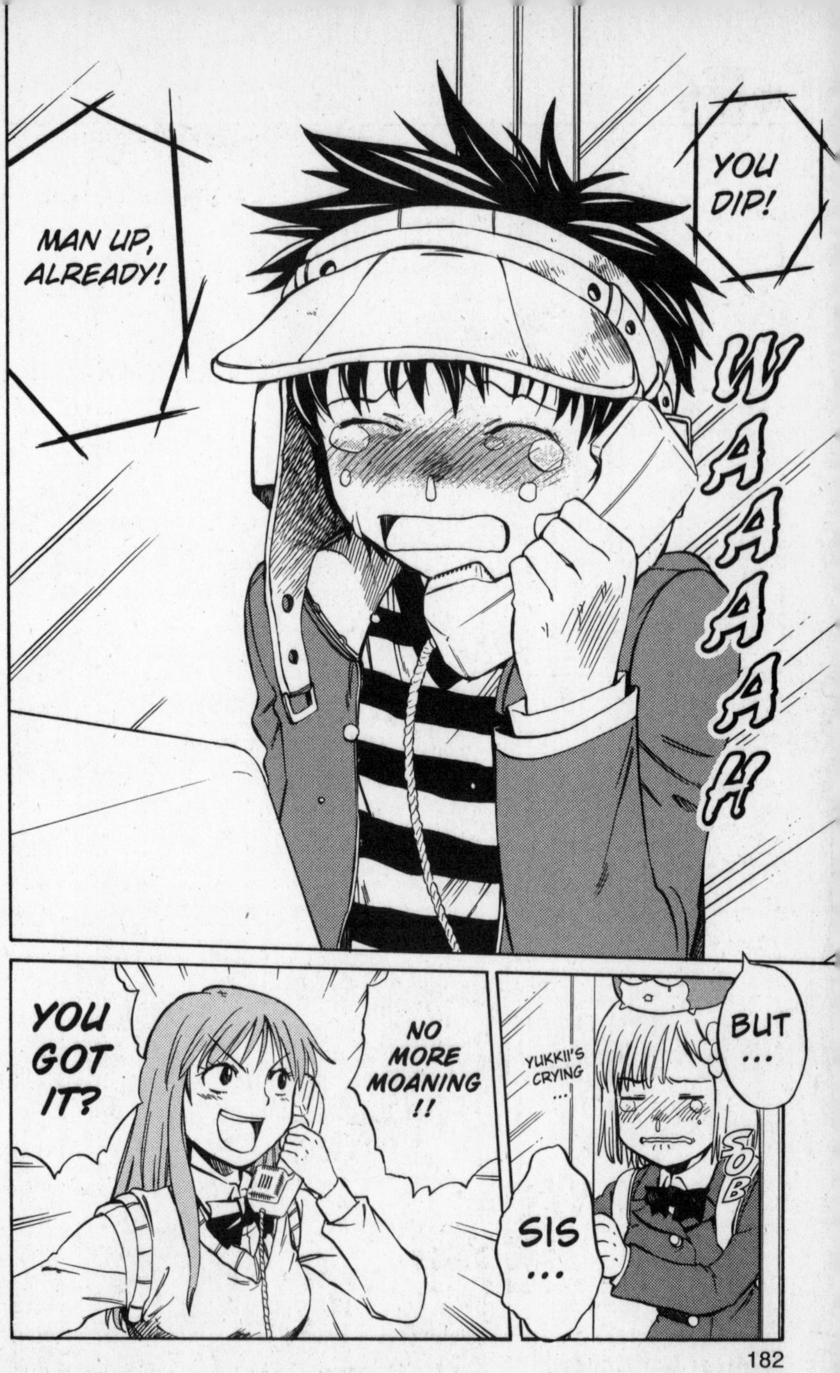
YOU DIP!
WAAAAAH
MAN UP, ALREADY!
BUT ...
SOB
YUKKII'S CRYING ...
SIS ...
NO MORE MOANING !!
YOU GOT IT?

READ THIS WAY

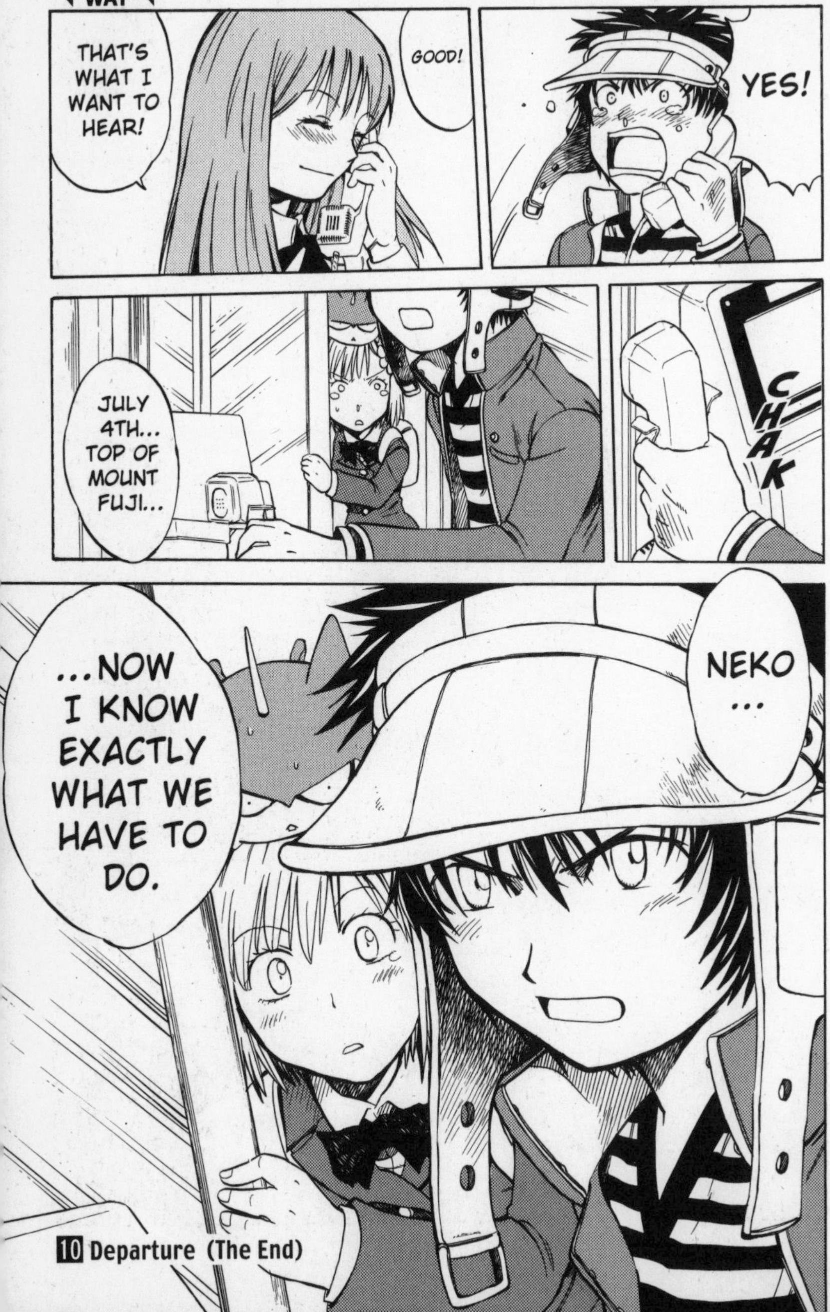
YES!
GOOD!
THAT'S WHAT I WANT TO HEAR!
CHAK
JULY 4TH... TOP OF MOUNT FUJI...
NEKO...
...NOW I KNOW EXACTLY WHAT WE HAVE TO DO.

10 Departure (The End)

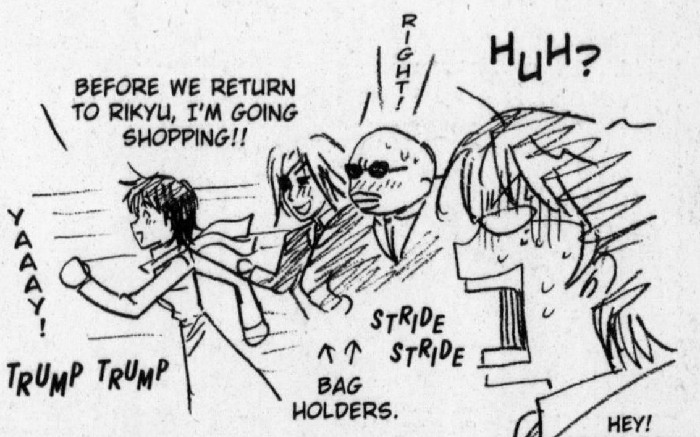
HUH?
HEY! CRISIS GOING ON HERE!
RIGHT!
STRIDE STRIDE
BAG HOLDERS.
BEFORE WE RETURN TO RIKYU, I'M GOING SHOPPING!!
YAAAAY!
TRUMP TRUMP

MEGURU, BEFORE PHONING TAKUMI.

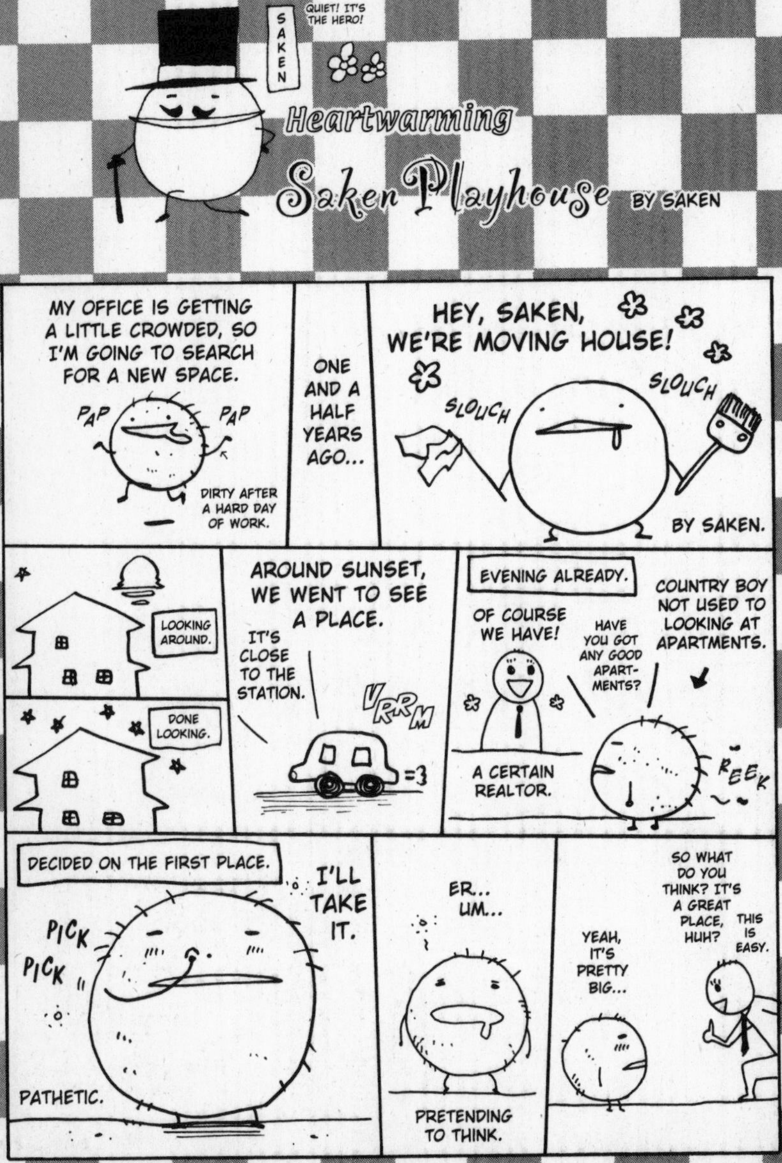
SAKEN
QUIET! IT'S THE HERO!
Heartwarming
Saken Playhouse
BY SAKEN
HEY, SAKEN, WE'RE MOVING HOUSE!
SLOUCH
SLOUCH
BY SAKEN.
ONE AND A HALF YEARS AGO...
MY OFFICE IS GETTING A LITTLE CROWDED, SO I'M GOING TO SEARCH FOR A NEW SPACE.
PAP
PAP
DIRTY AFTER A HARD DAY OF WORK.
EVENING ALREADY.
COUNTRY BOY NOT USED TO LOOKING AT APARTMENTS.
HAVE YOU GOT ANY GOOD APART-MENTS?
OF COURSE WE HAVE!
A CERTAIN REALTOR.
REEK
AROUND SUNSET, WE WENT TO SEE A PLACE.
IT'S CLOSE TO THE STATION.
VRRM
LOOKING AROUND.
DONE LOOKING.
SO WHAT DO YOU THINK? IT'S A GREAT PLACE, HUH?
THIS IS EASY.
YEAH, IT'S PRETTY BIG...
ER... UM...
PRETENDING TO THINK.
DECIDED ON THE FIRST PLACE.
I'LL TAKE IT.
PICK
PICK
PATHETIC.

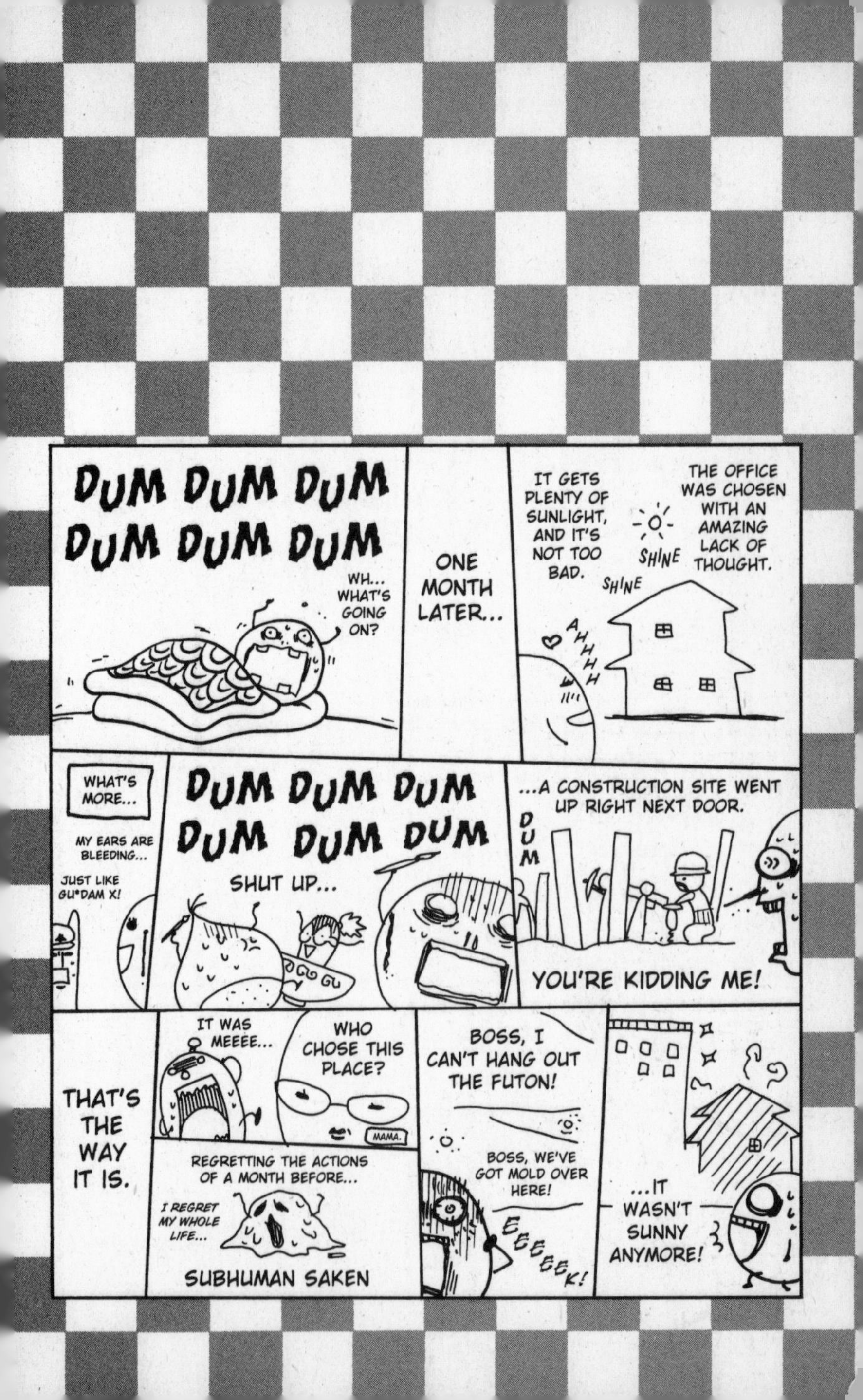
THE OFFICE WAS CHOSEN WITH AN AMAZING LACK OF THOUGHT.
IT GETS PLENTY OF SUNLIGHT, AND IT'S NOT TOO BAD.
SHINE
SHINE
AHHHH
ONE MONTH LATER...
DUM DUM DUM DUM DUM DUM
WH... WHAT'S GOING ON?
...A CONSTRUCTION SITE WENT UP RIGHT NEXT DOOR.
DUM
YOU'RE KIDDING ME!
DUM DUM DUM DUM DUM DUM
SHUT UP...
WHAT'S MORE...
MY EARS ARE BLEEDING...
JUST LIKE GU*DAM X!
...IT WASN'T SUNNY ANYMORE!
BOSS, I CAN'T HANG OUT THE FUTON!
BOSS, WE'VE GOT MOLD OVER HERE!
EEEEEK!
WHO CHOSE THIS PLACE?
IT WAS MEEEE...
MAMA.
REGRETTING THE ACTIONS OF A MONTH BEFORE...
I REGRET MY WHOLE LIFE...
SUBHUMAN SAKEN
THAT'S THE WAY IT IS.

Heartwarming

Saken Playhouse

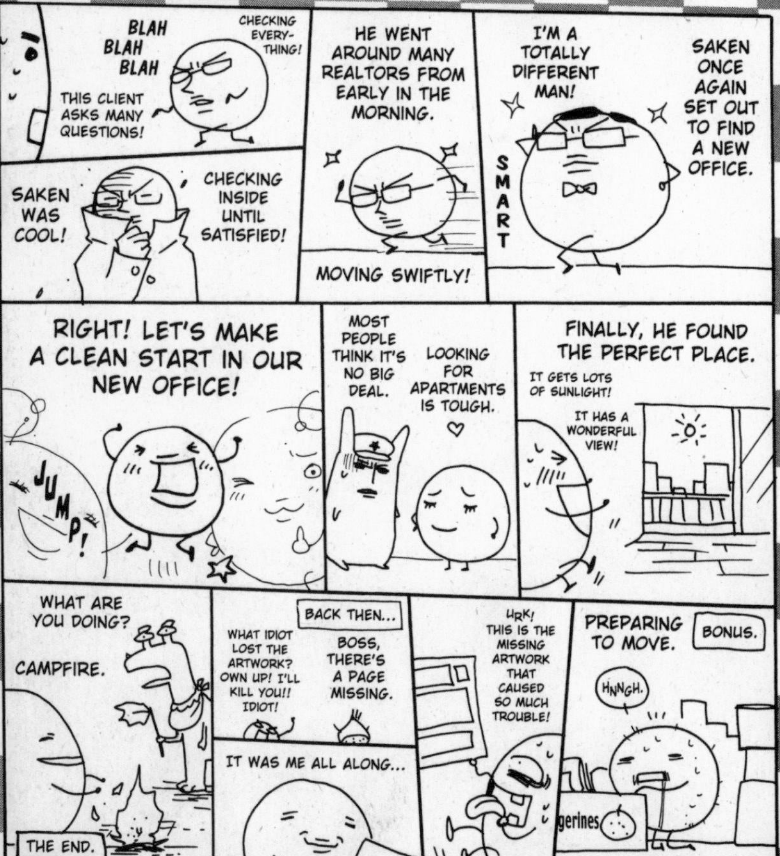

SAKEN ONCE AGAIN SET OUT TO FIND A NEW OFFICE.
I'M A TOTALLY DIFFERENT MAN!
SMART
HE WENT AROUND MANY REALTORS FROM EARLY IN THE MORNING.
MOVING SWIFTLY!
CHECKING EVERY-THING!
BLAH BLAH BLAH
THIS CLIENT ASKS MANY QUESTIONS!
CHECKING INSIDE UNTIL SATISFIED!
SAKEN WAS COOL!
FINALLY, HE FOUND THE PERFECT PLACE.
IT GETS LOTS OF SUNLIGHT!
IT HAS A WONDERFUL VIEW!
LOOKING FOR APARTMENTS IS TOUGH.
MOST PEOPLE THINK IT'S NO BIG DEAL.
RIGHT! LET'S MAKE A CLEAN START IN OUR NEW OFFICE!
JUMP!
BONUS.
PREPARING TO MOVE.
HNNGH.
gerines
URK! THIS IS THE MISSING ARTWORK THAT CAUSED SO MUCH TROUBLE!
BACK THEN...
BOSS, THERE'S A PAGE MISSING.
WHAT IDIOT LOST THE ARTWORK? OWN UP! I'LL KILL YOU!! IDIOT!
IT WAS ME ALL ALONG...
WHAT ARE YOU DOING?
CAMPFIRE.
THE END.

COMING NEXT VOLUME...

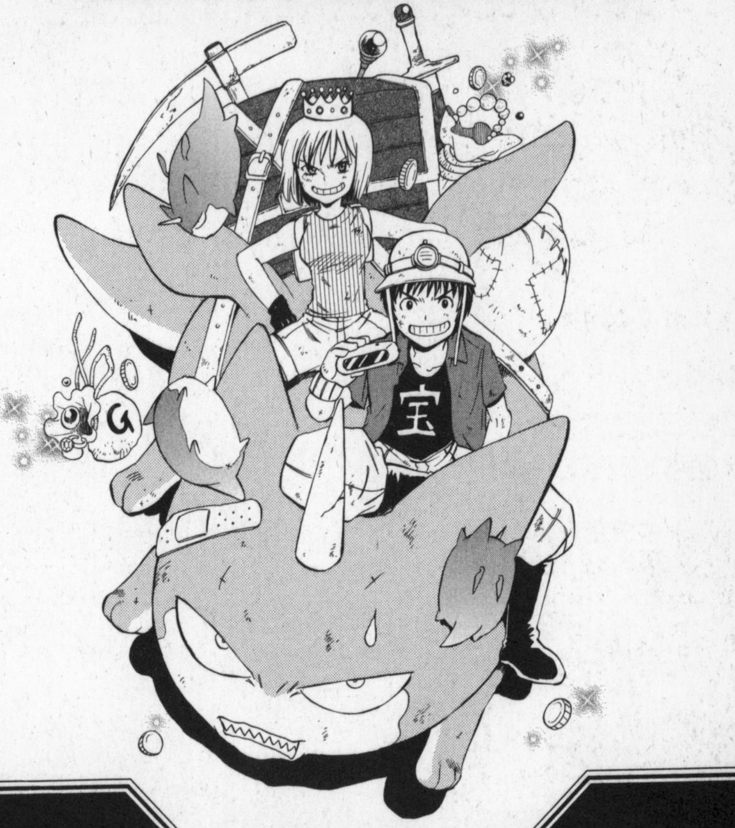
宝
G

As the directionally-challenged assassin Arisa slowly tracks Takumi down, Takumi and his friends set out on a mission of their own. How can they convince all the Raikoo masters in the world to gather at the top of Mount Fuji? And what will Takumi and Neko find in the strange world inside Raikoo's Dragon Drive card?

AVAILABLE IN DECEMBER 2008!

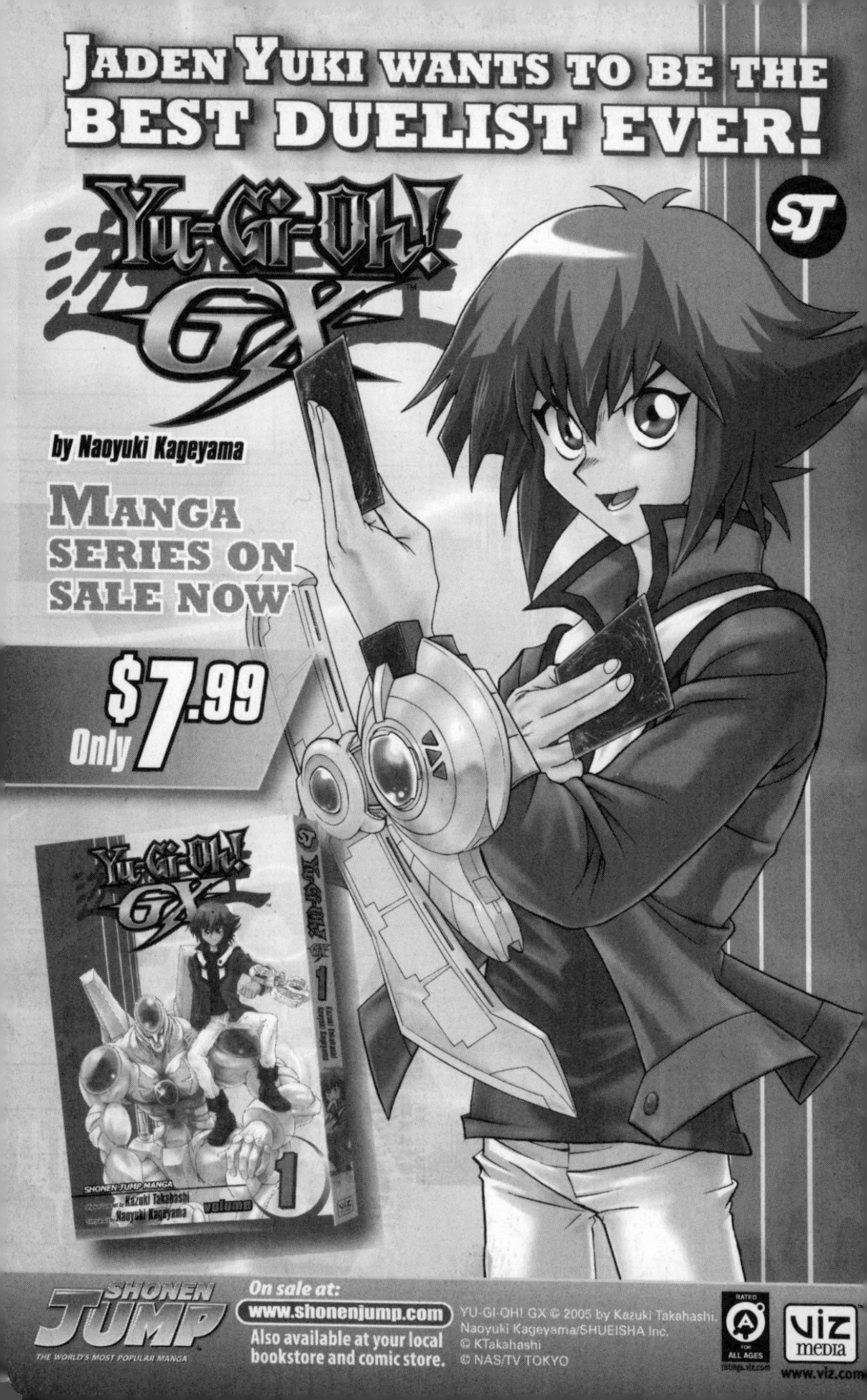
JADEN YUKI WANTS TO BE THE BEST DUELIST EVER!
SJ
YU-GI-OH! GX™
by Naoyuki Kageyama
MANGA SERIES ON SALE NOW
Only $7.99
YU-GI-OH! GX
SJ
1
SHONEN JUMP MANGA
Kazuki Takahashi
Naoyuki Kageyama
volume 1
SHONEN JUMP
THE WORLD'S MOST POPULAR MANGA
On sale at:
www.shonenjump.com
Also available at your local bookstore and comic store.
YU-GI-OH! GX © 2005 by Kazuki Takahashi, Naoyuki Kageyama/SHUEISHA Inc.
© KTakahashi
© NAS/TV TOKYO
RATED A FOR ALL AGES
viz media
www.viz.com

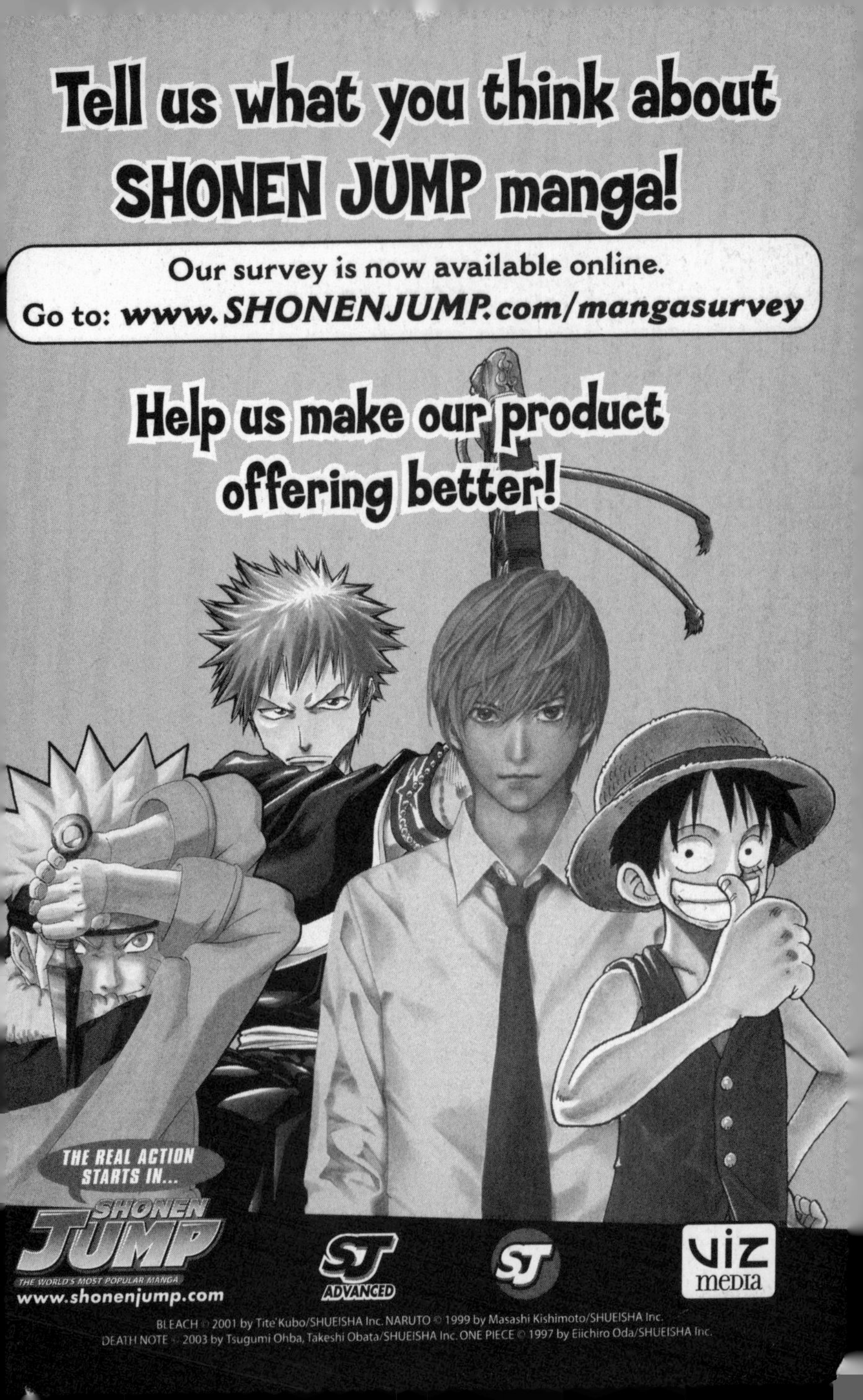
Tell us what you think about SHONEN JUMP manga!
Our survey is now available online.
Go to: www.SHONENJUMP.com/mangasurvey
Help us make our product offering better!
THE REAL ACTION STARTS IN...
SHONEN JUMP
THE WORLD'S MOST POPULAR MANGA
www.shonenjump.com
SJ ADVANCED
SJ
VIZ media
BLEACH © 2001 by Tite Kubo/SHUEISHA Inc. NARUTO © 1999 by Masashi Kishimoto/SHUEISHA Inc.
DEATH NOTE © 2003 by Tsugumi Ohba, Takeshi Obata/SHUEISHA Inc. ONE PIECE © 1997 by Eiichiro Oda/SHUEISHA Inc.

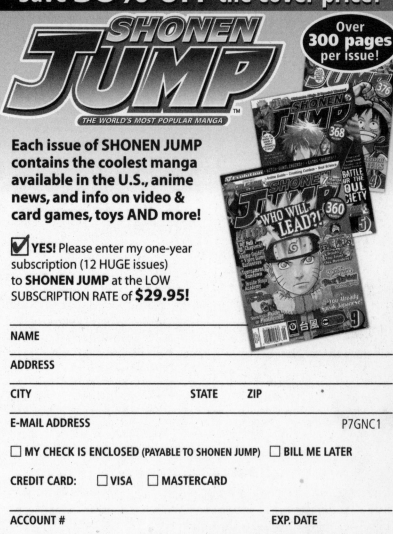

THE WORLD'S MOST POPULAR MANGA

WIN A TRIP TO JAPAN
through the SHONEN JUMP Experience Sweepstakes!

The year 2008 marks the 40th anniversary of *Weekly Shonen Jump*, the biggest manga magazine in Japan and the source for the English-language edition of *SHONEN JUMP*. *Weekly Shonen Jump* is the birthplace of the greatest manga artists and stories, and for 40 years has given the world amazing manga, including *NARUTO*, *BLEACH* and *SLAM DUNK*, to name just a few.

To celebrate this incredible milestone, we are giving away a **trip for one winner and a friend to Japan to attend Jump Festa 2009** (Dec. 20-21, 2008), **the ULTIMATE convention for everything SHONEN JUMP!**

(Entries must be postmarked by October 15, 2008 in order to qualify.)

(Please print clearly)

Name: _____

Street Address: _____

City: _____ State: _____ Postal Code: _____

Country: _____ Date of Birth (01/01/2000): _____

Phone number: _____

For mailing address information, visit www.shonenjump.com/wsj40.

BONUS!

Whether or not you win the sweepstakes, you can still get a GIFT!

COLLECT THREE (3) of the special bonus *Weekly Shonen Jump* stickers, stick them all on this form, enter your information on the other side, and mail this in for a surprise gift!* (ARV $10.00)

PLACE STICKER HERE

PLACE STICKER HERE

PLACE STICKER HERE

* While supplies last. Submissions must be postmarked by 10/15/08 and received by 10/31/08 in order to qualify. All three special round stickers must be mailed in on the same card in order to qualify for the surprise gift. Limit two submissions for surprise gift allowed per household. Allow 6-8 weeks from submission deadline for shipment of gift. No mechanical reproduction or copies of form or sticker allowed. Illegible or incomplete submissions will not be honored. Sponsor is not responsible for lost, late, mutilated, misdirected, or postage due mail or submissions. Void where prohibited.

viz media

www.viz.com